# LANGUAGES OF THE UNSAYABLE

## THE PLAY OF NEGATIVITY IN LITERATURE AND LITERARY THEORY

Edited by Sanford Budick
and Wolfgang Iser

Stanford University Press
Stanford, California

Stanford University Press
Stanford, California

© 1987 Columbia University Press
Reissued in paperback by Stanford University Press in 1996
by arrangement with Columbia University Press, New York

Printed in the United States of America
ISBN 0-8047-2483-0
LC 95-70818
This book is printed on acid-free, recycled paper.

Stanford University Press publications are distributed exclusively
by Stanford University Press within the United States, Canada,
Mexico, and Central America; they are distributed exclusively by
Cambridge University Press throughout the rest of the world.

"On the Negativity of Modern Poetry: Friedrich, Baudelaire,
and the Critical Tradition" copyright © 1989 Jonathan Culler.
"The Discourse of a Figure: Blakes's 'Speak Silence' in Literary
History" copyright © 1989 Geoffrey Hartman. The excerpt from
"Point of Departure" is reprinted by permission of North Point
Press from Variable Directions, copyright © 1989 Dan Pagis,
translated by Stephen Mitchell.

Original printing 1996
Last figure below indicates year of this printing:
04  03  02  01  00  99  98  97  96

*To the memory of Dan Pagis*

I think that not everything is in doubt.
I follow the moment, not to let it slip away.
. . . . . . . . . . . . . . . . . . . . . . . . . . . . . . . .

Beyond the door begins
the interstellar space which I'm ready for.
Gravity drains from me like colors at dusk.
I fly so fast that I'm motionless
and leave behind me
the transparent wake of the past.

Dan Pagis, *from* "Point of Departure."

# A Note on This Series

This is the paperback publication of the third in our series of volumes on topics in the Humanities. This volume originated in a research project on Negativity at the Institute for Advanced Studies, the Hebrew University, Jerusalem. I am grateful to former dean Terence D. Parsons of the School of Humanities and to former Executive Vice-Chancellor William J. Lillyman, both of the University of California, Irvine, for their support. For help with a broad range of problems, I am indebted to the Board of Directors of Irvine Studies in the Humanities, especially J. Hillis Miller and John Carlos Rowe. Jean Symonds gave our group secretarial support. Finally, I would like to thank Joel Reed for his work as copy editor and for compiling the index.

Robert Folkenflik, General Editor

# CONTENTS

    "THE TRUMPET PLACE"                                     209
        *Stéphane Moses*

9.  THE DISCOURSE OF A FIGURE: BLAKE'S
    "SPEAK SILENCE" IN LITERARY HISTORY                     225
        *Geoffrey H. Hartman*

10. UNDER THE SIGN OF LOSS: A READING OF
    FAULKNER'S *THE SOUND AND THE FURY*                     241
        *Shlomith Rimmon-Kenan*

11. DISLOCATIONS: THE CRISIS OF ALLEGORY IN
    THE *ROMANCE OF THE ROSE*                               259
        *Jon Whitman*

12. SOME WORDS IN GEORGE ELIOT: NULLIFY,
    NEUTRAL, NUMB, NUMBER                                   280
        *Neil Hertz*

13. TRADITION IN THE SPACE OF NEGATIVITY                    297
        *Sanford Budick*

    **PERFORMING**

14. THE PLAY OF THE TEXT                                    325
        *Wolfgang Iser*

15. NAUGHTY ORATORS: NEGATION OF
    VOICE IN *GASLIGHT*                                     340
        *Stanley Cavell*

    Contributors                                            379

    Index                                                   383

# INTRODUCTION

## The Critical Turn:
## Toward "Negativity" and the "Unsayable"

During the last two decades most of us have grown accustomed to recognizing the negative gestures that seem to be implicit in virtually all poetic, philosophical, and even historiographical language. The essays in this book primarily address two questions: Is there some power of dissemination or articulation that is inherent in the negative gestures themselves? To what extent might the phenomenon called "negativity" be an agent in bringing about such dissemination, thereby allowing the unsayable to speak for itself?[1] The critical turn mapped out in the following essays has to do with an all-too-easily forgotten part of our literary experience: the ways in which languages of the unsayable spotlight what has been excluded by that which is sayable and said. Historically speaking, this highlighting involves the recovery of the unspeakable elements in language glossed over by the linguistic turn that dominates twentieth-century thought. In many of the discussions that follow, a recuperation that allows for what has been shut out is sharply distinguished from an aesthetic recuperation that entails a predetermined integration (see Culler).[2] In its undetermined proliferation, *negativity* speaks for something that is arguably as real as anything else we know, even if it can be located only by carving out a void within what is being said.

Although this is not a book about Wittgenstein, it is useful to remind ourselves of the force of his final saying, or *unsaying*, in the *Tractatus*: "Whereof one cannot speak, thereof one must be silent." But far from relieving us of the burdens of the unsayable, Wittgenstein charges us with a double responsibility (see Derrida). Once we have encountered the limits of the sayable, we must acknowledge the existence of "unsayable things"[3] and, by means of a language somehow formed on being silent, articulate that which cannot be grasped. Since each of these salutary turns deserves and necessitates the other, this book aspires to cross the threshold between them, toward the unsayable.

## Modes of Negativity

Even if in its very nature negativity eludes conceptualization, a great deal can be said about and around it. The modern coinage *negativity*, or some equivalent means of eschewing indicative terminology, becomes inevitable when we consider the implications, omissions, or cancellations that are necessarily part of any writing or speaking. These lacunae indicate that practically all formulations (written or spoken) contain a tacit dimension, so that each manifest text has a kind of latent double. Thus, unlike negation, which must be distinguished from negativity, this inherent doubling in language defies verbalization. It forms the unwritten and unwritable—unsaid and unsayable—base of the utterance. But it does not therefore negate the formulations of the text or saying. Rather, it conditions them through blanks and negations. This doubling, to which we refer as negativity, cannot be deduced from the text or, in fact, from the world that it questions and that, to a lesser or greater degree, it necessarily casts in doubt. And, in all these operations, it cannot be conceived as preparing the way for any substantialist idea or positivity (see Iser). Indeed, it must be carefully discriminated from any ideological rupturings, from the negativity inherent in *theologia negativa*, from a *via negativa* and, equally, from any nihilism (see Derrida).

In order to evoke the multifariousness of negativity and to suggest how it can allow the unsayable to speak, negativity can only be described in terms of its *operations*, and not by any means in terms of a graspable entity. In many of these essays, therefore, negativity is shown to be operative in eliminating literalness and instilling in the exhibited position a self-consuming tendency. In others, it is examined in its function of marking a threshold in the ways of knowing, acting, and speaking. In most of the instances dealt with here negativity emerges as an erasure of being and as self-cancellation of its own discernible operation, thus standing out in relief against the motivations governing denials and negations.

A negativity which is traceable only through its impact exists in marked opposition to an Hegelian negativity whose dialectical concept appropriates negativity for the purpose of bringing about self-consciousness. Indeed, in the modern post-Hegelian tradition there is a tendency to reify negativity by conceiving of it as a determined negation or even as a kind of ordained enabling structure. Alternatively, it is defined as an antithesis to the empirical world which, as antithesis, incipiently affirms something that is as yet absent, though heralded. These are ideas to which Adorno, for example, seems to subscribe, sometimes in spite of himself (see Birus). In the phenomena of negativity, as distinguished in this volume, the multifacetedness of its operations opens up play even with what it brings about (see Iser). Since in these operations negativity undoes itself whenever it aspires determinatively to recuperation, the operations themselves can never be equated with nothing, nothingness, or denial, or with the aims of avoidance or nullifying. In the accounts offered in the present essays, it emerges that even when the modes of negativity are made apparent, they cannot be equated with an absolute of negativity, but are rather always in the process of transformation.

To account for such transformation in literary texts an approach is required that comes to grips with the sequential or temporal nature of the play movement itself. This movement turns the split signifier into a matrix for double meaning. In fact, only through play can difference as oscillation be manifested, because only play brings out the absent otherness that lies on the reverse side of all positions drawn into interaction. In the play of the text there is neither winning nor losing. Nor is there any fundamental change in the status of that which is absent. Instead there is a process of transforming positions which gives dynamic presence to the absence of otherness. In this way negativity not only shows that it is not negative, since it constantly lures absence into presence. While continually subverting that presence, negativity, in fact, changes it into a carrier of absence of which we would not otherwise know anything. Aesthetic reduction, as well as a totalization of the self, is avoided in this play of the text. Instead, the enacted transformation that we observe in literature makes it possible not so much to recuperate negativity or our identities as selves as to extend ourselves toward the inaccessible. Play as performance makes this inaccessibility both present and absent (see Iser).

By the same token, the unlimited negating potential of negativity excludes the possibility of elevating it into a fundamental principle. If it were to be conceived as such a principle, it would, indeed, be indistinguishable from those substances which, in the history of philosophy, have been posited as a be-all and end-all in order to explain everything that evolves from them. Here, quite the contrary, the accounts of negativity as an enabling structure do not impute to it the status of an origin. All the essays in this collection attempt to grasp different modes of negativity that are in play with one another. An emblem of this interplay is provided by the frame from *Gaslight,* which forms the frontispiece to this book.[4] Here the silent Ingrid Bergman, with her unformulated or unsayable knowledge of her husband's murderous identity, faces the silent gaslight, with its unutterable secret of vampirism, while both of them function under the sign of footsteps gouged out of the molding (which we as spectators cannot positively pronounce to be footsteps). There is no way of summing up these modes of negativity, much less arresting them and making them portable. The "still" form of the frame itself (and its hazy outlines) reminds us that what we appear to see here is in fact inaccessible. This image can *not* be seized upon as a reification of negativity, since this frame only acquires the sharp outline of meaning as one unfixable point in a sequence that cannot be arrested without destroying the particular kind of sense it makes.

The modes of negativity described individually in these essays similarly refuse the consolidation of negativity into something that can be appropriated. Yet, simultaneously, they adduce the wide-ranging adaptability of negativity, which can function equally as the *nihil originarium* and as the agent of world-making described by Heidegger as well as the Nothing of Revelation invoked by Scholem and Celan (see Motzkin, Bruns, Moses). As an enabling structure, as a means of recuperation, or as a play of the letter, negativity plays against something and thus bears the inscription of that something. Negativity does not so much indicate oppositions as combine negations with a resultant unforeseeability. It disperses what it undercuts and turns into a proliferating offshoot of what has been negated.

## Tropics of Negativity and the Unsayable

One kind of bridge between the functioning of negativity and the articulation of the unsayable can be located in the Platonic *khora* ("place"). This spatial interval (which resides deep within much of our culture and thought) neither dies nor is born. As space and place it receives all and participates in the intelligible in an enigmatic way. *Khora* is itself the atemporality of spacing, for it atemporalizes and calls forth a temporality, thus giving place to inscription. It signifies that there is something that is neither a being nor a nothingness. The spacing of *khora* introduces a dissociation or a difference in the proper meaning it renders possible. To receive all and to allow itself to be marked or affected by what is inscribed in it, *khora* must remain without form and without proper determination. Place of this kind is only a place of passage, a threshold. It allows us to speak about negativity as interval and hence as the place of inscriptions, while avoiding the fruitless attempt to speak or to figure negativity itself. In subtle but marked distinction to this figuration of the unfigurable or the allowing of the unsayable to speak, negative theology aims at a silent union with the ineffable. Yet the apophatic movement of negative theology cannot contain within itself the principle of its own interruption. This movement can only defer indefinitely the encounter with its own limits. If negative theology attempts to attain union with God, a speaking of that union becomes necessary, and whenever that speaking oc-

curs one is forced to speak of place, height, distance, and proximity (see Derrida).

In connection with a conception such as the khora a particular
definition of consciousness becomes prominent. One is tempted
to designate it as that place in which is retained the singular
power not to say what one knows. In this place there is always a
secret of denial and a denial of secrets. (Compare this with the
situation of the woman in Gaslight, as described by Cavell.) The
secret as such separates and institutes negativity. It is a negation
that denies itself; it de-negates itself. There is no secret as such,
but only in relation to what is to be denied (see Derrida).

Thinking about the limitless, impersonal khora in this way
may, however, be practically impossible for most writers, speakers, readers, and hearers. In the light of deconstruction we may
say that the "sense of an ending" appeals to everything in us that
desires a realm or place as something bounded. Place of this kind
is no doubt fallacious. It is only, after all, a simulacrum of presence. Yet even in the most implacable writing or speaking, construction must apparently always precede deconstruction. Con-
versely, though novels are built toward closure, they are never
finally or fully governed by it. It follows that there are protective
and deconstructive readings that depend on the hyperessential
and on the discourse of differance, respectively. In practice, we
do not usually have one without the other. A plot provides an
image of the world in which the essent becomes essent (see
Kermode).

A different instance of the place of negativity is provided by
the figure of apostrophe, which is always coded as both invocation and turning away, and which necessarily interrupts a previous discourse (spoken or mute). As a dimensionless midpoint
between discourses, it figures recurrence. It exists as a focus of
potential relatedness with other human experiences of the nothing. Yet in the conceptualization of relatedness that apostrophe
requires, reenforcement and subversion—which require over-
arching frameworks from which predications are made—are not
the operative terms. Predicative frameworks inevitably turn relationship into a representation of something other than itself. This
is what apostrophe escapes. Enabled by negativity, apostrophe

and its framework of rhetorical division give a shape to negativity. Each apostrophe is not only addressed to a double but also doubles its predecessor. As an empty space, apostrophe both invites the occupancy of what is different and conditions the linkage of negativity in which tradition consists. This linkage by means of negativity has been overlooked by the common understanding of tradition, which generally defines it as a form of handing down or replication of concepts. Thus apostrophe is not only a principal constituent of intertextuality, but a basic element in the grammar of tradition as well (see Budick).

In general we may say that in order to show the multifarious modes of negativity, the positions predicated in writing or speech are not deconstructed but translated to a negative realm. This has the effect of releasing a hitherto unnoticed network of relationships among these positions. But this can happen only when relationships are set free and not subsumed in what the positions stand for. Standing by themselves, these relationships turn into a matrix for generating a semantic potential that can only be pragmatically realized. In this way a relation of absence and presence comes to the fore in which exclusions both stabilize and challenge the pragmatic meanings reached. In its turn, this challenge points up the volatility, but not the meaninglessness, of all semantics.

## Languages of the Unsayable

What allows the unsayable to speak is the undoing of the spoken through negativity. Since the spoken is doubled by what remains silent, undoing the spoken gives voice to the inherent silence which itself helps stabilize what the spoken is meant to mean. This voicing of the unsayable is necessarily multilingual, for there is no one language by which sayings of things can be undone. As the modes of negativity are many, and the undoing of saying is manifold, so must the languages of the unsayable be diverse. These languages depend on whether the given saying is to be cancelled in relation to an addressee, a form of understanding, a prevailing pragmatics, and so on.

It would be unfair to the essays in this volume to try to reduce them—assuming we could—to rule and formula. But we would like to instance in advance some of the other conditions of occurrence or performance that the essays describe.

1. *The shifting of allegorical language, for all its instability, implies the existence of a tertium quid through which language can pass back and forth between negation and affirmation. Allegory develops a mode of articulation between the extremes of silence and fear. It qualifies either doubt or certainty by a continuity of voice, and finally evaluates that voice by an act of forbearance* (see Whitman).

2. In Blake, "speak silence" is a gesture to humanize the inhuman void. It intimates presence, not absence, and is part of Blake's quest for an original language (see Hartman). In George Eliot's search for the unrepresentable a dispersal into equivocation occurs that cuts like a corrosive liquid into whatever is said in order to nullify words and hollow them out. Everything fades into the sameness of numbers, which are themselves vehicles for approaching the neutral. The neutral, however, is never to be embodied. At best it can only be mimicked (see Hertz). The writings of Blake and George Eliot both seem to call for a certain performativity that results from the erasure of a single authority and the subsequent instituting of the play of the critic.

3. In Heidegger we hear that the work of art is marked by a rift that makes it impossible for the work to represent anything. The work of art occurs, rather, in the form of a double movement of disclosure and refusal, unconcealment and dissembling. The words in the work constantly break free, thus manifesting an uncontainability within language itself (see Bruns). In a parallel way, interruption is the very condition of sense-making in the poetry of Celan. The gap in space and the pause in signification make it possible for the pure phonic essence of voice to be heard in its originary violence. Thus, intervention as interruption creates an opening for the unpredictable to take place (see Moses). There is an analogous recuperation of unpredictable negativity in Beckett. His movement toward the suppression of figure and his silencing of language ultimately take place as the impossibility of their accomplishment and the inability to do so. Therefore Beckett's movement into silence constantly impels his texts into a different form of utterance, at a further remove from spoken language (see Wolosky). In a similar way, Faulkner too makes available a language that goes beyond words, expressed by a

voice that momentarily transcends the vicious cycle of loss and the repetition of absence. Yet in Faulkner's case it is often impossible to know if we are face-to-face with the recuperation of negativity or the restatement of negation (see Rimmon-Kenan).

4. In Gaslight self-reliance figures as the aversion to conformity. A pragmatized negativity is made present in the woman's freeing herself, through various forms of madness and irony, from her husband's control. The initial condition of the melodrama is set by the fact that the man intends to decreate the woman. The denial of her voice is the deprivation of her reason. Philosophy and film would replace voice in a mad itinerary to sanity. This itinerary takes into account the fact that conformity is voicelessness, hence a form of madness, and that writing and film-making in aversion to conformity are a continual turning away from society, which also means a continual turning toward society, as implicit reference. Therefore, philosophy and film perform a dervish's dance between madness and sanity. In a land (America) without an edifice of thought, in which the first cabins of thought are still under construction, there is no question of wishing to go back—historically, pedagogically, or archaeologically—to the days of thought's founding or to the metaphysical point of departure from madness. Hyperbolical doubt such as we encounter in Emerson or Thoreau, or in this film, is a turn to emptiness, a wish to exist outside language's games—not so much as it were beyond language as before it. Learning or providing for the possibility of the unsayable language of the other is, in any case, not the same as union or even conversation with the other. In the case of this film at least, the decreation of the woman, the theft of woman's knowledge, and the deprivation of her right to words can only be partially redeemed. That partial redemption, however, can serve as the condition for beginning to perform or sing (see Cavell).

Directly or indirectly, all of the essays in this collection emphasize that one cannot speak for the unsayable. It can only speak for itself. To say otherwise is to become imprisoned in one's own ventriloquism or gimmick. By the same token, there is no adequate substitute for listening to the languages of the unsayable. No one can fully do such listening for anyone else. Yet we trust that the following pages have provided many and varied opportunities for such listening.

. . . . . . .

FINALLY, SOME sayable words of acknowledgment and remembering. For continuous aid in carrying out the research for this book, we wish to thank Eliyahu Honig, Michael Ottolenghi, Amnon Pazi, Yoram ben-Porath, and, most particularly, Menahem Yaari, director of the Institute for Advanced Studies of the Hebrew University, where most of our work was done. Dalia Aviely, Shabtai Giron, and Bilha Guss, of the Institute staff, and Eva Vilarrubí and Ruth Fine, our research assistants, deserve special mention for their constant support and help. Jerusalem's Mishkenoth Shaananim guest house and Cinematheque graciously made available their marvelous facilities and resources. The Center for Literary Studies of the Hebrew University nurtured this project from beginning to end. We are grateful to our many colleagues in the Center, especially Lawrence Besserman, H. M. Daleski, and Gershon Shaked.

Robert Folkenflik, general editor of Irvine Studies in the Humanities, was of invaluable help in bringing our work to completion. Jennifer Crewe and Karen Mitchell, of Columbia University Press, saw the book through its final stages of preparation. This is also an opportunity to thank our anonymous readers, who will see that we benefited from their advice on many points. Emily Budick and Lore Iser blessedly gave counsel and encouragement throughout. Shirley Collier, always cheerful and optimistic, assured the continuity of our undertaking by establishing The Shirley Palmer Collier Endowment Fund for Literary Studies, in memory of her sister Jo (Palmer) Kaufman. At crucial junctures during the three years this volume was in the making, our work was facilitated by generous gifts from Sam and Lee Krupnick and from Max Zimmer.

This book is dedicated to the memory of our gentle colleague and friend, Dan Pagis. Dan participated energetically in our year-long deliberations. A few weeks after our collective work in Jerusalem was concluded, he succumbed to the illness he had suffered in silence.

S.B.
W.I.

## Notes

1. To consider these questions, the authors represented in this volume assembled in Jerusalem, at the Institute for Advanced Studies of the Hebrew University, over a period of ten months that culminated in a conference in June 1986. For reasons that have formed parts of some of the following essays, Jerusalem seemed a particularly appropriate place for extended deliberations on these matters.

2. In the interests of a panoptic view of the present volume, we have permitted ourselves this highly general form of reference to individual essays. We have referred to our authors in this way both where (as in this case) points we emphasize correspond closely to those made in the essays and where we are very much adapting or extending the arguments of the essays.

3. "Es gibt allerdings Unaussprechliches," he writes; *Tractatus Logico-Philosophicus*, ed. and trans. by D. F. Pears and B. F. McGuiness (London: Routledge and Kegan Paul, 1963), 6.522. For this sentence Pears and McGuiness offer, "There are, indeed, things that cannot be put into words" (p. 151), while Norman Malcolm adopts the translation "Unsayable things do indeed exist"; see *The Encyclopedia of Philosophy*, 8:333. Derrida's translator, Ken Frieden, employs yet a different wording in the first essay that follows.

4. A philosophical account of the meaning of *Gaslight* is provided in Cavell's essay.

Languages of the Unsayable

# UNSAYING

# 1

# HOW TO AVOID SPEAKING: DENIALS
## Jacques Derrida
### Translated by Ken Frieden

## I

EVEN BEFORE starting to prepare this lecture, I knew that I wished to speak of the "trace" in its relationship to what one calls, sometimes erroneously, "negative theology." More precisely, I knew that I *would have to* do this in Jerusalem. But what does such an obligation mean here? When I say that I knew that I would have to do it even before the first word of this lecture, I already name a singular anteriority of the obligation—is an obligation before the first word possible?—which would be difficult to situate and which, perhaps, will be my theme today.

Under the very loose heading of "negative theology," as you know, one often designates a certain form of language, with its *mise en scène*, its rhetorical, grammatical, and logical modes, its demonstrative procedures—in short a textual practice attested or rather situated "in history," although it does sometimes exceed the predicates that constitute this or that concept of history. Is there *one* negative theology, *the* negative theology? In any case, the unity of its legacy *(archive)* is difficult to delimit. One might try to organize it around certain attempts that are considered exemplary or explicit, such as the *Divine Names* of Dionysius the Areopagite (Pseudo-Dionysius). But as we shall see, for essential reasons one is never certain of being able to attribute to anyone a

*Editors' note:* The French version of this essay, "Comment ne pas parler: Dénégations," has appeared in Jacques Derrida, *Psyché: Inventions de l'autre* (Paris: Galilée, 1987), pp. 535–95.

project of negative theology *as such.*[1] Before Dionysius, one may search within a certain Platonic or Neoplatonic tradition; after him up to modernity in Wittgenstein and many others. In a less rigorous or less informed manner, then, "negative theology" has come to designate a certain typical attitude toward language, and within it, in the act of definition or attribution, an attitude toward semantic or conceptual determination. Suppose, by a provisional hypothesis, that negative theology consists of considering that every predicative language is inadequate to the essence, in truth to the hyperessentiality (the being beyond Being) of God; consequently, only a negative ("apophatic") attribution can claim to approach God, and to prepare us for a silent intuition of God. By a more or less tenable analogy, one would thus recognize some traits, the family resemblance of negative theology, in every discourse that seems to return in a regular and insistent manner to this rhetoric of negative determination, endlessly mutiplying the defenses and the apophatic warnings: this, which is called X (for example, text, writing, the trace, differance, the hymen, the supplement, the pharmakon, the parergon, etc.) "is" neither this nor that, neither sensible nor intelligible, neither positive nor negative, neither inside nor outside, neither superior nor inferior, neither active nor passive, neither present nor absent, not even neutral, not even subject to a dialectic with a third moment, without any possible sublation ("Aufhebung"). Despite appearances, then, this X is neither a concept nor even a name; it does *lend itself* to a series of names, but calls for another syntax, and exceeds even the order and the structure of predicative discourse. It "is" not and does not say what "is." It is written completely otherwise.

I have deliberately chosen examples that are close and, one might think, familiar to me. For two reasons. On the one hand, very early I was accused of—rather than congratulated for— resifting the procedures of negative theology in a scenario that one thinks one knows well. One would like to consider these procedures a simple rhetoric, even a rhetoric of failure—or worse, a rhetoric that renounces knowledge, conceptual determination, and analysis: for those who have nothing to say or don't want to

know anything, it is always easy to mimic the technique of negative theology. Indeed, this necessarily does include an apparatus
of methodological rules. In a moment I will try to show how
negative theology at least claims not to be assimilable to a technique that is subject to simulation or parody, to mechanical repetition. It would escape from this by means of the *prayer* that
precedes apophatic utterances, and by the address to the other, to
you, in a moment that is not only the preamble or the methodological threshold of the experience. Naturally, the prayer, invocation, and apostrophe can also be mimicked, and even give way,
as if despite themselves, to repetitive technique. In conclusion, I
will come back to this risk which, fortunately *and* unfortunately,
is also a piece of luck. But if the risk is inevitable, the accusation
it incurs need not be limited to the apophatic moment of negative
theology. It may be extended to all language, and even to all
manifestation in general. This risk is inscribed in the structure of
the mark.

There is also an automatic, ritualistic, and "doxic" exercise of
the suspicion brought against everything that resembles negative
theology. It has interested me for a long time. Its matrix includes
at least three types of objections:

a) You prefer to negate; you affirm nothing; you are fundamentally a nihilist, or even an obscurantist; neither knowledge nor
even theology will progress in this way. Not to mention atheism,
of which one has been able to say in an equally trivial fashion
that it is the truth of negative theology.

b) You abuse a simple technique; it suffices to repeat: "X is no
more this, than that," "X seems to exceed all discourse or predication," and so on. This comes back to speaking for nothing. You
speak only for the sake of speaking, in order to experience speech.
Or, more seriously, you speak thus with an eye to writing, since
what you write then does not even merit being said. This second
critique already appears more interesting and more lucid than the
first: to speak for the sake of speaking, to experience what happens to speech through speech *itself*, in the trace of a sort of
quasi-tautology, is not entirely to speak in vain and to say nothing. It is perhaps to experience a possibility of speech which the

objector himself must presuppose at the moment when he addresses his criticism. To speak for *nothing* is not: not to speak. Above all, it is not to speak to no one.

c) This criticism does not, then, threaten the essential possibility of the address or the apostrophe. It encompasses still a third possibility, less evident but no doubt more interesting. Here the suspicion takes a form that can reverse the process of the accusation: once the apophatic discourse is analyzed in its logical-grammatical form, if it is not merely sterile, repetitive, obscurantist, mechanical, it perhaps leads us to consider the becoming-theological of all discourse. From the moment a proposition takes a negative form, the negativity that manifests itself need only be pushed to the limit, and it at least resembles an apophatic theology. Every time I say: X is neither this nor that, neither the contrary of this nor of that, neither the simple neutralization of this nor of that with which it *has nothing in common*, being absolutely heterogeneous to or incommensurable with them, I would start to speak of God, under this name or another. God's name would then be the hyperbolic effect of that negativity or all negativity that is consistent in its discourse. God's name would suit everything that may not be broached, approached, or designated, except in an indirect and negative manner. Every negative sentence would already be haunted by God or by the name of God, the distinction between God and God's name opening up the very space of this enigma. If there is a work of negativity in discourse and predication, it will produce divinity. It would then suffice to change a sign (or rather to show, something easy and classical enough, that this inversion has *always already* taken place, that it is the essential movement of thought) in order to say that divinity is not produced but productive. Infinitely productive, Hegel would say, for example. God would be not merely the end, but the origin of this work of the negative. Not only would atheism not be the truth of negative theology; rather, God would be the truth of all negativity. One would thus arrive at a kind of proof of God—not a proof of the *existence* of God, but a proof of God *by His effects*, or more precisely a proof of what one calls God, or of the name of God, by effects without cause, by the *without cause*. The import of this word *without (sans)* will concern us in a moment. In the absolutely singular logic of this proof, "God" would name *that without which* one would not know how to account for any negativity: grammatical or logical negation, illness, evil, and finally neurosis which, far from permitting psychoanalysis to reduce religion to a symptom, would obligate it to recognize in the symptom the negative manifestation to God. Without saying that there must be at least as much "reality" in the cause as in the effect, and that the "existence" of God has no need of any proof other than the religious symptomatics, one would see on the contrary—in the negation or suspension of the predicate, even of the thesis of "existence"—the first mark of respect for a divine cause which does not even need to "be." And those who would like to consider "deconstruction" a symptom of modern or postmodern nihilism could indeed, if they wished, recognize in it the last testimony—not to say the martyrdom— of faith in the present *fin de siècle*. This reading will always be possible. Who could prohibit it? In the name of what? But what has happened, so that what is thus permitted is never necessary as such? In order that it be thus, what must the writing of this deconstruction be, writing according to this deconstruction?

That is a first reason. But I chose examples that are close to me for a second reason. I also wanted to say a few words about a quite long-standing wish: to broach—directly and in itself—the web of questions that one formulates prematurely under the heading of "negative theology." Until now, confronted by the question or by the objection, my response has always been brief, elliptical, and dilatory.[2] Yet it seems to me already articulated in two stages.

1. No, what I write is not "negative theology." First of all, *in the measure* to which this belongs to the predicative or judicative space of discourse, to its strictly propositional form, and privileges not only the indestructible unity of the word but also the authority of the name—such axioms as a "deconstruction" must start by reconsidering (which I have tried to do since the first part of *Of Grammatology*). Next, in the measure to which "negative theology" seems to reserve, beyond all positive predication, beyond all negation, even beyond Being, some hyperessentiality, a

being beyond Being. This is the word that Dionysius so often uses in the *Divine Names: hyperousios, -ôs, hyperousiotes.* God as being beyond Being or also God as *without* Being.[3] This seems to exceed the alternative of a theism or an atheism which would only set itself against what one calls, sometimes ingenuously, the existence of God. Without being able to return to the syntax and semantics of the word *without (sans)* which I have tried to analyze elsewhere, I limit myself here to the first stage of this response. No, I would hesitate to inscribe what I put forward under the familiar heading of negative theology, precisely because of that ontological wager of hyperessentiality that one finds at work both in Dionysius and in Meister Eckhart, for example, when he writes:

> Each thing works in its being [Ein ieglich dinc würket in wesene]; nothing can work above its being [über sîn wesen]. Fire can only work in wood. God works above Being [Got würket über wesene], in space, in which He can move. He works in non-being [er würket in unwesene]. Before there was Being, God worked [ê denne wesen wære, dô worhte got]; and He brought about being when there was no Being. Unrefined masters say that God is a pure Being [ein lûter wesen]; He is as high above Being as the highest angel is above a fly. I would be speaking as wrongly in calling God a being as I would in calling the sun pale or black. God is neither this nor that [Got enist weder diz noch daz]. A master says: if anyone thinks that he has known God, even if he did know something, he did not know God. But when I said that God is not being and that He is above Being [über wesen], I have not denied Him being [ich im niht wesen abegesprochen] but, rather, I have exalted Being in Him [ich hân ez in im gehœhet].[4]

In the movement of the same paragraph, a quotation from St. Augustine recalls the simultaneously negative and hyperaffirmative meaning of *without (sans):* "St. Augustine says: God is wise without wisdom [wîse âne wîsheit], good without goodness [guot âne güete], powerful without power [gewaltic âne gewalt]." *Without* does not merely dissociate the singular attribution from the essential generality: wisdom as *being*-wise in general, goodness as *being*-good in general, power as *being*-powerful in general. It does not only avoid the abstraction tied to every common noun and to the being implied in every essential generality. In the same word and in the same syntax it transmutes into affirmation its purely phenomenal negativity, which ordinary language, riveted to finitude, gives us to understand in a word such as *without,* or in other analogous words. It deconstructs grammatical anthropomorphism.

To dwell a bit longer on the first stage of my response, I thought I had to forbid myself to write in the register of "negative theology," because I was aware of this movement toward hyperessentiality, beyond Being. What *differance,* the *trace,* and so on "mean"— which hence *does not mean anything*—is "before" the concept, the name, the word, "something" that would be nothing, that no longer arises from Being, from presence or from the presence of the present, nor even from absence, and even less from some hyperessentiality. Yet the onto-theological reappropriation always remains possible—and doubtless *inevitable* insofar as one speaks, precisely, in the element of logic and of onto-theological grammar. One can always say: hyperessentiality is precisely that, a supreme Being who remains incommensurate to the being of all that is, which *is* nothing, neither present nor absent, and so on. If the movement of this reappropriation appears in fact irrepressible, its ultimate failure is no less necessary. But I concede that this question remains at the heart of a thinking of differance or of the writing of writing. It remains a question, and this is why I return to it again. Following the same "logic," and I continue with the first stage of this response, my uneasiness was nevertheless also directed toward the promise of that presence given to intuition or vision. The promise of such a presence often accompanies the apophatic voyage. It is doubtless the vision of a dark light, no doubt an intuition of "more than luminous [hyperphoton] darkness,"[5] but still it is the immediacy of a presence. Leading to union with God. After the indispensable moment of prayer (of which I will speak again later), Dionysius thus exhorts Timothy to *mystika theamata:*

This is my prayer. And you, dear Timothy, exercise yourself
earnestly in mystical contemplations, abandon all sensation
and all intellectual activities, all that is sensed and intelligible, all non-being and all being [panta ouk onta kai onta];
thus you will unknowingly [agnôstos] be elevated, as far as
possible, to the unity of that beyond Being and knowledge
[tou hyper pasan ousian kai gnôsin]. By the irrepressible
and absolving ecstasis [extasei] of yourself and of all, ab-
solved from all, and going away from all, you will be purely
raised up to the rays of the divine darkness beyond Being
[pros ten hyperousion tou theiou]. (MT, ch. 1:998b–1000a)

This mystic union, this act of unknowing, is also "a genuine
vision and a genuine knowledge [to ontôs idein kai gnôsai]" (MT,
ch. 2: 1025b). It knows unknowing itself in its truth, a truth that
is not an adequation but an unveiling. Celebrating "what is beyond Being in a hyperessential mode [ton hyperousion hyperou-
siôs hymnesai]," this union aims to "know unveiled [aperikalup-
tôs; in an open, unhidden manner] this unknowing [agnosian]
which conceals in every being the knowledge which one can have
of this Being" (MT, ch. 2:1025bc). The revelation is invoked by
an elevation: toward that contact or vision, that pure intuition of
the ineffable, that silent union with that which remains inaccessible to speech. This ascent corresponds to a rarefaction of signs,
figures, symbols—and also of fictions, as well as of myths or
poetry. Dionysius treats this economy of signs as such. The Symbolic Theology is more voluble and more voluminous than the
Mystical Theology. For it treats "metonymies of the sensible which
stand for the divine [ai apo tôn aisthetôn epi ta theia metonu-
miai]" (MT, ch. 3:1033a); it describes the signification of forms
(morphai) and figures (skhemata) in God; it measures its discourse against "symbols" which "demand more words than the
rest, so that the Symbolic Theology was necessarily much more
voluminous than the Theological Sketches and than the Divine
Names." With the elevation beyond the sensible, one gains in
"conciseness," "because what is intelligible presents itself in a
more and more synoptic manner" (MT, ch. 3:1033b). But there is
also something beyond this economical conciseness. By the passage beyond the intelligible itself, the apophatikai theologai aim

toward absolute rarefaction, toward silent union with the ineffable:

> Now, however, that we are to enter the darkness beyond
> intellect, you will not find a brief [brakhylogian] discourse
> but a complete absence of discourse [alogian] and intelligi-
> bility [anoesian]. In affirmative theology the *logos* descends
> from what is above down to the last, and increases according
> to the measure of the descent toward an analogical multi-
> tude. But here, as we ascend from the highest to what lies
> beyond, the *logos* is drawn inward according to the measure
> of the ascent. After all ascent it will be wholly without
> sound and wholly united to the unspeakable [aphthegktô].
> (*MT*, ch. 3:1033bc)

This economy is paradoxical. In principle, the apophatic
movement of discourse would have to negatively retraverse all
the stages of symbolic theology and positive predication. It would
thus be coextensive with it, confined to the same quantity of
discourse. In itself interminable, the apophatic movement cannot
contain within itself the principle of its interruption. It can only
indefinitely defer the encounter with its own limit.

Alien, heterogeneous, in any case irreducible to the intuitive
*telos*—to the experience of the ineffable and of the mute vision
which seems to orient all of this apophatics, including the prayer
and the encomium which prepare its way—the thinking of differance would thus have little affinity, for an analogous reason, with
the current interpretation of certain well-known statements of the
early Wittgenstein. I recall these words often quoted from the
*Tractatus*, for example, "6.522—The inexpressible, indeed, exists [Es gibt allerdings Unaussprechliches]. It *shows itself*; it is
the mystical." And "7.—Concerning that about which one cannot
speak, one must remain silent."

The nature of this "one must" (*"il faut"*) is significant here: it
inscribes the injunction to silence into the order or the promise
of a "one must speak," "one must—not avoid speaking"; or rather,
"it is necessary (*il faut*) that there be a trace." No, "it is necessary
that there *have been* a trace," a sentence that one must simultaneously turn toward a past *and* toward a future that are as yet

unpresentable. It is (now) necessary that there *have been* a trace (in an unremembered past; because of this amnesia, the "necessity" of the trace is necessary). But also, it is necessary (from now on, it will be necessary; the "it is necessary" always also points toward the future) that in the future there will have been a trace.

But we should not be too hasty. In a moment it will be necessary to differentiate between these modalities of the "it is necessary."

2. Turning to what was often the second stage of my improvised responses: the general name of "negative theology" may conceal the confusions it causes and sometimes gives rise to simplistic interpretations. Perhaps there is within it, hidden, restless, diverse, and itself heterogeneous, a voluminous and nebulous multiplicity of potentials to which the single expression "negative theology" yet remains inadequate. In order to engage oneself seriously in this debate, I have often responded, it would be necessary to clarify this designation by considering quite dissimilar corpuses, scenes, proceedings, and languages. As I have always been fascinated by the supposed movements of negative theology (which, no doubt, are themselves never foreign to the experience of fascination in general), I objected in vain to the assimilation of the thinking of the trace or of differance to some negative theology, and my response amounted to a promise: one day I would have to stop deferring, one day I would have to try to explain myself directly on this subject, and at last speak of "negative theology" *itself*, assuming that some such thing exists.

Has the day come?

In other words, how is it possible to avoid speaking about negative theology? How can one resolve this question, and decide between its *two* meanings? 1. How is it possible to avoid speaking of it henceforth? This appears impossible. How could I remain silent on this subject? 2. How, if one speaks of it, to avoid speaking of it? How *not* to speak of it? How is it necessary not to speak of it? How to avoid speaking of it without rhyme or reason? What precautions must be taken to avoid errors, that is, inadequate, insufficient, simplistic assertions?

I return to my opening words. I knew, then, what I would *have to* do. I had implicitly promised that I would, one day, speak directly of negative theology. Even before speaking, I knew that I was committed to doing it. Such a situation leaves room for at least two possible interpretations. 1. Even before speech, in any case before a discursive event as such, there is necessarily a commitment or a promise. This event presupposes the open space of the promise. 2. This commitment, this word that has been given, already belongs to the time of the *parole* by which I "keep my word," or "*tiens parole,*" as one says in French. In fact, at the moment of promising to speak one day of negative theology, I already started to do it. But this is only an as yet confused hint of the structure that I would like to analyze later.

Having already promised, *as if in spite of myself,* I did not know *how* I would keep this promise. How to speak suitably of negative theology? Is there a negative theology? A single one? A regulative model for the others? Can one adapt a discourse to it? Is there some discourse that measures up to it? Is one not compelled to speak of negative theology according to the modes of negative theology, in a way that is at once impotent, exhausting, and inexhaustible? Is there ever anything other than a "negative theology" of "negative theology"?

Above all, I did not know when and where I would do it. Next year in Jerusalem! I told myself, in order to defer, perhaps indefinitely, the fulfillment of this promise. But also to let myself know —and I did indeed receive this message—that on the day when I would in fact go to Jerusalem it would no longer be possible to delay. It would be necessary to do it.

Will I do it? Am I in Jerusalem? This is a question to which one will never respond in the present tense, only in the future or in the past.[6]

Why insist on this postponement? Because it appears to me neither avoidable nor insignificant. One can never decide whether deferring, as such, brings about precisely that which it defers and alters (*diffère*). It is not certain that I am keeping my promise today; nor is it certain that in further delaying I have not, nevertheless, already kept it.

In other words, am I in Jerusalem or elsewhere, very far from the Holy City? Under what conditions does one find oneself in Jerusalem? Is it enough to be there physically, as one says, and to live in places that carry this name, as I am now doing? What is it to live in Jerusalem? This is not easy to decide. Allow me to cite Meister Eckhart again. Like that of Dionysius, his work sometimes resembles an endless meditation on the sense and symbolism of the Holy City: a logic, a rhetoric, a topology, and a tropology of Jerusalem. Here is an example among many others:

> Yesterday I sat in a place where I said something [dâ sprach ich ein wort] that sounds incredible—I said that Jerusalem is as near to my soul as the place where I am now [mîner sele als nâhe als diu stat, dâ ich nû stân]. In truth, that which is a thousand miles beyond Jerusalem is as near to my soul as my own body; I am as sure of this as of being a man.[7]

I will speak of a promise, then, but also within the promise. The experience of negative theology perhaps holds *to* a promise, that of the other, which I must keep because it commits me to speak where negativity ought to absolutely rarefy discourse. Indeed, why should I speak *with an eye to* explaining, teaching, leading—on the paths of a psychagogy or of a pedagogy—toward silence, toward union with the ineffable, mute vision? Why can't I avoid speaking, unless it is because a promise has committed me even before I begin the briefest speech? If I therefore speak of the promise, I will not be able to keep any metalinguistic distance in regard to it. Discourse on the promise is already a promise: *in* the promise. I will thus not speak of this or that promise, but of that which, as necessary as it is impossible, inscribes us by its trace in language—before language. From the moment I open my mouth, I have already promised; or rather, and sooner, the promise has seized the *I* which promises to speak to the other, to say something, at the extreme limit to affirm or to confirm by speech at least this: that it is necessary to be silent; and to be silent concerning that about which one cannot speak. One could have known as much beforehand. This promise is older than I am. Here is something that appears impossible, the theoreticians of speech acts would say: like every genuine performative, a promise must be made in the present, in the first person (in the singular or in the plural). It must be made by one who is capable of saying *I* or *we*, here and now, for example in Jerusalem, "the place where I am now" and where I can therefore be held responsible for this speech act.

The promise of which I shall speak will have always escaped this demand of presence. It is older than I am or than we are. In fact, it renders possible every present discourse on presence. Even if I decide to be silent, even if I decide to promise nothing, not to commit myself to saying something that would confirm once again the destination *of* speech, and the destination *toward* speech, this silence yet remains a modality of speech: a memory of promise and a promise of memory.

I knew, then, that I could not avoid speaking of negative theology. But how and under what heading would I do it? One day, at Yale, I received a telephone message:[8] it was necessary for me to give a title on the spot. In a few minutes I had to improvise, which I first did in my language: "Comment ne pas dire . . . ?" The use of the French word *dire* permits a certain suspension. "Comment ne pas dire?" can mean, in a manner that is both transitive and intransitive, how to be silent, how not to speak in general, how to avoid speaking? But it can also mean: how, in speaking, not to say this or that, in this or that manner? In other words: how, in saying and speaking, to avoid this or that discursive, logical, rhetorical mode? How to avoid an inexact, erroneous, aberrant, improper form? How to avoid such a predicate, and even predication itself? For example: how to avoid a negative form, or how not to be negative? Finally, how to say something? Which comes back to the apparently inverse question: How to say, how to speak? Between the two interpretations of "Comment ne pas dire . . . ?" the meaning of the uneasiness thus seems to turn again: from the "how to be silent?" (how to avoid speaking at all?) one passes—in a completely necessary and as if intrinsic fashion—to the question, which can always become the heading for an injunction: how not to speak, and which speech to avoid, in order to speak *well*? "How to avoid speaking" thus means, at once or successively: How must one not speak? How is it necessary to speak? (This is) how it is necessary not to speak. And so on. The "how" always conceals a "why," and the "it is necessary" ("*il faut*") bears the multiple meanings of "should," "ought," and "must."

I thus improvised this title on the telephone. Letting it be dictated to me by I do not know what unconscious order—in a situation of absolute urgency—I thus also translated my desire to defer still further. This "fight or flight" reaction reproduces itself on the occasion of every lecture: how to avoid speaking, and yet from the outset to commit oneself by giving a title even before writing one's text? But also, in the economy of the same gesture: how to speak, how to do this *as is necessary, comme il faut*, assuming the responsibility for a promise? Not only for the arch-originary promise which establishes us *a priori* as people who are responsible for speech, but for this promise: to give a lecture on "absence and negation," on the *not* ("how not to," "ought not," "should not," "must not," etc.), on the "how" and the "why" (of the) *not*, the negation and the denial, and so on, and thus to commit oneself to giving a title *in advance*. Every title has the import of a promise; a title given in advance is the promise of a promise.

It was thus necessary for me to respond, but I assumed responsibility only while deferring it. Before or rather within a double bind: "how to avoid speaking" since I have already started to speak and have always already started to promise to speak? That I have already started to speak, or rather that at least the trace of a speech will have preceded this very speech, one cannot deny. Translate: *one can only deny it*. There can only be denial of this which is undeniable. What, then, do we make of negations and of denials? What do we make of them before God, that is the question, if there is one. Because the posing of every question is perhaps secondary; it perhaps follows as a first, reactive response, the undeniable *provocation*, the unavoidable denial of the undeniable provocation.

To avoid speaking, to delay the moment when one will have to say something and perhaps acknowledge, surrender, impart a secret, one amplifies the digressions. I will here attempt a brief digression on the secret itself. Under this title, "how to avoid speaking," it is necessary to speak of the secret. In certain situations, one asks oneself "how to avoid speaking," either because one has promised not to speak and to keep a secret, or because one has an interest, sometimes vital, in keeping silent even if put to the rack. This situation again presupposes the possibility of speaking. Some would say, perhaps imprudently, that only man is capable of speaking, because only he can *not* show what he could show. Of course, an animal may inhibit a movement, can abstain from an incautious gesture, for example in a defensive or offensive predatory strategy, such as in the delimitation of sexual territory or in a mating ritual. One might say, then, that animals can *not* respond to the inquisition or requisition of a stimulus or of a complex of stimuli. According to this somewhat naive philosophy of the animal world, one may nevertheless observe that animals are incapable of keeping or even having a secret, because they cannot *represent as such*, as an *object* before consciousness, something that they would then forbid themselves from showing. One would thus link the secret to the objective representation (*Vorstellung*) that is placed before consciousness and that is expressible in the form of words. The essence of such a secret would remain rigorously alien to every other nonmanifestation; and, notably, unlike that of which the animal is capable. The manifestation or nonmanifestation of *this* secret, in short its possibility, would never be on the order of the symptom. An animal can neither choose to keep silent, nor keep a secret.

I will not take up this immense problem here. To deal with it, it would be necessary to account for numerous mediations, and then to question in particular the possibility of a preverbal or simply nonverbal secret—linked, for example, to gestures or to mimicry, and even to other codes and more generally to the unconscious. It would be necessary to study the structures of denial before and outside of the possibility of judgment and of predicative language. Above all, it would be necessary to reelaborate a problematic of consciousness, that thing that, more and more, one avoids discussing as if one knew what it is and as if its riddle were solved. But is any problem more novel today than that of consciousness? Here one would be tempted to designate, if not to define, consciousness as that place in which is retained the singular power not to *say* what one knows, to keep a secret in the form of representation. A conscious being is a being capable of lying, of not presenting in speech that of which it yet has an articulated representation: a being that can avoid speaking. But in order to be able to lie, a second and already mediated possibility, it is first and more essentially necessary to be able to keep for (and say to) oneself what one already knows. To keep something to oneself is the most incredible and thought-provoking power. But this keeping-for-oneself—this dissimulation for which it is already necessary to be multiple and to differ from oneself—also presupposes the space of a promised speech, that is to say, a trace to which the affirmation is not symmetrical. How to ascertain absolute dissimulation? Does one ever have at one's disposal either sufficient criteria or an apodictic certainty that allows one to say: the secret has been kept, the dissimulation has taken place, one has avoided speaking? Not to mention the secret that is wrested by physical or mental torture, uncontrolled manifestations that are direct or symbolic, somatic or figurative, may leave in reserve a possible betrayal or avowal. Not because everything manifests itself. Simply, the nonmanifestation is never assured. According to this hypothesis, it would be necessary to reconsider all the boundaries between consciousness and the unconscious, as between man and animal and an enormous system of oppositions.

But I will avoid speaking of the secret as such. These brief allusions to the negativity of the secret and to the secret of denegation seemed necessary to me in order to situate another problem. I will only touch upon it. "Negative theologies" and everything that resembles a form of esoteric sociality have always been infortuitously associated with phenomena of secret society, as if access to the most rigorous apophatic discourse demanded the sharing of a "secret"—that is, of an ability to keep silent that would always be something more than a simple logical or rhetorical technique that is easily imitated and has a withheld content —and of a place or of a wealth that it would be necessary to conceal from the many. It is as if divulgence imperiled a revelation promised to apophasis, to this deciphering which, to make the thing appear uncovered (aperikalyptôs), must first find it hidden. A recurrence and a rule-governed analogy: today, for example, those who still denounce "deconstruction"—with its thinking of differance or the writing of writing—as a bastardized resurgence of negative theology are also those who readily suspect those they call the "deconstructionists" of forming a sect, a brotherhood, an esoteric corporation, or more vulgarly, a clique, a gang, or (I quote) a "mafia." Since a law of recurrence operates here, up to a certain point the logic of suspicion may be formalized. Those who lead the instruction or the trial say or tell themselves, successively or alternatively:

1. Those people, adepts of negative theology or of deconstruction (the difference matters little to the accusers), must indeed have a secret. They hide something since they say nothing, speak in a negative manner, respond "no, it's not that, it's not so simple" to all questions, and say that what they are speaking about is neither this, nor that, nor a third term, neither a concept nor a name, in short is not, and thus is nothing.

2. But since this secret obviously cannot be determined and is nothing, as these people themselves recognize, they have no secret. They pretend to have one in order to organize themselves around a social power founded on the magic of a speech that is suited to speaking in order to say nothing. These obscurantists are terrorists who remind one of the Sophists. A Plato would be of use in combating them. They possess a real power, which may be situated inside or outside the Academy: they contrive to blur even this boundary. Their alleged secret belongs to sham, mystification, or at best to a politics of grammar. Because for them there is only writing and language, nothing beyond, even if they claim to "deconstruct logocentrism" and even start there.

3. If you know how to question them, they will finish by admitting: "The secret is that there is no secret, but there are at least two ways of thinking or proving this proposition," and so on. Experts in the art of evasion, they know better how to negate or deny than how to say anything. They always agree to avoid speaking while speaking a lot and "splitting hairs." Some of them appear "Greek," others "Christian"; they have recourse to many languages at once, and one knows some who resemble Talmudists. They are perverse enough to make their esotericism popular and "fashionable." Thus ends a familiar indictment.

One finds hints of this esotericism in the Platonism, and Neo-platonism, which themselves remain so present at the heart of Dionysius' negative theology. But in the works of Dionysius himself, and in another way in those of Meister Eckhart, one may say that no mystery is made of the necessity of the secret—to be kept, preserved, shared. It is necessary to stand or step aside, to find the *place* proper to the experience of the secret. This detour through the secret will lead, in a moment, to the question of the *place* that will henceforth orient my talk. Following the prayer that opens his *Mystical Theology*, Dionysius frequently names the secret of the divinity beyond Being, the "secrets" *(cryphio-mystiques)* of the "more than luminous darkness of silence." The "secret" of this revelation gives access to the unknowing beyond knowledge. Dionysius exhorts Timothy to divulge the secret neither to those who know, think they know, or think they can know by the path of knowledge, nor *a fortiori* to the ignorant and profane. Avoid speaking, he advises him in short. It is thus necessary to separate oneself twice: from those who know—one could say here, from the philosophers or the experts in ontology —and from the profane, who employ predicative language as naive idolaters. One is not far from the innuendo that ontology itself is a subtle or perverse idolatry, which one will understand, in an analogous and different way, through the voice of Levinas or of Jean-Luc Marion.

The paragraph I will read has a surfeit of interest in defining a beyond that exceeds the opposition between affirmation and negation. In truth, as Dionysius expressly says, it exceeds *position* (thesis) itself, and not merely curtailment, subtraction *(aphairesis)*. At the same time, it exceeds privation. The *without* of which I spoke a moment ago marks neither a privation, a lack, nor an absence. As for the *beyond (hyper)* of that which is beyond Being *(hyperousios)*, it has the double and ambiguous meaning of what is above in a hierarchy, thus both beyond and more. God (is) beyond Being but as such is more (being) than Being: *no more being* and *being more than Being*: being more. The French expression *plus d'être* (more being, no more being) formulates this equivocation in a fairly economical manner. Here is the call to an initiatory secret, and the warning:

Disclose this not to the *uninitiated* [tôn amuetôn]: not to those, I say, who are entangled in beings [tois ousin], imagine nothing to be hyperessentially [hyperousiôs] beyond beings, and claim to know by the knowledge in them "Him who has made the dark his hiding place" [Ps. 18:12]. If the divine mystical initiations are beyond these, what about those yet more profane, who characterize the cause which lies beyond all [hyperkeimenen aitian] by the last among beings, and deny it to be preeminent to their ungodly phantasies and diverse formations [polyeidôn morphomatôn] of it? For while to it, as cause of all one must posit and affirm all the positions of beings, as beyond be-ing, beyond all, one must more properly deny all of these. Think not that affirmations and denials are opposed but rather that, long before, the cause transcends all privation [tas stereseis], since it *situates* itself beyond all affirmative and negative position [hyper pasan kai aphairesin kai thesin]. (*MT*, ch. 1:1000ab; my italics)

It *situates* itself, then. It situates itself *beyond* all position. What is thus this place? Between the place and the place of the secret, between the secret place and the topography of the social link which must protect the nondivulgence, there must be a certain homology. This must govern some (secret) relation between the topology of what stands beyond Being, without being — without Being, and the topology, the initiatory politopology which at once organizes the mystical community and makes possible the address to the other, this quasi-pedagogical and mystagogical speech, which Dionysius singularly directs to Timothy (*pros Timotheon*: the dedication of the *Mystical Theology*).

In this hierarchy,[9] where does the speaker stand, and where the one who listens and receives? Where does the one stand who speaks while *receiving* from the Cause which is also the Cause of this community? Where do Dionysius and Timothy stand, both they and all those who potentially read the text addressed by one of them to the other? Where do they stand in relationship to God, the Cause? God resides in a place, Dionysius says, but He is not this place. To gain access to this place is not yet to contemplate God. Even Moses must retreat. He receives this order from a place that is not a place, even if one of the names of God can sometimes

designate place itself. Like all the initiated, he must purify himself, step aside from the impure, separate himself from the many,
join "the elite of the priests." But access to this divine place does
not yet deliver him to passage toward the mystical Darkness
where profane vision ceases and where it is necessary to be silent.
It is finally *permitted* and *prescribed* to be silent while closing
one's eyes:

> It [the good and universal Cause] lies hyperessentially be-
> yond all, it is truly and undisguisedly manifested only to
> those who step beyond all that is pure and impure, scale
> every ascent of the holy summits, relinquish every divine
> light, celestial sounds and *logoi,* and enter into the divine
> darkness. . . . It is not to be taken lightly that the divine
> Moses was *ordered first to purify himself,* and again *to be
> separated* from those who were not pure; after every purifi-
> cation he hears the many sounded trumpets, he sees the
> many pure lights which flash forth and the greatly flowing
> rays. Then he is *separated* from the many and, with *those
> who are sacred and select* [tôn ekkritôn iereôn], he overtakes
> the summits of the divine ascents. Yet with these he does
> not come to be with God Himself; *he does not see God—for
> God is unseen* [atheatos gar]—*but the place* [topon] *where
> God is.* This signifies to me that the most divine and highest
> *of what is seen and intelligible* are hypothetical logoi of
> what is subordinate to that beyond-having all. Through these
> is shown forth the presence [parousia] of that which walks
> upon the intelligible summits of His most holy *places* [tôn
> agiôtatôn autou topôn].
>   And then Moses abandons those who see and what is seen
> and enters into the really mystical darkness of unknowing
> [tes agnôsias]; in this he shuts out every knowing apprehen-
> sion and comes to be in the wholly imperceptible and invis-
> ible, be-ing entirely of that beyond all—of nothing, neither
> himself or another, united most excellently by the com-
> pletely unknowing inactivity of every knowledge, and
> knowing beyond intellect by knowing nothing. (*MT,* ch.
> 1:1000cd; my italics)

I will take up three motifs from this passage.
1. To separate oneself, to step aside, to withdraw with an elite,

from the start this topolitology of the secret obeys an order. Moses "was ordered first to purify himself, and again to be separated from those who were not pure." This order cannot be distinguished from a promise. It is the promise itself. The knowledge of the High Priest—who intercedes, so to speak, between God and the holy institution—is the knowledge of the promise. Dionysius makes this more precise, in the *Ecclesiastical Hierarchy*, on the subject of the prayer for the dead. *Epaggelia* signifies both the commandment and the promise: "Knowing that the divine promises will infallibly realize themselves [tas apseudeis epaggelias], he teaches all the assistant priests that the gifts for which he supplicates by virtue of a holy institution [Kata thesmon ieron] will be abundantly granted to those who lead a perfect life in God."[10] Earlier, it was said that "the grand priest knows well the promises contained in the infallible Scriptures" (*ibid.*, p. 561d).

2. In this topolitology of the secret, the figures or *places* of rhetoric are also political stratagems. The "sacred symbols," the compositions (*synthemata*), the signs and figures of the sacred discourse, the "enigmas," and the "typical symbols" are invented as "shields" against the many. All of the anthropomorphic emotions which one attributes to God, the sorrows, the angers, the repentances, the curses, all negative moments—and even the "sophistries" (*sophismata*) which He uses in the Scripture "to evade His promises"—are nothing but "sacred allegories [iera synthemata] which one has had the audacity to use to represent God, projecting outward and multiplying the visible appearances of the mystery, dividing the unique and indivisible, figuring in multiple forms what has neither form nor figure [kai typôtika, kai polymorpha tôn amorphôtôn kai atypôtôn], so that one who could see the beauty hidden in the interior [of these allegories] would find them entirely mystical, consistent with God and full of a great theological light" (Letter 9:1105b et seq.). Without the divine promise which is also an injunction, the power of these *synthemata* would be merely conventional rhetoric, poetry, fine arts, perhaps literature. It would suffice to doubt this promise or transgress this injunction in order to see an opening—and also a closing upon itself—of the field of rhetoricity or even of literariness, the lawless law of fiction.

doubtless even precedes their distribution? At the intersection of the secret and of the nonsecret, what is the secret?

At the crossing point of these two languages, each of which *bears* the silence of the other, a secret must and must not allow itself to be divulged. It can and it cannot do this. One must not divulge, but it is also necessary to make known or rather allow to be known this "it is necessary," "one must not," or "it is necessary not to."

*How not to divulge a secret?* How to avoid saying or speaking? Contradictory and unstable meanings give such a question its endless oscillation: what to do in order that the secret remain secret? How to make it known, in order that the secret of the secret—as such—not remain secret? How to avoid this divulgence itself? These light disturbances underlie the same sentence. At one and the same time stable and unstable, this sentence allows itself to be carried by the movements which here I call *denial (dénégation),* a word that I would like to understand prior even to its elaboration in the Freudian context. (This is perhaps not easy and assumes at least two preconditions: that the chosen examples extend beyond both the predicative structure and the onto-theological or metaphysical presuppositions which sustain the psychoanalytic theorems.)

There is a secret of denial and a denial of the secret. The secret as such, *as secret,* separates and already institutes a negativity; it is a negation that denies itself. It de-negates itself. This denegation does not happen to it by accident; it is essential and originary. And in the *as such* of the secret that denies itself because it appears to itself in order to be what it is, this de-negation gives no chance to dialectic. The enigma of which I am speaking here —in a manner that is too eliptical, too "concise," Dionysius would say, and also too verbose—is the *sharing of the secret.* Not only the sharing of the secret with the other, my partner in a sect or in a secret society, my accomplice, my witness, my ally. I refer first of all to the secret shared *within itself,* its partition "proper," which divides the essence of a secret that cannot even appear to one alone except in starting to be lost, to divulge itself, hence to dissimulate itself, as secret, in showing itself: dissimulating its

dissimulation. There is no secret *as such*; I deny it. And this is
what I confide in secret to whoever allies himself to me. This is
the secret of the alliance. If the theo-logical necessarily insinuates
itself there, this does not mean that the secret itself is theo-logical.
But does something like the secret *itself*, properly speaking, ever
exist? The name of God (I do not say God, but how to avoid
saying God here, from the moment when I say the name of God?)
can only be *said* in the modality of this secret denial: above all, I
do not want to say that.

   3.  My third remark also concerns the place. The *Mystical Theology* thus distinguishes between access to the contemplation of
God and access to the place where God resides. Contrary to what
certain acts of designation may allow one to think, God is not
simply His place; He is not even in His most holy places. He is
not and He does not take place ("il n'est pas et il n'a pas lieu"),
or rather He is and takes place, but without Being and without
place, without being His place. What is the place, what takes
place or gives place to thought, henceforth, in this word? We will
have to follow this thread in order to ask ourselves what an event
can be—*ce qui a lieu* or that which *takes place*—in this atopics
of God. I say *atopics*, hardly even playing: *atopos* is the senseless,
the absurd, the extravagant, the mad. Dionysius often speaks of
God's madness. When he cites Scripture ("God's madness is wiser
than human wisdom"), he evokes "the theologians' practice of
turning back and denying all positive terms in order to apply
them to God under their negative aspect" (*DN*, ch. 7:865b). For
the moment a single clarification: if God's place, which is not
God, does not communicate with the divine hyperessence, this is
not only because it remains either perceptible or visible. This is
also the case inasmuch as it is an intelligible place. Whatever
may be the ambiguity of the passage and the difficulty of knowing
whether "the place where God resides"—and which is not God
—does or does not belong to the order of the sensible, the conclusion seems unambiguous: "The presence" (*parousia*) of God situates itself "upon the intelligible summits of His most holy places
[tais noetai akrotesi tôn agiôtatôn autou topôn]" (*MT*, ch. 1:1000d).

# II

We are still on the threshold.

How to avoid speaking? ("Comment ne pas parler?") Why direct this question now toward the question of the place? Wasn't it already there? And isn't to lead always to give oneself over from one place to another? A question about the place does not stand outside place; it properly *concerns* the place.

In the *three stages* that now await us, I have thought it necessary to privilege the experience of the place. But already the word *experience* appears risky. The relation to the place about which I shall speak will perhaps no longer have the form of experience—if this still assumes the encounter with or crossing over a presence.

Why this privilege of the place? Its justifications will appear along the way, I hope. Nevertheless, here are some preliminary and schematic hints.

Since such is the *topos* of our colloquium in Jerusalem, poetry, literature, literary criticism, poetics, hermeneutics, and rhetoric will be at stake: everything that can articulate speech or writing, in the current sense, together with what I call here a trace. Each time, problems are inevitable: *on the one hand*, the immense problem of figurative spatialization (both *in* speech or writing in the current sense and in the space *between* the current sense and the other, of which the current sense is only a figure); and, *on the other hand*, that of meaning and reference, and *finally*, that of the event insofar as it takes place.

As we have already glimpsed, figuration and the so-called places *(topoi)* of rhetoric constitute the very concern of apophatic procedures. As for meaning and reference, here is another reminder —in truth, the recall of the other, the call of the other as *recall*. At the moment when the question "how to avoid speaking?" is raised and articulates itself in all its modalities—whether in rhetorical or logical forms of saying, or in the simple fact of speaking—it is already, so to speak, *too late*. There is no longer any question of not speaking. Even if one speaks and says noth-

ing, even if an apophatic discourse deprives itself of meaning or
of an object, it takes place. That which committed or rendered it
possible *has taken place*. The possible absence of a referent still
beckons, if not toward the thing of which one speaks (such is
God, who is nothing because He takes place, *without place, beyond Being*), at least toward the other (other than Being) who
calls or to whom this speech is addressed—even if it speaks only
in order to speak, or to say nothing. This call of the other, having
always already preceded the speech to which it has never been
present a first time, announces itself in advance as a *recall*. Such
a reference to the other will always have taken place. Prior to
every proposition and even before all discourse in general—
whether a promise, prayer, praise, celebration. The most negative
discourse, even beyond all nihilisms and negative dialectics, preserves a trace of the other. A trace of an event older than it *or* of a
"taking-place" to come, both of them: here there is neither an
alternative nor a contradiction.

Translated into the *Christian* apophatics of Dionysius (although other translations of the same necessity are possible), this
signifies that the power of speaking and of speaking *well of* God
already proceeds from God. This is the case even if to do this it is
necessary to avoid speaking in one manner or another, or even if,
in order to speak *rightly* or *truly*, it is necessary to avoid speaking
entirely. This power is a gift and an effect of God. The Cause is a
kind of absolute reference for it, but from the outset both an order
and a promise. The Cause, the gift of the gift, the order and the
promise are the same, that same to which or rather to Whom the
responsibility for who speaks and "speaks well" responds. At the
end of the *Divine Names*, the very possibility of speaking of the
divine names and of speaking of them in a correct manner returns
to God, "to That One who is the Cause of all good, to Him who
has first given us the gift to speak and, then, to speak well [kai to
legein kai to eu legein]" (*DN*, ch. 13:981c). Following the implicit
rule from this utterance, one may say that it is always possible to
call on God, to call this assumed origin of all speech by the name
of God, its required cause. The exigence of its Cause, the responsibility before what is responsible for it, demands what is demanded. It is for speech, or for the best silence, a request, a

demand, or a desire, if you wish, for what one equally well calls meaning, the referent, truth. This is what God's name always names, before or beyond other names: the trace of the singular event that will have rendered speech possible even before it turns itself back toward—in order to respond to—this first or last reference. This is why apophatic discourse must also open with a prayer that recognizes, assigns, or ensures its destination: the Other as Referent of a *legein* which is none other than its Cause.

This always presupposed event, this singular having-taken-place, is also for every reading, every interpretation, every poetics, every literary criticism, what one currently calls the œuvre: at least the "already-there" *(déjà-là)* of a phrase, the trace of a phrase of which the singularity would have to remain irreducible and its reference indispensable in a given idiom. A trace has taken place. Even if the idiomatic quality must necessarily lose itself or allow itself to be contaminated by the repetition which confers on it a code and an intelligibility, even if it *occurs only to efface itself*, if it arises only in effacing itself, the effacement will have taken place, even if its place is only in the ashes. *Il y a là cendre.*

What I have just alluded to seems to concern only the finite experience of finite works. But since the structure of the trace is *in general* the very possibility of an experience of finitude, I dare to say that the distinction between a finite and an infinite cause of the trace appears secondary here. It is itself an effect of trace or differance, which does not mean that the trace or differance (of which I have tried to show elsewhere that it is finite, insofar as it is infinite)[11] have a cause or an origin.

Thus, at the moment when the question "How to avoid speaking?" arises, it is already too late. There was no longer any question of not speaking. Language has started without us, in us and before us. This is what theology calls God, and it is necessary, it will have been necessary, to speak. This "it is necessary" *(il faut)* is *both* the trace of undeniable necessity—which is another way of saying that one cannot avoid denying it, one can only deny it —*and* of a past injunction. Always already past, hence without a past present. Indeed, it must have been possible to speak in order to allow the question "How to avoid speaking?" to arise. Having come from the past, language before language, a past that was

never present and yet remains unforgettable—this "it is necessary" thus seems to beckon toward the event of an order or of a
promise that does not belong to what one currently calls history,
the discourse of history or the history of discourse. Order or
promise, this injunction commits (me), in a rigorously asymmet-
rical manner, even before I have been able to say *I,* to sign such a
*provocation* in order to reappropriate it for myself and restore the
symmetry. That in no way mitigates my responsibility; on the
contrary. There would be no responsibility without this *prior
coming (prévenance)* of the trace, or if autonomy were first or
absolute. Autonomy itself would not be possible, nor would respect for the law (sole "cause" of this respect) in the strictly
Kantian meaning of these words. In order to elude this responsibility, to deny it and try to efface it through an absolute regres-
sion, it is still or already necessary for me to endorse or counter-
sign it. When Jeremiah curses the day he was born,[12] he must yet
—or already—*affirm.* Or rather, he must confirm, in a movement
that is no more positive than negative, according to the words of
Dionysius, because it does not belong to position *(thesis)* or to de-
position (privation, subtraction, negation).

Why three steps? Why should I now proceed in three stages? I
am certainly not bent on acquitting myself of some dialectical
obligation. Despite appearances, here we are involved in a thinking that is essentially alien to dialectic, even if Christian negative
theologies owe much to Platonic or Neoplatonic dialectic; and
even if it is difficult to read Hegel without taking account of an
apophatic tradition that was not foreign to him (at least by the
mediation of Bruno, hence of Nicholas of Cusa and of Meister
Eckhart, etc.).

The three "stages" or the three "signs" that I will now link
together, as in a fable, do not form the moments or signs of a
history. They will not disclose the order of a teleology. They
rather concern deconstructive questions on the subject of such a
teleology.

Three stages or three places in any case to avoid speaking of a
question that I will be unable to treat; to deny it in some way, or
to speak of it without speaking of it, in a negative mode: what do
I understand by negative theology and its phantoms in a tradition

of thought that is neither Greek nor Christian? In other words, what of Jewish and Islamic thought in this regard?[13] By example, and in everything that I will say, a certain void, the place of an internal desert, will perhaps allow this question to resonate. The three paradigms that I will too quickly have to situate (for a paradigm is often an architectural model) will surround a resonant space of which nothing, almost nothing, will ever be said.

## A

The first paradigm will be Greek.

I quickly mention its names, whether proper or not: Plato and the Neoplatonisms, the epekeina tes ousias of the Republic, and the khora of the Timaeus. In the Republic, the movement that leads epekeina tes ousias, beyond Being (or beyond beingness— a serious question of translation on which I cannot dwell here), no doubt inaugurates an immense tradition. One may follow its pathways, detours, and overdeterminations until arriving at what in a moment will be the second paradigm, the Christian apophases, and those of Dionysius in particular. Much has been written about this affiliation and its limits; this will not concern me here. In the short time that I have at my disposal, since there can be no question of allowing myself a minute study, or even of summarizing what I am attempting elsewhere—now, in seminars or texts in preparation—I will content myself with a few schematic traits. I choose them from our present standpoint, that of the question "How to avoid speaking?" such as I have started to define it: a question of the place as place of writing, of inscription, of the trace. For lack of time, I will have to lighten my talk, employing neither long quotations nor "secondary" literature. But this will not, we shall see, render the hypothesis of a "naked" text any less problematic.

In the Platonic text and in the tradition it marks, it seems to me that one must distinguish between two movements or two tropics of negativity. These two structures are radically heterogeneous.

1. One of them finds both its principle and its exemplification in the Republic (509b et seq.). The idea of the Good (idea tou

*agathou)* has its place beyond Being or essence. Thus the Good is not, nor is its place. But this not-being is not a non-being; one may say that it transcends presence or essence, *epekeina tes ousias*, beyond the beingness of Being. From what is beyond the presence of all that is, the Good gives birth to Being or to the essence of what is, *to einai* and *ten ousian*, but without itself being. Whence comes the homology between the Good and the sun, between the intelligible sun and the sensible sun. The former gives to beings their visibility, their genesis (growth and nutrition). But it is not in becoming; it is not visible and it does not belong to the order of what proceeds from it, either in regard to knowledge or in regard to Being.

Unable to get involved in the readings that this immense text demands and has already provoked, I will observe two points that concern me in this context.

*On the one hand*, whatever may be the discontinuity marked by this beyond *(epekeina)* in relation to Being, in relation to the Being of beings or beingness (nevertheless, three distinct hypotheses), this singular limit does not give place to simply neutral or negative determinations, but to a *hyperbolism* of that, beyond which the Good gives rise to thinking, to knowing, and to Being. Negativity serves the *hyper* movement that produces, attracts, or guides it. The Good is not, of course, in the sense that it is not Being or beings, and on this subject every ontological grammar must take on a negative form. But this negative form is not neutral. It does not oscillate between the *ni ceci—ni cela* (the neither/nor). It first of all obeys a logic of the *sur*, of the *hyper*, over and beyond, which heralds all the hyperessentialisms of Christian apophases and all the debates that develop around them (for example, the criticism of Dionysius by Saint Thomas, who reproaches him for having placed *Bonum* before or above *Ens* or *Esse* in the hierarchy of divine names). This maintains a sufficiently homogeneous, homologous, or analogous relationship between Being and (what is) beyond Being, in order that what exceeds the border may be compared to Being, albeit through the figure of hyperbole; but most of all, in order that what is or is known may *owe* its being and its being-known to this Good. This analogical continuity allows for the translation, and for the comparison of the Good to the intelligible sun, and of the latter to the perceptible sun. The excess of this Good which (is) *hyperekhon*, its transcendence, situates it at the origin of Being and of knowledge. It permits one to *take account*, to speak both of what is and of what the Good is. Knowable things draw from the Good not only the property of being known, but also Being *(einai)* and existence or essence *(ousia)*, even if the Good does not belong to essence ("ouk ousias ontos tou agathou") but to something that by far surpasses *(hyperekhontos)* Being in dignity, antiquity *(presbeia)*, and power ("all'eti epekeina tes ousias presbeia kai dynamei hyperekhontos"; *Republic*, 509b). The excellence is not so alien to Being or to light that the excess itself cannot be described in the terms of what it exceeds. A bit earlier, an allusion to a third species *(triton genos)* seems to disorient the discourse, because this is neither the visible nor sight or vision; it is precisely light (507e), itself produced by the sun, and son of the Good ("ton tou agathou ekgonon") which the Good has engendered in its own likeness ("on tagathon agennesen analogon"). This analogy between the perceptible and intelligible sun will yet permit one to have confidence in the resemblance between the Good *(epekeina tes ousias)* and that to which it gives birth, Being and knowledge. Negative discourse on that which stands beyond Being, and apparently no longer tolerates ontological predicates, does not interrupt this analogical continuity. In truth, it assumes it; it even allows itself to be guided by it. Ontology remains possible and necessary. One might discern the effects of this analogical continuity in the rhetoric, grammar, and logic of all the discourses on the Good and on what is beyond Being.

On the other hand, soon after the passage on what (is) *epekeina tes ousias* and *hyperekhon*, Glaucon addresses himself or pretends to address himself to God, to the god of the sun, Apollo: "Oh Apollo, what divine hyperbole [daimonias hyperboles: what daemonic or supernatural excess]!" We should not assign too much weight to this invocation or address to God at the moment when one speaks of that which exceeds Being. It seems to be made lightly, in a somewhat humorous manner *(geloiôs)*, as if to punctuate the scene with a breathing. I emphasize it for reasons that will become clear in a moment, when the necessity for every discourse on apophatic theology to begin with an address to God will become something completely other than a theatrical rhetoric: it will have the seriousness of a prayer.

Why have I just pointed out the allusion to the "third species" destined to play a role of analogical mediation, that of light between vision and the visible? Because in the *Sophist* (243b), this schema of the *third* also concerns Being. Of all the paired oppositions, one may say that each term *is*. The being *(einai)* of this *is* figures as a third that is beyond the two others ("triton para ta duo ekeina"). It is indispensable to the interweaving *(symploke)* or to the dialectical intersection of the forms or of the ideas in a *logos* capable of receiving the other. After having raised the question of non-being, which is in itself unthinkable *(adianoeton)*, ineffable *(arreton)*, unpronounceable *(aphtegkton)*, foreign to discourse and to reason *(alogon; 238c)*, one arrives at the presentation of dialectic itself. Passing through the parricide and the murder of Parmenides, this dialectic receives the thinking of non-being as *other* and not as absolute nothingness or simple opposite of Being (256b, 259c). This confirms that there cannot be an absolutely negative discourse: a *logos* necessarily speaks about something; it cannot avoid speaking of something; it is impossible for it to refer to nothing ("logon anagkaion, otanper è, tinos einai logon, mè dè tinos adunaton"; 262e).

2. I will distinguish the tropics of negativity, which I have just outlined in such a schematic manner, from another tropics in Plato's works; it is another manner of treating what is beyond *(epekeina)* the border, the third species, and the place. This place is here called *khora*; I am, of course, alluding to the *Timaeus*. When I say that this is found "in Plato's works," I leave aside, for lack of time, the question of whether or not it has its place at the interior of the Platonic text, and what "at the interior of" means here. These are questions that I will treat at length elsewhere in a future publication. From this work in progress,[14] I will permit myself to set off a few elements that are indispensable to the formulation of a hypothesis that relates to the present context.

*Khora* also constitutes a third species *(triton genos; Timaeus* 48e, 49a, 52a). This place is not the intelligible paradigm with which the demiurge inspires itself. Nor does it belong to the order of copies or sensible mimemes that it impresses in the khora. It is difficult to speak of this absolutely necessary place, this place "in which" the mimemes of the eternal beings originate by impressing themselves (typothenta) there, and it is difficult to speak of the impression (ekmageion) for all the types and all the schemas. It is difficult to adjust to it a true or firm logos. One glimpses it only in an "oneiric" manner and one can only describe it by a "bastard reasoning" (logismô tini nothô). This spatial interval neither dies nor is born (52b). Nevertheless, its "eternity" is not that of the intelligible paradigms. At the moment, so to speak, when the demiurge organizes the cosmos by cutting, introducing, and impressing the images of the paradigms "into" the khora, the latter must already have been there, as the "there" itself, beyond time or in any case beyond becoming, in a beyond time without common measure with the eternity of the ideas and the becoming of sensible things. How does Plato deal with this disproportion and heterogeneity? There are, it seems to me, two concurrent languages in these pages of the Timaeus.

To be sure, one of these languages multiplies the negations, the warnings, the evasions, the detours, the tropes, but with a view to reappropriating the thinking of the khora for ontology and for Platonic dialectic in its most dominant schemas. If the khora— place, spacing, receptacle (hypodokhè)—is neither sensible nor intelligible, it seems to participate in the intelligible in an enigmatic way (51a). Since it "receives all," it makes possible the formation of the cosmos. As it is neither this nor that (neither intelligible nor sensible), one may speak as if it were a joint participant in both. Neither/nor easily becomes both . . . and, both this and that. Whence the rhetoric of the passage, the multiplication of figures which one traditionally interprets as metaphors: gold, mother, nurse, sieve, receptacle, impression, and so on. Aristotle provided the matrix for many of the readings of the Timaeus and, since his Physics (bk. 4), one has always interpreted this passage on the khora as being at the interior of philosophy, in a consistently anachronistic way, as if it prefigured, on the one hand, the philosophies of space as extensio (Descartes) or as pure sensible form (Kant); or on the other hand, the materialist philosophies of the substratum or of substance which stands, like the *hypodokhè, beneath* the qualities or the phenomena. These readings, the wealth and complexity of which I can only touch upon here, are still possible, and up to a certain point justifiable. As for their anachronistic character, it seems to me not only evident but structurally inevitable. The *khora* is the atemporality (*l'anachronie*) itself of the spacing; it (a)temporalizes (*anachronise*), it calls forth atemporality, provokes it immutably from the pretemporal *already* that gives place to every inscription. But this is another story with which we cannot get involved here.

The other language and the other interpretive decision interest me more, without ceasing to be atemporal or anachronistic in their way. The synchronicity of a reading has no chance here and no doubt would lack exactly that to which it claimed to adjust itself. This other gesture would inscribe an irreducible spacing interior to (but hence also exterior to, once the interior is placed outside) Platonism, that is, interior to ontology, to dialectic, and perhaps to philosophy in general. Under the name of *khora*, the place belongs neither to the sensible nor to the intelligible, neither to becoming, nor to non-being (the *khora* is never described as a void), nor to Being: according to Plato, the quantity or the quality of Being are measured against its intelligibility. All the aporias, which Plato makes no effort to hide, would signify that *there is* something that is neither a being nor a nothingness; something that no dialectic, participatory schema, or analogy would allow one to rearticulate together with any philosopheme whatsoever, neither "in" Plato's works nor in the history that Platonism inaugurates and dominates. The *neither/nor* may no longer be reconverted into *both . . . and*. Hence the so-called "metaphors" are not only inadequate, in that they borrow figures from the sensible forms inscribed in the *khora*, without pertinence for designating the *khora* itself. They are no longer metaphors. Like all rhetoric which makes of it a systematic web, the concept of metaphor issues from this Platonic metaphysics, from the distinction between the sensible and the intelligible, and from the dialectic and analogicism that one inherits with it. When the interpreters of Plato discuss these metaphors, whatever may be the complexity of their debates and analyses, we never see them suspicious of the concept of metaphor itself.[15]

But to say that Plato does not use metaphor or sensible figures to designate the place does not imply that he speaks appropriately of the proper and properly intelligible meaning of khora. The import of receptivity or of receptacle which, one may say, forms the elementary nonvariable of this word's determination, seems to me to transcend the opposition between figurative and proper meaning. The spacing of khora introduces a dissociation or a difference in the proper meaning that it renders possible, thereby compelling tropic detours which are no longer rhetorical figures. The typography and the tropics to which the khora gives place, *without giving anything*, are explicitly marked in the *Timaeus* (50bc). Hence Plato says this in his way: it is necessary to avoid speaking of khora as of "something" that is or is not, that could be present or absent, intelligible, sensible, or both at once, active or passive, the Good *(epekeina tes ousias)* or the Evil, God or man, the living or the nonliving. Every theomorphic or anthropomorphic schema would thus also have to be avoided. If the khora receives everything, it does not do this in the manner of a medium or of a container, not even in that of a receptacle, because the receptacle is yet a figure inscribed in it. This is neither an intelligible extension, in the Cartesian sense, a receptive subject, in the Kantian sense of *intuitus derivativus*, nor a pure sensible space, as a form of receptivity. Radically nonhuman and atheological, one cannot even say that it *gives* place or that *there is* the khora. The *es gibt*, thus translated, too vividly announces or recalls the dispensation of God, of man, or even that of the Being of which certain texts by Heidegger speak *(es gibt Sein)*. Khora is not even *that (ça)*, the *es* or *id* of giving, before all subjectivity. It does not give place as one would give something, whatever it may be; it neither creates nor produces anything, not even an event insofar as it takes place. It gives no order and makes no promise. It is radically ahistorical, because nothing happens through it and nothing happens to it. Plato insists on its necessary indifference; to receive all and allow itself to be marked or affected by what is inscribed in it, the khora must remain without form and without proper determination. But if it is amorphous *(amorphon; Timaeus, 50d)*, this signifies neither lack nor privation. Khora is nothing posi-

understands by this word a certain relation to presence, whether
it is sensible or intelligible or even a relation to the presence of
the present in general—and, *on the other hand*, what one calls
the *via negativa* in its Christian stage?

The passage through the negativity of discourse on the subject
of the *khora* is neither the last word nor a mediation in service of
a dialectic, an elevation toward a positive or proper meaning, a
Good or a God. This has nothing to do with negative theology;
there is reference neither to an event nor to a giving, neither to an
order nor to a promise, even if, as I have just underscored, the
absence of promise or of order—the barren, radically nonhuman,
and atheological character of this "place"—obliges us to speak
and to refer to it in a certain and unique manner, as to the wholly-
other who is neither transcendent, absolutely distanced, nor immanent and close. Not that we are obliged to speak of it; but if,
stirred by an obligation that does not come from it, we think and
speak of it, then it is necessary to respect the singularity of this
reference. Although it is nothing, this referent appears irreducible
and irreducibly other: one cannot invent it. But since it remains
alien to the order of presence and absence, it seems that one
could only invent it in its very otherness, at the moment of the
address.

But this unique address is not a prayer, a celebration, or an
encomium. It does not speak to You.

Above all, this "third species" that the *khora* also is does not
belong to a *group of three*. "Third species" is here only a *philosophical* way of naming an X that is not included in a group, a
family, a triad or a trinity. Even when Plato seems to compare it
to a "mother" or to a "nurse," this always virginal *khora* in truth
does not couple with the "father" to whom Plato "compares" the
paradigms; the *khora* does not *engender* the sensible forms that
are inscribed in it and that Plato "compares" to a child (*Timaeus*,
50d).

To ask what *happens* between this type of experience (or the
experience of the *typos*) and the Christian apophases is neither
necessarily nor exclusively to think of history, of events, of influences. Indeed, the question that arises here concerns the historicity or eventuality (*événementialité*), that is, of significations for-

eign to the khora. Even if one wishes to describe "what happens" in terms of structures and relations, it is no doubt necessary to recognize that what happens between them is, perhaps, precisely the event of the event, the story, the thinking of an essential "having-taken-place," of a revelation, of an order and of a promise, of an anthropo-theologicalization which—despite the extreme rigor of the negative hyperbole—seems to dominate anew, even closer to the agathon than to the khora. And in Dionysius' works, for example, the trinitarian schema appears absolutely indispensable to ensure the passage through or crossing between discourses on the divine names, between the symbolic and mystical theology. The affirmative theologemes celebrate God as the Good, the intelligible Light, even the Good "beyond all light" (it is a "principle of all light and hence it is too little to call it light"; DN, ch. 4:701ab). Even if this Good is called formless (like the khora), this time it itself gives form: "But if the Good transcends all being, as is in effect the case, then it is necessary to say that it is the formless that gives form, and that the One who remains in Himself without essence is the height of the essence, and the reality without supreme life" (DN, ch. 4:697a). This Good inspires an entire erotics, but Dionysius warns us: it is necessary to avoid using the word erôs without first clarifying the meaning, the intention. It is always necessary to start from the intentional meaning and not from the mere words (DN, ch. 4: 708bc): "one should not imagine that we oppose Scripture in venerating this word of amorous desire [erôs]. . . . It even seemed to some of our sacred authors that 'amorous love' ['erôs'] is a term more worthy of God than 'charitable love' ['agapè']. For the divine Ignatius wrote: 'It is the object of my amorous love that they crucified' " (DN, ch. 4:708c–709b). The holy theologians attribute the same import, the same power of unification and gathering to erôs and to agapè, which the many poorly understand, which assigns desire to the body, to the division, to the carving up (ibid.). In God, desire is at once ecstatic, jealous, and condescending (DN, ch. 4:712a et seq.). This erotics leads forward and hence leads back to the Good, circularly, that is, toward what "is situated far beyond both being considered in itself and non-being" (DN, ch.

4:716d). As for Evil, "it belongs neither to Being nor to non-Being. Rather, it is more absent and estranged from the Good than non-Being; it is more greatly without being than non-Being" (ibid.). What is the more of this less in regard to what is already without essence? Evil is even more without essence than the Good. If possible, one should draw the full consequences of this singular axiomatics. For the moment, this is not my concern.

Between the theological movement that speaks and is inspired by the Good beyond Being or by light and the apophatic path that exceeds the Good, there is necessarily a passage, a transfer, a translation. An experience must yet guide the apophasis toward excellence, not allow it to say just anything, and prevent it from manipulating its negations like empty and purely mechanical phrases. This experience is that of prayer. Here prayer is not a preamble, an accessory mode of access. It constitutes an essential moment, it adjusts discursive asceticism, the passage through the desert of discourse, the apparent referential vacuity which will only avoid empty deliria and prattling, by addressing itself from the start to the other, to you. But to you as "hyperessential and more than divine Trinity."

I will distinguish at least two traits in the experiences and in the so manifold determinations of what one calls prayer. I isolate them here even if at the neglect of everything else, in order to clarify my talk. 1. In every prayer there must be an address to the other as other; for example—I will say, at the risk of shocking— God. The act of addressing oneself to the other as other must, of course, mean praying, that is, asking, supplicating, searching out. No matter what, for the pure prayer demands only that the other hear it, receive it, be present to it, be the other as such, a gift, call, and even cause of prayer. This first trait thus characterizes a discourse (an act of language even if prayer is silent) which, as such, is not predicative, theoretical (theological), or constative. 2. But I will differentiate it from another trait with which it is most often associated, notably by Dionysius and his interpreters, namely, the encomium or the celebration (hymnein). That the association of these two traits is essential for Dionysius does not signify that one trait is identical with the other, nor even in general inseparable from the other. Neither the prayer nor the encomium is, of course, an act of constative predication. Both have a performative dimension, the analysis of which would merit long and difficult expositions, notably as to the origin and validation of these performatives. I will hold to one distinction: prayer in itself, one may say, implies nothing other than the supplicating address to the other, perhaps beyond all supplication and giving, to give the promise of His presence as other, and finally the transcendence of His otherness itself, even without any other determination; the encomium, although it is not a simple attributive speech, nevertheless preserves an irreducible relationship to the attribution. No doubt, as Urs von Balthasar rightly says, "Where God and the divine are concerned, the word ὑμνεῖν almost replaces the word 'to say.' "[16] Almost, in fact, but not entirely; and how can one deny that the encomium qualifies God and *determines* prayer, *determines* the other, Him to whom it addresses itself, refers, invoking Him even as the source of prayer? How can one deny that, in this movement of determination (which is no longer the pure address of the prayer to the other), the appointment of the *trinitary* and hyperessential God distinguishes Dionysius' *Christian* prayer from all other prayer? To reject this doubtless subtle distinction, inadmissible for Dionysius and perhaps for a Christian in general, is to deny the essential quality of prayer to every invocation that is not Christian. As Jean-Luc Marion correctly remarks, the encomium is "neither true nor false, not even contradictory,"[17] although it says something *about* the thearchy, about the Good and the analogy; and if its attributions or namings do not belong to the ordinary signification of truth, but rather to a hypertruth that is ruled by a hyperessentiality, in this it does not merge with the movement of prayer itself, which does not speak *of*, but *to*. Even if this address is immediately determined by the discourse of encomium and if the prayer addresses itself to God by speaking (to Him) of Him, the apostrophe of prayer and the determination of the encomium form a pair, two different structures: "hyperessential and more than divine Trinity, You who preside over the divine wisdom. . . ." In a moment I will quote more extensively from this prayer which opens the *Mystical Theology* and prepares the definition of apophatic theologemes. For "it is necessary to start with prayers" (*eukhès aparkhesthai khreôn; DN,* ch. 3:680d), Dionysius says. Why? No doubt, to attain union with God; but to speak of this *union,* it is still necessary to speak of *places,* of height, of distance and of proximity. Dionysius proposes to his immediate addressee—or to the one to whom he dedicates his work, Timothy—to examine the name of Good, which expresses divinity, *after* having invoked the Trinity, that principle of Good which transcends all goods. It is necessary to pray in order to *approach* it, "most intimately"—that is, to raise oneself toward it—and receive from it the initiation of its gifts:

> It is necessary that we first be lifted up toward it, the source of good, by our prayers, and then, by drawing near to it, that we be initiated into the all-good gifts of what is founded around it. For while it is present to all, not all are present to it. Then, when we invoke it by our most holy prayers with an unpolluted intellect which is suited for the divine union, we shall be present to it. For it is not in a place, so that it would be absent from some beings or have to go from one being to another. Moreover, even the statement that it is "in" all beings falls far too short of its infinity, which is beyond all and encompasses all. (*DN,* ch. 3:680b)

By a series of analogies, Dionysius then explains that, in approaching and elevating ourselves thus, we do not traverse the distance that separates us from a place (since the residence of the Trinity is not localized: it is "everywhere and nowhere"). On the other hand, the Trinity draws us toward it, while it remains immobile, like the height of the sky or the depth of marine bedrock from which we will pull on a rope in order to come to it, and not to draw it toward us:

> before everything and especially before a discourse about God, it is necessary to begin with a prayer—not so that the power present both everywhere and nowhere shall come to us but so that by our divine remembrance and invocations we ourselves shall be guided to it and be united with it. (*ibid.*)

The principle of the Good is beyond Being, but it also transcends the Good (*DN*, ch. 3:680b). God is the Good that transcends the Good and the Being that transcends Being. This "logic"
is also that of the "without" which I evoked a moment ago in the
quotations from Meister Eckhart, citing Saint Augustine ("God is
wise *without* wisdom, good *without* goodness, powerful *without*
power") or Saint Bernard ("To love God is a mode *without* a
mode"). We could recognize in the negativity without negativity
of these utterances—concerning a transcendence which is nothing other (and wholly other) than what it transcends—a principle
of multiplication of voices and discourses, of disappropriation
and reappropriation of utterances, with the most distant appearing the closest, and vice versa. A predicate can always conceal
another predicate, or rather the nakedness of an absence of predicate—as the (sometimes indispensable) veil of a garment can at
once dissimulate and reveal the very fact that it dissimulates and
renders attractive at the same time. Hence the voice of an utterance can conceal another, which it then appears to quote without
quoting it, presenting itself as another form, namely as a quotation of the other. Whence the subtlety, but also the conflicts, the
relations of power, even the aporias of a politics of doctrine; I
want to say: a politics of initiation or of teaching in general, and
of an institutional politics of interpretation. Meister Eckhart, for
example (but what an example!) knew something about this. Not
to mention the arguments he had to deploy against his inquisito-
rial judges ("They tax with error everything they don't understand. . . ."), the strategy of his sermons put to work a multiplicity
of voices and of veils, which he superimposed or removed like
skins or garments, thematizing and himself exploring a pseudo-
metaphor until reaching that extreme flaying of which one is
never sure that it allows one to see the nakedness of God or to
hear the voice of Meister Eckhart himself. *Quasi stella matutina*,
which furnishes so many pretexts to the Cologne judges, stages
the drama of twenty-four masters (*Liber 24 philosophorum* of
pseudo-Hermes Trismegistus) who are reunited to speak of God.
Eckhart chooses one of their assertions: "God is necessarily above
Being [got etwaz ist, daz von nôt über wesene sîn muoz]."[18]
Speaking thus of what one of his masters says, he *comments* in a

voice that no longer permits one to decide that it is not his own. And in the same movement, he cites other masters, Christians or pagans, great or subordinate masters *(kleine meister)*. One of them seems to say, "God is neither being nor goodness [Got enist niht wesen noch güete]. Goodness clings to being and is not more comprehensive [breiter] than being; for if there were no being, there would be no goodness, and being is purer than goodness. God is not good, nor better, nor best. Whoever were to say that God is good, would do Him as great an injustice as if he called the sun black" *(ibid.,* 1:148). (The Bull of condemnation mentions this passage only in an appendix, without concluding that Eckhart truly taught it.) The theory of archetypes that forms the context of this argument attenuates its provocative character: God does not share any of the modes of Being with other beings (divided into ten categories by these masters), but "He is not thereby deprived of any of them [er entbirt ir ouch keiner]."

But here is what "a pagan master" says: the soul that loves God "takes Him under the garment of goodness [nimet in under dem velle der güete]," but reason or rationality *(vernunfticheit)* raises this garment and grasps God in His nakedness *(in blôz).* Then He is derobed *(entkleidet),* shorn "of goodness, of Being, and of all names" *(ibid.,* 1:152). Eckhart does not contradict the pagan master; nor does he agree with him. He remarks that, unlike the "holy masters," the pagan speaks in accordance with "natural light." Next, in a voice that appears to be his own, he differentiates—I do not dare say that he makes dialectical—the preceding proposition. In the lines that I am preparing to quote, a certain signification of unveiling, of laying bare, of truth as what is beyond the covering garment—appears to orient the entire axiomatics of this apophasis, at the end of ends and after all. Doubtless, here one cannot speak in full rigor of signification and axiomatics, since what orders and rules the apophatic course precisely exceeds the Good or goodness. But there is indeed a rule or a law: it is necessary to go beyond the veil or the garment. Is it arbitrary to still call truth or hyper-truth this unveiling which is perhaps no longer an unveiling of Being? A light, therefore, that is no longer elucidated by Being? I do not believe so. Consider:

I once said in the school that intellect [vernünfticheit] is
nobler than will, and yet both belong to this light. Then a
master in another school said that will is nobler than intellect, for will takes things as they are in themselves, while
the intellect takes things as they are in it. That is true. An
eye is nobler in itself than an eye painted on the wall. But I
say that intellect is nobler than will. The will apprehends
God under the garment [under dem kleide] of goodness. The
intellect apprehends God naked, as He is divested of goodness and being [Vernünfticheit nimet got blôz, als er entkleidet ist von güete und von wesene]. Goodness is a garment
[kleit] under which God is hidden, and will apprehends God
under the garment of goodness. If there were no goodness in
God, my will would not want Him. (ibid., 1:152–53)

Light and truth, these are Meister Eckhart's words. Quasi stella
matutina, that is what it is, and it is also a topology (height and
proximity) of our relation to God. Like the adverb quasi, we are
beside the verb that is the truth:

"As [als] a morning star in the midst of the mist." I refer to
the little word "quasi," which means "as" [als]; in school
the children call it an adverb [ein bîwort]. This is what I
refer to in all my sermons. The most appropriate [eigenlî-
cheste] things that one can say of God are word and truth
[wort und wârheit]. God called Himself a word [ein wort].
St. John said: "In the beginning was the Word," and means
that beside the word [wort], man is an adverb [bîwort]. In
the same way, the free star [der vrîe sterne] Venus, after
which Friday [vrîtac] is named, has many names. . . . Of all
the stars, it is always equally near to the sun; it never moves
farther from or nearer to it [niemer verrer noch næher], and
symbolizes [meinet] a man who wants to be near God always, and present [gegenwertic] to Him, so that nothing can
remove him from God, neither happiness, unhappiness, nor
any creature. . . .The more the soul is raised [erhaben] above
earthly things, the stronger [kreftiger] it is. Even a person
who knows nothing but the creatures would never need to
think of any sermons, for every creature is full of God and is
a book [buoch]. (ibid., 1:154–56)

In its pedagogical necessity and initiatory virtue, the sermon supplements—not so much the Word (Verbe), which has no need of it, but—the incapacity of reading in the authentic "book" that we are, as creatures, and the adverbial quality that we must hence be. This supplement of adverbial quality, the sermon, must be accomplished and oriented (as one orients oneself by the morning star) by the prayer or invocation of the trinitary God. This is at once the end and the orientation point of the sermon: "The soul is thus like an 'adverb,' working together with God and finding its beautification in the same self-knowledge that exalts Him. That for all time, may the Father, the Verbum, and the Holy Spirit help us to remain adverbs of this Verbum. Amen" (ibid., 1:158).

This is the end of the Sermon; the prayer does not directly address itself, in the form of apostrophe, to God Himself. In contrast, at the opening and from the first words of the *Mystical Theology*, Dionysius addresses himself directly to You, to God, from now on determined as "hyperessential Trinity" in the prayer that prepares the theologemes of the *via negativa*:

> O Trinity beyond being [Trias hyperousiè], beyond divinity [hyperthèe], beyond goodness [hyperagathè], and guide of Christians in divine wisdom [theosophias], direct us to the mystical summits more than unknown and beyond light. There the simple, absolved, and unchanged mysteries of theology lie hidden in the darkness beyond light of the hidden mystical silence, there, in the greatest darkness, that beyond all that is most evident exceedingly illuminates the sightless intellects. There, in the wholly imperceptible and invisible, that beyond all that is most evident fills to overflowing, with the glories beyond all beauty. The intellects who know how to close their eyes [tous anommatous noas]. This is my prayer ['Emoi men oun tauta eutkhtô]. And you, dear Timothy, be earnest in the exercise of mystical contemplation. (ch. 1:998a)

What happens here?

*After* having prayed (he writes, we read), he presents his prayer. He quotes it and I have just quoted his quotation. He quotes it in what is properly an *apostrophe* to its addressee, Timothy. The

*Mystical Theology* is dedicated to him; in order to initiate him, it must lead him on the paths toward which Dionysius himself has prayed to God to lead him, or more literally to *direct* him in a straight *(ithunon)* line. A pedagogy which is also a mystagogy and a psychagogy: here the gesture of leading or directing the *psyche* of the other passes through apostrophe. The one who asks to be led by God turns for an instant toward another addressee, in order to lead him in turn. He does not simply turn himself away from his first addressee who is *in truth* the first Cause of his prayer and already guides it. It is exactly because he does not turn away from God that he can turn toward Timothy and *pass from one address to the other without changing direction.*

The writing of Dionysius—which we presently believe we are reading or read in view of believing—stands in the space of that *apostrophe* which *turns aside* the discourse in the *same* direction, between the prayer itself, the quotation of the prayer, and the address to the disciple. In other words, it is addressed to the best reader, to the reader who ought to allow himself to be led to become better, to us who presently believe we are reading this text. Not to us as we are, at present, but as we would have to be, in our souls, if we read this text as it ought to be read, aright, in the proper direction, correctly: according to its prayer and its promise. He also prays—that we read correctly, in accordance with his prayer. None of this would be possible without the possibility of quotation (more generally, of repetition), and of an apostrophe that allows one to speak to several people at once. To more than one other. The prayer, the quotation of the prayer, and the apostrophe, from one you to the other, thus weave the *same* text, however heterogeneous they appear. There is a text because of this repetition.[19] Where, then, does this text have its place? Does it have a place, at present? And why can't one separate the prayer, the quotation of prayer, and the address to the reader?

The identity of *this* place, and hence of *this* text, and of *its* reader, comes from the future of what is promised by the promise. The advent of this future has a provenance, the event of the promise. Contrary to what seemed to happen in the "experience" of the place called *khora,* the apophasis is brought into motion—

it is *initiated*, in the sense of initiative and initiation—by the event of a revelation which is also a promise. This apophasis belongs to a history; or rather, it opens up a history and an anthropo-theological dimension. The *hyphen* ("trait d'*union*") unites *the* "new, adjunct writing with that which God himself dictated" (*DN*, ch. 3:681b); it marks the very place of this adjunction. This place itself is assigned by the event of the promise and the revelation of Scripture. It is the place only after what will have taken place—according to the time and history of this future perfect. The place is an event. Under what conditions is one situated in Jerusalem, we asked a moment ago, and where is the place thus named situated? How can one measure the distance that separates us from or draws us closer to it? Here is the answer of Dionysius, who cites Scripture in the *Ecclesiastical Hierarchy:* "Do not distance yourself from Jerusalem, but await the promise of the Father which you have heard from my mouth, and according to which you will be baptised by the Holy Spirit" (512c). The situation of this speech situates a place: he who transmitted the promise (Jesus, "divine founder of our own hierarchy") speaks of Jerusalem as the place that takes place since the event of the promise. But the place that is thus revealed remains the place of waiting, awaiting the realization of the promise. Then it will take place fully. It will be fully a place.

Hence an event prescribes to us the good and accurate apophasis: how to avoid speaking. This prescription is at once a revelation and a teaching of the Holy Scriptures, the architext before all supplementary "adjunction":

> with regard to the secret Deity beyond Being, *it is necessary to avoid all speech, that is, every incautious thought [ou tolmeteon eipein, oute men ennoesai],* beyond what the Holy Scriptures divinely reveal to us [para ta theoeidôs emin ek tôn ierôn logiôn ekpephasmena]. For in these sacred texts, the Deity itself manifested that which suited its Goodness. (*DN*, ch. 1:588c; my italics)[20]

This hyperessential goodness is not entirely incommunicable; it can manifest *itself*, but it remains separated by its hyperessentiality. As for those theologians who have "praised" its inaccessibility and penetrated its "secret infinity," they have left no "*trace*" (*ikhnous; ibid.*; my italics).

A *secret manifestation*, then, if some such thing is possible. Even before commanding the extreme negativity of the apophasis, this manifestation is transmitted to us as a "secret gift" by our inspired masters. We thus learn to decipher symbols, we understand how "the love of God for man envelops the intelligible in the sensible, what is beyond Being in being, gives form and fashion to the unformable and the unfashionable, and through a variety of partial symbols, multiplies and figures the unfigurable and marvelous Simplicity" (*DN*, ch. 1:592b). In brief, we learn to read, to decipher the rhetoric without rhetoric of God—and finally to be silent.

Among all these figures for the unfigurable, there stands the figure of the seal. This is not one figure among others; it figures the figuration of the unfigurable itself; and this discourse on the imprint appears to displace the Platonic typography of the *khora*. The latter gave rise to the inscriptions, to *typoi*, for the copies of the paradigms. Here the figure of the seal, which also seals a promise, is valid for the entire text of the creation. It carries over a Platonic argument, one of the two schemas that I have just tried to distinguish, into another order. God at once permits and does not permit participation in Him. The text of creation exists as the typographic inscription of the nonparticipation in participation:

> as the central point of a circle is shared by all the radii, which constitute the circle, and as the multiple imprints [ektypomata] of a single seal [sphragidos] share the original which is entirely immanent and identical in each of the imprints, not fragmenting itself in any manner. But the nonparticipation [amethexia] of the Deity, the universal cause, yet transcends all these figures [paradeigmata]. (*DN*, ch. 2:644ab)

For unlike what happens with the seal, here there is neither contact, community, or synthesis. The subsequent discussion recalls again, while displacing, the necessity for the *khora* to be without form and virginal. Otherwise, it could not suitably lend itself to the writing of the impressions in it:

One might object that the seal is not complete and identical in all its imprints [en olois tois ekmageiois]. I respond that this is not the fault of the seal which transmits itself to each one completely and identically; rather, the otherness of the participants differentiates between the reproductions of the unique, total and identical model [arkhetypias]. (DN, ch. 2:644b)

Thus everything will depend on the material or wax (keros) which receives the imprints. It must be receptive, soft, flexible, smooth, and virginal, in order that the imprint remain pure, clear, and lasting (DN, ch. 2:644b).

If one recalls that the khora was also described as a receptacle (dekhomenon), one may follow another displacement of this figure, the figure of figures, the place of the other figures. Henceforth the "receptacle" is at once *physical* and *created*. It was neither in Plato's works. Later, Saint Augustine once again assures the mediation, and Meister Eckhart cites him in his sermon *Renouamini spiritu:* "Augustine says that in the superior part of the soul, which is called *mens* or *gemüte*, God created, together with the soul's being, a potential [craft] which the masters call a receptacle [sloz] or screen [schrin] of spiritual forms, or of formal images."[21] The creation of the place, which is also a potential, is the basis for the resemblance of the soul with the Father. But beyond the Trinity, one may say, beyond the multiplicity of images and beyond the created place, the *unmovability without form*—which the *Timaeus* attributed, one may say, to the khora—is here found to suit God alone: "when all the images of the soul are pushed aside and it contemplates only the unique One [das einig ein], the naked being of the soul encounters the naked being without form [das blose formlose wesen] of the divine unity, which is the hyperessential Being resting unmoved in itself [ein uberwesende wesen, lidende ligende in ime selben]" (ibid., 3:437–438). This unmovability of the formless is the unique and wondrous source of our movability, of our emotions, of our noblest suffering. Thus we can suffer only God, and nothing other than Him: "Oh! wonder of wonders [wunder uber wunder], what noble suffering lies therein, that the being of the soul can suffer nothing else than the solitary and pure unity of God!" (ibid., 3:438).

Thus named, "God is without name [namloz]," and "no one can either speak of Him or understand Him." Of this "supereminent Being [uber swebende wesen]" which is also a "hyperessential nothingness [ein uber wesende nitheit]" (ibid., 3:441–42), it is necessary to avoid speaking. Eckhart allows St. Augustine to speak: "what man can say that is most beautiful in respect to God is that he knows how to be silent [swigen] on account of the wisdom of the internal [divine] wealth." Eckhart adds: "Because of this, be silent" (ibid., 3:442). Without that you lie and you commit sin. This duty is a duty of love; the apostrophe orders love, but it speaks out of love and implores the aid of God in a prayer: "You must love Him inasmuch as he is a Non-God, a Non-Intellect, a Non-Person, a Non-Image. More than this, inasmuch as He is a pure, clear, limpid One, separated from all duality. And we must eternally sink ourselves in this One, from the Something to the Nothing.

May God help us. Amen" (ibid., 3:448).

This is to speak in order to command not to speak, to say what God is not, that he is a non-God. How may one hear the copula of being that articulates this singular speech and this order to be silent? Where does it have its place? Where does it take place? It is the place, the place of this writing, this trace (left in Being) of what is not, and the writing of this place. The place is only a place of passage, and more precisely, a threshold. But a threshold, this time, to give access to what is no longer a place. A subordination, a relativization of the place, and an extraordinary consequence; the place is Being. What finds itself reduced to the condition of a threshold is Being itself, Being as a place. Solely a threshold, but a sacred place, the outer sanctuary (parvis) of the temple:

> When we apprehend God in Being, we apprehend Him in his parvis [vorbürge], for Being is the parvis in which He resides [wonet]. Where is He then in His temple, in which he shines in His sanctity [heilic]? Intellect [vernünfticheit: rationality] is the Temple of God.[22]

The soul, which exercises its power in the eye, allows one to see what is not, what is not present; it "works in non-being and follows God who works in non-being." Guided by this *psyche*, the eye thus passes the threshold of Being toward non-being in order to see what does not present itself. Eckhart compares the eye to a sieve. Things must be "passed through the sieve [gebiu-telt]." This sieve is not one figure among others; it tells the difference between Being and non-being. It discerns this difference, it allows one to see it, but as the eye itself. There is no text, above all no sermon, no possible predication, without the invention of such a filter.

# C

I thus decided *not to speak* of negativity or of apophatic movements in, for example, the Jewish or Islamic traditions. To leave this immense place empty, and above all that which can connect such a name of God with the name of the Place, to remain thus on the threshold—was this not the most consistent possible apophasis? Concerning that about which one cannot speak, isn't it best to remain silent? I let you answer this question. It is always entrusted to the other.

My first paradigm was Greek and the second Christian, without yet ceasing to be Greek. The last will be neither Greek nor Christian. If I were not afraid of trying your patience I would recall that which, in Heidegger's thinking, could resemble the most questioning legacy, both the most audacious and most liberated repetition of the traditions I have just evoked. Here I will have to limit myself to a few landmarks.

One could read *What Is Metaphysics?* as a treatise on negativity. It establishes the basis for negative discourse and negation in the experience of the Nothing which itself "nothings" ("das Nichts selbst nichtet"). The experience of anguish puts us in relation to a negating (*Nichtung*) which is neither annihilation (*Vernichtung*), nor a negation or a denial (*Verneinung*). It reveals to us the strangeness (*Befremdlichkeit*) of what is (being, *das Seiende*) as the wholly other (*das schlechthin Andere*). It thus opens up the possibility of the question of Being for *Dasein*, the structure of which is characterized precisely by what Heidegger calls transcendence. This transcendence, *Vom Wesen des Grundes* will

say, is "properly expressed" (eigens ausgesprochen) by the Platonic expression epekeina tes ousias. Unable to involve myself,
here, in the interpretation of the agathon subsequently proposed
by Heidegger, I merely wished to mark this passage beyond Being,
or rather beyond beingness, and the reinterpretation of negativity
that accompanies it. Heidegger specifies immediately that Plato
could not elaborate "the original content of the epekeina tes
ousias as transcendence of Dasein [der ursprüngliche Gehalt des
epekeina als Transzendenz des Daseins]." He makes an analogous
gesture with regard to the khora: in the Einführung in die Metaphysik, a brief parenthesis suggests that Plato fell short of thinking of the place (Ort) which, however, signaled to him. In truth,
he only prepared (vorbereitet) the Cartesian interpretation of place
or space as extensio (Ausdehnung).[23] Elsewhere I try to show
what is problematic and reductive about this perspective. Some
seventeen years later, the last page of Was heisst Denken? mentions khora and khorismos anew, without any explicit reference
to the Timaeus. Plato, who is supposed to have given the most
determinative Deutung for Western thought, situates the khorismos—the interval or the separation, the spacing—between beings
(Seiendes) and Being (Sein). But "e khora heisst der Ort," "the
khora means the place." For Plato, beings and Being are thus
"placed differently [verschieden geortet]." "If Plato takes the
khorismos into consideration, the difference of place [die ver-
schiedene Ortung] between Being and beings, he thus poses the
question of the wholly other place [nach dem ganz anderen Ort]
of Being, by comparison with that of beings." That Plato is afterward suspected of having fallen short of this wholly other place,
and that one must lead the diversity (Verschiedenheit) of places
back to the difference (Unterschied) and the fold of a duplicity
(Zwiefalt) which must be given in advance, without one ever
being able to give it "proper attention"—I can follow this process
neither at the end of Was heisst Denken? nor elsewhere. I merely
underscore this movement toward a wholly other place, as place
of Being or place of the wholly other: in and beyond a Platonic or
Neoplatonic tradition. But also in and beyond a Christian tradition of which Heidegger—while submerged in it, as in the Greek
tradition—never ceased claiming, whether by denial or not, that

it could in no case entertain a philosophy. "A Christian philosophy," he often says, "is a squared circle and a misconception
[Missverständnis]."[24] It is necessary to distinguish between, on
the one hand, onto-theology or theiology, and, on the other hand,
theology.[25] The former concerns the supreme being, the being *par
excellence*, ultimate foundation or *causa sui* in its divinity. The
latter is a science of faith or of divine speech, such as it manifests
itself in revelation *(Offenbarung)*. Heidegger again seems to distinguish between manifestation, the possibility of Being to reveal
itself *(Offenbarkeit)*, and, on the other hand, the revelation *(Offenbarung)* of the God of theology.[26]

Immense problems are screened behind these distinctions. One
may follow, through Heidegger's works, the threads that we have
already recognized: revelation, the promise, or the gift *(das Ge-
ben, die Gabe,* and the *es gibt,* which progressively and profoundly displace the question of Being and its transcendental
horizon, time, in *Sein und Zeit),*[27] or yet the *Ereignis* which one
sometimes translates, in such a problematic manner, by "event."
I will limit myself to the question that my title commands: *How
to avoid speaking?* More precisely: How to avoid speaking *of
Being?* A question in which I will underscore equally the importance of avoiding and that of Being, as if to grant them equal
dignity, a sort of common essentiality, which will not go without
consequences. These are the consequences that interest me.

What does the avoidance signify here? In regard to Being or the
word "Being," does it always have the mode that we have recognized for it in apophatic theologies? For Heidegger, would these
be examples of aberration or of the "squared circle"—namely
Christian philosophies or unacknowledged onto-theologies? Does
the avoidance belong to the category or to the diagnostic of denial
*(Verneinung),* in a sense determined this time by a Freudian
problematic ("least of all do I say that")? Or again: with regard to
the traditions and texts that I have just evoked, and in particular
those of Dionysius and Meister Eckhart,[28] does Heidegger stand
in a relationship of avoidance? What abyss would this simple
word, *avoidance,* then designate?

*(To say nothing,* once again, of the mysticisms or theologies in
the Jewish, Islamic, or other traditions.)

Twice, in two apparently different contexts and senses, Heidegger *explicitly proposed* to avoid (is there denial, in this case?) the word *being*. More exactly, not to *avoid* speaking of Being but to avoid *using* the word *being*. Even more exactly, not to avoid *mentioning* it—as certain speech-act theorists, who distinguish between mention and use, would say—but to avoid using it. Thus he explicitly proposes, not to avoid speaking of Being, nor in some way to avoid mentioning the word *being*, but to refrain from using it normally, one may say, without placing it in quotation marks or under erasure. And in both cases, we may suspect, the stakes are serious—even if they seem to hold to the subtle fragility of a terminological, typographical, or more broadly, "pragmatic" artifice. But in both cases, the *place* is at issue, and this is why I privilege them.

1. First, in *Zur Seinsfrage* (1952), precisely in regard to thinking the essence of modern nihilism, Heidegger reminds Ernst Jünger of the necessity for a topology of Being and of the Nothing. He distinguishes this topology from a simple topography, and he has just proposed a reinterpretation of the seal, of the *typos*, of the Platonic and of the modern typography. It is then that Heidegger proposes to write *Being*, the word *being*, under erasure, an erasure in the form of a crossing out *(kreuzweise Durchstreichung)*. The word *being* is not avoided; it remains readable. But this readability announces that the word may solely be read, deciphered; it cannot or must not be pronounced, used normally, one might say, as a speech-act of ordinary language. It is necessary to decipher it under a spatialized typography, spaced or spacing, printing over. Even if this does not avoid the strange word *being*, it should at least prevent and warn against, deviate from, while designating, the normal recourse (if such exists) to it. But Heidegger also warns us against the simply *negative* use of this *Durchstreichung*. This erasure does not, then, have *avoidance* as its essential function. No doubt, Being is not a being, and it reduces to its turns, turnings, historical tropes *(Zuwendungen)*; one must therefore avoid representing it *(vorzustellen)* as something, an object that stands *opposite (gegenüber)* man and then comes toward him. To avoid this objectifying representation *(Vorstellung)*, one will thus write the word *being* under erasure. It is

henceforth not heard, but is read in a certain manner. In what manner? If this *Durchstreichung* is neither a sign nor merely a negative sign ("kein bloss negatives Zeichen"), this is because it does not efface "Being" beneath conventional and abstract marks. Heidegger understands it as showing (*zeigen*) the four regions (*Gegenden*) of what he here and elsewhere calls the fourfold (*Geviert*): earth and heavens, mortals and the divine. Why does this written cross, according to Heidegger, have nothing of a negative signification? 1. In withdrawing Being from the subject/ object relation, it allows Being to be read, both the word and the meaning of Being. 2. Next it "shows" the fourfold (*Geviert*). 3. But above all it *gathers*. This gathering takes place and has its *place* (*Ort*) in the crossing point of the *Durchkreuzung*.[29] The gathering of the *Geviert*, in a place of crossing ("Versammlung im Ort der Durchkreuzung"), lends itself to writing and reading in an indivisible *topos*, in the simplicity (*die Einfalt*) of the point, of this *Ort* whose name appears so difficult to translate. Heidegger tells us elsewhere that this name "originally signifies" "the point of the sword,"[30] that toward which all converges and assembles. This indivisible point always assures the possibility of the *Versammlung*. It gives place to it; it is always the gathering, *das Versammelnde*. "The place gathers toward itself at the greatest height and extremity [Der Ort versammelt zu sich ins Höchste und Äusserste]."

Nevertheless, in order to think the negative appearance of this erasure, to gain access to the origin of negativity, of negation, of nihilism, and perhaps also of avoidance, it would thus be necessary to think the place of the Nothing. "What is the place of the Nothing [der Ort des Nichts]?" Heidegger has just asked. Now he specifies: the Nothing should also be *written*, that is to say *thought*. Like Being, it should also be written and read under erasure: "Wie das S~~ein~~, so müsste auch das Nichts geschrieben und d.h. gedacht werden."

2. Elsewhere, in an apparently different context, Heidegger explains the sense in which he would *avoid* speaking of Being, this time without placing it under erasure. More precisely, the sense in which he would avoid *writing* the word *being*. More precisely still (while remaining in the conditional mode, and this

counts for much here), the sense in which "the word 'being' [das Wort 'Sein']" should not take place, occur, happen *(vorkommen)* in his text. It is not a matter of "remaining silent," as one would prefer to do, he says elsewhere,[31] when the "thinking of God" (on the subject of God) is in question. No; the point is, rather, not to allow the word *being* to occur, on the subject of God.

The text is presented as a *transcription.* Responding to students at the University of Zürich in 1951, Heidegger recalls that Being and God are not identical, and that he would always avoid thinking God's essence by means of Being. He makes this more precise in a sentence in which I underscore the words *were,* *ought,* and *write:* "If I *were* yet to *write* a theology, as I am sometimes tempted to do, the word 'being' *ought* not to appear there [take place there, occur, figure, or happen there ] [Wenn ich noch eine Theologie *schreiben würde,* wozu es mich manchmal reizt, dann *dürfte* in ihr das Wort 'Sein' nicht vorkommen]."[32]

How may one analyze the folds of denial in this conditional of writing, in the course of an oral improvisation? Can one recognize the modalities in it without first departing from the foundation and from the thing itself—here, that is, from Being and God? Heidegger speaks in order to say what *would happen if he were to write* one day. But he knows that what he says is already being written. If he were to write a theology, the word *being* would not be under erasure; it wouldn't even appear there. For the moment, speaking and writing on the subject of what he *ought to* or *could* write regarding theology, Heidegger allows the word *being* to appear; he does not use it, but mentions it without erasure when he is indeed speaking of theology, of that which he would be tempted to write. Where does this, then, take place? Does it have place? What would take place?

Heidegger continues, "Faith has no need for the thinking of Being." As he often recalls, Christians ought to allow themselves to be inspired by Luther's lucidity on this subject. Indeed, even if Being is "neither the foundation nor the essence of God [Grund und Wesen von Gott]," the experience of God *(die Erfahrung Gottes)*—that is, the experience of revelation—"occurs in the dimension of Being [in der Dimension des Seins sich ereignet]."

This revelation is not that (*Offenbarung*) of which the religions speak, but the possibility of this revelation, the opening for this manifestation, this *Offenbarkeit* of which I spoke earlier and in which an *Offenbarung* can take place and man can encounter God. Although God is not and need not be thought from Being as His essence or foundation, the *dimension of Being* opens up access to the advent, the experience, the encounter with this God who nevertheless is not. The word *dimension*—which is also difference—here gives a measure while giving place. One could sketch a singular chiasmus. The anguished experience of the Nothing discloses Being. Here, the dimension of Being discloses the experience of God, who is not or whose Being is neither the essence nor the foundation.

How not to think of this? This dimension of disclosure, this place that gives place without being either essence or foundation —would not this step or passage, this threshold that gives access to God, yet be the "parvis" (*vorbürge*) of which Meister Eckhart spoke? "When we apprehend God in Being, we apprehend Him in His outer sanctuary [*parvis*], for Being is the *parvis* in which He resides." Is this a theological, an onto-theological, tradition? A theological tradition? Would Heidegger adopt it? Would he disown it? Would he deny it?

I do not intend to respond to these questions, nor even to conclude with them. More modestly, in a more hasty but also more programmatic manner, I return to the enigma of avoidance, of negation, or of denial in a scene of writing. Heidegger *says* (then allows to be written in his name) that if he *were to write* a theology, he would avoid the word *being*; he would avoid writing it and this word would not figure in his text; or rather should not be present in it. What does he mean? That the word would figure in it yet under erasure, appearing there without appearing, quoted but not used? No; it should not figure in it at all. Heidegger well knows that this is not possible, and perhaps it is for this profound reason that he did not write this theology. But didn't he write it? And in it did he avoid writing the word *being*? In fact, since Being is not (a being) and in truth is nothing (that is), what difference is there between writing *Being*, this Being which is

not, and writing *God*, this God of whom Heidegger also says that
He is not? Indeed, Heidegger does not merely say that God is not
a being; he specifies that He "has nothing to do here with Being
[Mit dem Sein, ist hier nichts anzusichten]." But since he recognizes that God announces Himself to experience in the "dimension of Being," what difference is there between writing a theology and writing on Being, of Being, as Heidegger never ceased
doing? Most of all, when he writes the word *being* under and in
the place *(Ort)* of the cancellation in the form of a cross? Hasn't
Heidegger written what he says he would have liked to write, a
theology *without* the word *being*? But didn't he also write what
he says should not be written, what he should not have written,
namely a theology that is opened, dominated, and invaded by the
word *being*?

   With and without the word *being*, he wrote a theology with
and without God. He did what he said it would be necessary to
avoid doing. He said, wrote, and allowed to be written exactly
what he said he wanted to avoid. He was not there without
leaving a trace of all these folds. He was not there without allowing a trace to appear, a trace that is, perhaps, no longer his own,
but that remains as if *(quasiment)* his own. *Not, without, quasi*
are three adverbs. *Quasiment*. Fable or fiction, everything happens as if I had wanted to ask, on the threshold of this lecture,
what these three adverbs mean and whence they come.

P.S. One more word to conclude, and I ask your pardon for it. I
am not certain that only rhetoric is at stake. But this also concerns
the strange discursive modality, or rather the *step of* (not) *writing
(pas d'écriture)*, Heidegger's pass, impasse, or dodge. What does
he do? He says to some students, in short: if I had to write a
theology (I have always dreamed of this, but I didn't do it and
know that I will never do it), I would not let the word *being* occur
*(vorkommen)*. It would not have a place, it would not have the
right to a place in such a text. I mention this word here but I have
never let it occur, it could not figure in all my work, except *in not
doing it*—since I always said that Being *is not* (a being, that is)
and that it *would have always had to* be written *under erasure*, a

rule that I did not in fact always observe, but which I should have respected in principle, starting from the first word, *dès le premier verbe*. Understand me: this is an erasure that would above all have nothing negative about it! And even less of denegation! Etc.

What is thus the discursive modality of this *step of* (not) *writing* and of this abyss of denial? Is it first of all a modality, a simple modality among other possible ones, or rather a quasi-transcendental recourse of writing? We should not forget that we are dealing with an oral declaration, later recorded from memory by Beda Allemann. Heidegger indeed approved this protocol, but while remarking that it did not render present the atmosphere of the discussion, nor would a "complete shorthand report" have done this: no writing could have rendered what had been said *there*.

What was said *there* was addressed to colleagues and students, to disciples, in the very broad sense of this word. Like the address of Dionysius, in his apostrophe to Timothy, this text has a pedagogical or psychological virtue. It remains a text (written or oral; no matter) only in this measure: as repetition or repeatability on an *agogic* path.

But there is never a prayer, not even an apostrophe, in Heidegger's rhetoric. Unlike Dionysius, he never says "you": neither to God nor to a disciple or reader. There is no place, or in any case there is no regularly assigned place, for these "neither true nor false" utterances that prayers are, according to Aristotle. This may be interpreted in at least two ways, which appear contradictory.

1. This absence signifies in effect that theology (in the sense in which Heidegger links it to faith and distinguishes it from theiology and from metaphysical onto-theology) is rigorously excluded from his texts. It is well defined there but excluded, at least in what ought to *direct* it, namely the movement of faith. And in fact, while thinking that solely the truth of Being can open onto the essence of the divinity and to what the word *god* means (one is familiar with the famous passage in the "Letter on Humanism"), Heidegger says no less: "At the interior of thought, nothing could be accomplished that would prepare for or contribute to

determining what happens in faith and in grace. If faith summoned me in this manner, I would close down shop. —Of course, interior to the dimension of faith, one yet continues to think; but thinking as such no longer has a task."[33] In short, neither faith nor science, as such, thinks or has thinking as its task.

This absence of prayer, or of apostrophe in general, also confirms the predominance of the theoretical, "constative," even propositional form (in the third-person, indicative present: S is P) in the rhetoric, at least, of a text which yet forcefully questions the determination of truth linked to this theoreticism and to this judicative form.

2. But at the same time, on the contrary, one can read here a sign of respect for prayer. For the formidable questions evoked by the essence of prayer: can or must a prayer allow itself to be mentioned, quoted, and inscribed in a compelling, *agogic* proof? Perhaps it need not be. Perhaps it must not do this. Perhaps, on the contrary, it must do this. Are there criteria external to the event itself to decide whether Dionysius, for example, distorted or rather accomplished the essence of prayer by quoting it, and first of all by writing it for Timothy? Does one have the right to think that, as a pure address, on the edge of silence, alien to every code and to every rite, hence to every repetition, prayer should never be turned away from its present by a notation or by the movement of an apostrophe, by a multiplication of addresses? That each time it takes place only once and should never be recorded? But perhaps the contrary is the case. Perhaps there would be no prayer, no pure possibility of prayer, without what we glimpse as a menace or as a contamination: writing, the code, repetition, analogy or the—at least apparent—multiplicity of addresses, initiation. If there were a purely pure experience of prayer, would one need religion and affirmative or negative theologies? Would one need a supplement of prayer? But if there were no supplement, if quotation did not bend prayer, if prayer did not bend, if it did not submit to writing, would a theology be possible? Would a theology be possible?

## Notes

Translator's note: I shall avoid the customary apologies and excuses, denials and disclaimers, instead merely acknowledging the assistance of Barbara Caulk and Ora Wiskind in revisions of this translation.

1. Who has ever assumed the project of the negative theology *as such*, reclaiming it in the singular under this name, without subjugating and subordinating it, without at least pluralizing it? On the subject of this title, *the* negative theology, can one do anything but *deny* it? Jean-Luc Marion contests the legitimacy of this title, not only for the ensemble of Dionysius' oeuvre—which goes without saying —but even for the places where there is a question of "negative theologies" in the plural ("tines oi kataphatikai theologiai, tines ai apophatikai") in chapter 3 of the *Mystical Theology.* Concerning "what it is suitable to call 'negative theology,' " Jean-Luc Marion notes: "To our knowledge, Dionysius employs nothing which may be translated by 'negative theology.' If he speaks of 'negative theologies,' in the plural, he does not separate them from the 'affirmative theologies' with which they maintain the relationship which one describes here." (See the *Mystical Theology,* 1032 et seq.) Marion, *L'idole et la distance* (Paris: Grasset, 1977), pp. 189 and 244.

2. This occurred in diverse passages and contexts. I will cite only one in order to clarify a point and, perhaps, to respond to an objection which has the merit of not being stereotypical. In "Différance" (1968), contained in my *Margins of Philosophy,* trans. Alan Bass (Chicago: University of Chicago Press, 1982), p. 6, I wrote: "So much so that the detours, locutions, and syntax in which I will often have to take recourse will resemble those of negative theology, occasionally even to the point of being indistinguishable from negative theology. Already we have had to delineate *that différance is not,* does not exist, is not a present-being *(on)* in any form; and we will be led to delineate also everything *that it is not,* that is, *everything;* and consequently that it has neither existence nor essence. It derives from no category of being, whether present or absent. And yet those aspects of *différance* which are thereby delineated are not theological, not even in the order of the most negative of negative theologies, which as one knows are always concerned with disengaging a hyperessentiality beyond the finite categories of essence and existence, that is, of presence, and always hastening to recall that God is refused the predicate of existence, only in order to acknowledge His superior, inconceivable, and ineffable mode of being" (translation modified slightly [KF]). After having quoted this last sentence, in *L'idole et la distance,* p. 318, Jean-Luc Marion objects: "What does 'one knows' mean here? We have seen, precisely, that the so-called negative theology, *in its depths* [my italics], does not aim to reestablish a 'hyperessentiality,' since it aims at neither predication nor at Being; how, *a fortiori,* could there be a question of existence and essence in Dionysius, who speaks a sufficiently originary Greek to see in it neither the idea nor the usage?" Here, too briefly, are some elements of a response. 1. In speaking of presence or absence, of existence or essence, I sought merely to specify, in a cursory manner, the different categories or modalities of presence in general, without precise historical reference to Dionysius. 2. Whatever may be the complex and quite enigmatic historicity of the distinction between essence and exis-

tence, I am not sure that it is simply ignored by Dionysius: how can one be certain of the *absence* of such a distinction at any stage of the Greek language? What does "a sufficiently originary Greek" mean? 3. What does "in its depths" mean here? What does it mean that "negative theology," in its depths, does not aim to reestablish a "hyperessentiality"? First of all, as Marion knows better than anyone else, it is difficult to consider accidental the reference to this hyperessentiality which plays a major, insistent, and *literal* role in so many texts by Dionysius—and by others, whom I will cite later. Next—beyond this obvious case, the only one to which I had to refer in a lecture that was not devoted to negative theology and did not even name Dionysius—it is necessary to elaborate an interpretive discourse as interesting and original as that of Marion, at the crossing, in the wake, sometimes beyond thoughts like those of Heidegger, Urs von Balthasar, Levinas, and some others, to distinguish the "depths" (the thinking of the gift, of paternity, of distance, of celebration, etc.) from what in the so-called "negative theology" still seems to be very concerned with hyperessentiality. But without being able to develop this third point here, I will return to it below, at least in principle and in an oblique fashion.

3. Concerning a paradoxical writing of the word *without (sans)*, notably in the work of Blanchot, I allow myself to refer to the essay "Pas" in *Gramma* (1976), nos. 3–4, reprinted in my *Parages* (Paris: Galilée, 1986). *Dieu sans l'être* is the magnificent title of a book by Jean-Luc Marion (Paris: Fayard, 1982), to which I cannot do justice in the space of a note or the time of a lecture. This title remains difficult to translate. Its very suspension depends on the grammatical vacillation that only French syntax can tolerate—precisely in the structure of a title—that is, of a nominal or incomplete phrase. L' may be the definite article of the noun *être* (*God without Being*), but it can also be a personal pronoun—object of the *verb* to be—referring to God, from God to God Himself who would not be what He is or who would be what He is *without being (it) (God without being God, God without being):* God with and without being. On the subject of a title's syntax, Levinas preferred to say—also in a most singular syntax, no doubt in order to avoid this ultimate precedence of Being or of the predicative sentence that would insinuate itself here—rather than "Being without Being," "God with or beyond Being," extra-essence, or hyperessence: *otherwise than Being.* Let us not forget these fairly recent, thought-provoking titles—*Dieu sans l'être* and *Autrement qu'être ou au-delà de l'essence* (1974–78)—which seek, in two very different ways, to avoid what Levinas calls the contamination by Being, in order to "hear God not contaminated by Being" for example. Grammar does not suffice, but it never reduces to an accessory instrumentality; by the word *grammar* one designates a discipline and its history, or more radically the modalities of writing—how one writes of God. The two cited titles lead the way to two major responses to the question I would like to raise: how not to say or speak? Otherwise, and implicitly: how not to speak Being (how to avoid speaking—of Being?)? How to speak Being otherwise? How to speak otherwise (than) being? And so on.

4. Meister Eckhart, *Quasi stella matutina.* All translations of Meister Eckhart's sermons are based on *Meister Eckharts Predigten,* ed. Josef Quint (Stuttgart: W. Kohlhammer, 1936), vols. 1–3. The present passage appears in 1:145–46.

5. Pseudo-Dionysius, *The Mystical Theology,* in *The Divine Names and Mystical Theology,* trans. John D. Jones (Milwaukee, Wis.: Marquette University Press, 1980), ch. 1:998a et seq. References to these two works, cited in the text as *MT*

and *DN*, are modified slightly from this translation [KF]. For obvious reasons, I will sometimes quote several words of the original text [JD].

6. Here the author alludes to the grammar of biblical Hebrew, which does not employ a present-tense form of the verb *to be*; the previous paragraph refers to a messianic motif in the Passover Haggadah [KF].

7. *Adolescens, tibi dico: surge*, in *Meister Eckharts Predigten*, 2:305.

8. Provenance of the call: Jerusalem. Sanford Budick had just called. He had to record a title, however provisory, on the program of the colloquium. I must associate the memory of this telephone call with that of a telegram. It also came from Jerusalem and was signed by Sanford Budick, who was then preparing the volume, which has since appeared, *Midrash and Literature* (New Haven, Conn.: Yale University Press, 1986). Having learned that in Seattle, during a colloquium devoted to Paul Celan, I had given what he called a "lecture on circumcision," he asked me: "could we have a portion of that lecture or some other piece you would be willing to give us however short stop midrash volume soon going to press."

9. Here it is not possible to become directly involved with this difficult problem of hierarchy, in particular concerning relations of translation or analogy—or regarding the rupture and heterogeneity between hierarchy *as such*, namely "the sacred ordinance," the principle or origin of sanctity, and, on the other hand, the sociopolitical order. One may follow Jean-Luc Marion as far as possible when he dissociates the "hierarchy, understood from the Theandric mystery of which the Church offers us the unique place" and the "vulgar concept" or the "common concept" of hierarchy (*L'idole et la distance*, p. 209). One might even agree with certain of his more provocative formulations ("the political model of hierarchy has nothing to do with the mystery of the hierarchy which opens onto the communion of saints. The deliberate or naive equivocation betrays the perversion of the look, and does not even merit refutation. At issue is only seeing, or not seeing"; p. 217). No doubt, but what it is also *necessary to see* is the historic, essential, undeniable, and irreducible possibility of the aforementioned perversity which is perhaps only considerable by first having been observable, as one says, "in fact." How is the "vulgar concept" constituted? This is what it is also necessary to see or not to not see. How is it possible that "distance"—in the sense Marion gives to this word and which also makes up the distance between the two hierarchies—can have let itself be overstepped or "traversed" and *give place to the analogical translation of one hierarchy into another*? Can one proscribe here an "analogy" which appears nevertheless to support all of this construction? And if the translation is bad, erroneous, "vulgar," what would be the good political translation of the hierarchy as a "sacred ordinance"? This is only a question, but it is not impossible that its matrix holds others of the same kind in reserve, on the subject of the trinitarian Thearchy of which the hierarchy would be "the icon, at once resembling and dissembling" (p. 224; and the entire exposition on pp. 207ff starting from the term "hierarchy" which "Dionysius mobilizes" and which "our modernity prohibits us from the outset from understanding correctly"); and thus on the subject of the trinitarian or patristic scheme sustaining a thinking of the gift that does not necessarily require it or that perhaps finds in it a strange and unfathomable *economy*, in other words a fascinating limit. Here I must interrupt this lengthy note on a noneconomy or an anarchy of the gift, which nevertheless has concerned me for a long time. In this regard I feel that Marion's thought is both very close and extremely distant; others might say opposed.

10. *Ecclesiastical Hierarchy*, p. 564a. Quotations from this work are translated from the French version cited by Derrida, as are a few short passages from the *Divine Names* and *Mystical Theology*.

11. "The infinite différance is finite." See Derrida, *Speech and Phenomenon and Other Essays*, trans. David Allison (Evanston, Ill.: Northwestern University Press, 1973), p. 102.

12. This allusion referred to a seminar on Jeremiah which had just taken place in Jerusalem (at the Institute for Advanced Studies), shortly before this colloquium, and to a large extent with the same participants. Concerning that which a question (be it the "piety of thought") must *already* contain in itself and which no longer belongs to the questioning, see my *De l'esprit: Heidegger et la question* (Paris: Galilée, 1987), pp. 147ff.

13. Despite this silence, or in fact because of it, one will perhaps permit me to interpret this lecture as the most "autobiographical" speech I have ever risked. One will attach to this word as many quotation marks as possible. It is necessary to surround with precautions the hypothesis of a self-presentation passing through a speech on the negative theology of others. But if one day I had to tell my story, nothing in this narrative would start to speak of the thing itself if I did not come up against this fact: for lack of capacity, competence, or self-authorization, I have never yet been able to speak of what my birth, as one says, should have made closest to me: the Jew, the Arab.

This small piece of autobiography confirms it obliquely. It is performed in all of my foreign languages: French, English, German, Greek, Latin, the philosophic, metaphilosophic, Christian, etc.

In brief, how not to speak of oneself? But also: how to do it without allowing oneself to be invented by the other? or without inventing the other?

14. A long introduction to this work in progress has appeared under the title *Chora*, in a volume in honor of Jean-Pierre Vernant.

15. See my essay "Le retrait de la métaphore," in *Psyché*, pp. 63–93.

16. Quoted by Jean-Luc Marion in *L'idole et la distance*, p. 249. Here I refer to this work, and in particular to the chapter "The Distance of the *Requisit* and the Discourse of Encomium: Dionysius." I must admit that I had not read this book at the time of writing this lecture. This book was in fact published in 1977, and its author had amicably sent it to me. Discouraged or irritated by the signs of reductive misunderstanding or injustice concerning me, which I thought I had immediately discerned, I made the mistake of not continuing my reading, thus allowing myself to be diverted by quite a secondary aspect (namely, his relationship to my work); today, after rereading Dionysius and preparing the present lecture, I better perceive the force and the necessity of this work—which does not always signify, on my part, an agreement without reservations. Since the limitations of this publication do not permit me to explain myself, I defer the matter until later. Nevertheless, the few lines in which I distinguish between prayer and encomium, like the references to *Dieu sans l'être*, were subsequently added to the exposition that I had devoted to prayer in the lecture read in Jerusalem. I did this in response and in homage to Jean-Luc Marion, who seems to me to give the impression all too quickly that the passage to the encomium is the passage to prayer itself, or that between these two the passage is immediate, necessary, and in some way analytic. Notably, when he writes: "Dionysius tends to substitute another verb for the *speaking* of predicative language, ὑμνεῖν, to praise. What does this substitu-

tion signify? It no doubt indicates the passage of the discourse to prayer, because 'prayer is a λόγος, but neither true nor false' (Aristotle)" (p. 232). What Aristotle says, as a matter of fact, in the *Peri Hermeneias* (17a), is that if all *logos* is significant *(semantikos)*, only one in which one can distinguish the true and false is *apophantic*, and constitutes an affirmative proposition. And he adds: this does not appertain to all *logos*; "thus prayer [eukhè] is a discourse [logos], but neither true nor false [all'outè alethès oute pseudes]." But would Aristotle have said that the encomium *(hymnein)* is not apophantic? That it is neither true nor false? That it has no relationship to the distinction between the true and the false? One may doubt this. One may even doubt it in the case of Dionysius. For if the encomium or the celebration of God indeed does not have the same rule of predication as every other proposition, even if the "truth" to which it lays claim is the higher truth of a hyperessentiality, it celebrates and names what "is" such as it "is," beyond Being. Even if it is not a predicative affirmation of the current type, the encomium preserves the style and the structure of a predicative affirmation. It says something about someone. This is not the case of the prayer that apostrophizes, addresses itself to the other and remains, in this pure movement, absolutely pre-predicative. Here it does not suffice to underscore the performative character of utterances of prayer and encomium. The performative itself does not always exclude predication. All the passages from the *Divine Names* or the *Mystical Theology*, to which Marion refers in a note (n. 65, p. 249) as "confirmation," involve an encomium or, as M. de Gandillac sometimes translates, a celebration that is not a prayer and that entails a predicative aim, however foreign it may be to "normal" ontological predication. One may even risk the following paradox: sometimes the celebration can go further than the prayer, at least in supplementing it where it cannot "accomplish" itself, namely, as Dionysius says, in the "union" *(DN,* ch. 2:680bcd). Even if the encomium cannot merely bring to light *(ekphainein)* or say, it says and determines—as that which it is—the very fact that it cannot show and know, and to which it cannot unite itself even by prayer. If prayer, at least according to Dionysius, tends toward union with God, the encomium is not prayer; it is at most its supplement. It is what is added to it, when union remains inaccessible or fails to occur, playing the role of substitute, but also determining the referent itself, which is also the cause (the Réquisit, Marion would say) of the prayer. It can incite to prayer, it can also follow it, but it is not identical with it. From many other possible examples, here I recall only the one Marion rightly quotes, underscoring a few words; "We must merely recall that this discourse does not aim to bring to light *(ἐκφαίνειν)* the hyperessential essence insofar as it is hyperessential (because it remains unspeakable, unknowable, and thus entirely impossible to bring to light, *eluding all union),* but much rather to praise the procession which makes the essences and which comes before all the beings of the [trinitary] thearchy, a principle of essence" *(DN,* ch. 5:816c; cited by Marion on pp. 249–50). This passage may be found on p. 128 of the (often different) translation by Maurice de Gandillac in the *Œuvres Complètes* of Pseudo-Dionysius the Areopagite (Paris: Aubier-Montaigne, 1943). Not to bring to light, not to reveal *(ekphainein),* not to make access to it by a revelation reaching "union": this is not exactly not to speak, not to name, nor even to abstain from attributing (even if this is beyond Being). This is not to avoid speaking. It is even to start to speak in order to determine the addressee of the prayer, an addressee who is also *aitia,* of course, and cause or *requisit*

25. Although this distinction is essential and stable, it does not always receive a terminological equivalent as clear as, for example, in Martin Heidegger, *Hegel's Concept of Experience* (New York: Harper and Row, 1970), p. 135: "The science Aristotle has described—the science that observes beings as beings—he calls First Philosophy. But first philosophy does not only contemplate beings in their beingness [Seiendheit]; it also contemplates that being which corresponds to beingness in all purity: the supreme being. This being, τὸ Θεῖον, the Divine [das Göttliche], is also with a curious ambiguity called 'Being.' First philosophy, as ontology, is also the theology of what truly is. It should more accurately be called theiology. The science of beings as such is in itself onto-theological." See also Heidegger's course on *Schelling* (1936; Tübingen: M. Niemeyer, 1971), pp. 61–62. Insofar as it is distinct from the onto-theological theiology, theology had been defined in *Sein und Zeit* (p. 10): a "more originary making explicit" of the being of man in his relation to God, starting from the "meaning of faith." See Heidegger's *Nietzsche* (Pfullingen: Neske, 1961), 2:58–59. In the preceding chapter, "Nihilismus, nihil und Nichts," Heidegger defines the essence of nihilism (from which Nietzsche will not have escaped): not to take seriously the question of the Nothing, "the essential non-thinking of the essence of the Nothing [das wesenhafte Nichtdenken an das Wesen des Nichts]" (*ibid.*, pp. 53–54).

26. See, in particular, the resumé of a session of the *Académie évangélique*, early in December 1953, in Hofgeismar, *Heidegger et la question de Dieu*, trans. Jean Greisch (Paris: Grasset 1980), p. 335.

27. *Es gibt die Zeit, es gibt das Sein*, says "Zeit und Sein" in 1962. Later printed in Martin Heidegger, *Zur Sache des Denkens* (Tübingen: Max Niemeyer, 1969), pp. 1–25. There is no question of reversing priority or a logical order and saying that the gift precedes Being. But the thinking of the gift opens up the space in which Being and time give themselves and give themselves to thought. Here I cannot enter into these questions, to which in the 1970s I devoted a seminar at the *École normale supérieure* and at Yale University ("Donner le temps"), which expressly orient all the texts I have published since about 1972.

28. Heidegger sometimes quotes Meister Eckhart, and frequently in regard to the thinking of the thing. "As the old master of reading and living, Meister Eckhart, says, in what is unspoken of their language [i.e., that of things] is 'God first God'" (Martin Heidegger, *Der Feldweg* [Frankfurt am Main: Vittorio Klostermann, 1953], p. 4; my italics). It is always on the subject of the thing that he associates the name of Dionysius (who, to my knowledge, he cites nowhere else), with that of Eckhart: "Meister Eckhart employs the word *dinc* both for God and for the soul. . . . Thereby this *master of thought* [my italics] by no means wishes to say that God and the soul are similar to a boulder: a material object; *dinc* is here the cautious and reserved name for something that is in general. Thus Meister Eckhart says, following a passage of Dionysius the Areopagite: *diu minne ist der natur, daz si den menschen wandelt in die dinc, die er minnet* [the nature of love is that it transforms man into the things he loves]. . . . Like Meister Eckhart, Kant speaks of things and understands, by this word, something that is. But for Kant, what is becomes an object of representation [Gegenstand des Vorstellens]" ("Das Ding," in *Vorträge und Aufsätze* [Pfullingen: Neske, 1954], p. 169). I quote this last phrase because, as we shall see, it is not without relation to the reason for which Heidegger writes the word *being* under erasure. Concerning the concept of *Gemüt* in Heidegger and a tradition that also leads back to Eckhart, among others,

see my *De l'esprit: Heidegger et la question* (Paris: Galilée, 1987), p. 125 and passim.

29. By an analogous but no doubt radically different gesture, Jean-Luc Marion inscribes the name of God under a cross in *Dieu sans l'être*, "crossing G⨯d with the cross which reveals Him only in the disappearance, His death and resurrection" (pp. 152–153). This is another thinking of the gift and of the trace, a "theology" which would be "rigorously Christian" by sometimes opposing itself to the most kindred thoughts, those of Heidegger in particular: "these questionings could join together in a topical, apparently modest question: does the name of G⨯d, who crosses Himself with a cross because He crucifies Himself, arise from Being? We say nothing of 'God' in general, or of thought which takes its starting-point from the divine, hence also from the fourfold; we speak of the G⨯d who crosses himself with a cross because He reveals Himself by His being placed on the cross, the G⨯d revealed by, in, and as Christ; in other words, the G⨯d of rigorously *Christian* theology" (p. 107). By placing a cross on "God" rather than on "Being," Marion proposes to subtract the thinking of the gift, or rather of the *trace* of the gift, because there is also and still at issue a thinking of the *trace*, from the Heideggerian fourfold: "G⨯d gives. The giving *[donation]*, giving one cause to guess how 'it gives,' a donation, provides the only accessible trace of Him who gives. Being / beings, like everything, if it is taken into view as a giving, can therein allow one to guess the trace of another gift. Here solely the model of the gift which one admits is important—appropriation or distance. In the former case, naturally, the agency of G⨯d could not intervene, since the giving *[donner]* is included in the fourfold. . . . There remains to be glimpsed—if not with Heidegger, at least from his reading and, if necessary, against him—that G⨯d does not belong to Being / beings, and even that Being / beings arises from distance" (pp. 153–54). This thinking of the trace is thus also that of a "distance" not reducible to the ontological difference.

30. See, among many other places, the first page of Martin Heidegger, "Die Sprache im Gedicht: Eine Erörterung von Georg Trakls Gedicht," in Martin Heidegger, *Unterwegs zur Sprache* (Pfullingen: Neske, 1959), p. 37. In English, see Martin Heidegger, *On the Way to Language*, trans. Peter D. Hertz (New York: Harper and Row, 1971), p. 159.

31. "Metaphysics is onto-theology. Whoever has experienced theology in its own roots—both the theology of the Christian faith and that of philosophy— today prefers, in the realm of thinking, to *remain silent* [schweigen] about God. For the onto-theological character of metaphysics has become questionable [frag-würdig] for thought, not on the basis of any atheism, but out of the experience of a thinking that has shown, in onto-theology, the as yet *unthought* unity of the essence of metaphysics." See the bilingual edition of Martin Heidegger's *Identity and Difference*, trans. Joan Stambaugh (New York: Harper and Row, 1969), pp. 54–55 and 121. I have underscored the words *remain silent*.

32. This seminar was translated and presented by F. Fédier and D. Saatdjian in the review *Po&sie* (1980), vol. 13, and the passage I quote was also translated in the same year by Jean Greisch in *Heidegger et la question de Dieu*, p. 334. The German text of the privately circulated edition was quoted, for the passage that interests us, by J.-L. Marion, in *Dieu sans l'être*, p. 93.

33. Report of a session of the Evangelical Academy in Hofgeismar, December 1953, trans. Jean Greisch, in *Heidegger et la question de Dieu*, p. 335.

# 2
# ENDINGS, CONTINUED
# Frank Kermode

...si j'entrouvre un de mes ouvrages, et si je le goûte, si je l'admire, c'est là me sentir inférieure à celui qui l'écrivit. Je me dis: Tu n'en ferais pas autant aujourd'hui, tu es ta propre diminution. C'est un sentiment très pénible. Que si, au contraire, le texte me semble absurde ou d'un style que je ne puis plus supporter, j'ai honte d'avoir été le malheureux qui l'a pu écrire. ... On n'y échappe point. Il faut pleurer dans les deux cas, ou celui que l'on est, ou celui qu'on fut, et le moment présent a toujours les deux visages d'un Janus, tous deux fort tristes.

(Valéry, *Mon Faust*)

VALÉRY, OR rather his Faust,[1] expresses accurately the discomfort an author may feel in looking back at early works of which he does not clearly remember either the writing or the argument, let alone what was thought at the time to be good or bad about them. I myself try to avoid such occasions; when I can't I find myself in precisely the plight described by Valéry, now thinking sadly that I couldn't do *that* any more, now squirming at my kinship with someone who once supposed he could get away with *that*.

Such are my feelings when I look once more at *The Sense of an Ending*.[2] It is over twenty years old, for the lectures contained in it were given in the autumn of 1965. The book was published

in 1967, a year that in the opinion of many should be as celebrated in the history of criticism as 1798 in the history of poetry;
for it was in 1967 that Jacques Derrida published the three books
which were soon, with the aid of many successors from his hand,
and with the support of enthusiastic disciples, to end one epoch
and begin another, in which the sort of literary theory represented
by The Sense of an Ending might perhaps look at best a little
archaic. The book is still in print, having I daresay a sort of paleo-
technological interest—rather as if someone had designed an
advanced new airplane propellor at the very moment when the
jet engine arrived on the scene; or an archaeological interest, as if
a Louis Agassiz might offer to demonstrate the fixity of species in
1859, the year of Darwin's Origin.

What induced me to risk the double sorrow of Valéry's Faust
was a suggestion that the book, which had appeared without
revision in several other languages, might now be translated into
German, provided it could be shored up by an additional chapter
offering a few hints as to how the reader could update its mus-
ings, or contrast them as they were and are with what they might,
with more luck, have been.

It so happened that this notion came up at a conference in
Jerusalem in the early summer of 1986, an occasion notable,
among other things, for an extraordinary performance by Derrida.
His topic was, very roughly indeed, the relation between his
thought and the negative theology of Christian tradition. I was
asked to comment on this vast lecture,* and it was subsequently
suggested that I might usefully combine that task with the other
one of updating The Sense of an Ending. And that is what I have
attempted in this paper.

IT IS possible, and also I believe reasonable, to maintain a resistance to certain literary applications of deconstruction while continuing to admire—and, let us translate, wonder at—the achievements of Derrida, whose virtuosity is such that one sometimes

---

* Editors' note: The reference is to the preceding essay in this volume, Derrida's
"How to Avoid Speaking: Denials," which has been revised slightly from its
original lecture form.

feels genuinely embarrassed at claiming membership not only of the same profession but even of the same species. *De la Grammatologie* continues to strike me as an astonishing intellectual feat, quite beyond the conceptual capacities even of the sort of mind we should in the ordinary way, and with justification, call distinguished. I do not mean this characterization of the philosopher as a sort of superman of pure intellection to be taken as vacuous eulogy; my point will come to be seen as a different one, namely that a continual attention to the operations of differance, even supposing that it is always provided by thinkers of the highest quality, even supposing that it is necessary by the purest standards of intellectual hygiene, may not be humanly supportable; that even if this is the way things really are most of us may still have to behave as if they were otherwise.

Summary accounts of the new philosophy, by persons better qualified than I am to provide them, are easily available. Here I concern myself only with aspects that seem to have a bearing on the topics I considered, though in so different a mode, in my old book. I can begin with the Jerusalem lecture. In it Derrida took up an issue that had exercised him for a long time, though he had not hitherto dealt with it so extensively. He called his lecture "Comment ne pas dire?" or, in English, "How to Avoid Speaking: Denials." In the course of the lecture he made frequent use of the term *apophasis,* which the *Oxford English Dictionary* glosses as *denial.* The dictionary distinguishes two main senses of the word. It was a technical term in rhetoric for "a kind of Irony, whereby we deny that we say or doe that which we especially say or doe" —to quote an example of 1657 cited by the OED. Derrida, who has a special interest in multiple senses, and in the "slippage" between them, undoubtedly had something like this definition in mind as a description of his own method in the paper. But the other main sense of the word, which he kept in the foreground, is theological, and has to do with the method of "negative theology" —"knowledge of God obtained by way of negation," as in this OED example of 1961: "negative or apophatic theology . . . certainly does not lead to complete ignorance."

Now Derrida had much earlier considered the possibility that since to describe *différance* means forever saying what it is not, his philosophy might be taken (mistaken) for an exercise in negative theology. In his essay "Différance,"[3] he remarked that

> the detours, phrases, and syntax that I shall often have to resort to will resemble—will sometimes be practically indistinguishable from—those of negative theology. . . . We have noted that differance is not, does not exist, and is not any sort of being-present *(on)*. And we will have to point out everything that it is not, and, consequently, that it has neither existence nor essence. And yet what is thus denoted as differance is not theological, not even in the most negative order of negative theology. The latter . . . is always occupied with letting a supraessential reality go beyond the finite categories of essence and existence, that is, of presence, and always hastens to remind us that, if we deny the predicate of existence to God, it is in order to recognize him as a superior, inconceivable, and ineffable mode of being. Here there is no question of such a move . . . [Differance] is not a being-present. . . . It commands nothing, rules over nothing, and nowhere does it exercise any authority. It is not marked by a capital letter. Not only is there no realm of differance, but differance is even the subversion of every realm. This is obviously what makes it threatening and necessarily dreaded by everything in us that desires a realm, the past or future presence of a realm. And it is always in the name of a realm that, believing one sees it ascend to the capital letter, one can reproach it for wanting to rule. (pp. 134–53)

As I read these rather eerie words I become conscious of a remote resonance, some memory stirred by what may be merely rhythmical association:

> Nothing, nothing, attaches to them, and their reputation . . . does not depend on human speech. . . . Nothing is inside them . . . if mankind grew curious and excavated, nothing, nothing would be added to the sum of good or evil. One of them is rumoured within the boulder that swings on the summit of the highest of the hills; a bubble-shaped cave that has neither ceiling nor floor, and mirrors its own darkness in every direction infinitely.

These are Forster's caves, "older than anything in the world," "unspeakable," bearing "no relation to anything dreamt or seen." Shortly I shall have to speak of *place*, of what Derrida names *khora;* and the caves are a kind of figure of that place, always already in place, without dimension or direction, not a realm, not a being-present yet not an absence; the rhythms are the rhythms of negativity itself.

The purpose of Derrida's idiomatic pronouncement is to claim that differance is not negative in the same measure as the God of negative theology; for it is so in much greater measure—indeed it cannot properly be thought of as negative at all; it is outside negativity as it is outside everything. Only by an intellectual error —induced by a sort of metaphysical paranoia, a fear for the security of that "realm"—could anybody suppose that differance has a design on us, or a desire to make itself into some sort of presence. (Yet it *is* granted a sort of negative status as a person; it does not command, rule, exercise authority; it subverts and can seem threatening.) The centrally important need is to distinguish it from the negativity of the theologians, into which there will always be smuggled the comforting notion of hyperessentiality.

Accordingly Derrida labors to make us see that despite an apparently inevitable similarity of vocabulary and figure what he is talking about is different from any philosophy or theology that invokes some form of hyperessentiality, or gives to the "without," which is inevitably used over and over again to speak of the negative attributes of God, a quasi-positive sense: "the simultaneously negative and hyperaffirmative meaning of *without*," as he put it in the Jerusalem lecture. When Augustine, echoed by Meister Eckhart, describes God as "wise without wisdom, good without goodness, powerful without power," "purely phenomenal negativity" is being transmuted into "affirmation." But differance, as Derrida remarked in the earlier essay, is quite different; it cannot (or should not) be so transmuted; it casts not the slightest shadow of positivity. Its difference lies in the fact that differance is *not* a way of positing a supraessential reality beyond existence, beyond essence.

This rather hectic and repeated emphasis may suggest that it is Derrida himself rather than the opponents he cites (without nam-

ing them) who most obstinately brings up this question of negative theology and its resemblances to differance. It is as if he were
self-threatened with a theology, or an atheology—with the desire
for a realm, however vacant—and finds the prospect disturbing.
He therefore attaches exceptional importance to this work of dis-
crimination. He does not want differance, under any of its aliases,
to be in place of God, or in a place resembling that of God, or
indeed in any *place* at all.

One of the objections attributed in the Jerusalem speech to
some imaginary opponent is precisely that such a discourse as
this of Derrida's, though its object is to forestall any such convergence, inevitably verges on divinity. Derrida of course contests
this "onto-theological reappropriation," while admitting that,
trapped in the same language and logic, one can't avoid it when
speaking of something that is preconceptual, independent of
presence or even absence, etc.; it is because the difficulty is real
that he now risks returning to it.

I cannot trace every step of his route, taken with much calculated hesitation, and somewhat in the mode of apophatic irony,
as he wonders how to speak about the almost unspeakable, wonders how not to speak when he is already speaking, when indeed
he has effectively been doing so even before beginning to. Instead,
to serve my own ends, I shall here consider what he says about
*place.* He tells us that God "is not and He does not take place ('il
n'a pas lieu') or rather He is and takes place, but without Being
and without place." He is certainly above all places. What happens when one speaks of many discourses, including negative
discourse on God, and discourse that in certain respects resembles that negative discourse on God, taking place in the place
Jerusalem, which is not simply a place but a kind of origin and a
kind of end? As in all discourse on God, even the most apophatic,
there is a trace. The power of negative theology to speak in its
own way of God comes from God as its necessary cause. He is
called upon in consequence of an irrepressible desire for a referent, a desire for meaning. "This is what God's name always
names . . . : the trace of the singular event that will have rendered
speech possible." That is why apophatic discourse must open
with a prayer. Without that preliminary prayer the negative dis-

course would be directionless, a desert wandering. God, and his Derridean antimetaphysical analogues (which are not truly analogous, but which, *rather* like God, are beyond being and do not take place) must nevertheless *have* place, in a certain unique mode of doing so, for which Derrida, with characteristic resource, finds a name in the *Timaeus.*

The word is *khora,* the place (which is yet not a place) or the receptacle (which is not a receptacle) in which the mimemes of the forms are impressed on matter; the "place" that must therefore have been there already, in a "there" outside time and becoming, neither in the eternity of the ideas nor in the becoming of the sensible things. (Plato at this point does sound rather Derridean.) The *khora* is something of which we have only a dreamlike sense, as if it existed and did not, were there and not there, neither positive nor negative, neither passive nor active, the receptacle or place of the inscription of the forms, yet not a receptacle and not a place; although the word *khora* existed already, it here denotes none of the things it formerly denoted. One must think of the *khora* as Dionysius thought of the good: as the formless which confers form. It is in this respect that it seems to resemble the *place* to which negative theology hopes to be directed by prayer as it passes through the wilderness of discourse.[4]

In imagining the *place* as Jerusalem, offering another figure for the unfigurable—Being reduced to a place, the place as a trace of "that which committed or rendered it possible," as the taking place of "a reference to the other"—Derrida perhaps remembers his earlier, more rhapsodic, essay on "Edmond Jabès and the Question of the Book."[5] Jews, the "race born of the Book" (p. 64), can say "God separated himself from us in order to let us speak . . . this negativity in God is our freedom" (p. 67). And "Writing is the moment of the desert as the moment of Separation." "The desert-book is made of sand, *'of mad sand'* " (p. 68). In his reflections on the poetry of Jabès Derrida seems to approve these figures, and he goes on to speculate that the Book might be "an *epoch* of Being, Being come to an end, radically outside the book, books as the dissipation of Being, incapable of the interrogation of God" (p. 77), separated from presence, the word (not the Word) in the desert.

It is at least evident from this, as from his whole posture, that Derrida is unlikely to have much time for the idea of a book as a place, another figure for the unfigurable; itself a sort of Jerusalem, constituting a city, having limits and order or traces of them, having even reference. Part of his attack on structuralism was indeed founded on the perception that "a structuralism, by its own activity, always presupposes an appeal to the theological simultaneity of the book, and considers itself deprived of the essential when this simultaneity is not accessible . . . simultaneity is the myth of a total reading or description, promoted to the status of a regulatory ideal" (p. 24). The whole essay from which I quote, "Force and Signification,"[6] clearly places the book as a theological repression of differance and of writing; and the point is spelt out in *Of Grammatology:*[7]

> The idea of a book is the idea of a totality, finite or infinite, of the signifier; this totality of the signifier cannot be a totality, unless a totality constituted by the signified preexists it, supervises its inscriptions and its signs, and is independent of it in its ideality. The idea of the book, which always refers to a natural totality, is profoundly alien to the sense of writing. It is the encyclopaedic protection of theology and of logocentrism against the disruption of writing, against its aphoristic energy, and . . . against difference in general. If I distinguish the text from the book, I shall say that the destruction of the book, as it is now under way in all domains, denudes the surface of the text. That necessary violence responds to a violence that was no less necessary. (p. 18)

The epochal supersession of the book as the enemy of writing— perhaps these are early days, but it has not made decisive progress, at least "in all domains"—-seems to leave the book in much the same plight as the onto-theological tradition and the metaphysics of presence: that is, in *place,* as part of an aporetic necessity, an inevitable collaborator in its own destruction, the reward of collaboration being survival, the price a major undecidability.

HERE I would draw attention to the prominence in the discourse under consideration of certain words other than *God* and *Being* and *writing* and *place;* for example, *realm* ("everything in us that desires a realm") and *desert*—the desert outside the city walls of Cairo (in the essay on Jabès) or of Jerusalem, where, on one side, the wilderness laps against the walls. Realms and cities have limits, like books; they resist free play, seek to halt difference and deferral. But the play of difference and deferral has to be conducted in terms of the already limited, *as if* it were possible to halt them; and of course the users of such discourse are well aware of this "as if"—aware of the metaphoricity that infects their own discourse as well as the discourse to be deconstructed.

"Everything in us that desires a realm"—it is a variant of a familiar Nietzschean position, "the kind of error without which a certain species of living being could not live." "The value for *life* is ultimately decisive";[8] there are of course other aphorisms making similar points ("The most strongly believed a priori 'truths' are for me—*provisional assumptions;* e.g., the law of causality, a very well acquired habit of belief, so much that not to believe in it would destroy the race. But are they for that reason truths? What a conclusion! As if the preservation of man were a proof of truth!")[9] Yet if to "preserve man" is desirable, or if it is biologically impossible to eliminate that project whether it is desirable or not, then we behave, except in the unusual circumstances of doing radical philosophy, as if we have forgotten that well-acquired habits of belief are not truths, or as if life-preserving habits of belief were what mattered rather than truth. If the truth is in endless signifying chains and not in ordered sense, in shifting sand, not city walls and accepted limits—if it consists in a perpetual challenge to that which Milton's Satan, after traversing the wilderness of Chaos, identified as the "proud limitary cherub"— then the realm we desire is one in which the truth is repressed in the interest of self- or species-preservation, even perhaps of simple comfort.

What is the fate attendant on denying "everything in us that desires a realm"? Partly, as I have suggested, to engage in an unending struggle against the language of the realm in the language of the realm, appropriately skewed, *sous rature,* and always on the verge of "reappropriation." But more important in the

present context is the necessary acceptance of finalities believed
to be false. Deferral must, in human terms, have a stop, and the
stop of deconstructive discourse is the aporia; the universal terminus is undecidability. To treat text as a guarded meaning-
construct, as a willed *civitas* or perhaps oasis, as proportioned
and limited, is the plot of those who yield to the call of "everything in us that desires a realm"; to treat it as something that
must be untied and exposed as interminably frayed, the exposure
being itself a kind of end, an end that makes sense of the untying,
is the plot of those who are mastered by a desire more subtle, yet
still a desire for a realm, which, for them, will replace that *mensonge véridique* of which Lacan speaks, and which Derrida dis-
likes. For Lacan thought of the unconscious as a *place*, even *the*
place, of truth, what the signifiers signify; a concept as illicit as
the theologians' hyperessentiality. To mentalities less severe it
might seem a poor satisfaction to destroy a city and erect, as its
monument, an aporia: *solitudinem faciunt, pacem appellant.*

If we want to avoid, even as we admire, this austerity, we may
be thrown back on a defense of *mensonge véridique*, or *vérité
mensongère*, that will involve Nietzsche in a different sort of
argument. On either side, say the Lacanian and the Derridean,
there is, despite all the ingenious and honorable attempts to
prevent it, an inevitable suspicion of bad faith. Derrida's translator and interpreter, Gayatri Spivak, notes that the desire to deconstruct may be a desire of mastery, a desire to teach the text a
lesson by showing that it does not mean what it says (unlike the
text of the demonstration, which must be privileged); and Derrida
is of course always aware of this. And Spivak adds that another
allure of deconstruction is the Poe-like pleasure and fear of contemplating the abyss—"the lure of the abyss as freedom." Deconstruction is itself *sous rature* (*Of Grammatology*, pp. lxxvii–lxxviii).
It is a tormented and somewhat desolating way to power and
pleasure. Is it indeed what we should invariably choose instead
of the easier means that survive from an epoch said to be closed?
May we not admit that our acts are slaves to limit? May we not
speak of places or realms, and of books and perhaps of lives and
of the world at large, as having recognizable though fictive bounds,

as affording instances of the kind of error without which a certain species of being cannot live?

LOOKING NOW at *The Sense of an Ending*, one cannot avoid discovering a kind of naive confidence that was originally far from evident. If I now briefly recount some of its arguments it will at once be plain how many assumptions made in them are nowadays put to the question. First of all, it seemed to me that the matter of fictional endings had been curiously neglected. There is, one might say, a tendency on the part of writers and readers to wish upon endings the status of ends; mere cessation is not satisfying—one hankers after entelechy, some sense that a potential has been actualized, that the ending has conferred order and consonance on the beginning and the middle. To express the matter as simply as possible, this completion is also what we should want in our own lives and deaths, however skeptical we may be about the possibility of achieving it.

For these fictive operations I found a kind of model in apocalypse, and especially in the biblical Apocalypse, the end of a book which begins with Genesis and has been found to be inexhaustibly full of concords. (I did not claim to discover the connection between fictions of apocalypse and fictions about death; it was pointed out by St. Augustine.) By such means we "humanize the common death." And such is our need of ends that we habitually impose them on successive time, sometimes as epochs, sometimes as other kinds of fiction.

Our attachment to such fictions is so habitual that when apocalyptic predictions are disconfirmed we make up new ones, or adapt the old ones, in the interests of restored consonance and credibility. But I also argued that we are at the same time highly skeptical of these operations, and reconcile credulous desire with the operations of critical intellect by means of fictions, notably literary fictions, which are, in Vaihinger's expression, consciously false, known to be *vérités mensongères*. Such fictions, I added, require to be distinguished from myths; "myths are the agents of stability, fictions the agents of change. Myths call for absolute, fictions for conditional assent." Myths are agents of communal action by believers; fictions are tentative and act in private. But the acceptability of fictions no doubt lies in their power to satisfy under criticism, and under criticism to change, in order to go on satisfying our persistent and perhaps barely conscious need to make sense of our lives. We seek this sense even when the search requires us, in the interest of completeness and final order, to invent threats and terrors that reflect the realities of death, as apocalypse does. And we always risk the disappointments attendant on disconfirmation. The historical perpetuation of the apocalyptic paradigms in various forms, with their repetitive Terrors and anti-Christs and their endlessly recurring disconfirmations, testifies to the truth of this observation; the book seems not to make the point explicitly, but it is strongly implied.

Part of what I said about plot depends on the argument that when we speak of the tick-*tock* rather than the tick-*tick* of a clock we are replacing mere successive time with a significant duration, creating a fictive temporal structure by inventing an end; tick is a genesis, tock an apocalypse. Tock-tick is meaningless, or at least we do not choose to hear it; it is merely successive time, outside the organization to which we give our attention. In the same way a fictional plot creates out of, or against the background of, successive time a "season" that is *humanly* more interesting than unaccented temporal flow, and is made so by the equivalent of the fictive tock. The fullness of time I called *pleroma,* as that word is used in the New Testament, meaning that this is the special quality given to the fictions by the fictive tock that satisfies our sense of an ending.

As to the special character of time when it is subjected to such manipulations, I suggested that there were precedents in the Scholastic doctrine of *aevum,* the time of the angels brought to earth by medieval lawyers, who found it useful for various constitutional and legal purposes, chiefly relating to the fictive perpetuity of monarchs and corporations. I remember hearing a good deal of talk about tick-tock and clerkly skepticism, and also about the idea that fictions can regress into myth, which was indeed treated rather critically; but *aevum* didn't seem to catch on. It is a third order of duration, standing between eternity and time. Angels are independent of time and succession but act within time, rather like characters in novels. I was anxious to find a term that could replace the notion of "spatial form" with its oversimple assumption of a fictive simultaneity (it is a fiction that has, as we've seen, attracted the critical attention of Derrida). It seemed useful, but "spatial form" still had some life in it and was not superseded.

Books and plots (alike slaves to fictive limits) are, I proposed, fictive models of the temporal world as humanly dealt with, and their effects might be compared with the effects of other "concord-fictions." Of course I was keen to qualify the character of our belief in them, and to point out that apocalyptic thought was always subject to "clerkly skepticism," a force that insists on change, on the alterations necessary to continued credibility. In fact, a good deal of the *The Sense of an Ending* is concerned with just such issues; but I daresay I have said enough about it to make possible a few guesses as to how it might be assailed by deconstructive critics.

THE IMPOSSIBILITY of my undertaking in *The Sense of an Ending* was deconstructively suggested by J. Hillis Miller in a brief article that served as the leading contribution in a 1978 issue of *Nineteenth Century Fiction*,[10] which was dedicated to the question of endings. Professor Miller showed, with practiced ease, that there was no way of distinguishing the Aristotelian operations of *desis* and *lusis*, tying and untying, and consequently that no means existed by which one could decide when a given narrative is complete; "analysis of endings leads always, if carried far enough, to the paralysis of the inability to decide" (p. 7). This leaves the whole question at the point I mentioned earlier, which is habitually regarded as terminal by deconstructive analysis: namely, paralysis. Not wishing the volume to end with its dismissive opening chapter, its editor, Alexander Welsh, pointed out that by means of the sort of argument Miller had deployed it would be right to say "that the terms East, Midwest, and West have no clear denotation because the regions they represent merge imperceptibly on the map, or that the tides that lap the shores of the continent obscure the distinction between dry land and wet." Moreover, the argument that analysis, "if carried far enough," must inevitably lead to an impasse, has at some point to yield to convenience, "as is recognized in all the sciences. The appropriate level of analysis depends on the uses of 'literary investigations' " (p. 9). It appears that Aristotle himself found some difficulty in sorting out *desis* and *lusis*, but he knew that it was the dramatist's job to get them right: "Many do the *lusis* badly after doing the *desis* well; and yet the two things ought to be fitted together."[11] Admittedly the *lusis* has to be distinguished from the later term *dénouement* and starts much farther back, as G. F. Else points out, so that the dividing line between tying and untying might be hard to determine, but Aristotle (and the playwrights he was discussing) evidently supposed it possible to decide what belonged to one and not the other—just as we confidently distinguish land and sea despite the tendency of the land nearest the sea to get wet—and did not see their "fitting together" as constitutive of an aporia. Perhaps Aristotle did not carry the analysis far enough to reach a paralysis, deeming the level at which he discussed the matter to be the appropriate one.

It is at this point that the relatively easygoing theory of the last epoch confronts the ludic-puritanical challenge of the new, the paralysis of aporia preferred to the *lusis* that used, in the era between Aristotle and 1967, to seem appropriate. Welsh defines it as occurring at the level appropriate to "the uses of literary investigations," hinting that this level is lower than the one on which Hillis Miller wishes to conduct the analysis "far enough."

However, on Hillis Miller's views there is no real sense in a book about endings, since they don't, in the form presupposed, exist, or exist only as evasions of aporia. On the Derridean view there are even stronger reasons for abstention, which may be inferred from his campaign, reported above, against the very notion of the book. For the book imposes limit; if it did not do so there could be no endings or indeed beginnings, and none of those concordant structures it was once our habit to seek. The book presents itself as a totality, which it cannot be unless constituted by a preexistent signified which controls it. It is therefore the enemy of writing; it is described as a violence used to resist the violence of writing, of differance; it checks deferral and masks difference. It is a false *epoch*. It imposes simultaneity on that which cannot be simultaneous. It appeals to everything in us that desires a realm; it is a false *place*, a simulacrum of *presence*. Even the most refined claims that could be made for it would still be subject to the kind of critique applied to the theologian's hyper-essentiality. Its thematic concords are indeed theological, the product of a "theological simultaneity . . . the myth of a total reading or description." An instance of the bad faith of the book as structure is indeed its fictive simplification of time.

In the intention of deconstruction the textual processes of construction and deconstruction go ahead simultaneously, the text deconstructing itself in the process of construction, and this is what the analyst has to point out. But as many have remarked, the deconstructive reading cannot in practice begin until a constructive reading (serving the myth of a total reading) is in place. John Searle's speech-act theory had to be constructed and in place before Derrida could deconstruct it by indicating its self-deconstruction; Rousseau's devious candor had to be on the page before its more or less latent self-critique could be expounded. This practical measure of priority accounts, in part at least, for the obstinacy with which practitioners choose canonical works to deconstruct; there must be something to subvert, and there must be in existence some doubtless naive established reading of the constructive sort Derrida describes as "a doubling of the commentary," an attempt to protect the text and prevent us from saying absolutely anything we like about it; to reduce its infinite openness. ("This moment of doubling commentary should no doubt have its place in a critical reading. To recognize and respect all its classical exigencies is not easy and requires all the instruments of traditional criticism. Without this recognition and this respect, critical production would risk developing in any direction at all and authorize itself to say almost anything. But this indispensable guardrail has always only *protected*, it has never *opened*, a reading" [*Of Grammatology*, p. 158, where there occurs also the famous pronouncement "il n'y a pas de hors-texte"].)

In an interesting paper in the issue of *Nineteenth Century Fiction* mentioned above ("*Little Dorrit* and the Question of Clo-

sure," pp. 110–30) Alistair Duckworth sought a compromise between the protective and the deconstructive ways of reading, or
between limit and openness. Duckworth makes many conces-
sions; he disowns Hirsch's emphasis on authorial intention, and
allows much to Derrida—for example, he agrees that criticism
which in spite of the evident complexities and untidiness of plots
still discovers thematic unities, still sees an end that confers
order and meaning on the whole, can rightly be called "eschatological" and condemned as an attempt to "conceive of structure
from the basis of a full presence which is out of play" (quoting
Derrida).[12] Duckworth, in arguing for compromise rather than
confrontation between a necessary though limited protection and
"openness" expresses his fear that what he says will be "construed as [in] the interests of a dated humanism." But as I have
suggested, the presence of a stable "crafted text" protected by
constructive readings is hard to deny and is allowed even by
Derrida; and in any case it may be time to stop apologizing for
"humanism," even though it connotes a desire for a realm, and a
proneness to the kind of error without which a certain species of
human being could not live—one of those illusions which, like
the "metaphysics of presence," are so deeply ingrained that they
can be thought of as among those Nietzschean lies that turn into
truth for the benefit of a hapless non-superhuman humanity. This
is a view to which I still incline. It entails an acceptance of realm,
place, and limit in books as not necessarily repressive—in many
fictions, which we after all described as fictions in *The Sense of
an Ending.*

IF I were trying to write such a book now I should of course make
it very different; I wouldn't want to talk about the same texts, and
I should certainly be more interested in all that makes for "openness" and goes beyond "doubling." But I should still, though on
grounds that had probably not occurred to me in 1965, and in a
manner refined, I hope, by a greater awareness of hermeneutic
problems, think of interpretation as subject to constraint. Take,
for example, the question of endings which appear to be faked, or
manipulated certain ways, by an author who counts on a stock

response. D. A. Miller doubts whether closure can really effect
what he calls that "transcendence"[13] of the narrative material
which, as he thinks, is assumed in my book and in others by
Genette, Kristeva, Barthes, and Sartre (though the last two named
at least corrected themselves). He thinks that one may take for
transcendence what is "merely a deluded transcendence effect."
He argues that "once the ending is enshrined as an all-embracing
cause in which the elements of a narrative find their ultimate
justification, it is difficult for analysis to assert anything short of
total coherence." What is needed is a recognition that although
"novels 'build' towards closure . . . they are never fully or finally
governed by it."

This will hardly be contested, since an attempt to justify that
"fully and finally" would be insane; what is more interesting is
the confident distinction between "transcendence" and "transcendence effect"; for it is not easy to see how the former could
be established except in terms of the latter, nor is it easy to decide
who is "deluded." Nevertheless it is possible to identify endings
which can be seen to be in a sense imposed on the reader by
identifiable authorial fiat; so that they feel different from endings
that are, so to speak, properly earned—either by "thematic" means
(though these are frowned upon by Derrida) or simply by a *lusis*
that seems, before analysis proceeds toward paralysis, to be satisfying. The "effect," one might say, is an effect and nothing more
—a trick, an illusion.

I had myself given some thought to these pseudo- or illusory
endings; too late for my book I came across Shklovsky's remarks
on the subject. He spoke of the ease with which writer can induce
reader to credit the story with an ending, or effect his own closure, by making some weighty observation about the scenery or
the weather. Shklovsky calls this device the "illusory ending."[14]
It depends on obedience to a coded rhetorical gesture: "the river
ran on," "it was still raining," and the like. The interest of such
devices is that they induce one to believe in an end when the
tale, raveled but not unraveled, might otherwise be thought to
have merely stopped. There is of course a metatextual end to all
written discourses, including stories; you run out of printed mat-

ter, there's no more to read. But even if a narrative comes close to merely petering out in this way (a famous example is *Women in Love*) nobody is really disposed to accept the drying-up of reading matter as an *end*, and in the case of Lawrence's novel we are in fact told, in the manner of final chapters, that "Gerald was taken to England to be buried," and that "Gudrun went to Dresden," and that Ursula and Birkin stayed behind and had the conversation reported on the last page. This happens to be about Birkin's need for "eternal union with a man" as well as with a woman. Here, as so often throughout the novel, Ursula is skeptical, indeed hostile to Birkin's theory of his needs, and so, in a suitably low tone (they are mourning) a major conflict is remembered in a coda, and the book ends on a discord we could easily show to be "thematic" if we allowed ourselves to think in such terms. In other words we are willing to find what we want, even when the author makes a gesture, as was Lawrence's habit, toward denying it to us. By the same token it could be argued that Shklovsky's remarks assume the argument of *The Sense of an Ending;* there has to be a *desire* for such endings before the rhetorical trick will work.

To Derrida such maneuvers would be typical of the *bricolage* of all constructions, and no different from all other "thematic" effects in narrative; all "thematizations" are the product of the wrong sort of interpretation. But you can equally well think of it if you happen to approve of it, identifying it with what Henry James called "the finer tribute"—that degree of devotion in the reader which goes beyond "the simpler . . . forms of attention"; that "miraculous windfall, the fruit of a tree he [the author] may not pretend to have shaken." It was James who said that the reader's share was "quite half," and part of the contribution must be to work on endings, for the author cannot make "revelations stop," only draw "the circle within which they shall happily *appear* to do so," the conversion of appearance into something like reality being, no doubt, part of the reader's share, the rest being his or her willingness to accept the simultaneous structures which are suggested but cannot, insofar as his book is a fraud violently perpetrated against "writing," really exist. For James at any rate the perfect reader would, however fraudulent, be intensely protective. He or she is the weapon by which the book resists the reciprocal violence of writing.

The difference between the "protective" and the "deconstructive" readings mirrors that between the discourse which depends on the hyperessential and the discourse of differance. But, as we have seen, these discourses are hard to distinguish, even by the observer best placed to distinguish them; and it seems that in practice you can't have one without the other. Just as the discourse of differance is defined by its not being the discourse of apophatic theology, and therefore, in the mind of its inventor, must continually be referred to that discourse, so the discourse of deconstruction depends on the discourse of construction, the superhuman on the human. That the protective reading will be in some severe sense "ideological" is hard to deny. Its assumptions may not invariably be "species-specific," but cultural, and it will have to change over time, though it seemed to me worthwhile looking for more universal determinants, such as the desire for a realm. The assumption, which may seem ignoble, is that "human kind / Cannot bear very much reality," or live without a certain kind of error. Not every individual can be as contemptuous of the need or will to live as Nietzsche was.

SOMETIMES, REFLECTING on endings, I remember Ben Jonson's disapproval of the habit of aposiopesis, the utterance of sentences that do not end and so are not sentences; he saw a connection between slovenly language and public riot. Our notions of well-formedness may somehow stem from our lifelong power to produce and understand well-formed sentences—another violence committed against writing. In rhetoric, aposiopesis is defined as an artifice in which "the speaker comes to a sudden halt, as if unwilling or unable to proceed, though something not expressed must be understood" (OED). (It is a device very much part of Derrida's own rhetorical armoury.) Clearly the rhetorical uses of aposiopesis are various: you can use it when, like Derrida, you wish to draw attention to the actual predicament of the speaker, hindered by the very processes of his own thought from moving on, from saying what comes next, even though it is already written, forbidden by one's own doctrine from ever coming to an end (though in fact Derrida is very good at endings, as he is at writing books against books). Of course you can also use it when you genuinely haven't anything more to say, but, thinking you ought to have, try to make it appear that you are using the standard device, and throw the burden of completion upon your audience ("an excellent figure for the ignorant, as 'what shall I say?' when one has nothing to say, or 'I can no more' when one really can no more," as Pope jokes in *The Art of Sinking*). For whatever reason, aposiopesis substitutes silence for speech, in a recognized convention, and may be expected to appear as part of the rhetoric of narrative, still bearing the small burden of ambiguity it has in oratory.

However, if the habit were common at the level of spoken language, we might never learn to speak at all, and it may be that we should find it impossibly difficult to learn something that had no complete syntax or system. And stories have system, even when paratactic or episodic, and their structure is at least in some measure determined by their ends. Given an end that has some of the quality, or the delusive appearance, of an entelechy, one does have that (illusion of) structure, of a sort of simultaneous totality. Derrida is quite right, in his own terms, to call this "the encyclopaedic protection of theology . . . against the disruption of writing." He blames Claudel for saying that creators and poets have, like God, "a taste for things that exist together"—a desire to frustrate the operations of differance—and he censures Rousset for thinking that the reader should overcome the "natural tendency of the book [i.e., to present itself sequentially] and see it as a simultaneous network of reciprocal relationships." "It is then that the surprises emerge," says Rousset. "What surprises?" asks Derrida. "How can simultaneity hold surprises in store? Rather, it neutralizes the surprises of nonsimultaneity. . . . Simultaneity is the myth of a total reading or description, promoted to the status of a regulatory ideal"—which must be a false ideal because of the indefinite referral of signifier to signifier ("Force and Signification," pp. 24–25). However, he does say that "surprise emerges from the dialogue between the simultaneous and the nonsimultaneous," and the realm in which that coexistence occurs is that which I named *aevum* in my book, though the name was probably too obscure, or too hard to pronounce, to catch on.

The dialogue between the simultaneous and the nonsimultaneous must take place in a condition of simultaneous simultaneity and nonsimultaneity. And it is certainly not the case that all the surprises occur in the sphere of the nonsimultaneous; unless, of course, one discounts those discovered relationships (as James remarked, they stop nowhere) which constitute the "surprise" concealed in the presentation of the simultaneous. They become readable when the successiveness stops, when the *work* ends, ceases for our purposes to be simply text and becomes a book, properly equipped, since it is in good theological standing, with a genesis and an apocalypse and a human concern for death and its types and figures. The flow of the successive contains small mimemes of this plot, ticks that become tocks, seasons that replace mere seconds, antitypes fulfilling remote types. Thus are prepared the surprises of the simultaneous. The New Testament, being the part of the book that is always announcing and providing an end, is full of small typological completions; the texture accordingly becomes not a matter of succession or repetition, but of fulfilment; these reciprocities as recorded in the nonsimultaneous are figures for the larger fulfilments of what I think of as *aeval* simultaneity. So the imitation of this process in secular plots can, as I've suggested, very reasonably be called theological, even though anybody with a vested interest in random successiveness and interminable deferral would prefer to call it repressive. What I tried to show was that it was human; that it is disgraceful only from a superhuman perspective to prefer system to aggregation, as even Kant, thinking of history, admitted that he did.

HEIDEGGER SAYS that "a fundamental characteristic of the essent is *to telos,* which means not aim or purpose but end. Here 'end' is not meant in a negative sense, as though there were something about it that did not continue, that failed or ceased. End is ending in the sense of fulfilment [Vollendung]. Limit and end are that wherewith the essent begins to be. It is on this basis that we must understand the supreme term that Aristotle used for being, *entelecheia*—the holding (preserving)-itself-in-the-ending. . . . That which places itself in its limit, completing it, and so stands, has form, *morphe*. Form as the Greeks understood it derives its essence from an emerging placing-itself-in-the limit." He goes on to say that the German word translating the Greek *parousia*, being or presence, is *An-wesen*, "which also designates an estate or homestead, standing in itself or self-enclosed."[15] Derrida would of course differ from this view, but I quote it for comfort, and because this homestead sounds like the *place*, and the *realm* we have it in us to desire, in so far as we are "a certain species." A plot provides an image of the world in which the essent becomes essent; its closure might be an entelechy, its structure a form, its recognition an unconcealment or truth.

ONE OLD signification of the word *presence* was the confines of a royal court—the king's ceremonial chamber, or simply the stated limits or area in which his person resided. Certain rules of conduct, a certain etiquette, were absolutely enforced within these limits, not merely for security but in the interest of dignity. The presence could as well be a field or a ship as a palace, but the rules were the same. The ruler's personal presence was deemed to extend to these limits, ending at a particular wall or tent; this was a shared legal-ceremonial fiction, binding on all.

Such are the ceremonial arrangements acceptable to a certain species. It attaches similar force to many other kinds of ceremony; its members are deemed to change their state at set moments, when they make promises or exchange rings, for instance. They have not, in any other than this very arcane and ceremonial sense, changed, though the community will in certain cases require them to behave as if they had. All such fictions are the enemies of difference and the allies of presence, aspects of the great myth by which we are said to have been enslaved. If they are revealed as subterfuges, illusions, attempts (like those Derrida identifies in Rousseau) to smuggle presence into the present, are they still not *there*, and still humanly interesting, like some ceremonies concerning realms, places, and states? And do not our bookish fictions, our ends and structural reciprocities, our defeats of never-present time, have a dignity of the same sort, which is undeniably a human sort?

SO MUCH by way of speaking up for my old book, written before anybody knew there were radically other ways of writing about writing, in the hope that it is still a place, or in place. I may seem to have taken the long way round, yet the idea is essentially very simple. Let us say that there is no *hors-texte*, not even death, not even life; so there are no ends, no undeconstructible concords, no such thing as being in the midst. We could allow this to be the case, yet live within our necessary limitations and persist in our necessary illusions, our ways of making sense of the ways in which sense is made of the world. Indeed it was in that spirit, and with a due sense of the illusory character of those illusions, that *The Sense of an Ending* was written.

## Notes

1. The epigraph above is from Paul Valéry, *Mon Faust (Ebauches)* (Paris: Gallimard, 1946), p. 57.

2. Frank Kermode, *The Sense of an Ending* (New York: Oxford University Press, 1967). Page references will be cited in the text.

3. Jacques Derrida, "Différance," in Derrida, *Speech and Phenomena and Other Essays on Husserl's Theory of Signs*, trans. David B. Allison and Newton Garver (Evanston: Northwestern University Press, 1973), pp. 129–60. Page references will be cited in the text. (This was originally published as *La Voix et le phénomène* [Paris: Presses Universitaires de France, 1967]).

4. See also "Plato's Pharmacy," in *Dissemination*, trans. B. Johnson (Chicago: University of Chicago Press, 1981), pp. 167–68, where the "undecidable" there, beyond being, inaccessible, is related to Plato's *epekeina tes ousias*, which is also obviously related to apophatic aspirations. *Dissemination* (p. 235) speaks of supplementarity as "the essential nothing from which the whole . . . can surge into appearance."

5. Jacques Derrida, "Edmond Jabès and the Question of the Book," in Derrida, *Writing and Difference*, trans. Alan Bass (London: Routledge and Kegan Paul, 1978), pp. 64–78. Page references will be cited in the text.

6. Jacques Derrida, "Force and Signification," in *Writing and Difference*, pp. 3–30.

7. Jacques Derrida, *Of Grammatology*, trans. G. C. Spivak (Baltimore: Johns Hopkins University Press, 1976; first published Paris: Minuit, 1967).

8. Friedrich Nietzsche, *The Will to Power*, trans. Walter Kaufmann and R. J. Hollingdale (New York: Vintage Books, 1968), p. 272.

9. *Ibid.*, p. 273.

10. J. Hillis Miller, "The Problematic of Ending in Narrative," *Nineteenth Century Fiction* (1978), 33:3–7.

11. G. F. Else, *Aristotle's Poetics: The Argument* (Leiden: E. J. Brill, 1967), p. 539.

12. Jacques Derrida, "Structure, Sign, and Play," in R. Macksey and Eugenio Donato, eds., *The Languages of Criticism and the Sciences of Man* (Baltimore: Johns Hopkins University Press, 1970), p. 248.

13. D. A. Miller, *Narrative and Its Discontents* (Princeton: Princeton University Press, 1981), pp. xii–xiv.

14. See Viktor Shklovsky, "La construction de la nouvelle et du roman," in T. Todorov, ed., *Théorie de la littérature* (Paris: Seuil, 1965), pp. 170–79.

15. Martin Heidegger, *An Introduction to Metaphysics*, trans. Ralph Manheim (New Haven, Conn.: Yale University Press, 1959), pp. 60–61.

# 3

# HEIDEGGER'S TRANSCENDENT NOTHING
## Gabriel Motzkin

MARTIN HEIDEGGER was the first major twentieth-century thinker to reconsider the problem of the relation of ontological Nothingness to Being. In order to expose his perspective, it may be useful to begin by contrasting his position on this issue to that implicit in Jacques Derrida's paper in this volume, "How to Avoid Speaking: Denials."

The aim of Derrida's paper is to expose how the Platonic philosophical tradition, especially its Christian Neoplatonic variant, considered two issues together: the Being that is beyond beings, and the possibility or impossibility of saying anything about that Being. For that tradition, the One (God), as expounded by Derrida, cannot be a direct referent in speech. The reason God cannot be a direct referent in speech is that He is transcendent to any world, since any world must be a created world. Language, however, can only take place within a world. Therefore we can turn toward that which is beyond being, for example in prayer, but we cannot say anything about it. What Derrida does not elaborate is whether this impossibility of speaking about what is beyond being is not a result of our being created beings: this impossibility holds not only for us, but for all the angels and Ideas as well.

The concept of the transcendent that Derrida consequently applies is a concept of the transcendent as the other. The beyond Being is transcendent to Being, but are we transcendent to Being? The concept of the Nothing that informs Derrida's text then follows from this fundamental ontological difference: the Nothing is neither the Beyond-being nor Being, for the relation between these two is neither one of Being to Nothingness nor one of simple opposition.

Derrida does not state baldly where he locates the Nothing in the architectonic of the ontology he discerns in the mystical tradition. But his placement of the relation between Being and what is beyond being as a relation to the other and his rejection of opposition as the model for this relation allow us to understand what is meant by saying, with Meister Eckhart, that God is a non-God. The reciprocal relation between self and other is such that one can only *be* insofar as all he can *say* is that the other *is* not. The beyond-being is beyond predication; therefore it can be "predicated" as being the completely receptive place wherein all things can happen. True negativity is the negativity that is the threshold between language as being with a world and its other as the transcendent which is without a world. It is because God is without a world that he *is* not.

Martin Heidegger does not really belong to this tradition, because he did not set transcendence as equivalent to what is beyond being. He did distinguish between Being and entities, and one could read this distinction as the distinction between being and what is beyond being in the Neoplatonic scheme. But the essential character of Heidegger's transcendence is that it is world-making, indeed that the concepts of transcendence and the world cannot be thought of separately because it is the world itself that is transcendent. Therefore it is the sensible and intelligible entities within the world that do not have a world because they cannot have a world. Therefore the problem of addressing the beyond-being is never the problem of addressing what is beyond understanding, even though Heidegger would agree with Derrida that the frame of reference is one that is beyond predication. What is beyond predication, however, is not what is beyond the world, but rather the world itself. Therefore, while Heidegger would agree with Derrida that the moment of negativity is essential to the process of constitution, he would never characterize it as a moment of receptivity. Rejecting the notion that the other is what is beyond being, Heidegger rather identified the other with the whole of what is, counterposing the other as all entities within the world to the Nothing as world-defining. In what follows, I aim to decipher Heidegger's specific conception of Nothingness in terms of its world-making role.

AT THE conclusion of the Transcendental Analytic, Kant discusses the "concept of an object in general . . . without its having been decided whether it is something or nothing."[1] To help us be able to decide whether a concept is something or nothing, Kant distinguishes between four concepts of nothing: 1. the empty concept without object, *ens rationis*; 2. the empty object of a concept, *nihil privativum*; 3. the empty intuition without object, *ens imaginarium*; and 4. the empty object without concept, *nihil negativum*. Kant terms the *ens rationis* and the *nihil negativum* empty concepts, and the *nihil privativum* and the *ens imaginarium* empty *data* for concepts. With respect to these last two, the *nihil privativum* and the *ens imaginarium*, Kant continues, "Negation and the mere form of intuition, in the absence of a something real, are not objects."[2]

This paper will make two arguments. The second is that Heidegger's concept of the Nothing can be understood in terms of these two concepts which Kant had grouped together, the *nihil privativum* and the *ens imaginarium*. Such a specification of Heidegger's concept of the Nothing has value because the Nothing is the precondition for the activity of conferring and recovering meaning in his thought. My first argument will be that Heidegger's concept of the Nothing only makes sense in terms of his concept of transcendence. Therefore an elucidation of the role of transcendence in Heidegger's philosophy is a prerequisite for a specification of the function of Nothing in his conception of the meaning-process.

I will concentrate on those of Heidegger's writings which focus on these two concepts, transcendence and the Nothing. These lectures and essays all stem from the period between 1927 and 1929. The exposition of the relation between transcendence and Nothing in Heidegger's philosophy during these years may contribute to a better understanding of the well-known reversal or *Kehre* in his thinking, which is usually dated at 1930.

THREE CONCEPTS of transcendence had been developed in the philosophical tradition: 1. absolute transcendence, i.e., the self-subsisting realm above and beyond the world of sense; 2. immanent transcendence, i.e., the incarnation of the absolutely transcendent in this world; 3. transcending, i.e., the presumed human capacity to move beyond this world.

The Catholic philosopher, Maurice Blondel, writing toward the close of the nineteenth century, emphasized immanent transcendence in order to show that we are not the source of our own capacity to transcend.[3] Contemporaneously, Edmund Husserl sought to anchor truth in an ideal so absolutely transcendent that it could not be modified in either space or time.[4] Husserl's "secularization" of absolute transcendence, which secured meaning by making it transcendent to sense-reality, was absorbed by Emil Lask.[5] Lask bequeathed this doctrine to his disciple, Martin Heidegger, with two significant modifications: first, influenced by the neo-Kantian, Heinrich Rickert, he concluded that the source of this transcendence must be sought within the world;[6] second, reading Neoplatonism through the eyes of Eduard von Hartmann, he argued that the location of the source of meaning in a primordial world that is transcendent to subjectivity requires that logical affirmation and negation be derived from an ontological source in this primordial world.[7]

Martin Heidegger endorsed both of these positions, but, whereas Lask had rejected both immanent transcendence and transcending, retaining only the absolute transcendence of the primordial world as the origin of meaning, Heidegger elaborated a concept of transcendence that integrated absolute transcendence and transcending while rejecting immanent transcendence. His motive for doing so was his desire to anchor transcendence in the nature of time.

Heidegger's solution to the nineteenth-century problem of the world's transcendence to us, and its consequent possible inaccessibility, was to reverse the order, and to suggest that it is not objects that are transcendent to consciousness, but rather human being, *Dasein*, that is transcendent to things.[8] Dasein's transcendence, however, is human. It is not an eternal and immobile self-contemplation, but is rather dynamic and incessant, and as such time-bound, and as time-bound, finite. Its being finite, however, does not make it any the less absolutely transcendent, for this activity can never be other than transcendent.

What Heidegger meant by making Dasein absolutely transcendent to things was that Dasein's world, as the sum total of Dasein's possibilities, can never be determined in terms of things that are within that world (BP, pp. 162, 165). With respect to those things, the world is an antecedent and transcendent determination, with the reservation that the world does not produce the things we meet in the world (BP, p. 165).

Such a world can only exist if Dasein exists (BP, p. 166). It is precisely because Dasein is the world that it is forever beyond itself (BP, pp. 168, 170).[9] The analysis of transcendence must therefore begin with the concept of world.

Heidegger conceived of transcendence in relation to the world as that process which makes the world one as a world of meaning, a world that is forever beyond itself, but that is always already understood (BP, pp. 165, 296). In relation to this concept of world, transcendence is a process of understanding, i.e., transcending is the process through which significance becomes explicit (BP, pp. 300, 302). Even the concept of self is a structure of significance which can only be made explicit on the basis of transcending (BP, p. 300).[10]

This apparent demotion of the self to the level of a construct and the assignment of the cardinal function of world unification to transcendence forced Heidegger to grapple again and again with the problem of unity, whether of the world, of time, or of transcendence.[11] The assumption of the one world that is unified by transcendence would seem to indicate that for a given human being there exists only one transcendence. However, the act-character of transcending appears to require a multiple transcendence, and perhaps multiple worlds of significance devolving from many acts of meaning.

This problem of the nature of the link between transcendence —that which gives unity to something—and that something itself goes back to the Scholastic discussion of transcendental determinations. For the Scholastics, transcendental determinations meant such determinations as were necessary for the existence of an entity but could not exist apart from it. Thus my being one is necessary for my existence, but my oneness cannot be said to have a possible existence apart from me. The Scholastics were aware that setting the individual one as a transcendental determination could prove problematic not merely with regard to oneness conceived as a universal and general determination, but also with regard to the plurality of ones. Should multiplicity also be considered as a transcendental determination?

Heidegger had examined one response to this problem in his habilitation, namely Scotus' theory of disjunctive transcendentals, which are related to each other, for example, in that the one is the privation of the many and the many is the privation of the one.[12] If this privative conception of unity were combined with an act-conception of transcendence, the consequence would be that there are many transcendences which are inherently privative and which are related to each other disjunctively. Heidegger did think that the instantiation of transcendence is multiple: One thing transcendence does is that it "makes possible coming back to entities" (BP, p. 300). Since Heidegger held that an entity can only be *identified* as such after reversion to the entity from the world, transcendence requires multiplicity (BP, p. 299).[13]

Heidegger's epistemological theory consequently separated understanding from identification. He justified this distinction ontologically by denying both the uniformity of being between the knower and the known and the division between the knower and the known according to the degree of knowledge possessed by the knower. Instead, he drew a sharp distinction between meaning and physical being. The meaning-process is transcendent to the entities that are interpreted in its terms. This transcendence of the meaning-process means that the entities are understood before they are interpreted. Interpretation presumes the connectedness of the entities to an enframing activity. This enframing activity, which is transcendent to the entities, is both synonymous with understanding and a necessary condition of our being in a world.

This priority of sense over determinate reference to the entities identified within a world would, however, be ontologically indistinguishable from the priority of the knower over the known in

the Kantian epistemological picture, unless the world is identified with the totality of sense and not with the totality of references. For such a totality of sense, the repeated reversion implicit
in reidentification through multiple reference to the same entity
is meaningful, for no two acts of identification can be identical,
albeit the sense remains invariant.

In sum, Heidegger substituted meaning for knowledge, and
identified the world with the meaning-process and not with an
unsignified totality of entities which would somehow lie beyond
that process as an unmeant totality from which a world or a
context of significance is then individuated. Whereas the neo-
Kantian theory of knowledge had viewed as identical the determination of the entity as known and the determination of the
limit of knowledge, i.e., the determination of the limit of the
world of knowledge, Heidegger's separation between the regional
determination and the reidentification of the individual entity
dissolved this double character of the act of knowing, a double
character which, as Hegel had seen, could ultimately be legiti-
mated only dialectically. Instead, Heidegger had made the world
transcendent to the entity.

This transcendence of the world is absolute, but this world is
Dasein's world, and as such is in time (BP, pp. 297, 302). Since
Dasein's basic temporal mode is futurity, Dasein's relation to its
world takes place in terms of the ecstatic temporal mode, which
as ecstatic is transcendent, i.e., always beyond itself (BP, p 302).
This ecstatic character of time, which is most readily apparent in
our relation to our futures, is then antecedent to transcendence as
a way of relating to the world (BP, p. 302).[14]

This theory has several interrelated consequences. First, time
is transcendent to the entity. Second, this transcendence is not a
transcendence of one substance to another, but a transcendence
of meaning. Third, meaning as world-making is ontologically
prior to the being of the individual entity.

The unity of meaning as world-making is a transcendental
unity rather than an essential unity, i.e., transcendent meaning is
a necessary condition for the possibility of something like a world,
but it can never be considered separately from the world of which
it is a condition. This transcendental unity is then a condition of

understanding; correlatively each world is a world of meaning, and as such prior to the being of the individual entity. Implicitly, that being cannot exist apart from meaning. In *The Basic Problems of Phenomenology*, Heidegger wrote: "The transcendence of being-in-the-world is founded in its specific wholeness on the original ecstatic-horizonal unity of temporality. If transcendence makes possible the understanding of being and if transcendence is founded on the ecstatic-horizonal constitution of temporality, then temporality is the condition of the possibility of the understanding of being."[15]

In *The Metaphysical Foundations of Logic*, Heidegger focused on the relation between the transcendent world and the entity that is encountered within it.[16] He argued that an entity is perceived by a transcending being only when it has already been transcended (*MA*, p. 212). Entities can only "appear" if they have already been surpassed, and therefore they can never be said to be "present" for the transcending activity. The individuation of an entity, in contrast to the human entity for which it is individuated, can only take place retrospectively; that is, the entity can only be identified after it has already been encountered, and therefore each identification is in reality a reidentification, for no entity can be encountered outside of its contextual determination. Transcending then means the surpassing of an entity or object that is encountered in the same world to which I belong. The telos of transcendence is then not the entity, but the world itself. Dasein, already in a world, transcends to that world (*MA*, p. 212).

Heidegger was careful to point out that by beginning his analysis with Dasein as being already in a world, he did not mean to begin the analysis of human existence with the contingent existence of a particular human being, as if, for the purposes of the analysis, that human being were in any way necessary or determinate: "It does not lie in the idea of man that he really exists, i.e. is in a world; it is merely possible that such an entity as human Dasein is in a world . . . it does not belong to the essence of Dasein as such that it exists factically; it is rather its essence that this entity can always be factically non-existent."[17]

Transcendence, being-in-the-world, is therefore prior to existence, for it has possibilities of existence and of non-existence

(*MA*, p. 217). The transcendent possibility of non-existence is
therefore prior to any real, factical existence. The idea of transcendence is thus carefully separated from the idea of actuality.
For Heidegger, the primacy of possibility over actuality was cardinal; it saved him from the pitfall of subjective Idealism, for if
his theory were a theory of actuality, then he would have been
driven to the conclusion that no world can exist except as a
consequence of determinate human existence.

On the other hand, since world designates the totality of the
entity in the totality of its possibilities, these possibilities must
be specified not in terms of the actuality of an entity, from which
they cannot be derived, but rather as what they are, namely
human possibilities for meaning-conferral (*MA*, pp. 231, 247).
Without this link to human meaning-conferral, the world as the
totality of possibilities could not be conceived as a whole, given
that the world as the totality of possibilities far exceeds any
totality of actualities. How can this world be conceived as a
whole? Heidegger's response was that this totality of possibilities
can only have significance in relation to a being for which world
is a fundamental mode of its being (*MA*, p. 233).

Here the objection could be raised that Heidegger had introduced a fundamental distinction between human beings taken as
entities and all other entities, or more strictly between an individual human being and all that is external to it. Heidegger discerned
this objection, and responded by asserting that transcending does
not only mean transcending other entities but also Dasein's transcending itself (*MA*, p. 234). Transcending has then a double role
for Heidegger. First, transcending means transcending the entity
that Dasein encounters in a world that it itself defines, while the
entity that it encounters is not itself Dasein. The entity is not
transcendent to Dasein, but is rather immanent to Dasein's world.
It can be located in Dasein's world only because that world is
itself transcendent. Second, since Dasein is itself an entity that it
encounters in such a world in the same way as it encounters
other entities, Dasein transcends itself, that is, the structure of
significance transcends physical being.

Since the concept of a self is a structure of significance, this
result means that Dasein can only be a self insofar as it transcends

its physical being (*MA*, pp. 234, 243–44). This gap between physical being and the self is a sign of Dasein's surplus of possibilities. This gap only becomes manifest through transcending.

If the world as the totality of Dasein's possibilities always surpasses any real entity, each entity is then revealed in its actuality as a restriction or limitation on Dasein's possibilities (*MA*, p. 248). The realization of the possible is, as thing-in-itself, a restriction of the universe of the possible *(ibid.)*. Each determination is a negation, but a negation not of the actual, but rather of the totality of the possible. Each entity is thus revealed as being by its very nature insufficient or deficient. It is deficient, however, not in relation to a plenitude of being, but rather in relation to a surplus of possibilities. If all actual entities in any possible world are always deficient insofar as they are real, then reality is by nature deficient.

Heidegger's substitution of the surplus of possibilities for the plenitude of being as the transcendent sphere required a redefinition of intelligibility, for intelligibility could no longer be conceived in terms of a being with a plenitude of determinations, that is, an intelligible world or entity about which we could know everything. Instead, Heidegger conceived the ideal of intelligibility in terms of an entity with a deficiency of determinations (hence everything can be known about it within a given context of significance) in its relation to a being with a surplus of determinations of being (hence the contexts of significance are functionally infinite).

The question arises whether the infinite field of possibilities is bounded or unbounded. While Heidegger restricted the set of actualities in comparison to the field of possibilities, at the same time he located the set of infinite possibilities in Dasein, saving Dasein from being a god only by denying it the power to create an infinite actuality parallel to its infinite possibilities. Actuality is nothing in which Dasein can become immanent: Dasein's bounded infinity of possibilities is not transformed into something else by the encounter with the restriction of actuality.

If Dasein's existence is thus located before actuality, then the possibility of endowing objects with meaning is given before the objects themselves. (I experience my existence as the primordial given from which ontological analysis begins, but I am certain of my existence only as my most certain possibility, never as a restrictive actuality of the type I would have to derive from my actual being as an entity.)

Heidegger hence concluded that the entity's entry into a world (*Welteingang*), the concept that he substituted for immanence, means possible entry (*MA*, p. 249). If entry into the world is then only possible rather than necessary, it is therefore only occasional, for the qualification of possibility assumes that the situation of nonentry into a world can also occur (*MA*, p. 250). It is important to note that this entry is not a possibility for Dasein, but rather for entities, including Dasein in its aspect as an entity. Dasein as such always remains transcendent; entities have the possibility of either becoming immanent, i.e., entering a world or not, in this case Dasein's world (*MA*, p. 251). Heidegger thus distinguished completely between transcendence and immanence by attributing them to ontologically different beings, whereas one great traditional problem had been how an entity can pass from one condition to the other. Furthermore, Heidegger's determination of Dasein as the only transcendent entity meant that every other entity has to be considered as immanent, since transcendence is not a possibility for an entity encountered in the actual world.

If transcendence is not a possibility for the entity, the entity's possibility of entry into a world is completely dependent for realization on Dasein. Transcendent Dasein makes it possible for nontranscendent entities to become immanent in a world. This actual entry is not a defining characteristic of the entity itself, for the entity as such has no need of Dasein's world of significance, all the more so since the world the actual entity has entered is a world of pure possibility (*ibid.*)

This problem of the possible entry of an entity into a world of human significance led Heidegger to specify the ontological distinction between the world and the entity that is within it.

Since the entity is not affected by Dasein's meaning-process, the world as such does not exist in terms of the entity. Hence, from the point of view of a philosophy of substance, the world is nothing at all (*MA*, p. 252). If the world is not an entity, it is then also not a nonentity. However, while the world in relation to the entity is nothing as all, all the same as Being it is something (*ibid.*).

Heidegger began his investigation of the nothingness of the world with this determination that the world can have no physical being as an individuated entity, and yet nonetheless does have being. It has being in the way that all meaning must have being. If the world is really nothing, then so is Dasein, so is transcending, and so is meaning. This null being of the world must then be spelled out, for its being spelled out is the condition for the possibility of a discourse in which meaning can be given to the surplus of unrealized possibilities over realizations.

It was clear to Heidegger that this Nothing cannot be the simply negative "not," nor a dialectically determinate negation, for meaning can never become an entity, nor an entity create a world. The world's not being an entity means that the world has no substance. However, the world is also not absolutely nothing in Kant's sense of a *nihil negativum* (*ibid.*).

Heidegger elaborated the concept of nothingness he needed in order to secure the transcendence of the meaning-process in relation to the concept of time. "Time as primordial temporality is the inner possibility of transcendence" (*ibid.*). This simple assertion does not, however, clarify the relation between time and negativity. Here Heidegger made his next original move: he defined temporality as the *nihil originarium* (*ibid.*).

Before continuing, we should recall Heidegger's model of the relation between Dasein and entities. Heidegger rejected two models of the subject's relation to the world, the immanent relation to an external world and the intentional relation to an object (*MA*, p. 253). Heidegger had rejected the first model because he viewed it as privileging the temporal mode of the present, and he rejected the second model because it posed a world outside of time as mediating between the subject and the external world. In *Being and Time*, it had appeared as if his basic model was one that took as its basic datum Dasein's existence together with other entities in one world. The further emphasis on transcendence, however, seemed to correct this misimpression, for it located a dividing line between the world, now understood as belonging to Dasein, and entities or objects.

Anytime a world is posed, necessarily that world as a coherent concept must be delimited. One such limit appears to be the object, which serves as a restriction on the world, as noted above (see also *MA*, p. 254). What restricts the world from the other direction? Any argument for a world must relate such an external limit to the world as something that is included in the said world. It is necessary to include the limit in the world, for otherwise any concept of a world is incoherent, i.e., there would then be two limits, a limit that does not belong to the world and a limit that does. Heidegger, like so many others before him, had to reject the possibility that what lies at the limit of the world is absolute nothingness, for that would make the limit a nothing. On the other hand, such a limit must be absolutely inclusive, that is, no entity can exist that is excluded from the world, not even a Kantian noumenon.

Heidegger conceived of the limit as dynamic. The difficulty with this dynamic limit was that it could be argued that the existence of such a limit necessarily changes the structure of the individual entities it circumscribes at any given moment, as both Hegel and Cohen had in fact maintained.

In that case, one could argue that no real ontological distinction exists between a world and whatever is found within it. Against this last position Heidegger set out to find a response that would secure this distinction while retaining the necessity of a relation to entities despite the primacy of possibility. Otherwise a world with no entities could be imagined. In order to establish, first, the necessity of the relation to entities; second, the ontological distinction between the world and the individuals within it; and third, the inapplicability of absolute nothingness as that which circumscribes the world, Heidegger turned to the analysis of temporality.

Heidegger rejected the various conceptions of time as linear, or subjective, or belonging to sensibility (thus leaving spirit and reason outside of time), or as contrasted to eternity (*MA*, pp. 254–55). He enunciated five characteristics of his concept of time:

first, time is ecstatic; second, as ecstatic, time necessarily has a
horizon (limit); third, time neither passes nor stands still, but
rather temporalizes; fourth, time must include reason and spirit
as well as sensibility; fifth, time has a personal direction (MA, p.
256). That does not mean that the person creates time, but rather
that time is directed towards factical, i.e., actual existence, and
therefore it is directed to persons (ibid.).

Heidegger asserted further that the modes of time are not modes
of consciousness of time, but that each mode of time, making
past, making present, and making future, is time itself (MA, p.
263). This division of time into modes raises the question of
whether there is one time, whether the modes of time can be
unified. The problem of unity is aggravated because Heidegger
held that the verb to be cannot be predicated in the ordinary way
of time (MA, p. 264). This move is reminiscent of Brentano's
argument that no unity can possibly exist between different predicative uses of the verb to be, i.e., the predicative is is an illusion
of grammar.[18] In the same way, Heidegger argued that time cannot
be predicated.

Heidegger nonetheless remained within traditional metaphysics by defending time's fundamental unity. Temporality is the
unity of modes that first unifies itself primordially through temporalization (MA, p. 264). Heidegger needed unity in order to
protect time against the misconception that time is temporary,
which Heidegger saw as a deeper illusion than the notion that
time is present.[19] If time were to dissolve into different modalities, then one such authentic modality would necessarily have to
include the notion that time is temporary.

Heidegger thought that temporal expressions reveal a primordial temporality (MA, pp. 264–65). If we attach words such as
then or now to an entity, we see that their reference is not completely circumscribed by that entity, for they always refer away
from the entity to somewhere else (Darüberwegweisen; ibid.).
Heidegger believed that this referentiality away from . . . does not
come from the entity, but must belong to primordial temporality.
What this referentiality away from . . . shows is that a fundamental character of time is displacement (Entrückung; MA, p. 265).
Heidegger argued that this displacement is primordial and that it

must have preceded any possible entity in advance, i.e., that it in a sense has already anticipated the entire field of possibility (ibid.). Thus one can speak of two properties of primordial temporality; displacement and anticipation.

The ecstatic aspect of temporality as anticipatory or expectant is such that a fissure, a *raptus*, as Heidegger called it, is created by temporality itself (ibid.). This rapture is a gap in time itself, since it is characteristic of time that it is always out of itself, that its referentiality is away from itself. Heidegger believed that this ecstatic, transcending quality of time is what provides the world with its unity (MA, 266). Each temporal ecstasy, which is the condition for the possibility of a world, circumscribes itself (MA, p. 269). The displacement posed by an ecstasy does not determine anything, yet the ecstasy is already faced with a possibility. However, the ecstasy does not produce from itself any certain possibility. What it does is provide the horizon, i.e., the limit of possibility, in which a certain possibility can be expected (ibid.).

Heidegger emphasized the point that the horizon is not spatially or temporally localizable (ibid.). It cannot be found at any entity. He thus made a clear distinction between the entity as restriction and the horizon as a limit on the sum total of possibilities. Having determined that the horizon is not characterizable through any determination whatsoever of the entity, he then drew a further distinction between "is" and temporalization. Since the horizon temporalizes itself, it "is" not (ibid.). Thus the normal "is" of existence cannot be applied to it.

The horizon, however, is not identical with the temporal *ecstasis*. If it were, Heidegger's theory of temporality would be subjective, for he would have identified the act of temporalization with its limit. What the horizon does is to provide the ecstases with their unity. Thus the unity of time is not the same as its modality. Yet the horizon appears together with and in the ecstasis. Heidegger defined the horizon in relation to the ecstases as their *ecstema* (ibid.).

It now becomes clear why Heidegger distinguished between the temporalization of time and its unity. Namely, the ecstematic unity of the horizon of temporality is the temporal condition of the possibility of the world as a unity (MA, pp. 269–70). In a sense, Heidegger had elaborated two transcendent structures: primordial temporality and its horizon, the horizon being the condition for the possibility of the world.

The structure of the ecstematic unity of the horizon shows how the world belongs essentially to transcendence (ibid.). Since transcendence is the basic condition for the possibility of a world, it is prior to the world, but it is not prior to temporality. Both ecstatic temporality and the ecstematic unity of the horizon of temporality are prior to transcending. The ecstases surpass anything that can enter a world, and hence they of themselves are not the immediate conditions for the possibility of a world. It is their ecstematic unity, i.e., the unity of time, that is world-making (MA, p. 270). Entry into the world is thus based on the structure of the temporalization of temporality. In this way, Heidegger located the source of transcendence as far away as possible from immanence. Hence he also had had to make his world as transcendent as possible.

Having anchored transcendence and world in temporality, Heidegger turned to the question of what it means to say that the world is a nothing. He did not contrast nothingness to temporality; he rather opposed nothing (Nichts) to something (Etwas) (MA, p. 271).

Heidegger specified that the world is nothing in the sense that it is not an entity (MA, p. 272). Whereas he had linked transcendence to a determinate entity, Dasein, which has both transcendent and ontic aspects, the world posed a problem for Heidegger in that it has no ontic aspect, no being as an entity, and yet nonetheless presupposes a relation to entities in its very conception. If entities can enter a world, how in turn can that world serve as the ground for those entities? The relation of the concept of transcendence to entities focuses on the power to go beyond them. The world may be the same phenomenon seen from a different point of view, but the question from this different point of view is not how entities are surpassed, but how they are grounded.

An individuated entity is a restriction of the field of possibility, whereas the world is the unity of that field. As that unity, its subject is not an entity, but rather temporality temporalizing itself. The object of this temporalization, what this temporalization temporalizes, is the unity of its horizon, that is, time temporalizes itself as a unity. Since this unity of the horizon of time is synonymous with the world, and since the world is also the unity of the field of possibility, the unity of the horizon of time is synonymous with the unity of the field of possibility. As the ecstematic unity of the horizon of time, the world originally temporalizes itself. As the unity of the field of possibility, the world is not derivable from actual entities, and is therefore a nothing. Hence Heidegger called it the *nihil originarium (ibid.)*. This *nihil originarium* is the ground for entities, and is transcendent to them. Given Heidegger's concept of transcendence, a *nihil originarium* that is transcendent to entities can never be characterized as a substance or a subject; the basis for entities is not something. However, entities could not appear as entities except on the basis of this constitutive and transcendent world which is synonymous with the *nihil originarium*.

Temporality produces not a something, but rather a nothing, a nothing that is the world. Since what time then produces is not entities but worlds, the character of time is not read out from entities, but rather from worlds, i.e., totalities of possibilities.

In the third section of *Vom Wesen des Grundes*, Heidegger discussed the negative structure of transcendence, which he conceived as privative.[20] He began by asserting that Dasein's field of possibilities is always greater than the reality that it already possesses. (*WG*, p. 104). Being situated among other entities, Dasein always appropriates and possesses. This factical being-situated, however, means that Dasein has always already been deprived of other possibilities. This privation of certain possibilities occurs solely because of Dasein's own facticity, which thus serves as one kind of limit on the range of its possibility. And yet this privation of certain possibilities of Dasein's potentiality for being-in-the-world is what makes Dasein confront the "really" graspable possibilities of world-making as its world.[21] The transcendent structure of world-making is thus simultaneously surpassing and privative, excessive and deficient, for each projection of a world is transcending, but it can only be appropriated and possessed as privative.

This characteristic of transcendence as being both surpassing and privative is necessary to the capacity to recover the meaning that has been conferred on something (WG, p. 105). Surpassing and privation are both requisite for the capacity to pose the famous question of why anything exists, and not, rather, nothing (ibid.). In other words, what joins the projection of a world to the relation to entities, which appear as two different things, is the possibility of attaching ontological significance to entities, that is, of projecting the world onto the entities within it. What unites the world to the entities within it is Dasein's possibility of querying the significance of the factical, privative conditions that it confronts.

This querying has two conditions. The first is the ontological difference between Being and entities. However, this condition alone is insufficient for questioning the meaning of existence because the ontological difference itself exists as a possibility, while in actuality the ontological difference only appears as a privation, i.e., as an absence. The second condition for questioning is finite human freedom (WG, p. 106). If transcendence is restricted on one side by actuality as the privation of possibility, on the other side it is limited by the finitude of its own potentiality for being. Heidegger did not think that this finitude characterizes only entities; he believed that it belongs to the essence of possibility, and therefore of the possibility of questioning. This finitude characterizes possibility because it characterizes temporality, i.e., it is a condition of the temporalization of temporality that it temporalizes itself as finite; the world is finite. That means that transcendence cannot be said to originate from somewhere. This conclusion is another reason for calling the origin a nihil originarium.

In What Is Metaphysics? Heidegger applied the same figure of thought to nothingness that he had applied to time in the Metaphysical Foundations of Logic.[22] He argued that we experience in anxiety the ungraspability of the Nothing as coinciding with the whole of what is (BW, p. 104). That is so because, in this experience, we must turn back, revert (BW, p. 105).[23] This reversion occurs because the Nothing cannot be an object of reference. However, we cannot derive this rejection of all referentiality from a logical negation. Hence his dictum that the Nothing nihilates means that it rejects the qualification of being a limit because it is transcendent to all referentiality. It is because the Nothing is not a limit that it discloses the whole of what is as absolutely other than the Nothing *(ibid.)*. As the object of transcending, that which is beyond entities, the Nothing thus unifies ecstematically. Heidegger did not think that transcendence can bridge the gap between us and the Nothing, that we can transcend our finitude, but he did think that transcendence is directed to this nothingness.

The Nothing, however, is not simply something to be counterposed to entities, i.e., to what is. The Nothing belongs to the Being of what is *(BW,* pp. 12, 17).[24] If that Being is transcendent, then the Nothing is also transcendent. The Nothing makes us revert to entities because it is a transcendent negation.

It should be recalled that the Nothing is the ecstema of transcendence; that is, the Nothing is not a substantial structure with objective existence, but a meaning-structure, and as such necessarily transcendent to entities as the ultimate horizon of our world. This characterization has the following implication for the question of why anything exists rather than nothing. At first, it would seem as if this question must be interpreted to mean that each entity has a surplus of possibilities of not-being over being. Therefore its existence is especially odd. However, a more compelling interpretation may be that, if Heidegger is correct about the directionality of Dasein's meaning-structure, the fact that things exist, despite Dasein's being among them, is a paradox.

As an ecstema, the transcendent negation is an object of the temporal ecstasis, indicating that the temporal ecstasis, the event of temporalization, is itself ungrounded. Temporalization is its own ground, but because it is transcendent, it can never be reflexive. Heidegger believed that Dasein as well can never be reflexive, can never return home. Dasein's reversion from the Nothing to entities within a world *first* constitutes Dasein as a self.

This reversion from the disclosed world to the entities within it that first constitutes Dasein as a self, like any entry into a world, reflects the structure of temporalization as being finite and having a horizon. This structure of temporalization, however, must remain transcendent to any actual world; it therefore never appears as itself. In Kant's terms, the world, which includes all of what is, is an *ens imaginarium*, which is derived from the *nihil privativum*, given that transcending is privative. Heidegger would not have fully accepted this formulation because he distinguished between the *nihil originarium* and the *nihil privativum*, the latter being the nothing within the world. In these terms, Heidegger's order of things would then be: *nihil originarium* (primordial temporality), *ens imaginarium* (world), *nihil privativum* (Dasein, man).

Only in these lectures and essays spanning the years 1927 to 1929 did Heidegger attempt to develop a systematic account of the relation between transcendence and nothingness. The problem of the world would continue to preoccupy him in the following period, but more and more in relation to the history of Being etched by primordial temporality (the *nihil originarium*). His analysis of the concept of the Nothing had driven him from the consideration of the relation between the world and what is within it, an intimate question for human Dasein, to the problem of the relation between time and nothingness, which is the history of Being.

## Notes

1. Immanuel Kant, *Critique of Pure Reason*, trans. N. Kemp Smith (New York: St. Martin's Press, 1929), p. 294: A290, B346.

2. *Ibid.*, p. 296: A292, B349.

3. Bernard Reardon, *Liberalism and Tradition: Aspects of Catholic Thought in Nineteenth-Century France* (Cambridge: Cambridge University Press, 1975), p. 231.

4. Edmund Husserl, *Logical Investigations* trans. J. N. Findlay (London: Routledge and Kegan Paul, 1970), vol. 1, ch. 4, sec. 22.

5. See Lask's main works: *Die Logik der Philosophie und die Kategorienlehre* and *Die Lehre vom Urteil*, reprinted in Emil Lask, *Gesammelte Schriften*, ed. Eugen Herrigel (Tübingen: J. C. B. Mohr [Paul Siebeck], 1923), vol. 2.

6. See Heinrich Rickert, *Der Gegenstand der Erkenntnis* (1st eds.; Tübingen: J. C. B. Mohr [Paul Siebeck], 1892), pp. 8, 15–19; Lask, *Lehre vom Urteil*, ch. 3, sec. 1, pp. 413–26.

7. Lask, *Kategorienlehre*, pp. 223 and 236, acknowledges Hartmann's influence; see especially Eduard von Hartmann, *Geschichte der Metaphysik*, published as vols. 11 and 12 of Eduard von Hartmann, *Ausgewählte Werke* (Leipzig: Hermann Haacke, 1899). For Lask's theory of affirmation and negation see *Lehre vom Urteil*.

8. Martin Heidegger, *The Basic Problems of Phenomenology*, trans. A. Hofstadter (Bloomington, Ind.: Indiana University Press, 1982), pp. 65, 162; *Die Grundprobleme der Phänomenologie* (Frankfurt: Klostermann, 1975), pp. 91, 230. Further page references to *Basic Problems (BP)* will be cited in the text, with corresponding pages in *Grundprobleme (GP)* cited in the notes.

9. *GP*, pp. 230, 235; p. 235; p. 237; pp. 239, 241–42.

10. *GP*, pp. 235–36, 420; pp. 425, 429–30; pp. 425–26.

11. On the self, see *BP*, pp. 301–2, 159; *GP*, pp. 428–29, 226–27. "The self is there for the Dasein before all reflection," but "rather, as the Dasein gives itself over immediately and passionately to the world, its own self is reflected to it from things." On selfhood being founded on transcendence, see *BP*, p. 302; *GP*, p. 428. On the centrality of unity, see *BP*, pp. 302, 307; *GP*, pp. 429, 436.

12. Martin Heidegger, *Die Kategorien- und Bedeutungslehre des Duns Scotus*, Habilitationsschrift, Freiburg im Breisgau, 1915 (Tübingen: J. C. B. Mohr [Paul Siebeck], 1916). Heidegger thought that the author of the manuscripts he was analyzing was Duns Scotus, but the author of *De rerum principio* is now thought to have been Vital du Four. Compare Frederick Copleston, *A History of Philosophy*, vol. 2, *Medieval Philosophy*, part 2, *Albert the Great to Duns Scotus* (Garden City, N.Y.: Doubleday, 1962), p. 201, and Frederick Copleston, *A History of Medieval Philosophy* (New York: Harper and Row, 1972), p. 215. The author of the *Grammatica Speculativa*, which is the main work Heidegger discussed in his habilitation, is now thought to have been Thomas of Erfurt. See Copleston. On Duns Scotus' theory of transcendentals, see Heinrich Knittermeyer, *Der Terminus transzendental in seiner historischen Entwickelung bis zu Kant* (1914; Marburg: S. Hamel, 1920), pp. 46–63, especially p. 59.

13. *GP*, p. 426; p. 424.

14. *GP*, pp. 422, 429; p. 428; p. 429.

15. *BP*, p. 302; *GP*, p. 429: "Die Transzendenz des In-der-Welt-seins gründet in ihrer spezifischen Ganzheit in der ursprünglichen ekstatisch-horizontalen Einheit der Zeitlichkeit. Wenn Transzendenz das Seinsverständnis ermöglicht, Transzendenz aber in der ekstatisch-horizontalen Verfassung der Zeitlichkeit gründet, dann ist diese die Bedingung der Möglichkeit des Seinsverständnisses."

16. Martin Heidegger, *Metaphysische Anfangsgründe der Logik im Ausgang von Leibniz* (Frankfurt: Klostermann, 1978). Further page references to *Metaphysische Anfangsgründe (MA)* will be cited in the text.

17. *MA*, p. 216: "es liegt nicht in der Idee des Menschen, dass er wirklich existiert, d.h. in einer Welt ist; es ist lediglich möglich, dass so ein Seiendes wie menschliches Dasein in einer Welt ist; ... es gehört nicht zum Wesen von Dasein überhaupt, dass es faktisch existiert, sondern es ist gerade sein Wesen, dass dieses Seiende je faktisch auch nicht existent sein kann."

18. Franz Brentano, "The First Draft of the Theory of Categories," in *The Theory of Categories*, trans. Roderick M. Chisholm and Norbert Guterman (The Hague: Martinus Nijhoff, 1981), 1:151; *Kategorienlehre* (Hamburg: Felix Meiner, 1933), vol. 1.

19. All of Heidegger's strictures on the vulgar conception of time attack the conception of time as temporary (*MA*, pp. 254–55).

20. Martin Heidegger, *Vom Wesen des Grundes* (1st ed.; Beitrag zur Festschrift für Edmund Husserl zum 70. Geburtstag: Ergänzungsband zum Jahrbuch für Phi-

losophie und phänomenologische Forschung, Halle, 1929), pp. 71–110. This work will be cited hereafter in the text as *WG*. It is also included in Martin Heidegger, *Wegmarken* (Frankfurt: Klostermann, 1970), pp. 22–70.

On Heidegger's use of *Entzug* and *entziehen* for Greek *steresis* (privation), see Martin Heidegger, *Aristoteles, Metaphysik, Theta 1–3, Von Wesen und Wirklichkeit der Kraft, Gesamtausgabe, 2. Abteilung: Vorlesungen 1923–1944* (Frankfurt: Klostermann, 1981), 33:109: "in einem Entzug stehen-steresis. . . . Entzug (esteremenon)." See also *WG*, p. 104: "Die Transzendenz ist entsprechend den beiden Weisen des Gründens überschwingend-entziehend zumal."

21. "Aber gerade dieser in der Eingenommenheit vom Seienden beschlossene *Entzug* gewisser Möglichkeiten seines In-der-Welt-sein-könnens bringt erst die 'wirklich' ergreifbaren Möglichkeiten des Weltentwurfs dem Dasein als seine Welt entgegen" (*WG*, p. 104).

22. See Martin Heidegger, *Was ist Metaphysik?* in *Wegmarken*, pp. 1–19; *Basic Writings*, ed. D. F. Krell (New York: Harper and Row, 1977), pp. 95–112. Further page references to *Basic Writings* (*BW*) will be cited in the text.

23. *Wegmarken*, pp. 10–11.

24. *Ibid.*, pp. 106, 110.

# 4

# DISAPPEARED: HEIDEGGER AND THE EMANCIPATION OF LANGUAGE
## Gerald L. Bruns

## I

BASIC TO linguistics, semiotics, and analytic philosophy of language is the idea of exposing language to view, laying bare the underlying or deep structure of its sentences, or constructing models of the system of rules or ensemble of relations that makes signification, or anyhow the speaking of a language, possible. This (essentially Kantian) task is at once theoretical and emancipatory: to bring language under conceptual control is to demystify it. There is nothing mysterious about language; it is a calculus of signs or global semantic system capable of producing chains of signifiers of such endless variety that there is nothing that cannot occur in language, and nothing that cannot be explained. Even *Finnegans Wake* can be normalized as "a metaphor for the process of unlimited semiosis."[1]

The later writings of Martin Heidegger are a consistent parody of this Kantian or analytic-semiotic tradition. I mean that Heidegger does not so much repudiate this tradition as appropriate it in arguably comic ways. Already in *Being and Time* (1927) he had called for "the liberation of grammar from logic," that is, not the abandonment of grammar but the emancipation of it from what he would later call the framework or En-framing (*Ge-stell*) of "representational-calculative thinking" (*SD*, p. 65/58).[2] I think that in "Der Weg zur Sprache" (1959), Heidegger's last major essay on language, we get something very like this emancipated or parody-grammar. At the outset of this essay Heidegger introduces what he calls his *Wegformel: "Die Sprache als die Sprache zur Sprache bringen"* (*US* p. 242/112). The "way to language," Heidegger says, is given in this formula, but not in the way we imagine. Bringing language as language to language is not the same as bringing it into view or laying bare its deep structures, nor does it mean constructing a new metalanguage. Rather, the *Wegformel* points to a "web of relations" in which we are always entangled, never more so than when we try to talk about language. This web is "the pre-determined realm in which . . . all linguistic science, all theory and philosophy of language, must live" (*US*, p. 242/112–13). In fact this web is, as a good structuralist would say, nothing less than language itself, and we are always enmeshed in it. Not to worry, however, because our task is not to extricate ourselves from this web, say by mounting a critique of the usual sort, but to lose ourselves in it. For what matters is not our freedom but the freedom of language, if "language" is the right word. Heidegger says: "Perhaps there is a bond running through the web which, in a way that remains strange, unbinds and delivers language into its own [in ihr Eigentümliches entbindet]. The point is to experience the unbinding bond within the web of language" (*US*, p. 243/113).

What is this bond that runs through the web and unbinds language, releasing it into its own (into language)? What is it to experience this releasement? And where does this leave us with respect to language? Whatever the sense of these questions, they appear to be basic to Heidegger's para-Kantian grammar.

## II

In the Kantian tradition the concept of concepts is that of the sign or its equivalents (the significant form, the logical term, the element as nexus, gap, place, or difference in the chain, fence, frame, system, web or prison-house of signifiers). But instead of speaking of the sign (*Zeichen*), Heidegger recurs to his mysterious word, *der Riss*, that is, the sign as rift, which in "Der Weg zur Sprache" takes the form of *Aufriss* or *Auf-Riss*, the design or design that "structures," not language exactly, but *das Sprachwesen*, which is Heidegger's way of no longer quite saying the "being" or "nature" or "essence" of language (his way, in other words, of no longer quite doing philosophy of language). "Most of us," he says,

> know the word "sign" ["Riss"] only in its debased meaning
> —lines on a surface [Riss in der Wand]. But we make a
> design also when we cut a furrow into the soil to open it to
> seed and growth. The design is the whole of the traits of that
> drawing which structures and prevails throughout the open,
> unlocked freedom of language [Der Auf-Riss ist das Ganze
> der Züge derjenigen Zeichnung, die das Aufgeschlossene,
> Freie der Sprache durchfügt]. (US, p. 252/121)

There is no short and easy way of making sense of Heidegger's "rift." The word turns up for the first time in "Der Ursprung des Kunstwerkes" (1934–35) as a way of figuring the conflict of earth and world, that is, the strife (which belongs to the essence of truth) between that which closes itself up or refuses itself and that which opens or is self-disclosing. "The conflict," Heidegger says,

> is not a rift [Riss] as a mere cleft is ripped open; rather, it is
> the intimacy with which opponents belong to each other.
> This rift carries the opponents into the source of their unity
> by virtue of their common ground [Dieser Riss reisst die
> Gegenwendigen in die Herkunft ihrer Einheit aus dem eini-
> gen Grunde zusammen]. It is a basic design, an outline sketch
> that draws the basic features of the rise of the lighting of
> beings [Er ist Auf-riss, der die Grundzüge des Aufgehens der
> Lichtung des Seienden zeichnet]. This rift does not let op-
> ponents break apart; it brings the opposition of measure and
> boundary into their common outline [Umriss]. (HW, p. 51/
> 63)

The rift turns up again in "Die Sprache" (1950) as the painful "dif-ference [Unter-schied]" of world and thing, where "dif-ference" is no longer a term of distinction or relation, no longer categorical or structural difference, but simply the "between" that "holds apart the middle in and through which world and thing are at one with each other" (US, p. 25/202). In "Das Wesen der Sprache" (1957), the rift is the "delicate and luminous difference

[Differenz]" that holds poetry and thinking apart, "each in its own darkness." Here Heidegger asks us to imagine an incision *(Schnitt)* that cuts poetry and thinking "into the design [Aufriss] of their neighboring nature," as if they were engraved or drawn or "signed" *(eingezeichnet)* in wood. "This drawing is the rift [Diese Zeichnung ist der Riss]. That cut assigns poetry and thinking their nearness to one another [Er reisst Dichten und Denken in die Nähe zueinander auf]" (*US*, p. 196/90).

It is hard to picture the rift because the word *Riss* is a pun that takes in both form and rupture. "The rift/design is the drawing together, into a unity, of sketch and basic design, breach and outline [Der Riss ist das einheitliche Gezüge von Aufriss and Grundriss, Durch- und Umriss]" (*Hw*, p. 51/63). Thus the work of art is said to inscribe the rift within itself as its *Gestalt* (*Hw*, p. 52/64); the work is, so to speak, "structured" or "de-signed" as a strife of earth and world insofar as its work is to open up a world even as, at the same time, earthlike, it withdraws itself, shows its reserve, refuses itself, solitary and strange, closing itself up before every effort that we make, in our usual analytical style, to lay it open to view. The work in this respect is not an aesthetic object. It does not represent anything or say anything to us; it does not stand before us as an object of our gaze. Heidegger speaks of it instead as "self-standing," belonging only to itself. It possesses thingly and equipmental features, to be sure, but the *truth* of the work occurs only in its *work*, that is, it occurs in the form of a double movement of disclosure and refusal, unconcealment and dissembling. The work *is*, but not as a being that is; rather, the work *works*, and the more that it does so, that is, the more that it thrusts itself into the open, say into the "is," if that is what it is, "the more cleanly does it seem to cut its ties to human beings" (*Hw*, p. 54/66).

For Heidegger, the work of art is something like a model for thing, world, and language. Thing and world are not beings of any sort; we cannot say of them that they exist, or anyhow it is not enough to say this. Rather, as the work *works*, so the thing *things* and the world *worlds*. (Compare the odd sentence: "It rains," where the substantive disappears into the verb). Categories of existence, presence, objectivity, representation, and meaning are absorbed in all that happens in this event—called, famously, *Ereignis*. Paul Ricoeur, following Otto Pöggeler and others, thinks of *Ereignis* as a "philosopher's metaphor" like the analogy of being.[3] In fact, like much else in the later Heidegger that Ricoeur "deplores," *Ereignis* is a pun so dense that no one has been able to unpack it. Whatever it is, it is, to borrow a line from Emmanuel Levinas, "otherwise than being."[4]

At all events the world is not to be thought of as a place or container for things. The thing is worldless, self-standing like the work of art, separated from the world by a rift that nevertheless draws thing and world into a mutual belonging. The thing is not a Kantian object but an event, nor is the world anything constituted according to the forms of time and space and categories of explanation. We are beyond representation and explanation. In his essay "Das Ding" (1950), Heidegger puts together a parody of picturing that designs, sketches, or rifts the world in a wild mixture of metaphors and puns in which earth and sky, gods and mortals come together out of Hölderlin's poetry into a "mirror-play" and "round dance" that unites them, or rather "rings" them, as the fourfold (*das Geviert*). This mirror-play of the fourfold is the world, the round dance of *Ereignis* in which everything comes together, belongs together—not, however, as interlocking elements in a system; rather, each comes into its own and dwells in its own apartness: "Das Spiegel-Spiel von Welt ist der Reignen des Ereignens." Heidegger thinks of this event as the setting free of the thing: "Out of the ringing mirror-play the thinging of the thing takes place" (*VA*, p. 173/180).

Now it is to this strange idiom of thinging and worlding that the speaking of language belongs: *Die Sprache spricht* in the same way that *Das Ding dingt* and *Die Welt weltet*. Heidegger's first essay on language, "Die Sprache," is devoted to the question of what it is for this speaking to occur. The first and hardest thing to understand is that we are not involved in this speaking as speakers who make it happen; or at all events our linguistic competence does not take the form of any sort of construction, whether of sentences or speech-acts or whatever. Language speaks as a calling, where calling is like the raining that occurs without a rainer. In *Being and Time* Heidegger speaks of conscience as a calling in which "the caller maintains itself in conspicuous absence. . . . The peculiar indefiniteness of the caller and the impossibility of making more definite what the caller is, are not just nothing; they are distinctive for it in a *positive* way. They make known to us that the caller is solely absorbed in summoning us to something, that it is *heard only as such*, and furthermore that it will not itself be coaxed [into view]" (SZ, pp. 74–75/319). The caller withholds itself, refuses itself in the earthly manner of the work of art. The German word for this is *Sichversagen*, which is a kind of saying. And as the work of art is absorbed in its working, or as the rain is absorbed, if that is the word, in its raining, so is the caller in its calling. And so are we. I mean that we are absorbed or appropriated by this event, we disappear into it, we are overwhelmed and transformed by it, transported out of the sphere of our ordinary comportment, estranged from ourselves, out of control, a little mad perhaps, or perhaps, Hölderlin- or Nietzsche-like, not just a little. Heidegger calls this having an "experience [Erfahrung] with language," which is the subject of his second essay on language, "Das Wesen der Sprache."

Now, in "Der Weg zur Sprache," we have the rift or rift-design of language—or, more accurately, of the *Aufriss des Sprachwesens* (US, p. 252/121). *Der Aufriss des Sprachwesens* means, roughly, how language, taken on its own or by itself, *is*, or—in the lingo of the structuralists—how it puts itself together, or how it works. However, Heidegger the para-structuralist draws or sketches this *Aufriss* for us in the form of a pun rather than as a picture—namely, *Zeichen-zeigen* (sign versus showing). The rift in language, taken on its own, can be traced in the difference or, one should say, the dif-ference (the rift) that this pun inscribes. Or, better, the dif-ference can be traced in the line of puns that the word "sign" sets in motion: *Zeichen—Zeigen—Eigen—Eignen—Ereignis*. The movement back and forth along this line may turn out to be the way to language, or the way it works.

For now, let us trace this line as follows: We speak, say, by means of the manipulation of signs, that is, in the terms of language, but what gets said cannot be accounted for simply by a doctrine of signification, since it is always the case that what we say gets away from us and something more (or something else) gets said than what is simply stated. "Der Weg zur Sprache" picks this up by stressing what Heidegger calls the "manysidedness" of what is spoken: "Das Gesprochene bleibt indes vielfältig" (US, p. 251/120). This sounds like the commonplace idea that what we say always exceeds what we mean, but in fact manysidedness is not a semantic or polysemantic phenomenon. Rather, it has to do with the distinction that Heidegger draws in *Was heisst Denken* (1961) between words *(Worte)* and terms *(Wörter)*. Terms are what words become when we contain them within the logical forms of sentences and contexts or otherwise situate them within this or that conceptual framework that, for the time being, fixes their usage. Heidegger's point is that we can certainly do these things with words, but words nevertheless resist such usage: they are not containable within the forms and frameworks that we construct in order to make sense of things. They are always breaking free of the logical function of signification. Plato called this uncontainability the "weakness of the logos" (*Seventh Letter*, 342e), but for Heidegger this uncontainability is part of the *Aufriss des Sprachwesens.*

In the idiom of normal structuralism, one would say that terms are signifiers within a system of differences, that is, within a network of diacritical relations that make possible infinite discriminations of meaning. Heidegger, by contrast, would say that terms mean one thing and not another, but not the word, which resonates so as to sound not like one word but many. The word is more like a pun than a signifier. As Gadamer says, besides the Platonic dialectic of the One and the Many that makes possible the fragile unity of predication,

> there is another dialectic of the word, which assigns to every word an inner dimension of multiplication [Vervielfachung]: every word breaks forth as if from a center and is related to a whole, through which alone it is a word. Every word causes the whole of the language to which it belongs to resonate and the whole of the view of the world which lies behind it to appear. Thus every word, in its momentariness, carries with it the unsaid, to which it is related by responding and hinting [winkend].[5]

Here is structuralism with a difference. For what is it for a word to have "an inner dimension of multiplication"? It is not just that words are polysemantic; it is that it is hard to tell where one word leaves off and another begins. This is especially so when we take words as sounds and not just by sight. As Heidegger says in "Das Wesen der Sprache": "It is just as much a property of language to sound and ring and vibrate as it is for what is spoken [Gesprochenes] to carry a meaning" (US, p. 205/98). Words do not so much carry meanings as steal them and hide them away forever. This is one reason why the Heraclitean fragment is the model text for Heidegger: its words are lost to us. Philology cannot recover their meanings (VA, p. 211/69). Thus the old Greek word phusis does not mean nature; rather, as Heraclitus says, phusis kruptesthai philei (Fr. 123): phusis loves to hide. What Heidegger wants to understand is the way in which phusis belongs to the Aufriss des Sprachwesens.

Heidegger asks us to imagine a language whose each word internalizes, not so much its own meaning, that is, its own structural difference from other words in the system, as the sounds of all the other words in the language. Sound a word and others answer, as in the pun. Hence the uncanniness of ordinary language where no word is just itself but is always threatening to turn into another. In this event it is not enough to characterize words as elements in a signifying system. Language is not a network of implications that differential analysis could explicate. Words are not discrete elements but, like puns, they are multiple and dialogical. Imagine language as an infinite conversation in which words talk endlessly back and forth, picking up hints from one another, playing to one another, internalizing one another, sounding and resounding in one another so that nothing can ever be said quite in the same way twice by virtue of the way words are always echoing differently. One could not write a grammar for such a language; that is, one could not say in what the logic of such a language could conceivably consist. This is not a language for speaking; it is a language for listening.

Just so, Heidegger pulls deliberately away from linguistics and philosophy of language toward an antique way of taking language —the way of mystery rather than of system. "Everything spoken," he says, "stems in a variety of ways from what is unspoken" (*US*, p. 251/120). Or, again,

> What is unspoken is not merely something that lacks voice, it is what remains unsaid, what is not yet shown, what has not yet reached its appearance. That which must remain wholly unspoken is held back in the unsaid, abides in concealment as unshowable, as mystery. That which is spoken to us speaks as saying in the sense of something imparted, something whose speaking does not even require to be sounded [Das Zugesprochene spricht als Spruch im Sinne des Zugewiesenen, dessen Sprechen nicht einmal des Verlautens bedarf]. (*US*, p. 253/122)

This is very strange, this talk, but to situate it we can say that before Aristotle, with his Organon (that is, before the invention of logical grammar), there was Heraclitus, whose words we can sound but no longer understand, and whose theory of the sign is like nothing we know because it has nothing to do with meaning (or what we think of as meaning: signifying, saying something). "The Oracle at Delphi does not speak, it gives a sign [semainei]" (Fr. 93), only this sign is not the sign of anything—it is nothing logical, nothing semiotic, nothing that can be diacritically or conceptually determined or put into a statement (made to function semantically). The Heraclitean sign is dark, more word than term; it is, as Heidegger emphasizes every time he takes up Heraclitus, something like a hint (*Wink*). It works not by meaning but by opening.

Whatever it is, or does, it is close to what "Der Weg zur Sprache" is about. *"The essential being of language,"* Heidegger says, *"is Saying as Showing [Das Wesende der Sprache ist die Sage als die Zeige].* Its showing character [deren Zeigen] is not based on signs [Zeichen] of any kind" (*US*, p. 254/123). Signs belong to human speaking, that is, to the making of statements and the closing of contexts; they belong to logos, but not to language. And so it hurts the mind when we try to imagine what it would be to speak such a language, a language not made of signs or signifying elements. But speaking, Heidegger says, is finally *not* making statements or constructing contexts. Oh, it is *that*, anyhow there is no other way (in theory) to figure it. "But speaking," Heidegger says, is at the same time also listening [zugleich Hören]. It is the custom to put speaking and listening in opposition; one speaks, the other listens. But such listening accompanies and surrounds not only speaking such as takes place in conversation. The simultaneousness of speaking and listening has a larger meaning. Speaking is itself a listening. Speaking is listening to the language which we speak. Thus, it is a listening not *while* but *before* we are speaking. This listening to language also comes before all other kinds of listening that we know, in a most inconspicuous manner. We do not merely speak *the* language—we speak *by way of it* [wir sprechen *aus ihr*]. We can do so because we always have already listened to the language. What do we hear there? We hear language speaking. (US, p. 254/123–124)

Die Sprache spricht: language speaks, but nothing gets said, that is, nothing gets signified; rather, in the stillness of nothing spoken, things make their appearance, come into their own, that is, they *thing* in the manner of self-disclosure or self-showing *(Sich-zeigen = Das Ding dingt)*. The thinging of things is the worlding of the world, the ringing of the fourfold, the round-dance of earth and sky, gods and mortals—and there we are: that's us moving among them, mortal as we are.

Only here we are getting away from "Der Weg zur Sprache," which (strangely) doesn't say a word about such things—doesn't so much as hint at earth and world, the near and the remote, thinging things and worlding world, the simple onefold of the fourfold: not a word of it. Heidegger's weird lingo—put into play as long ago as "Der Ursprung des Kunstwerkes" and carefully elaborated in the first and second essays on language and in the collateral essays on "Bauen Wohnen Denken" and "Das Ding"— is dropped. All that remains is *der Riss*, echoing in the quasi- or paragrammatical notion of the *Aufriss des Sprachwesens*, the rift of sign and showing, the spoken and the unspoken, speaking and saying, sound and stillness, structure and event. What remains strange, or anyhow unphilosophical, is the priority of listening, and even this Heidegger makes an effort to philosophize:

Language speaks by saying, that is, by showing [Die Sprache spricht, indem sie sagt, d.h. zeigt]. ... We, accordingly, listen to language in this way, that we let it say its Saying to us. No matter in what way we may listen besides, whenever we are listening to something *we are letting something be said to us [Sichsagenlassen]*, and all perception and conception are already contained in that act. In our speaking, as a listening to language, we say again the Saying we have heard. We let its soundless voice come to us, and then demand, reach out, and call for the sound that is already kept in store for us. (*US*, p. 255/124)

One could say that listening is Heidegger's way of going beyond structuralism. But now what sense can we make of this?

## III

In the essay "Logos (Heraklit, Fragment 50)," Heidegger picks up on the pun in ge*hören*: "We have *heard [gehört]* when we *belong to [gehören]* the matter addressed [Zugesprochenen]" (*VA*, p. 207/66). In "Der Weg zur Sprache," Heidegger picks up on this again: "We hear Saying," he says, "only because we belong within it [Wir hören sie nur, weil wir in sie gehören]" (*US*, p. 255/124).

And "all perception and conception are contained in that act."

Say then that our relationship to the world is not first that of seeing but of listening. Not that we don't (can't) see and conceive how things are, but because of how we are situated (in the mode of hearing) we may not be in a position to get a good look at things; we may not be able to produce the picture we want (for example, an exact likeness, or a clear and distinct idea). Seeing and conceiving are already contained in listening, not so much in the sense of *implied* as in the (darker) sense of being situated in an alien mode. For listening is not the spectator's mode; listening means involvement and entanglement, participation or belonging for short. The ear's mode is always that of conspiracy, that is, of getting caught up in something (a tangled plot), being overtaken or taken over and put to use. The ear is exposed and vulnerable, at risk, whereas the eye tries to keep itself at a distance and frequently from view (the private eye). The eye appropriates what it sees, but the ear is always expropriated, always being taken over by another ("lend me your ears"). The ear gives the other access to us, allows it to enter us, occupy and obsess us, putting us under a claim, driving us mad or something like it, as when we let (cannot do otherwise than let) "a soundless voice come to us, and then demand, reach out and call for the sound that is already kept in store for us." Imagine hearing such a thing! Seeing is objectifying and possessive; hearing means the loss of subjectivity and self-possession, belonging to what we hear. Think of the call. The ear puts us in the mode of being summoned, of being answerable and having to appear. It situates us. It brings us into the open, puts us at risk, whereas the eye allows us to stand or hang back, seeing but unseen (the transparent eyeball: imagine being an eyeball!).

What is it to be taken over (call it "appropriated") in this way? It is usual to think of appropriation (Aneignung) as an act of possessive individualism, as one subject appropriating another: I make my own what belongs to someone else, that is, I take ownership of another's property (even take another as property). For Heidegger, however, appropriation is Ereignis rather than Aneignung—roughly so, anyhow, since Ereignis is the word for event. Think of Ereignis not as a subjective act of appropriation but as an event in which we are caught up (appropriated, if you like)— or, say, expropriated, in the sense of being taken out of ourselves and put into play.

Play is a good analogy. As Gadamer has shown, play is like (but not quite the same as) the event of appropriation. Play, he says, "is not to be understood as a kind of activity. . . . The actual subject of play is obviously not the subjectivity of an individual who among other activities also plays, but [is] instead the play itself" (TM, p. 99/93). Thus Gadamer speaks of "the primacy of play over the consciousness of the player" (TM, p. 100/94): "all playing is a being played. The attraction of the game, the fascination that it exerts, consists precisely in the fact that the game tends to master the players. . . . The game is what holds the player in its spell, draws him into play, and keeps him there" (TM, pp. 101–2/95–96). One could explicate listening as a kind of play— as against, for example, the seriousness of seeing.

Think, however, of the difference between hermeneutical and empirical experience (Erfahrung versus Empfindung). This is the distinction Heidegger has in mind when he speaks about "undergoing an experience with language":

> To undergo an experience with something—be it a thing, a person, or a god—means that this something befalls us, strikes us, comes over us, overwhelms and transforms us. When we talk of "undergoing" an experience, we mean specifically that the experience is not of our own making; to undergo here means that we endure it, suffer it, receive it as it strikes us and submit to it. It is this something itself that comes about, comes to pass, happens. (US, p. 159/57)

And naturally one thinks here of what Heidegger calls "the gambling game of language, where our nature is at stake" (WD p. 87/128).

However, this loss of subjectivity does not mean self-annihilation. On the contrary, Gadamer speaks of the buoyancy, the sense of abandonment and freedom from constraint, the ontological release that is possible when one enters fully into the spirit of the game. Gadamer wants to say: the essence of play is freedom. The game does not so much annihilate the subject as let it go; the game takes us out of ourselves and, putting us into play, brings us out into the open, not in the sense that we are therefore objectified—playing is not self-expression, or making inwardness visible; rather, in playing, what is in reserve is called upon and brought out. As in the fulfillment of a task or in responding to a challenge, we come into our own.

The loss of subjectivity means self-annihilation only if we hold to the Cartesian outlook of the pure subject—pure in the sense of disembodied and free of all environment and contingency. Descartes' motto, *cogito ergo sum*, carries with it the angelic corollary that thinking, and therefore being, can do without the body, has no need for it, cannot, in any case, picture itself that way as having or being in a body; has not language of embodiment in which to sort out the tangle of whether one is "in" or whether one "has" a body, which is just the age-old question of ownership or mastery. How we connect up with the body is just as mysterious as how we connect up with language. The body, in the modernist or Manichean view, is a negative entity; like language, it is just that which gets in the way of knowledge (and of being, since the body always lets us down when we want to live, as when it grows old and weak and dies). The body means historicality and the finitude of consciousness. It means belonging to horizons. One cannot say that one has a body or is in it, as if the body were something objective, an entity apart, a form of containment or prison-house. It is true perhaps that in virtue of our bodies we are brought up against otherness, our own temporality, where we are always turning into someone else. But this just means that the body does not seal us off from whatever is apart; it is our mode of being temporal, of entering into apartness, which is to say: our mortality, our being mortal. It is in virtue of our bodies that we come into our own, that is, appear as what we are (situated, historical, contingent, mortal). The body (the outward and visible sign, not of the soul, but of mortality) catches us up, absorbs us, incarnates us and carries us along, not, however, as its burden or its passenger but as its dancer. Think of the dance as a carrying away, bodily, as by the sheer exuberance or over-flowing of embodiment, a releasement. It is no accident that Heidegger figures the belonging-together of earth and sky, gods and mortals (that is, the world) as a dance. The body is our mode of dancing, that is, our mode of belonging to the round-dance of the fourfold; it is our mode of belonging to the world, fitting into it, being appropriate to it, owning up to it, acknowledging or accepting it. One could say: the body is our mode of belonging to Saying, whose "soundless voice" calls upon us to speak (or sing) aloud, as with the body.

Think of embodiment not as imprisonment but as releasement in Heidegger's sense of *Gelassenheit* or the letting go of things. Heidegger says: "Saying [Sage] sets all present beings *free* into their given presence, and brings what is absent into their absence. Saying pervades and structures the openness of the clearing [das *Freie* der Lichtung] which every appearance must seek out and every disappearance must leave behind, and in which every present or absent being must show, say, announce itself [sich herein-zeigen, sich einsagen muss]" (*US*, p. 257/126). One should say: the truth of Saying is the event (*Ereignis*) in which everything comes into its own, even that which withdraws and conceals itself—*phusis*, for example, which loves to hide; or, for all of that, language. In "Das Wesen der Sprache," Heidegger says that "only because in everyday speaking language does *not* bring itself to language [die Sprache selber sich *nicht* zur Sprache bringt) but holds back, are we able to go ahead and speak a language, and so to deal with something and negotiate something by speaking" (*US*, p. 161/134). So it is with Saying, which "will not let itself be captured in any statement" (*US*, p. 266/134).

Even Being itself is caught up in this play. This was already Heidegger's point in *Identität und Differenz* (1957), where *Ereignis* was introduced as the event in which "Man and Being are appropriated to one another" (*ID*, p. 23/31). The relationship of Man and Being is not to be thought of as a formal connection or a grounding in some primal unity; rather, it is a "belonging-together [Zusammengehören]" in which the notion of ground gives way to the notion of mutual participation in an event in which Being makes a claim upon Man and itself "arrives" only insofar as Man "listens to" the claim, answers to it, belongs to it, as if Man and Being were caught up in a dialogue and were nothing apart from it: either in play or nothing. This is what Heidegger means when he says that Man and Being are "mutually appropriated [übereignet]" (*ID*, p. 25/33). They are "delivered over to each other" (*ID*, p. 28/36). They are not beings but occurrences in the event of appropriation—which, for its part, is not itself "a happening, or occurrence," but is now to be understood "as a *singulare tantum*" (ID, p. 29/36), that is, "that realm, vibrating within itself, through which Man and Being reach each other in their nature, achieve their nature by losing those qualities [subjectivity and objectivity, for example] with which metaphysics has endowed them" (*ID*, p. 30/37). *Ereignis* as a *singulare tantum* is untranslatable: a word, say, that cannot be made into a term. The English translation, "event of appropriation," is thus not wrong exactly, but neither is it close to saying what the word means, since *Ereignis* is a pun whose soundings cannot be assimilated into any formal unity (cannot, certainly, be "captured" in any statement).

Basic to the pun, however, is *Eignen* (owning), in which, of course, *Zeichen* and *Zeigen* also resound. Heidegger says: "The

moving force in Showing of Saying is Owning [Das Regende im
Zeigen der Sage ist das Eignen]" (US, p. 258/127). It is as if it
were the eigen in Zeigen that gave Zeigen its force; or perhaps not
"as if," but just so: das Eignen, Heidegger says, "is what brings
all present and absent beings each into their own [in jeweilig
Eigenes], from where they show themselves in what they are, and
where they abide according to their kind. This owing which
brings them there, and which moves Saying as Showing in its
showing, we call Appropriation [heisse das Ereignen]" (US p.
258/127). And again, echoing Identität und Differenz: "The appropriating event is not the outcome (result) of something else,
but the giving yield whose giving reach alone is what gives us
such things as a 'there is' ['es gibt'], a 'there is' of which even
Being itself stands in need to come into its own as presence" (US,
p. 258/127).

And not Being only, but also language: Die Sprache als die
Sprache zur Sprache bringen. At the outset I asked about the
"unbinding bond" in the "web of language" that "delivers language into its own." This bond is the rift, that is, der Auf-Riss des
Sprachwesens, that both divides and joins, brings together and
sets free each into its own, Saying and speaking, the unspoken
and the spoken, showing and signification, earth and world, world
and thing, poetry and thinking. Put it as follows: For man to come
into his own means to enter into a dialogue, not with Being (as
Heidegger once figured it) but with Saying. In Saying, nothing
gets said, but this does not mean that Saying remains unspoken.
Saying appropriates man in the sense that man now enters into
the event of Saying and gives voice to it. Saying claims man for
its own, and man responds—answers with what is his own:
namely, as Heidegger says,

> the sounding of the word. The encountering saying of mor-
> tals is answering. Every word spoken is already an answer:
> counter-saying, coming to the encounter, listening saying
> [Gegensage, entgegenkommendes, hörendes Sagen]. When
> mortals are made appropriate for Saying, human nature is
> released into that needfulness out of which man is used for
> bringing soundless Saying to the sound of language [Die

Vereignung der Sterblichen in die Sage entlässt das Mensch-
enwesen in den Brauch, aus dem der Mensch gebraucht ist,
die lautlose Sage in das Verlauten der Sprache zu bringen].
(*US*, p. 260/129)

Here, however, is the surprise: What Heidegger calls "the way
to language" turns out not to be our way, that is, not our access to
the essence of language—not the "right approach," as we would
call it, as if the way to language were the way to know it. There
is, just to put it flatly, no way of knowing it, certainly not in the
sense of grammatical representation. On the contrary, "the way to
language," Heidegger says, "belongs to Saying," not to us. *Ereignis* is a "way-making" movement that "lets . . . Saying reach
speech" (*US* p. 260/120). The German text reads: "Das Ereignis
lässt in der brauchenden Vereignung die Sage zum Sprechen
gelangen. Der Weg zur Sprache gehört zu der aus dem Ereignis
bestimmten Sage." This is the meaning of the *Wegformel: Die
Sprache als die Sprache zur Sprache bringen.* Moreover, in this
movement, the being or essence or whatever of language *(das
Sprachwesen)*, that is, what belongs to language essentially, *conceals itself:* "In diesem Weg, der zum Sprachwesen gehört, ver-
birgt sich das Eigentümliche der Sprache" (*US*, pp. 260–61/129).
Bringing language as language to language does not mean objectifying it. Language, Heidegger wants to say, is untheorizable. It
cannot be contained within the logical framework of representational-calculative thinking, that is, within the *Ge-Stell*. Indeed,
philosophy of language shows as much with its distinction between natural and formalized or "gerrymandered" languages: it
throws the one away because it is only possible to frame a theory
for the other. Of course, having a theory of language means, in
this context, having a theory of meaning or truth, that is, a theory
of how language links up with reality, or how it encodes infor-
mation about a world outside of it. The assumption of the *Ge-
Stell* is that language is for framing representations of an independent reality. But suppose language doesn't "link up" with reality,
or with anything at all? What if it just stands on its own?

What is called "natural language" must be excluded from the
theory of language, as, analogously, *parole* must be excluded from

linguistics, and surface structures set aside from deep structures. But no matter: Heidegger isn't talking about natural languages, or about speech. Rather, he is talking about what belongs to language essentially, that is, *das Eigentümliche der Sprache*. And this means that he is talking about, among other things, *us*: we belong to (*gehören*) language:

> In order to be who we are, we human beings remain committed to and within the being of language [das Sprachwesen], and can never step out of it and look at it from somewhere else. Thus we always see the nature of language [Sprachwesen] only to the extent to which language itself has us in view, has appropriated us to itself. That we cannot know language—know it according to the traditional concept of knowledge defined in terms of cognition as representation—is not a defect, however, but rather an advantage by which we are favored with a special realm, that realm where we, who are needed and used to speak language, dwell as mortals. (US, p. 266/134)

To belong to language means that we disappear into the event of way-making as consciousness disappears into play, as spectatorship is dissolved by participation, or as the dancer is carried away by, disappears into, the dance. Bringing language as language to language is not a function that we perform; it is not an achievement of usage. Indeed, it would not be too much to say that letting Saying reach speech runs counter to the whole idea of usage as the exercise of linguistic competence or the show of mastery. Letting Saying reach speech involves "renunciation [Verzichten]." It means setting language free.

## IV

The "way-making movement . . . delivers Saying to speech": we don't do it. The way-making movement is not a performative activity; it is an event in which we are caught up, to which we belong, into which we disappear. We can't picture ourselves in what Heidegger has to say about language, can't recognize ourselves, because *that* is what it means to belong to language. What belongs to language essentially *conceals itself*: and so it is with us. Not only can we not know language in this event, we cannot know ourselves, that is, cannot know in the traditional sense of cognition as representation. We disappear into the way-making movement as consciousness disappears into play, as the dancer disappears into the dance.

So Heidegger: "Language, thus delivered into its own freedom, can be concerned solely with itself" (*US*, p. 263/131), that is, with Saying—whatever that is. Saying is not anything about which we can frame a theory. All Heidegger says is that "Saying is the mode in which *Ereignis* speaks: mode not so much in the sense of modus or fashion as melodic mode, the song that singing says [das Lied, das singend sagt]" (*US*, p. 266/135). Saying is the song of *Ereignis*. The point is to understand that this song is not the product of expression; rather, we enter into it by way of renunciation.

Let me conclude by trying to clarify this last sentence with a reference to the essay "Das Wort," where Heidegger explicates the word *Verzichten* as it occurs in the final couplet of Stefan George's poem "Das Wort": "So lernt ich traurig den verzicht: / Kein ding sei wo das wort gebricht" (*US*, p. 220/140). Renunciation means giving up language as logos, that is, as the power of framing representations. It means giving up signs as "darstellende Worte" that "rule over things" (*US*, p. 225/144). By means of renunciation, the poet opens onto "a different rule of the word," one that is not based on signs and has nothing to do with signification. "The poet," Heidegger says, "must relinquish the claim to the assurance that he will on demand be supplied with the name for that which he has posited as what truly is. This positing and that claim he must now deny himself. The poet must renounce having words under his control as the representational names for what is posited. As self-denial [Sichversagen], renunciation is a Saying which says to itself: 'Where word breaks off no thing may be' ['Kein ding sei wo das Wort gebricht']" (*US*, pp. 227–28/146–47).

Which is to say that poetry participates in, or rather belongs to (listens to)—comes into its own within—"that higher rule of the word which first lets a thing be as thing." Renunciation is the way poetry enters or is taken over by the movement that allows Saying to reach speech. Poetry means letting language go, which is the same as letting language speak and things thing: "Das Wort bè-dingt das Ding zum Ding" (US, p. 232/151). Peter Hertz translates this line as "The word makes the thing into a thing," as if to turn Heidegger back into Kant, but the word is not constitutive of things. Poetry is not world-making. "Renunciation," Heidegger says, "commits itself to the higher rule of the word which first lets a thing be as thing. The word 'be-things' the thing. We should like to call this rule of the word 'bethinging' ['Bedingnis']" (US, p. 232/151).

Now what is important about *Bedingnis* is that it is no longer the sign of anything; it is a word but not a term. Logically it is a nonentity. "This old word," Heidegger says, "has disappeared from linguistic usage" (US, p. 252/151). We no longer know what it means, what it signifies, and so for us it is dead; but precisely for this reason the word comes alive for Heidegger. It is a word that has withdrawn itself, secluded itself in darkness—call it a word of self-refusal, as if this dark word could become the word of words, the word for "the higher rule of the word," or, as Heidegger says, the word for "the word's mystery" (US, p. 233/151). Call it a word that language speaks, or a word for language speaking—but not a word for us. As a word, it leaves us in the dark. But we mustn't be afraid. Sound the word and hear the pun or the parody of *bedingen,* which is to say that hoary old philosophical activity of postulation or the laying down of conditions of possibility (Kantian bethinging, or objectification, thing as representation). "In this context, however," Heidegger says,

> bethinging says something different from talking about a condition. A condition is the existent ground for something that is. The condition gives reasons, and it grounds. It satisfies the principle of sufficient reason. But the word does not give reasons for the thing. The word allows the thing to presence as thing [Das Wort lässt das Ding als Ding anwesen]. We shall call this allowing [lassen] bethinging. The poet does not explain what this bethinging is. But the poet commits himself, that is, his Saying to this mystery of the word. (US, pp. 232–33/151)

Thus renunciation does not mean disavowal; rather it means something like acknowledgment or acceptance—call it openness to mystery. "There is no word for this mystery," Heidegger says, "that is, no Saying which could bring the being of language to language [Für dieses Geheimnis fehlt das Wort, d. h. jenes Sagen, das es vermöchte, das Wesen der Sprache—zur Sprache zu bringen]" (*US*, p. 236/154). Like *phusis*, Saying loves to hide.

In "Das Wesen der Sprache" Heidegger had said that "the essential nature of language [das Wesen der Sprache] flatly refuses to put itself in words—in the language, that is, in which we make statements about language." This, however, is not a statement about the impossibility of grammar or the phantom of metalanguage; it rather has to do with the nature of language itself, its earthliness or reserve.

> If language everywhere withholds its nature in this sense [refuses to put itself in words], then such withholding belongs to the very nature of language [dann gehört diese Verweigerung zum Wesen der Sprache]. Thus language not only holds back when we speak it in the accustomed ways, but this its holding back is determined by the fact that language holds back its own origin and so denies its being [Wesen] to our usual notions. But then we may no longer say that the being of language is the language of being [das Wesen der Sprache sei die Sprache des Wesens], unless the word "language" in the second phrase says something different, in fact something in which the withholding of the being of language—speaks [worin die Verweigerung des Sprachwesens—spricht]. (*US*, p. 186/81).

So when language speaks it does not do so (if we can imagine this) by means of language; rather, it is *die Verweigerung des Sprachwesens* that speaks, that is, its *Sichversagen*. And we must take poetry as a mode of belonging to the self-refusal of language, or to the *Verweigerung des Sprachwesens*. The hard part is that we can't translate this way of taking poetry into a description of the formal features of a text. As an object of our analytical gaze, poetry has, along with everything else (ourselves included), disappeared.

# Notes

1. Umberto Eco, "The Semantics of Metaphor," in Robert E. Innis, ed., *Semiotics: An Introductory Anthology* (Bloomington: Indiana University Press, 1985), p. 252.

2. References to Heidegger's works are given in the text following quotation. The first page number is to the German text, the second to the English translation. Abbreviations are as follows:

ID *Identität und Differenz* (Pfullingen: Neske, 1957). English translation by Joan Stambaugh, *Identity and Difference* (New York: Harper and Row, 1969).

Hw *Holzwege* (Frankfurt: Klostermann, 1950). The English translation of "Der Ursprung des Kunstwerkes" is by Albert Hofstadter, "The Origin of the Work of Art," in *Poetry, Language, Thought* (New York: Harper and Row, 1971), pp. 15–87.

SD *Zur Sache des Denkens* (Tübingen: Max Niemeyer, 1969). English translation by Joan Stambaugh, *On Time and Being* (New York: Harper and Row, 1969).

SZ *Sein und Zeit* (Tübingen: Max Niemeyer, 1984). English translation by John Macquarrie and Edward Robinson, *Being and Time* (New York: Harper and Row, 1962).

US *Unterwegs zur Sprache* (Pfullingen: Neske, 1959). English translation by Peter D. Hertz, *On the Way to Language* (New York: Harper and Row, 1971). The translation of the essay "Die Sprache" is by Albert Hofstader, "Language," in *Poetry, Language, Thought*, pp. 189–210.

VA *Vorträge und Aufsätze* (Pfullingen: Neske, 1954). English translation of "Das Ding" by Albert Hofstader, "The Thing," in *Poetry, Language, Thought*, pp. 165–86; and of "Logos (Heraklit Fragment 50)," by David Krell and Frank A. Capuzzi, "Logos (Heraclitus Fragment 50)," in *Early Greek Thinking* (New York: Harper and Row, 1965), pp. 59–78.

WD *Was heisst Denken?* (Tübingen: Max Niemeyer, 1984). English translation by J. Glenn Gray, *What Is Called Thinking?* (New York: Harper and Row, 1968).

3. Paul Ricoeur, *The Rule of Metaphor: Multidisciplinary Studies in the Creation of Meaning*, trans. Robert Czerny et al. (Toronto and Buffalo, N.Y.: University of Toronto Press, 1977), p. 313.

4. Emmanuel Levinas, *Otherwise Than Being or Beyond Essence*, trans. Alphonso Lingis (The Hague: Martinus Nijhoff, 1981), p. 59. The temptation is to translate *Ereignis* as "Being," as if Heidegger were simply trying to speak (of) Being in another language in order to escape a way of speaking, say a philosophical way of speaking (called "metaphysics"), that Being itself eludes or evades—a game Being will not play. A pun, however, is not a species of analogy; it is not translatable. Even to speak of it as being "so dense" that no one can "unpack" it is to misconceive it, because a pun is all surface and no depth. The exegete slides across it and frequently slips and falls. Think of the pun as parodistic, a comic-ironic double of the concept, or perhaps a whole region of language sounding at once in the tiny space of a single word whose meaning at first seems plain but then is suddenly withdrawn. One does not so much speak such words as hear them. Puns happen. We don't cause them; on the contrary, to speak is to prevent them from happening. *Ereignis* is a happening that Heidegger does not prevent,

that is, it is not a word for another word (or thing)—not an expression or piece of speech—but a sounding whose limits can't be determined because we can't get a position on it, can't get a fix on where it's coming from or where it belongs or what it's for (as if it were just a term in a dictionary, say the German word for happening). So *Ereignis* is not just a way of *not* saying "Being," either. There's no saying what the word says or doesn't say. What is this condition of not being able to say what a word says or doesn't say? Whatever it is, it is the condition in which language always places us; that is, all talk of linguistic competence aside, language does all it can to keep us from speaking it. Grammar and logic were invented in order to help us get the upper hand so that speaking can become (logically) possible. Paradoxically, the arts of language were designed to keep language from happening, that is, they are part of our effort to bring language under our control so that it will only happen when we want it or when we say it does. Now Heidegger comes along with his uncontrollable language to undo centuries— whole metaphysical epochs—of hard work, emancipating grammar from logic. But of course puns and poetry and things like *Finnegans Wake* have been undoing this work all along, only we haven't been listening.

5. Hans-Georg Gadamer, *Truth and Method,* ed. Garrett Barden and John Cumming (New York: Seabury Press, 1975), pp. 415–16. Further references to this volume (abbreviated as TM) will be given in the text.

# 5

# ADORNO'S "NEGATIVE AESTHETICS"?

## Hendrik Birus

### I

ADORNO's *Aesthetic Theory*,[1] which was published posthumously in 1970, is widely regarded as the most decisive German version of the "aesthetics of the negative" dominant in France at the time.[2] And indeed, aside from such concepts as "subject/object," "consciousness," "experience," and "society," there is scarcely a term in this wide-ranging work that is used as lavishly as the concept of "negativity" in all its permutations. To be sure, the term is used here to express an exceptionally broad variety of concepts, from the antitraditionalist and anti-ideological negativity of bourgeois art, to the formal and significative negativity of the autonomous work, to the ontological and theological negativity of the work of art as such; it is even used to describe the theoretical standing of *Aesthetic Theory* in relation to the tradition of philosophical aesthetics. Analysis of the conceptual variety of the term "negativity" reveals both its theoretical potential and its dubiety as a fundamental principle of aesthetics, thus calling into question the current interpretation of Adorno's *Aesthetic Theory* as the realization of a program of "negative aesthetics."

The most obvious and least surprising of the meanings of "the negative" in Adorno is its use in the sense of a "critique of ideology," for this is, after all, the common ground between the aesthetician Adorno and the other members of the Frankfurt School. According to this view, art is "the social antithesis to society"

(*AT*, p. 19), the "social protest against society" (*GS*, 10:350). Criticism, contradiction, protest—the negative character of art is justified as the negation of the "absolute power of negation" (*GS*, 4:170): Art must be negative in order to critically "bear witness to the negativity of social existence" (*GS*, 14:52). It is in this sense that Adorno interprets in particular the asocial "useless and fragile beauty" of decadent lyric poetry as a "protest against an insensitive, reified society" (*GS*, 14:53) and as a negation of the marketplace (*GS*, 10:220).

The opposite of the negativity of art so conceived is "vile affirmation" (*GS*, 11:424), quite in keeping with Herbert Marcuse's neo-Marxist critique of the "affirmative nature of culture."[3] "Since reality has become so misshapen, the affirmative nature of art, though inescapable, has become intolerable" (*AT*, p. 10); "the a priori character of the affirmative is the ideological dark side of art" (*AT*, p. 240). For this reason, the mere number of affirmative works of art—"practically the whole array of traditional art" (*AT*, p. 239), as he admits—is a cause of some aggravation to him.[4] And Adorno more or less refuses to "jump to their defense by using the all too abstract argument that they are also critical and negative because they stand in vivid contradiction to empirical fact" (*AT*, p. 239). This, however, does not keep him from making the "all too abstract" assertion shortly thereafter that "all works of art, even those that are affirmative, are a priori polemical. The idea of a conservative work of art is something of a contradiction in terms" (*AT*, p. 264).[5]

Elsewhere, however, he attenuates his own theory of the universal dominance of social "constraint"[6] and allows that "some historical periods granted greater opportunities for reconciliation than the present, which rejects it radically" (*AT*, p. 283). That aspect of traditional affirmative art which is no longer valid in our society still retains some truth for us, but it is accessible to modern consciousness only through negation (*AT*, p. 383). In Adorno's subtle variant of the Marxist concept of "legacy," which he himself opposed, it forms, if it serves any function at all, a "reserve" for a liberated and reconciled mankind in the future (*AT*, pp. 67, 290; *GS*, 11:190).

Moreover, in Adorno's opinion, the bond between art and so-

ciety does not exhaust itself in the negative relationship inherent
in criticism; like Lukács' traditionalist concept of "art as the self-
consciousness of mankind's development,"[7] works of art for
Adorno are in a positive sense the "unconscious historiography
of an age" (*AT*, p. 272; see also *AT*, p. 384). They are able to
exercise this function because the "opposition of the work of art
to power" is at the same time a "mimesis of it": "They must
adjust to dominating behavior in order to produce something
qualitatively different from the world of domination" (*AT*, p. 430;
see also AT, p. 66). The crystallization of history in such works
of art is, however, not an affirmatively posited content but "only
a negative one" (*AT*, p. 200). What binds the critical and the
mimetic moments in art and allows them to coexist, even to
coincide, is the Hegelian operation of "determined negation":[8]
"It is based [at least in Adorno's nonspeculative reading] on the
experience of the impotence of criticism as long as it limits itself
to generalities. . . . Only the critical thought that sets free the
energy stored in its own object is fertile" (*GS*, 5:318).

As Dieter Henrich has noted in his review of *Negative Dialectics*, Adorno is admittedly only working with the "minimal in-
ventory of Hegelianism"[9] when he reduces dialectics to "the
organized spirit of contradiction" (*GS*, 5:12, 287)—and Hegel's
fundamental speculative operation of autonomous negation[10] to
"criticism" (*GS*, 5:276).

Correspondingly, Adorno also describes the historicity of art
by means of the "dialectic figure of determined negation": "One
work of art is the mortal enemy of another" (*AT*, p. 60). The
"negation of the monumentum aere perennius" (*GS*, 11:167) is a
readily predictable consequence of Adorno's criticism of the affirmative nature of traditional art. But it is precisely in its own
antithesis that tradition can live on: "It is present precisely where
it is rejected" (*GS*, 14:138). As support for his assertion that
authentic current production can be regarded as the "determined
negation" of tradition, Adorno can call above all, at least as far as
literature is concerned, on Beckett's parodic transformation of
traditional dramatic form in all its aspects.

This radically negativistic understanding of tradition is by no
means consistently maintained by Adorno, and his "canon of the

forbidden" for modern art which he advanced in The Philosophy
of the New Music (GS, 12:40) is repeated only in diminished form
in Aesthetic Theory: "Determined negation" has "become almost
[!] a prescriptive canon again for deciding what is to be done"
(AT, p. 58). Between these works lay the sobering experience of
"The Aging of the New Music" (GS, 14:143–67), which was a
result of the purely "abstract negation" of the traditional vocabulary of music in serial compositions by Webern followers after
1945 (GS, 14:151): "Mere newness can stagnate, can turn into
uniformity" (AT, p. 41). Adorno's demand that in the event of
such stagnation "the direction of innovation must be changed,
shifted to another dimension" (ibid.), comes close to the theory
of literary evolution as formulated by the Russian Formalists,
though it lacks the concreteness of the latter. Such a change was
indeed realized in the music of the 1960s through a development
that was for Adorno unforeseeable—the productive assimilation
of the anarchistic impulses of John Cage and the compositions of
Charles Ives, which cannot be compared with anything in the
New Music. In clear mitigation of his own concept of negativity,
Adorno writes in his late work: "The history of art is no boxing
match in which the younger contestant knocks out the older one;
nor is the encounter that agonistic among the avant-garde, where
one work appears [!] to criticize another" (GS, 11:444).

In fact, Adorno even goes a step further when he draws attention to the fact that "anything that is qualitatively modern is not
only ahead of its time but is also a remembrance of the forgotten.
. . . The advanced, in contrast to the merely up to date, is always
also the past" (GS, 16:446).[11] The proximity of such ideas to those
of Benjamin and (in spite of all the material and stylistic differences) to those of Heidegger is unmistakable; they cannot be
derived from even the most refined dialectical concept of "determined negation."

For Adorno, negativity is also the central feature of aesthetic
form; it characterizes its relationship both to social reality and
artistic tradition and is, in fact, the essence of form itself. As far
as the first point is concerned, Adorno stated emphatically in his
very early essay "On the Social Situation of Music" (GS, 18:729–
77):

At present, music can do nothing other than represent social
antinomies in its own structure. . . . Music will be that much
better the more profoundly it is able to formulate the power
of those contradictions and the necessity of overcoming them
socially, that much better the more purely it gives expression through the antinomies of its own form to the plight of
society, thus calling for change through the cryptic language
of suffering. (GS, 18:731)

And he expresses himself similarly even in the *Aesthetic Theory*:
"The unresolved antagonisms of reality recur in works of art as
the immanent problems of their form. It is this and not the injec-
tion of objective aspects that defines the relationship between art
and society" (*AT*, p. 16; see also *AT*, p. 479).

Negativity also defines the relationship of the form of each
individual work to received tradition. For as a "negation of the
bad generality of the norm," art allows of no "normal artifacts"
and "also therefore of no artifacts that are mediocre in that they
correspond to the norm or that they are to be defined in terms of
their deviation from it" (*AT*, p. 280). On the other hand, form can
not simply be regarded as the "negation of aesthetic universals"
(*AT*, p. 325); for the organizational principle of Adorno's *Didactic
Writings on the Practice of Music* (*GS*, 15:157–402, collected
under the title *The Faithful Music Coach*) is, in effect, that one
"rediscovers moments of general validity, a participation in the
typical that remains hidden to the work itself" just when one is
analyzing pieces "that are individualized in the extreme and that
reject all schematic norms" (*GS*, 6:164).

But even beyond that, aesthetic form as such—in spite of its
"non-violence" (*AT*, p. 19)—is negative in Adorno's eyes: "Aesthetic harmony is negative in relation to its elements" (*AT*, p.
236). "The synthesis extrapolated from the manifold, which potentially carries that synthesis within it, is unavoidably also its
negation" (*AT*, p. 252). It is in this sense that Adorno describes
such musical forms as counterpoint (*GS*, 16:164 ff) and the developing variation (*GS*, 14:412) as the "determined negation" of the
elements they synthesize.

Here, too, however, Adorno gives with one hand and takes
with the other, for if form converges on the one hand with cri-

tique (AT, p. 216) as negative, it is nevertheless supposed to be a positive witness to the possibility of reconciliation (GS, 1:119): "As a nonrepressive integration of divergent tendencies . . . , the work of art transcends the antagonisms of existence without pretending that they no longer exist" (AT, p. 283). This understanding of the artistic creation of forms as the "salvation of the many in the one" (AT, p. 284), familiar to us from classical aesthetics, can be reconciled with Adorno's global concept of negativity only by means of a dialectical equation of opposites, the result of which is a view of art as the "salvation of nature or immediacy through their negation, that is, complete mediation" (AT, p. 428): "Reconciliation with the object succeeds if at all only through its negation" (GS, 10:323).

"If at all"—for Adorno, the growing impossibility of achieving such an equilibrium finally leads in modernism to a critical dissolution of the "idea of the well-rounded work": "The only oeuvres that matter today are those that are no longer oeuvres" (GS, 12:37). The quality of formal consistency is, to be sure, essential to aesthetic success (AT, p. 280), but "this consistency breaks down in the face of a higher authority, that of the truth of content" (AT, p. 73). Reading the resulting fissures as the "language of truth" (GS, 13:309), even as the "code of the unnamable supreme truth" (GS, 16:455), is an impassioned endeavor (inspired by Benjamin's concept of allegory) of Adorno's philosophy of music.

Adorno's epigrammatic formulation, that "the stigmata of disorder are the seal of authenticity of the modern" (AT, p. 41), is applicable not only to art. For he also says of Hegelian philosophy that the "stigmata of its failure" were "forged by truth itself" (GS, 5:294) and regards paradoxical "failure" as a "measure of Husserl's philosophical rank" (GS, 5:193). Yet this negation of authorial intention as a measure of interpretation is primarily located in Adorno's theory of art.

Drawing on his basic thesis that "no work of art . . . can be described and explained in terms of categories of communication" (AT, p. 167), Adorno concludes that the aesthetics of production has absolute priority over the aesthetics of reception (AT, p. 338).[12] Further, this orientation toward the work itself results in a diminished concern with the intentions of the author as against the content of the work, which may even run counter to those intentions. "The whole is realized contrary to intention; it integrates through the negation of every individual, indeterminable [intention]" (GS, 16:254). The formulation applies to music, Adorno's model of autonomous art (GS, 4:252), but in his interpretations of poetry as well he is constantly concerned with the line from the determined negation of meaning, which is the objective vehicle of intentions (AT, p. 227), to the truth content of the work (GS, 11:451).[13]

Analogous to the negation of formal harmony, the "strict negation of meaning [may] create something like meaningfulness in the second degree" (GS, 11:443); as a matter of fact, "in the work of art the negation of meaning has its justification alone in the fact that the negation itself is meaningful" (GS, 16:618). Here again the "emphatically absurd work" of Beckett is exemplary in that it marks the "point of indifference between meaning and its negation" (GS, 10:450–51). In contrast to Beckett, in Adorno's opinion, are efforts—for example, in the music of the postwar period—in which "meaninglessness per se is turned into a program . . . at times supported by the tenets of existential philosophy: in place of subjective intentions, Being itself supposedly spoke" (GS, 14:157). But elsewhere he must concede that it is difficult to "judge whether the negativeness of this music expresses the social element and in so doing transcends it, or whether it imitates social negativeness, unconsciously in its thrall. In the end, the two cannot be distinguished by the probing of critical thought" (GS, 14:379). "There is no strict criterion that defines the border between the determined negation of meaning and the wretched positivism of meaninglessness as a studious perseverance for its own sake" (GS, 11:426–27).

Although Adorno has good reason to shy away from proclaiming "that the line of progressive negativity—negation of objectively binding meaning—is the direction of progress in art" (AT, p. 239), and although he asks "whether art is possible at all after the fall of theology and without a theology" (AT, p. 403), he does place the aesthetic in a fundamentally negative relation to theology by defining "all art" as "the secularization of transcendence" (AT, p. 50) or of "revelation" (AT, p. 162): "Works of art are neutralized and therefore qualitatively altered epiphanies" (AT, p. 125). Or as it is epigrammatically expressed in Minima Moralia: "Art is magic, liberated from the lie of being truth" (GS, 4:252). In any case, works of art "only became what they are by negating their origin" (AT, p. 12). As neutralized epiphanies, however, works of art take on the character of "aesthetic semblance [Schein]." Admittedly, in Adorno's opinion everything "that is said by mortal beings about transcendence . . . is only a semblance of it, but as Kant realized, it is a necessary semblance. For that reason, the salvation of appearance, the object of aesthetics, takes on an incomparable metaphysical relevance" (GS, 6:386). Insofar as art fully renounces "theology, the undiminished claim to the truth of salvation," for the sake of its own development, it damns itself to the affirmation of the existing, of that which is (AT, p. 10; see also GS, 6:104–5).

It is precisely because of its ever more radical theological negativity that Adorno regards the essence of art—that is, ontological negativity in the face of the factually existent—as being in jeopardy. For the single negative unifying principle of all art is its "antithesis to the empirical world" (GS, 10:448). This means first the "practical" "negation of practical being" (AT, p. 358), thanks to which art is not only "a critique of social practice when it is the rule of brutal self-preservation" but also "the representative of a better practice than that which has existed up to now" (AT, p. 26).

Yet, even though Adorno refers to art as the "promesse du bonheur," in allusion to Stendhal and Nietzsche, art means more for him "than that current practice hampers happiness: Happiness would then exist outside all practice" (AT, p. 26). Drawing on psychoanalysis for support, he therefore calls the work of art "the negation of the principle of reality" (AT, p. 379) since it "negates . . . reality by becoming a reality sui generis. Art realizes its protest against reality through its objectivation" (AT, p. 414). When Adorno insists that "what is true is only what does not suit this world" (AT, p. 93), and that "what is true in art is a nonbeing" (AT, p. 198), such eccentric formulations mark the most extreme position on the ontological horizon of his negative aesthetics, that of an "ontology of despair" (GS, 11:598). It is in this sense that he interprets the truth in Beckett's (*AT*, p. 517; *GS*, 11:319) and Celan's work (*AT*, p. 477) as radically negative.

As Adorno admits, however, even "the purest negativity of content . . . contains a grain of affirmation" (*AT*, p. 347), not only in the sense of an actual "adulteration" of the idea of the negative work of art but by conceptual implication: "Negation and contradiction are not to be regarded as absolutes. Unity is as necessary to a concept of them as contradiction is to unity" (*GS*, 16:225). But with this simple assertion of mutual implication between negative and positive, if not of the primacy of the latter, [14] the program of a "negative aesthetics" is robbed of its point. Here, if not earlier, one sees the problematics of Adorno's reduction of Hegel's constructive dialectic to a mere "organized spirit of contradiction" and of the concept of autonomous and double negation (in the sense of an "*absolute* negativity")[15] to mere "criticism." For how, except as a rhetorical exaggeration, can we speak of an "absolute negativity" by means of which art is supposed to give expression to the "inexpressible," to "utopia" (*AT*, p. 56)?

Finally, such radical negativity is attributed not only to art as the object of the *Aesthetic Theory* but to the latter itself as theory. And here we find the connection between this work and the program advanced in the *Negative Dialectics* three years before, "the determined negation [one is tempted to say 'deconstruction'] of traditional philosophical problems. . . . Yet this negation will be chained to their questions" (*GS*, 6:28). In his book on Husserl, *Metacritique of Epistemology* (*GS*, 5:7–245), Adorno had already formulated this approach in relation to the traditional conceptual framework of philosophy:

> Even worn epistemological concepts point beyond themselves. Even in their supreme formalism and particularly in their failure they are a piece of unconscious historiography, to be preserved by being led to self-consciousness in opposition to what they mean themselves. This salvation, the commemoration of the suffering that settles in the concepts, awaits the moment of their disintegration. (*GS*, 5:47; cf. *GS*: 148)

Accordingly, he writes in the "Early Introduction" to the *Aesthetic Theory*, as its methodological maxim:

In an age in which traditional aesthetics and contemporary art are irreconcilable, the philosophical theory of art has no other choice, to paraphrase Nietzsche, than to consider decaying categories as transcendent categories in determined negation. All that is left to contemporary aesthetics is the reasoned and concrete dissolution of the accepted aesthetic categories; at the same time, dissolution sets free the transformed truth of those categories. (AT, p. 507)

Some of the essentials of Adorno's critique of Husserl come close to Derrida's "deconstructive" reading of this philosopher: e.g., the criticism of the philosophy of origin in its scientific form as a theory of cognition (GS, 5:29–30), the constitutive function of subjectivity (GS, 5:194, 200), the primacy of objective consciousness (GS, 5:173), and the central concepts of the "elementary" (GS, 5:28) and "evidence" (GS, 5:63–64) as well as the recognition of the discovery of historicity in the late Husserl (GS, 5:218–19). Moreover, Adorno's overall program of "determined negation" of traditional philosophical problems and concepts actually seems to converge with Derrida's undertaking to "deconstruct" the basic concepts developed during the entire history of philosophy.[16] Just as for Adorno the negativity of art, as of theory, aims at the utterance of the unutterable in utopian fashion (AT, p. 56), "deconstruction" is ultimately concerned with "groping one's way through inherited concepts toward the ineffable,"[17] whereby its "reserves have to be drawn from the very same logic it is deconstructing,"[18] or (as Derrida graphically puts it) "using the tools or stones against the house that are available in the house, that is, in the language."[19]

In spite of the things they have in common, a profound rift opens up between the two enterprises over the shibboleth of Heidegger. While the program of "deconstruction" demonstratively picks up the "task of a destruction of the history of ontology" sketched in Sein und Zeit,[20] Adorno expressed only scorn for the "harmlessness" of the "respectful destruction of the traditional in Heidegger" (GS, 5:19; see also GS, 6:361). In comparison, however, Adorno's attempt at a negative-dialectical self-reflection of metaphysical tradition may be neither respectful enough nor sufficiently destructive.

Not respectful enough: Derrida, in any case, began his first published essay with a reflection on the danger of questioning a way of thinking before one has listened to it carefully, which, he says, is always an act of aggression and disloyalty, even if it is meant to discover or uncover the sense of a labor latent in the text.[21] He later claims that for the "deconstruction" of philosophy it is indispensable to "think the structured genealogy of its concepts in the most precise, most immanent way possible."[22] Adorno, on the other hand, rejects the idea of "philology as *ephexis* [restraint] in interpretation" as called for by Nietzsche, who pleads for this "art of being able to read off a fact without falsifying it by interpretation, without losing caution, patience, or subtlety in the desire for understanding";[23] he proceeds from an initial conflation of "reading" and "criticism" and on the assumption that any idea that "criticism is based on understanding" is false and "deduced from pedagogical convenience and authoritarian prejudice" (GS, 5:373; see also GS, 5:391). The danger, however, is that criticism would no longer experience resistance and that the critic would always be right.

Insufficiently destructive: Derrida, in any case, does not stop at the accurate "repetition" of the implicit in traditional metaphysics but describes the "double gesture" of deconstruction as an attempt "to respect the inner and orderly play of these philosophemes and epistemes as strictly as possible by pursuing them, without abusing them, to the point of their irrelevance, exhaustion, and closure."[24] In Adorno, on the other hand, "the dissolution of the common aesthetic categories" as the only possible "form of current aesthetics" is supposed to set positively free the "transformed truth of those categories" (AT, p. 507). The "negativity" of Adorno's dialectics as well as of his aesthetics basically consists in the "inversion" of classical conceptual hierarchies common since the time of Feuerbach and the early Marx: "materialism" (instead of "idealism"); the "primacy of the object" (instead of "constitutive subjectivity"); the "nonidentical" (instead of the "identity of subject and object") as the Absolute; and "negation" (instead of "affirmation"), etc., as well as the blurring of conceptual differences. The field covered by these oppositions remains, however, more or less intact. Disruption or shifting of

this field would have required a "radical" destruction of traditional concepts, one that went back to the roots in Greek thought;
such "destruction" was undertaken by both Heidegger and Derrida, while Adorno, with the exception of a global design for the
*Dialectics of the Enlightenment* and a liberal sprinkling of Greek
and Latin terms, scarcely ever deals with the genealogy of the
concepts he criticizes, at least not beyond the philosophy of
consciousness developed by Descartes; indeed, it is scarcely ever
dealt with in pre-Kantian philosophy. Adorno thus remains bogged
down in the oppositions of traditional metaphysics and the repeated invocation of "negativity," in spite of his attempt at their
critical dissolution. This stands quite in contrast to Derrida, who
initially proclaimed a most radical negativity, tamed by no Hegelian dialectics, as the "unhistorical basis of history,"[25] but then
freed himself of the "metaphysical or romantic pathos of negativity" (in the wake of his reading of Artaud and Bataille),[26] finally
arriving at a programmatic designation of "deconstruction" as
"affirmation."[27]

## II

However, there is more to both the *Aesthetic Theory* and the
*Negative Dialectics* than universal negativism, for the *Aesthetic
Theory* aims at "saving appearance" and therefore at the "emphatic right of art, the legitimation of its Truth" (*AT*, p. 164). And
even the *Negative Dialectics* makes the transition to metaphysics
as a kind of *theologia negativa*,[28] which culminates in the idea of
the self-dissolution of dialectics (*GS*, 6:397–400): for "in view of
the concrete possibility of a utopia, dialectics is the ontology of
the false state of affairs. A proper one would be liberated from
dialectics, system no less than contradiction" (*GS*, 6:22). Dialectics would then "end in reconciliation. This would liberate the
non-identical, would even release it from spiritualized constraint,
would first open up the variety of difference over which dialectics would no longer have any power" (*GS*, 6:18). The "Non-
identical"—for Adorno both the "individuum ineffabile" (*GS*,
6:148) and the "Absolute . . . as metaphysics conceives of it" (*GS*,
6:398)—is "experienced in an unreconciled state . . . as negative"

(GS, 6:41), but is "secretly . . . the telos of identification, that which is to be preserved in it" (GS, 6:152). However, it is immediately accessible to thought neither as positive nor through the negation of negation (GS, 6:161). Yet, if "irreconcilable thought . . . remains paired with the hope of reconciliation" (GS, 6:31), it finds itself in a situation that Adorno once described as follows: "Whatever one does is wrong; first one must develop an awareness of dilemma" (GS, 16:508). Adorno here sees the dilemma of two equally valid convictions, the one articulated in the maxim "Without hope there is no good" (GS, 6:272), and the other in Grabbe's dramatic aphorism "And nothing / But despair can save us!"[29]

This dilemma finds unrivaled expression in the final section of the *Minima Moralia* (GS, 4:281):

> *At the end.* —The only form of philosophy acceptable in the face of despair would be an attempt to see and present all things as they would present themselves from the point of view of salvation. Knowledge has no light except that which shines upon the world from salvation: everything else exhausts itself in reconstruction and remains merely a piece of technology. Perspectives ought to be established in which the world displaces and alienates itself, reveals its cracks and fissures as it will one day appear, disfigured and in need, in the Messianic light. The only thing that matters to thought is the establishment of such perspectives without arbitrariness and force, purely by being in touch with the objects. It is the simplest of all things, since the situation calls urgently for such knowledge, since indeed complete negativity, once it has been fully recognized, crystallizes into the mirror image of its opposite. But it is entirely impossible because it presupposes a position at least minimally outside the thrall of existence, while any possible knowledge not only has to be wrested from existence in order to be binding but for this very reason is simultaneously marked by the same need and disfigurement it is seeking to avoid. The more passionately thought seals itself off from its conditionality for the sake of the unconditional, the less consciously and therefore the more fatefully it falls back into the world. It must understand its own impossibility for the

sake of the possible. Compared to the demand thus placed on thought, the question of the reality or irreality of salvation itself is almost irrelevant.

In order to construct such a hypothetical eschatology, thought in Adorno's view depends not only in a purely dialectical manner on a reading of the "mirror image" of the "complete negativity" of existence.[30] For although it has no fixed Archimedean point that is removed from "the sphere of being . . . to even a slight degree," it still cannot do completely without the scattered positive traces of transcendence within the "absolute negativity" of the existing world (GS, 6:354):

> That is why thought seeks shelter in texts. The withheld own [intention] discovers itself in them. But the two are not the same: What is discovered in the texts does not prove that which is concealed. The negative—impossibility—expresses itself in just such a difference, in an Oh, if it were only so—which is just as far from the assurance that it is so as from an assurance that it is not. An interpretation does not make the claim that what it finds is prevailing truth, and yet it knows that there would be no truth without the light whose traces interpretation follows in the texts. . . . The stance of interpretative thought is like Lichtenberg's "neither deny nor believe," which shouldn't be plowed under as mere skepticism. . . . The treatment of profane texts as sacred is the answer to the fact that all transcendence has immigrated into the land of profanity and liberates only where it conceals. (GS, 11:129)

It is no accident that Adorno calls here, at the pole opposite his dialectical negativism, on Ernst Bloch's concept of "symbolic intention" (ibid.), which Bloch had defined in The Principle of Hope as "a flash of the utopian final condition."[31] And just as this is related in Bloch to quite insignificant events and everyday circumstances,[32] such "metaphysical experience" (GS, 6:366) is exemplified in Adorno not primarily in art but in the childlike promise of happiness contained in such village names as Otterbach, Watterbach, Reuenthal, and Monbrunn: "If you were to go there, you would reach fulfillment, as if that existed. When you are really there, promise recedes like a rainbow. And still you are not disappointed; you feel rather that you must be too close to be able to see" (ibid.).[33] In art, however, and here Adorno refers to Proust's Recherche and Berg's Wozzeck and Lulu (GS, 6:366–68), the evidence of such transitory experience takes on permanent form.

THE TEXTS Adorno has in mind in his quoted apology for "Alexandrianism" as the "interpretive submersion in traditional writing" (GS, 11:129) are above all poetic texts. For only as works of art are they for him "images of a changed mankind despite all mediation, all negativity" (AT, p. 358)—and not just a product of helpless longing (AT, p. 422). In fact, in his "Short Commentaries on Proust" (GS, 11:203–15), Adorno formulates his view as follows: "Great works of art make us feel that their content cannot possibly not be true; their success and authenticity themselves point to the reality of that for which they stand" (GS, 11:214).

As an explication of such aesthetic experience and as a "saving" of the appearance of truth embodied in it, Adorno's theory of art eludes the label of a "negative aesthetics." Significant as the parallels in both terminology and method in Negative Dialectics and Aesthetic Theory are, with respect to their subject matter the relationship is almost complementary: "Art rectifies conceptual knowledge by achieving, in absolute isolation, what knowledge vainly seeks from the non-visual, subject-object relationship, that is, that the objective reveal itself through subjective effort" (AT, p. 173). Works of art therefore contain that for which Negative Dialectics makes its vain efforts, the Absolute; but it is indiscernible. "For discursive knowledge truth is unconcealed, but it does not possess it; knowledge that is art does possess it, but as something incommensurable with it" (AT, p. 191). It follows for Adorno, on the other hand, that because the truth of works of art is concealed, it can "only be reached by way of philosophical reflection. This and nothing else justifies aesthetics" (AT, pp. 193, 507; GS, 11:433, 452). It cannot be "the task of a philosophical interpretation of works of art to make them identical with a concept, to consume them in it; but the work develops in its truth through such interpretation" (GS, 6:25).[34]

For this reason, Adorno's asserted "convergence of philosophy and art . . . in their truth" (*AT*, p. 197)[35] does not mean a transformation of philosophy into aesthetics. If Adorno postulates that "genuine aesthetic experience must become philosophy or it is nothing" *(ibid.)*, the reverse does not also apply. On the contrary —a difference in principle between philosophy and art is one of the constants of Adorno's thought. In his first book, *Kierkegaard: Construction of the Aesthetic* (GS, 2:7–213), he gave programmatic expression to the position: "In view of the mere possibility of confusion . . . , the primary task of a construction of the aesthetic in Kierkegaard's philosophy is to distinguish philosophy from poetry" (GS, 2:1); and emphasizes, as late as in his *Negative Dialectics*, that:

> The affinity between philosophy and art does not entitle the former to borrow from the latter. . . . Philosophy that imitated art or that wanted to be art would end in self-abrogation. . . . Transcending their mutual opposition, each remains loyal to its essence: art by resisting all meaning, philosophy by rejecting all immediacy. (GS, 6:26–27)

To be sure, for philosophy the aesthetic aspect is not a matter of chance (GS, 6:26), inasmuch as the tension between "stringency" and "expression" is essential to it (GS, 11:389). Therefore, while Wittgenstein closes his *Tractatus Logico-Philosophicus* with the sentence: "Whereof one cannot speak, thereof one must be silent,"[36] Adorno replies: "Philosophy can be defined, if at all, as the attempt to utter the unspeakable, to help give expression to the non-identical, although expression always identifies it" (GS, 5:336).

As a counter to the "constant denunciation of rhetoric by nominalism," Adorno also defines dialectics as the "attempt to provide a critical salvation of the rhetorical aspect: to approximate thing and expression so closely that difference disappears" (GS, 6:64). Though this applies to philosophy as a whole, it is even more important for dialectical aesthetics, "just as it would scarcely be possible to speak of aesthetics unaesthetically—ignoring all affinity for the thing itself—without succumbing to Philistinism and a priori losing touch with the subject" (GS, 11:11). The title

*Aesthetic Theory* promises both: not only a "theory of aesthetics" but an "aesthetic theory."

From the time he began writing, Adorno moved back and forth between philosophy and art in an intermediate field he describes programmatically in "The Essay as Form," the opening essay of the *Notes on Literature* (GS, 11:9–33). Here he polemicizes against the idea of a *prima philosophia*, against the Cartesian ideal of method, against making philosophy a science, above all against regarding it as logical analysis and epistemology, and in general against the "ideal of cleanliness and meticulousness that are common to the exercise of a True philosophy whose measure is the eternal, of an unassailable and thoroughly organized science, and of a nonconceptual, concrete art" (GS, 11:14). At the same time he evidences a keen sense of the "verbal nature" of philosophy and its "either open or simply latent dependence on texts" (GS, 6:63); seen together with his carefree motto "Truth that has been abandoned by play would be mere tautology" (GS, 11:29), this is a perfect example of Richard Rorty's concept of "Philosophy as a Kind of Writing."[37] Similarly, he proclaims a "pleasure principle of thought," under whose rule the "dubious transitions of rhetoric" (e.g., "association, ambiguity, the slackening of logical synthesis") "are fused with the truth of the essay" (GS, 11:30–31). In keeping also is the sleight-of-hand answer to the desperate Δός μοι ποῦ στῶ at the end of the *Minima Moralia*: "The essay as genre cleverly positions itself among the texts, as if they were absolutely there and had authority. The essay thus gains a firm if dubious footing without the pretense of being primal, comparable to the former theological exegesis of scripture. The tendency, however, is toward the opposite" (GS, 11:29). "Heresy" is the "essay's innermost law of form" (GS, 11:33).

Adorno's program of an "individuation of knowledge" (GS, 6:55) goes back above all to this subversive tradition, which runs counter to the main trend of modern thinking. Individuation of knowledge means on the one hand conscious effort with regard to the "form of representation" (GS, 11:26) and to "incisive subjective expression" (GS, 11:31); for in Adorno's opinion and "in stark contrast to the usual ideal of science . . . , the objectivity of dialectical knowledge requires not less but more subjectivity;

otherwise philosophical experience withers" (GS, 6:50). The rejection of established scientific rules is admittedly like walking a tightrope: "Free thought is not protected against the risk of slipping off into arbitrariness; nothing guarantees that it has saturated itself with the subject sufficiently to survive the risk. But the consistency of execution, the density of the texture contributes towards its hitting the mark" (GS, 6:45).

"Individuation of knowledge" means, on the other hand, the "accentuation of the partial"—in general the fragmentary, changing, and ephemeral, which has been regarded as "unworthy of philosophy" since Plato (GS, 11:17). In his best essays on literature and music, Adorno actually does succeed "in illuminating, through submersion in fragments, something of that content that gains its immortality from nothing other than the color of the hic et nunc" (GS, 11:204) in accordance with his essayistic maxim: "Philosophical activity is not to be directed at the concrete but to spring from it" (GS, 6:43).

IF WE measure it by this standard, the *Aesthetic Theory* is a somewhat disappointing book, both in the "consistency of execution" of its negativistic program as well as in the "density of the fabric" of concepts and concrete detail, and finally also in terms of the courage with which it advances the "pleasure principle of thought" and "heresy"—and this not just because it was never finished. Rather, disappointment is a result of the book's "positiveness," its tendency toward a systematic conclusiveness, toward being a "major work," a tendency Adorno the essayist had so energetically resisted (GS, 11:26). Instead, the *Aesthetic Theory*, according to the editors, "along with *Negative Dialectics* and a projected book on moral philosophy 'represent' what Adorno wished 'to put on the scales' " (AT, p. 537).

At the same time Adorno was fond of quoting from Walter Benjamin's *One-Way Street*: "All the decisive blows will be landed with the left hand."[38] But then again, in his late "Bibliographical Caprices" (GS, 11:345–57), he notes with a certain self-irony, albeit seriously: "an old antipathy toward books whose titles are printed lengthwise along the spine. Humane books should have it printed crosswise. . . . —Only on some of the books I've written

could my wish for the latter be fulfilled. . . . The reason may well
have been my own resistance to thick tomes" (GS, 11:353–54).
With his two last works Adorno was able to fulfill the desire for
this (however precarious) "expression of permanence" (GS,
11:353).[39] Essayistic "resistance to thick tomes," however, was
undoubtedly his better part.

In his late essay "Stravinsky: A Dialectical Sketch," dedicated
to the memory of Walter Benjamin (GS, 16:382–409), Adorno
revised the earlier judgment of Stravinsky expressed in *The Philosophy of the New Music* (GS, 12:127–96). In the later essay, he
allows the revision to meld into an imaginary "corriger la fortune"
in order to bring to mind the negative utopian potential of the
early Stravinsky, who had not yet been overcome by the "curse
of the positive." The passage begins: "The old player tempts one
to playfully imagine how different things might have been" (GS,
16:406–07). And so the rules might also allow us to imagine what
it would have been like if, after his return from exile, Adorno had
not tried increasingly to be academic, with the concomitant pride
in the "development of a school" (GS, 11:591)[40] and concern
about the "permanence" of what he had "to put on the scales," a
concern that cast a shadow not only over his thick volumes but
also over many of his late treatises and prefaces. It might allow us
to imagine what would have happened had he followed the line
that culminated in the *Minima Moralia*, a "collection of aphorisms," which, in Habermas' neat formulation, "one can in good
conscience study as if it were a Summa."[41] A body of work that
took its inspiration from the most ephemeral, was conversant in
all areas of philosophy, literature, and music, one that "deter-
minedly negated" the German tradition but was above all extremely "literary," could have been realized, an *oeuvre* that would
have been most closely comparable to the late work of Roland
Barthes, rejecting all scientific pretension and yet steeped in theory, radically autobiographical and at the same time "artificial,"
one oriented toward the *plaisir du texte*. The alternative would
have been a strictly theoretical articulation and empirical examination of those aphoristic anticipations, not just an "essayistic"
exploitation of Hegel's speculative dialectics and the interdisci-

plinary research program of the early "Critical Theory."[42] But Adorno never committed himself to either.

Instead, the *Aesthetic Theory* is a book impressive in its complexity, rich in illuminating insights and brilliant formulations, but rather tormenting as a whole: neither a collection of "aesthetic fragments" without any pretended agenda nor a consistently theoretically articulated discourse. The planned revision would scarcely have provided a remedy. Neither in its formal structure nor in the conceptual application of the principle of "negativity"—a concept that constantly oscillates, tending now toward the absolute, now toward the relative, that emphasizes here one aspect of meaning, there another—does the work represent a convincing realization of "negative aesthetics." But was this indeed the point of Adorno's last work-in-progress?

During his youth Adorno noted aphoristically: "To couple the idea of the dodecaphonic technique with the feeling of a child hearing Madame Butterfly on the grammophone should be the goal of musical understanding" (GS, 16:269). What he said here about music is a precise and graphic formulation of the two foci of Adorno's aesthetic experience as the "arena" (*AT*, p. 513) for his *Aesthetic Theory*. A program of "negative aesthetics," however, cannot be inferred from it and is, in fact, scarcely compatible with it.

## Notes

1. Theodor W. Adorno, *Ästhetische Theorie*, 2d ed., ed. Gretel Adorno and Rolf Tiedemann, (Frankfurt am Main: Suhrkamp, 1971) (*Gesammelte Schriften*, vol. 7); referred to hereafter as *AT*. Further page references will be given in the text. Adorno's other writings are cited from the *Gesammelte Schriften* (hereafter GS), vols. 1–20 (Frankfurt am Main: Suhrkamp, 1970–1986); volume and page numbers will be given in the text. Adorno's *Ästhetische Theorie* in the English translation (*Aesthetic Theory*, trans. C. Lenhardt, ed. Gretel Adorno and Rolf Tiedemann [London, Boston, Melbourne, and Henley: Routledge and Kegan Paul, 1984]) was consulted while preparing the final English version of this essay—for which I would like to express my appreciation to Melanie Richter-Bernburg; I would also like to thank Ruth K. Angress and Leonard M. Olschner for their helpful advice.

2. Hans Robert Jauss, *Ästhetische Erfahrung und literarische Hermeneutik*, 2d ed. (Frankfurt am Main: Suhrkamp, 1984), pp. 27, 44–47, and 54.

3. Herbert Marcuse, "Über den affirmativen Charakter der Kultur" in Marcuse, *Schriften*, vol. 3: *Aufsätze aus der Zeitschrift für Sozialforschung, 1934–1941* (Frankfurt am Main: Suhrkamp, 1979), pp. 186–226.

4. See Jauss, *Ästhetische Erfahrung*, p. 47.

5. Compare the similarly abstract and therefore almost empty assertion that "all art [is] sad, especially that which thinks itself cheerful and harmonious" (*AT*, p. 50).

6. "On the other hand, we would be consenting all too readily to the unidirectionality of the Weltgeist if we were to reduce it to the mere notion of domination" (*AT*, p. 310).

7. Georg Lukács, *Über die Besonderheit als Kategorie der Ästhetik* (Berlin and Weimar: Aufbau-Verlag, 1985), pp. 247–61; see also Lukács, *Die Eigenart des Ästhetischen* (Berlin and Weimar: Aufbau-Verlag, 1981), 1:540–83.

8. Georg Wilhelm Friedrich Hegel, *Phänomenologie des Geistes*, 6th ed., ed. Johannes Hoffmeister (Hamburg: Meiner, 1952), p. 69; and Hegel, *Wissenschaft der Logik*, ed. Georg Lasson (reprint of the 1936 ed.; Hamburg: Meiner, 1975), 1:36.

9. Dieter Henrich, "Diagnose der Gegenwart: Definition der kritischen Theorie —Theodor W. Adorno: 'Negative Dialektik,' " *Frankfurter Allgemeine Zeitung*, No. 235, October 10, 1967, p. 7L. In similar fashion, Adorno had already criticized Lukács' "narrow instrumentarium, drawn on the whole from Hegel" (*GS*, 11:257).

10. See in particular Dieter Henrich, "Hegels Grundoperation: Eine Einleitung in die 'Wissenschaft der Logik,' " in Ute Guzzoni, Bernhard Rang, and Ludwig Siep, eds., *Der Idealismus und seine Gegenwart, Festschrift für Werner Marx zum 65. Geburtstag* (Hamburg: Meiner, 1976), pp. 208–30.

11. Albrecht Wellmer would have met with no resistance from Adorno when he argued that "in the fixation of art in a progressive negation of meaning there is again an implicit overall construction of the progress of art." See Wellmer, *Zur Dialektik von Moderne und Postmoderne: Vernunftkritik nach Adorno* (Frankfurt am Main: Suhrkamp, 1985), p. 69.

12. Adorno thus follows Benjamin, whose programmatic essay "Die Aufgabe des Übersetzers" begins as follows: "Nowhere does consideration of the recipient prove to be fruitful for the understanding of the art work or the art form. . . . For no poem is addressed to the reader, no picture to the viewer, no symphony to its hearers." See Walter Benjamin, *Gesammelte Schriften*, 5 vols., ed. Rolf Tiedemann and Hermann Schweppenhäuser in cooperation with Theodor W. Adorno and Gershom Scholem (Frankfurt am Main: Suhrkamp, 1980, 1983], vol. 4, pt. 1, pp. 9–21; quotation here from p. 9.

13. "Truth is the death of intention," as Benjamin had already written in the introduction to his *Ursprung des deutschen Trauerspiels* (Benjamin, *Gesammelte Schriften*, vol. 1, pt. 1, pp. 203–430, here p. 216).

14. "The mediated is not implied in immediacy the way the immediate which would be mediated is implied in mediation. Hegel ignored this distinction" (*GS*, 6:173).

15. See Henrich, "Hegels Grundoperation," especially pp. 214–16; in contrast, see Adorno's fundamental rejection of the theorem of "negation of negation" as a principle of construction (*GS*, 6:9), though he does grant it at most a limited validity for the "subjective progress of philosophical knowledge" (*GS*, 6:161 n.) as well as for the "realm of aesthetics" (*AT*, p. 60).

16. See Jacques Derrida, "La structure, le signe et le jeu dans le discours des sciences humaines," *L'écriture et la différence* (Paris: Seuil, 1979), pp. 409–28, here p. 416 (although Derrida here uses the term "dé-constituer" along with "destruction" and "dé-construction"; see *ibid.*, p. 414). Parallels between Adorno's *Negative Dialectics* and Derrida's "deconstruction" are noted by Rainer Nägele in "The Scene of the Other: Theodor W. Adorno's Negative Dialectic in the Context of Poststructuralism," *Boundary 2* (1983), 11:59–79, and more generally and polemically in Jürgen Habermas, *Der philosophische Diskurs der Moderne: Zwölf Vorlesungen*, 3d ed. (Frankfurt am Main: Suhrkamp, 1986), pp. 219–24.

17. "... s'enfoncer, en tâtonnant à travers les concepts hérités, vers l'innomable" (Jacques Derrida, *La voix et le phénomène: Introduction au problème du signe dans la phénoménologie de Husserl* [Paris: Presses Universitaires de France, 1967], p. 86).

18. "Elle doit pour le reste puiser ses ressources dans la logique qu'elle déconstruit" (Jacques Derrida, *De la grammatologie* [Paris: Minuit, 1967], p. 443).

19. "... en utilisant contre l'édifice les instruments ou les pierres disponibles dans la maison, c'est-à-dire aussi bien dans la langue" (Jacques Derrida, "Les fins de l'homme," *Marges de la philosophie* [Paris: Minuit, 1972], pp. 129–64, here p. 162).

20. Martin Heidegger, *Gesamtausgabe*, section 1: *Veröffentlichte Schriften 1914–1976*, ed. Friedrich-Wilhelm von Herrmann (Frankfurt am Main: Klostermann, 1976– ), 2:27–36, section 6. Cf. Jacques Derrida, "Ousia et grammè: Note sur une note de Sein und Zeit," *Marges de la philosophie*, pp. 31–78, especially 33ff; Derrida, "Les fins de l'homme," pp. 162–63; and Derrida, *Positions: Entretiens avec Henri Ronse, Julia Kristeva, Jean-Louis Houdebine, Guy Scarpetta* (Paris: Minuit, 1972), especially pp. 18–20 and 73.

21. Jacques Derrida, " 'Genèse et structure' et la phénoménologie," in Derrida, *L'écriture et la différence*, pp. 229–51, here p. 229.

22. " 'Déconstruire' la philosophie ce serait ainsi penser la généalogie structurée de ses concepts de la manière la plus fidèle, la plus intérieure"; Derrida admittedly does not stop there (as will be explained) but continues: "mais en même temps depuis un certain dehors par elle inqualifiable, innommable, déterminer ce que cette histoire a pu dissimuler ou interdire, se faisant histoire par cette répression quelque part intéressée" (Derrida, *Positions*, p. 15).

23. Friedrich Nietzsche, *Der Antichrist: Fluch auf das Christenthum*, in Nietzsche, *Sämtliche Werke: Kritische Studienausgabe*, ed. Giorgio Colli and Mazzino Montinari (Munich, Berlin, and New York: Deutscher Taschenbuch, Verlag, de Gruyter, 1980), 5:165–254, here p. 233 (section 52). On this subject, see Hendrik Birus, "Nietzsche's Concept of Interpretation," *Texte: Revue de critique et de théorie littéraire* (1984), 3:87–102, especially pp. 91–92; and Birus, "Nietzsche's Hermeneutical Considerations," in Volker Dürr, Reinhold Grimm, Kathy Harms, eds., *Nietzsche: Literature and Values* (*Monatshefte* Occasional Volume, no. 6) (Madison: University of Wisconsin Press, 1988), pp. 66–80, especially pp. 68–70.

24. "... par ce double jeu ... j'essaie donc de respecter le plus rigoureusement possible le jeu intérieur et réglé de ces philosophèmes ou épistémes en les faisant glisser sans les maltraiter jusqu'au point de leur non-pertinence, de leur épuisement, de leur clôture" (Derrida, *Positions*, pp. 14–15).

25. ". . . la négativité . . . , qui est le fonds non historique de l'histoire" (Jacques Derrida, "Cogito et histoire de la folie," *L'écriture et la différence*, pp. 51–97, here p. 55 and pp. 89–90).

26. "Avec tous les risques mais sans le pathos métaphysique ou romantique de la négativité" (Derrida, *Positions*, p. 121).

27. ". . . interprétation déconstructrice, c'est-à-dire affirmative" (Jacques Derrida, *Éperons: Les styles de Nietzsche*, préface de Stefano Agosti [Paris: Flammarion, 1978], p. 28). In comparable fashion, the thought of Jean-François Lyotard leads to a suggested "affirmative aesthetics," motivated to a large degree by the reception and criticism of Adorno's *Negative Dialectics* and *Aesthetic Theory*. But that is another subject. . . .

28. See Michael Theunissen, "Negativität bei Adorno," in *Adorno-Konferenz 1983*, ed. Ludwig von Friedeburg and Jürgen Habermas (Frankfurt am Main: Suhrkamp, 1983), pp. 41–65, especially 57–59. On the relationship between "deconstruction" and "negative theology," see Jacques Derrida, "Violence et métaphysique: Essai sur la pensée d'Emmanuel Levinas," *L'écriture et la différence*, pp. 117–228, especially pp. 170–71 and 216; Derrida, "La différance," in Derrida, *Marges de la philosophie*, pp. 1–29, especially p. 6; and, particularly, Derrida's contribution to this volume.

29. Christian Dietrich Grabbe, *Herzog Theodor von Gothland*, in *Werke: Historisch-kritische Gesamtausgabe*, I, ed. Alfred Bergmann (Emsdetten: Lechte, 1960), pp. 9–208, here p. 95 (act 3, Sc. 1, verses 406–7); cited in slightly modified form in *GS*, 17:273 and used as the closing sentence in a radio broadcast discussion with Arnold Gehlen: "Is Sociology a Science of Man? A Debate" (printed as an appendix in Friedemann Grenz, *Adornos Philosophie in Grundbegriffen: Auflösung einiger Deutungsprobleme*, 2d ed. [Frankfurt am Main: Suhrkamp, 1975], p. 251).

30. Theunissen speaks in this context of a "proleptic eschatology" (in the sense of an "anticipation of the future in the present") in contrast to Adorno's usual "apocalyptic eschatology" (Theunissen, "Negativität bei Adorno," pp. 54–56). On the relationship between "eschatological discourse" and "enlightenment," see Jacques Derrida, *D'un ton apocalyptique adopté naguère en philosophie* (Paris: Galilée, 1983), especially pp. 57–59 and 63–65.

31. Ernst Bloch, *Werkausgabe*, 16 vols. and one supplementary volume (Frankfurt am Main: Suhrkamp, 1985), 5:336–38.

32. See Ernst Bloch, *Geist der Utopie: Faksimile der Ausgabe von 1918*, in Bloch, *Werkausgabe*, 16:364–65; and Bloch, *Spuren*, in Bloch, *Werkausgabe*, 1:216–18; however, these examples from the everyday are usually mediated in Bloch through literature (e.g., through Dostoevsky and Hamsun).

33. See Adorno's autobiographical notes in "Amorbach" (*GS*, 10/1:302–9); on this point and on the anticipatory nature of names in Proust's *Recherche*, see Hendrik Birus, *Poetische Namengebung: Zur Bedeutung der Namen in Lessings "Nathan der Weise"* (Göttingen: Vandenhoeck und Ruprecht, 1978), pp. 49–53.

34. Adorno is evidently thinking here of Benjamin, who decreed in a letter to Florens Christian Rang (December 9, 1923): "I define: criticism is the mortification of works. Not the intensification of consciousness in them (romantic!) but the locating of knowledge in them" (Walter Benjamin, *Briefe*, ed. Gershom Scholem and Theodor W. Adorno [Frankfurt am Main: Suhrkamp, 1966], 1:323). And, similarly, in *Ursprung des deutschen Trauerspiels* (*Gesammelte Schriften*, vol. 1,

pt. 1, p. 357), Benjamin continues: "Beauty that lasts is an object of knowledge. And although it is questionable whether beauty that lasts can still be called that, the only thing that is certain is that without a center worthy of knowledge there is no beauty."

35. Thus, in Benjamin's opinion, art criticism searches for the "sisters of the art work": "And all authentic works have their sisters in the realm of philosophy. For those are the ideal forms their problems take on" ("Goethes Wahlverwandtschaften," in Benjamin, *Gesammelte Schriften*, Vol. 1, pt. 1, pp. 123–201, here p. 172).

36. Ludwig Wittgenstein, *Werkausgabe*, 8 vols. (Frankfurt am Main: 1984), 1:7–85, especially p. 85. As a corrective to an all too simple reading of this statement, see, for example, the notes for a "Vortrag über Ethik" (1919/30): "Astonishment at the very fact of the world. Every attempt to express it leads to nonsense. —Man has a tendency to assault the limits of language. This assault points to ethics" (*Ludwig Wittgenstein und der Wiener Kreis: Gespräche, aufgezeichnet von Friedrich Waismann*, ed. B. F. McGuinness, in Wittgenstein, *Werkausgabe*, 3:92–93). Or, formulated even more drastically under the heading "Zu Heidegger": "Everything we want to say can only be nonsense. And still we assault the limits of language. Kierkegaard recognized this assault and even defined it in similar fashion as an assault on paradox. This assault on the limits of language is what we call ethics. . . . But the tendency, the assault, points to something. St. Augustine already knew it when he said: What? You clod, you don't want to talk nonsense? Go ahead and talk nonsense, it doesn't make any difference!" (Wittgenstein, "Zu Heidegger," in Wittgenstein, *Werkausgabe*, 3:68–69.)

37. See Richard Rorty, "Philosophy as a Kind of Writing: An Essay on Derrida" in Rorty, *Consequences of Pragmatism (Essays: 1972–1980)* (Minneapolis: University of Minnesota Press, 1982), pp. 90–109. As reductionist as Rorty's Derrida interpretation is, it could have called on Derrida's demand (inspired by Valéry) that philosophy also be regarded as a "genre littéraire particulier": "étudier le texte philosophique dans sa structure formelle, dans son organisation rhétorique, dans la spécificité et la diversité de ses types textuels, dans ses modèles d'exposition et de production. . . ." (Jacques Derrida, "Qual Quelle: Les sources de Valéry," in Derrida, *Marges de la philosophie*, pp. 325–63, here pp. 348–49). This by no means leads to a subordination of philosophy to rhetoric, as Habermas claims (*Der philosophische Diskurs der Moderne*, especially pp. 224–27 and 240–43). Though Rorty does question calling Derrida a "philosopher of language," he nevertheless asserts quite unmistakably that "he does have something to say—but it is something about philosophy, not about language" ("Philosophy as a Kind of Writing," p. 105).

38. Benjamin, *Gesammelte Schriften*, vol. 4, pt. 1, pp. 83–148, here p. 89 ("Chinawaren").

39. However, Adorno himself had emphasized in the *Aesthetic Theory* that "the idea of the permanence of works is an imitation of categories of possession, ephemeral in a bourgeois manner" (p. 265).

40. See also Adorno's laudatory review "Fällige Revision" (*GS*, 20:257–61) of the "Habilitation" of his student Hermann Schweppenhäuser (*Kierkegaards Angriff auf die Spekulation: Eine Verteidigung* [Frankfurt am Main: Suhrkamp, 1967]).

41. Jürgen Habermas, "Theodor W. Adorno: Ein philosophierender Intellektueller (1963)," in Habermas, *Philosophisch-politische Profile: Erweiterte Ausgabe,* 3d ed. (Frankfurt am Main: Suhrkamp, 1984), pp. 160–62, here p. 162.

42. On this subject, see Helmut Dubiel, *Wissenschaftsorganisation und politische Erfahrung: Studien zur frühen Kritischen Theorie* (Frankfurt am Main: Suhrkamp, 1978), as well as the related Habermas, *Der philosophische Diskurs der Moderne,* pp. 143–44 and 153–57.

# 6

# SAMUEL BECKETT'S FIGURAL EVASIONS
## Shira Wolosky

IF BECKETT'S novels seem extended exercises in reduction, his late prose texts may seem reductions reduced. Despite its seeming absence of technique, however, this art of the minimal actually entails complex strategies of apotropism—the turning away from figures. Such apotropism is pursued on every level, from a meticulously constructed language to entire textual structures. Yet it extends beyond technique; for it invokes a broad context and history of negative mysticisms as a framework. Eventually, Beckett's apotropisms arrive at something that is decidedly not the nothingness they at first seem to suggest, although it is also not the metaphysical something toward which figural language traditionally points us.

Stanley Cavell offers one important avenue into the reductive methods of Beckett's language in his essay "Ending the Waiting Game," where he notes a tendency in Beckett to pure denotation: "Beckett shares with positivism its wish to escape connotation, rhetoric, the noncognitive, the irrationality and awkward memories of ordinary language, in favor of the directly verifiable, the isolated, the perfected present."[1] This denotative or positivist use of language governs texts such as "Fizzles," in which a protagonist makes his way through what seems an underground labyrinth of walks and turns and sudden sheer falls. The action of "Fizzles" is comprised of this and only this activity; its plot, that is, becomes exactly plotting a course through space: "He halts, for the first time since he knows he's under way, one foot before the other, the higher flat, the lower on its toes, and waits for a decision. Then he moves on."[2] Temporal succession is in turn entirely defined within the space the protagonist traverses, step by step: "But see how now, having turned right for example, instead of turning left a little further on he turns right again. And see how now again, yet a little further on, instead of turning left at last he turns right yet again. And so on until, instead of turning right yet again, as he expected, he turns left at last" ("Fizzles 1," p. 10). Now, again, yet, until, at last: these words of temporal measure here only mediate the stops and starts, the twists and turns of strict, unmitigated spatial progression. Indeed, the passage seems constructed to explore just how curtailed and restricted the meanings of such terms can become when allowed to function only within the limits of spatial context. As for the protagonist—if one can continue so to call a figure who himself seems only a function of the labyrinth he traverses—his very life too becomes a compilation of the space he crosses, in the time it takes him to do so. In this way

> little by little his history takes shape, with if not yet exactly its good days and bad, at least studded with occasions, passing rightly or wrongly for outstanding, such as the straightest narrow, the loudest fall, the most lingering collapse, the steepest descent, the greatest number of successive turns the same way, the greatest fatigue, the longest rest, the longest—aside from the sound of the body on its way—silence. . . . In a word all the summits. ("Fizzles 1," pp. 13–14)

In this passage—both as text and as action—what occurs is the sustained elimination of any sense not confined within the spatial motion that it alone admits. Indeed, there seems a radical de-figuration of a whole tradition of literary journeys in which progress is presented physically in order to re-present progress of a moral, emotional, religious, or psychological kind. Here the inverse occurs. Terms of judgment such as "good" and "bad" are assimilated into the term "outstanding," which emerges in its physically determined sense. Words that in other contexts open into metaphysical or psychical meanings—"the straightest narrow," "fall," "descent,"—lose any sense but that of physical dimension and direction. And even words that retain some figurative usage—"studded" with occasions, "passing rightly," "summits"—are turned back toward a physical, literal sense. Personal "history," then, is nothing more than a series of shifts in position. The inner life and the very terms for formulating it do not mediate the external world but are mediated by it. And yet, the force of this insistent physicality and literalism depends on the figural level that such a literary journey inevitably evokes. Figuration has not been so much eliminated as pointedly denied, a palpable evasion creating an absence within which this passage continues to resonate—and which accounts for its humor as well.

What "Fizzles 1" accomplishes in a miniature of miniatures *The Lost Ones* carries out more extensively, again both as text and as action. *The Lost Ones* posits a complete cosmos, a cylinder-world constructed out of elemental forces and governed by their laws: light, which oscillates between darkness and a dim yellowness; heat, which rises and falls with the light; and time, in seconds. These physical conditions determine not only the space in which the lost ones live but every aspect of the lives they live there:

> One body per square metre or two hundred bodies in all round numbers. Whether relatives near and far or friends in varying degree many in theory are acquainted. Seen from a certain angle these bodies are of four kinds. Firstly those perpetually in motion. Secondly those who sometimes pause. Thirdly those who short of being driven off never stir. . . . Fourthly those who do not search or non-searchers.[3]

Hugh Kenner has remarked that Beckett's bodies, like Newton's, are either in motion or at rest.[4] Inertia, resistance, and, in the text's apocalyptic end, entropy, when "the temperature comes to rest not far from freezing point" (*LO*, p. 62) and the last mobile figure's motion ceases, become life's governing forces. They determine all that takes place, making personal identity a function of the same degrees, measures, modulations, and oscillations that define the system's light and heat. The conduct of life has become not only subordinate to, but utterly indistinguishable from, physical conditions. And these in turn constitute a mode of discourse,

establishing the context for and determining the resonance of
such words as "relatives," "in varying degrees," and "ac-
quainted." The nature and kind and indeed very definition of
relationship becomes a matter of relation in space, of physical
proximity and juxtaposition. What indeed can "man and wife"
even mean when "man and wife are strangers two paces apart to
mention only this most intimate of bonds. Let them move on till
they are close enough to touch and then without pausing on their
way exchange a look. If they recognize each other it does not
appear" (*LO*, p. 36). "Intimate," "bonds," "exchanges": these
words, in this context, can only register relative distances while
moving and pausing. And of what, in this context, would recognition even consist? Just so, "passion" in *The Lost Ones* is the
"passion to search"; the word is returned to its etymological
origin as passing, undergoing, but only from place to place "such
that no place may be left unsearched" (*LO*, p. 50). "What principle of priority," the text asks, "obtains among the watchers always in force and eager to profit by the first departure from among
the climbers" (*LO*, p. 51). But the text's linguistic situation makes
only one principle of priority possible, that involving exactly the
order in which the watchers stand on line and no more.

Beckett's late texts seem, at least in their art, meditations on
such words, on how they can mean, given the situations he gives.
In "Enough," the romance between "he" and "she" transpires by
podometer. "Total milage divided by average daily milage. So
many days. Divide" (p. 59). The two lives accordingly take shape
as "immediate continuous communication with immediate redeparture. Same thing with delayed redeparture. Delayed continuous communication with immediate redeparture" (p. 57), where
communication can mean only stops taken side by side for so
many moments in the course of covering average daily distances.
Listening to sounds of crawling and falling, the voice of *Company*
stops to wonder "what in the world such sounds might signify."[5]
But in the world of *Company* they signify crawling and falling
only, almost in a short circuit of signification akin to tautology—
one figure Beckett retains in all its emptiness.

This delimiting of the sense of his words to an unmitigated
literalism—while always including, as part of its intention, the

"figurative" meanings the words might otherwise convey—meets in Beckett another almost opposite and yet strangely converging evasion of figure. This second evasive strategy involves Beckett's puzzling and pervasive use of mathematical figures, figures that control large portions of such texts as *The Lost Ones*, "Ping," "Imagination Dead Imagine," "Enough," "All Strange Away," *Ill Seen Ill Said*,[6] etc. "No way in, go in, measure," "Imagination Dead Imagine" invites: "Diameter three feet, three feet from ground to summit of the vault. Two diameters at right angles AB CD divide the white ground into two semicircles ACB BDA. Lying on the ground two white bodies, each in its semicircle" (p. 63). Here as elsewhere, Beckett reduces space and any activity within it to pure extension—to purely geometrical and mathematical elements. To such mathematical treatment all other considerations are subordinated. Thus, the only interaction between the two white bodies of "Imagination Dead Imagine" consists in the random spatial intersection of their two gazes, when exactly once "the beginning of one overlapped the end of the other for about ten seconds" (pp. 65–66). The assimilation of body to geometry in "All Strange Away" extends from the mathematization of bodily position—"For nine and nine eighteen that is four feet and more across in which to kneel, . . . Arse to knees, say diagonal ac, feet say at d, head on left cheek at b"—to the grotesque mathematization of sex: "Back of head against face when eyes on cunt, against breasts when on hole, and vice versa, all most clear" (pp. 43–44). "Ping," if possible, goes still further in identifying dimensions of the self with dimensions of place: "Bare white body fixed one yard ping fixed elsewhere white on white invisible heart breath no sound" (p. 70). "All Strange Away" formulates the principle: "A place, then someone in it, that again"; and then proceeds to give it flesh: "Five foot square, six height, no way in, none out, try for him there. . . . Sitting, standing, walking, kneeling, crawling, lying, creeping, in the dark, in the light" (p. 39).

This further reduction from matter to mathematical figure suggests a rigorous method that is not entirely Beckett's own invention. For Beckett seems to proceed by a programmatic elimination of all secondary qualities. His later texts thus omit all that resists quantitative expression: passion, hope, grief, pleasure. Only num-

ber, figure, magnitude, and duration remain. Like Descartes, puzzling in his *Second Meditation* over the onotology of wax until
he comes to eliminate all "that sweetness of honey," "that pleas-
ant odor of flowers," "that whiteness," "that shape," "that sound,"
to leave "only a body, extended, flexible, and movable,"[7] Beckett
similarly eliminates all experiences except as they can be assimilated to trajectories pursued, paths demarcated, measures taken.
The vision of love in *Company* thus quickly becomes a calculation of "the height or length you have in common [as] the sum of
equal segments" (p. 41). As the yellow light of *The Lost Ones*
throbs to its lull and all activity accordingly ceases,

> the fists on their way to smite in anger or discouragement
> freeze in their arcs until the scare is past and the blow can
> be completed or volley of blows. Similarly without entering
> into tedious details those surprised in the act of climbing or
> carrying a ladder or making unmakable love or crouched in
> the niches or crawling in the tunnels as the case may be. But
> a brief ten seconds at most and the throbbing is resumed
> and all is as before. Those interrupted in their coming and
> going start coming and going again and the motionless relax.
> The lovers buckle to anew and the fists carry on where they
> left off. The murmur cut off as though by a switch fills the
> cylinder again. (pp. 37–38)

Anger and love hover here. But they can only take place as
geometric figure in mathematical space: fists "freeze in their arcs";
climbing, carrying, crouching, or crawling, activities themselves
restricted by the parameters of extension, are equated with attempts at "making unmakable love"—what the text elsewhere
clearly establishes as a matter of "penetration" and "erection"
(*LO*, p. 53). And when the figures are once more set in motion,
the "throbbing" of the light that activates them cannot be distinguished from the "throbbing" of life or of love; sexual partners
then "buckle to," a pun both of whose senses register only shape
and momentum, while the fists "carry on," but only in their arc.
Through a similar technique, the hands of a woman in "All
Strange Away" present "no real image but say like red no grey
say like something grey and when again squeeze firm down five

seconds say faint hiss then silence then back loose two seconds
and say faint pop and so arrive though not true image at small
grey punctured rubber ball" (p. 57). Red and grey, pop and hiss,
tension increased and relaxed, the hand becomes nothing but a
"small grey punctured rubber ball."

This writing, in which, as Beckett explains, "little by little all
strange away" ("ASA," p. 57), seems akin to the reduction to
corporeality of Beckett's literalist, denotative language. Yet the
further step into mathematics remains a radical one, and represents a nearly inverse, although no less reductive, procedure with
regard to figuration. Jacques Derrida, discussing the structure of
metaphor in "White Mythology," notes that "metaphor remains
. . . a metaphysical concept." Derrida cites Heidegger (in *Der Satz
vom Grunde*) where he says that metaphor is "a transposition
into the non-sensible of the supposedly sensible": "The notion of
'transposition' and of metaphor," Heidegger asserts, rests on "the
distinction, not to say the separation" between the "sensory and
the non-sensory, between the physical and the non-physical." It
is a basic feature of what is called "metaphysics" and "confers
upon Western thought its essential characteristics." Derrida argues that the "transposition from the proper sensory meaning to
the proper spiritual meaning by means of the detour and of figures" is nothing but "a movement of idealization" in a "framework" that "sets to work the oppositions . . . sensual/spiritual,
sensible/intelligible, sensory/sense *(sinnlich/Sinn)*." Moreover in
an aside with special resonance for Beckett, Derrida remarks: "it
is difficult to conceive" how the "mathematical text" could fur-
nish "metaphors in the strict sense, since it is attached to no
determined ontic region and has no empirical sensory content."[8]
In these terms, if radical literalism strives to eliminate any figurative level, mathematics may be said to strive oppositely, toward
the elimination of the literal level, or what Derrida calls "sensible
or empirical content." That is, mathematics swings toward the
opposite "metaphysical" pole of figuration: toward the nonsensible, the nonphysical, toward "sense" *(Sinn)* itself. But in this it is
not outside the as it were metaphysical structure of metaphor. It
remains within it, by way of incompletion. For Beckett's mathematical figures, in omitting what one may call the concrete level

of human experience, reduce the dual structure of figuration to one dimension, but this one implies a second which is, however, felt as lacking.

Yet "metaphysical" here is not "only" figurative. Rather, the metaphysics of figuration here takes on full force. For mathematics in the Western tradition has in fact had a privileged role in relation to the realms of higher ontological being. While falling below the very highest class of intelligible entities defined in the *Republic* (book 6) as the first principles, i.e., the objects of reason, as Plato says, that make "no use whatever of any object of sense but only of pure ideas moving on through ideas to ideas and ending with ideas" (511), Plato nevertheless places mathematical entities in the intelligible realm, above the sensible realm of objects and their images. In that mathematics employs visible figures, it is not entirely independent of sense impressions. Yet ultimately it remains directed not toward the visible but rather toward "those realities that can be seen only by the mind" (*Republic*, 510).[9] Thus mathematics—especially in its aspect as theoretical mathematics, as distinct from the technical art of calculation concerned with applications to sensible things—acquires an intermediate position between the intelligible and sensible realms, yet does so as an avenue into the intelligible. In the *Republic* Plato accordingly distinguishes between numbers when applied to objects of sense and numbers as they are in themselves, grasped, he says, "by thought alone" (525). In this latter sense, mathematical entities partake of the realm of unchanging being which alone, because permanent, constitutes the true object of knowledge. Plato even claims for mathematical entities an independent existence, prior to sensible things; and he further grants to them, as *mathema*, or things to be learned, a special heuristic role, as a paradigm for philosophy's "turning" away (*Republic*, 518) from the things of daily life toward the realm of being and knowledge.[10]

This noetic and even ontologically independent status of mathematics, despite some criticism from Aristotle, enters into Neo-Platonism, and emerges, for example, in St. Augustine, who distinguishes between "numbers as they are used in counting things" and the "principle of number by which we count." The latter, he insists, is not derived from "images of things which the eye of my body has reported to me." Rather, "we know them simply by recognizing them inside ourselves without reference to any material object. . . . It is not an image of the things we count, but something which is there in its own right."[11] And Descartes, whose figure haunts Beckett's texts and Beckett studies, similarly seems to grant to mathematics a noetic character. He repeatedly insists that his conception of wax, in terms of pure geometrical extension, is achieved "by my understanding alone"; that its apprehension is not in "a vision, a touch, nor an imagination, . . . but is solely an inspection by the mind . . . comprehend[ed] solely by the faculty of judgment which resides in my mind."[12] Like Plato, he distinguishes between the abstract number and counted things: "number is not the thing enumerated"; "a unit is not a quantity." For, as he explains in Rule 12, the pure intellect is pure exactly as the "abstract beings" it represents are "free of all admixture of images or representations," "divorced from the aid of any bodily image." Rather, the mind "beholds some one of the ideas which are within itself," the "simple things purely intellectual."[13]

Beckett himself does not directly invoke any such history in his own use of mathematical figures. In this, in fact, we encounter yet another kind of figural evasion prominent in Beckett—the evasion of allusion. Beckett characteristically will proffer an invitation to allusion; and yet it remains an invitation that must ultimately be declined. For Beckett generally refuses to provide quite enough material to permit the definite location of a specific source for his allusive hints. His intertextual gestures thus remain suspended, seeming to intend some prior text yet never fully pointing to any single one. Or, some element from a prior context may be introduced, but without enough elaboration to bring the Beckett text into systematic relation to some prior one. In this, as in many ways, Beckett's methods suggest a tangent to Joyce's. Like Joyce, he would send readers and scholars to compiling lists of allusions—but will leave them with no more than notations followed by question marks, with echoes that cannot be firmly established.

There are numberless instances of such incomplete allusions

in Beckett, ranging from single allusive words to entire textual structures. *The Lost Ones* provides an example of the latter. With its underground caverns and the vain wish to escape from them, the entire text wavers between an evocation of Dante's *Inferno* and of Plato's cave, with both suspicions supported by the rumours circulating among the lost "that there exists a way out," about which, however, there are "two opinions":

> One school swears by a secret passage branching from one of the tunnels and leading in the words of the poet to nature's sanctuaries. The other dreams of a trapdoor hidden in the hub of the ceiling giving access to a flue at the end of which the sun and other stars would still be shining. (p. 18)

Tunnel or trapdoor, Dante or Plato; and a possible ascent to the sun and stars does little to resolve the matter—although, as the text adds, the choice between them has "so little effect on the comportment of either sect that to perceive it one must be in the secret of the gods" (p. 19). For, in either case, the hope of escape is utterly defeated, with no notion of which tunnel to follow, and the ceiling in any event out of reach.

These hints are sufficiently pointed almost to validate our suspicion that a Platonic or Dantesque reference and even substratum extends almost systematically throughout *The Lost Ones*. But it can be very difficult to gauge such extents. To consider the *Texts for Nothing* only, "Text 10" offers a vision of suspended souls—"souls being licked into shape, souls swooned away, or sick with over-use, or because no use could be found for them, but still fit for use, or fit only to be cast away . . . or it has knelled here at last for our committal to flesh."[14] The text invokes Platonic, Neoplatonic, and Virgilian myths of souls waiting to be reborn, but no one myth can be cited, and none comes to full realization. "Text 6" inserts what seems to recall some gnostic myth: "Blot, words can be blotted and the mad thoughts they invent, the nostalgia for the slime where the Eternal breathed and his son wrote, long after, with divine idiotic finger, at the feet of the adulteress" ("Text 6," p. 103). But it is impossible to determine which gnostic myth and which gnostic figures—which father, which son, which adulteress—may be indicated here, and, again, the passage cannot sustain determinate extrapolation.

Countless other passages entice the reader into similar intertextual quicksand. Beckett offers endless elicitations of figures from philosophy, although the attributions hardly approximate footnotes, while the systematic implications remain centrifugal. *Murphy*, for example, offers many references to Pythagoreanism. Neary is the author of a tractate called *The Doctrine of the Limit*, and is in search of Pythagorean harmony (Apmonia, he calls it). He refers to his beloved as a "tetrakyt,"[15] the sum of root numbers $(1 + 2 + 3 + 4)$ constituting the Pythagorean decade. And he warns Wylie against the fate of Hippasos, "drowned in a puddle for having divulged" the Pythagorean secret of "the incommensurability of side and diagonal" (p. 47). Murphy is himself called a "surd," an incommensurable, and, as Hugh Kenner points out, this very incommensurability was called alogon, "unnameable."[16]

These allusions, however, are not systematically developed, and citing them toward full articulated structures remains problematic—an attempt to construct a master system which this, and most Beckett texts, simply refuse to sustain. A similar caution must be observed regarding mathematics as a whole in relation to its history, which Beckett at most sporadically invokes. Rather, the attempt to situate mathematics is but one instance of the reader's endless and endlessly defeated efforts to "place" Beckett's allusive hints—and indeed, many aspects of his texts—in order to try to make sense of them. The incomplete and evasive figures traced by Beckett's allusions in this join with what Wolfgang Iser calls a general pattern of negativity in Beckett's prose: the "relentless process of negation, which in the novels applies even on the level of the individual sentences themselves, which follow one another as a ceaseless rejection and denial of what has just been said."[17] The narrators are consciously engaged in this unrelenting process of retraction; but the reader too must ceaselessly undo his own readings, the constructions with which he tries to encompass and order the texts before him, as in the attempt to trace allusions. As Iser writes elsewhere, "the moment one tries to restrict [the texts] to a specific meaning they slide away in a new direction."[18] This process, as Iser argues, finally implies an equivocal status for fiction making itself. The constant retraction of the ordering structures we erect reveal them to be fictions; and yet we can never penetrate beyond them: "this mode of comprehension is the only one possible, even though real comprehension is not possible."[19] Our fictions thus emerge as inescapable, but also necessarily false: "We cannot abandon our fictions, but nevertheless ought to realize that they are fictions, as this is the only certain knowledge we can hope to obtain. . . . We are still searching for certainty where we know there can be none and . . . in spite of this knowledge we still take the image for the truth."[20]

Beckett's technique of incomplete and unstable allusion certainly follows this pattern of negativity, especially in the experience of reading. But his use of allusions may also be said to open a further dimension, one that reflects back upon its own activity. For it suggests a context for Beckett's own efforts at figural evasion. There is in fact a tradition of such figural evasion, indeed of negativity, rooted in just such equivocation as Iser outlines—the tradition of apophasis, to which Beckett no less alludes. "First I'll say what I'm not," declares the Unnamable, "that's how they taught me to proceed, then what I am."[21] This apophatic method is repeatedly both cited and accomplished through the novel. Litanies of negation—"Feeling nothing, knowing nothing, capable of nothing, wanting nothing" (U, p. 348); "bereft of speech, bereft of thought, and feel nothing, hear nothing, know nothing, say nothing, are nothing, that would be a blessed place to be, where you are" (U, p. 374)—inevitably call to mind similar litanies from Pseudo-Dionysius, St. Augustine, Basil, John of the Cross —all figures Beckett cites, or at least names that he invokes. Again, Beckett's texts resist any definitive source attributions. It is, for example, difficult to distinguish—for good historical reasons—between Neoplatonist and Christian apophaticism when the Unnamable describes his effort to arrive at "some idea of the elements to be eliminated from the setting, in order for all to be empty and silent. That was always the way. . . . It's a lot to expect of one creature, it's a lot to ask, that he should first behave as if he were not, then as if he were, before being admitted to that peace where he neither is nor is not" (*U*, p. 334). Moreover, these apophatic gestures take their place beside innumerable other theological echoes, pagan, Christian, and heterodox, none sufficient for constructing stable metaphysical frameworks for the texts. Yet the apophatic echoes are both especially pervasive and particularly suggestive, touching the very core of Beckett's own methods—his figural evasions, the equivocation they reflect, and the issues raised by them. For apophasis represents the effort to abolish all form, all figure, indeed ultimately all language as inevitably and necessarily inadequate to that ultimate truth and unity—truth as unity—which stands in its essence beyond form, figure, and utterance, indeed beyond the differentiation and temporality which entail form, figure, and utterance and in which these are articulated. As the Unnamable remarks at the outset, "I shall have to banish them in the end, the beings, things, shapes, sounds and lights with which my haste to speak has encumbered this place. In the frenzy of utterance the concern with truth" (*U*, pp. 299–300).

Within this structure, figuration and even articulation remain in an equivocal position and at best retain an equivocal value. For in it representation remains essentially other than the truth it would hope to represent—an otherness regarded at best as an accommodation and at worst as an obstacle. The general ambivalence of metaphor which Jacques Derrida describes as a "risk of interruption of the semantic plenum" and of the essential knowledge which ideally would be known in itself and which in its unity would always stand beyond the language that expresses it, becomes in the apophatic structure ever more acute.[22] Plato, especially in the *Sophist*, emphasizes accommodation, insisting that the changing world of becoming still retains some ontological status and that images based upon it are still able to express some degree of truth—if only an intermediate one; but in the Neoplatonist development the status of figuration becomes more problematic. As Plotinus remarks: "Who, if he is able to contemplate what is truly real will deliberately go after the image?" Indeed, because images may draw attention to themselves and away from true reality, they finally impede its pursuit.[23]

Apophasis becomes one mode for both addressing and affirming this figural problematic. In the face of the absolute unity of
the Neoplatonic One, even predication becomes suspect as an
intrusion of limits and divisions, while discourse in general only
contributes to the unity's fragmentation.[24] Accordingly, Plotinus
declares: "If anyone attributes to [the One] anything at all, be it
essence or intelligence or beauty, by that attribution one takes
away from Him. Therefore, let us take away everything from Him
and let us affirm nothing of Him." The One—"ineffable, unnameable, unable to be grasped by thought" in Plotinus' formulation—
cannot be positively described; indeed, doing so detracts from
Him. Therefore, it is best to detract from Him, to speak of Him, if
at all, only by way of abstraction, stripping away, removal: "We
say what He is not, but what He is we do not say."[25] It is worth
noting that mathematics once again plays an important role here:
fundamentally, through the Pythagorean influence in formulating
the very notion of the unity of the One;[26] but also as a model of
apophatic abstraction as such, a function not unrelated to mathematical figures as they tend toward the nonsensible pole of figuration. "The first method of forming a conception of God," Albinus states, "will be by remotion of these [sensible predicates of
God] in the same way we form a conception of a point by its
abstraction from the sensible, namely by first forming the conception of a surface, then that of a line, and finally that of a point."
Albinus thus models his negative description of God on Euclid's
negative definition of a point as that "which has no parts."[27]
     Within Neoplatonism the poles distinguishing sensible lan-
guage and the nonsensible truth it would represent become increasingly remote from each other, and the apophatic way becomes ever more strained as it attempts less to negotiate this gap
than to emphasize and insist upon it. Damascius, for example,
came to feel that even a negative relation remains a relation and
therefore compromises the utter transcendence of the One, so that
neither affirmative nor negative expressions could be adequate to
the ultimate principle.[28] Etienne Gilson insists that in the Christian Neoplatonic tradition such extremes tend to be mitigated by
a positive identification of God with Being;[29] but the Neoplatonic

One is similarly an ultimate rather than a nonbeing—a hyperessentiality, not a nonessence, while the "Being" of God in a figure such as the Pseudo-Dionysius can be difficult to distinguish from the supra-Being of his Neoplatonic antecedents, as, for example, in the conclusion to his treatise *Mystical Theology*: "Neither is He of things which are not, nor of things which are. . . . Neither is there utterance of Him, nor name, nor knowledge; Neither is He darkness nor light nor falsehood nor truth; Neither is there any entire affirmation or negation that may be made concerning Him."[30] But even so normative a figure as St. Augustine assumes an absolute distinction and tension between the language of utterance and the immutability of God, whose Word, as he writes in the *Confessions*, is not "subject to time and change" but rather is "silent and eternal," and as such is "far, far different from these words which sound in time. They are far beneath me; in fact, they are not at all, because they die away and are lost. But the Word of my God is above me and endures forever."[31]

Beckett does not so much work within or out of this tradition as reflect back upon it—"Ah, the old questions, the old answers, there's nothing like them," as Hamm puts it in *Endgame*, or, as the Unnamable muses, "the old thoughts, . . . it's visions, shreds of old visions" (p. 405). In Beckett's work the apophatic process, while no less old thoughts and shreds, acquires a particularly commanding persistence. It is most extensively enacted in the evasions of figures of the self that control the novels, especially *The Unnamable*, but also many *Texts for Nothing. The Unnamable* traces the endless retraction of every character the narrator invents for himself and of himself, characters he projects only to deny them at once, insisting they are not his representations: "If only I were not obliged to manifest. . . . Why did I have myself represented in the midst of men, the light of day?" (pp. 296–97), the Unnamable laments. These questions and qualms reappear repeatedly in *The Unnamable*: "When I think of the time I've wasted with these bran-drips, beginning with Murphy, who wasn't even the first, when I had me" (pp. 390–91). Or, as the narrator continues in the *Texts for Nothing*, which seem in so many ways palimpsests of the Unnamable's unending discourse, "What am I doing, talking, having my figments talk, it can only be me" ("Text 4," p. 93).

In this constant tension between "me" and "my figments," the narrator attempts to turn away from his figures, and in so doing to arrive at some pure, essential self, independent of them, a self that would not dissipate itself in what the Unnamable calls his "delegates" (p. 297). He assumes that somewhere prior to and outside these representations there is a true self, the signified that these representations merely signify, and in so doing distort and betray. As he pleads in *Texts for Nothing*, "Leave it, leave it, . . . I'll never get anywhere. . . . When I labored, all day long and let me add, before I forget, part of the night, when I thought that with perseverance I'd get at me in the end" ("Text 6," p. 102). His fictions seem so many detours in the road to the self, detours he attempts to avoid so as to leave only a quintessential "me in the end." And yet, each time he embarks toward this solitary "me," he inevitably finds himself accompanied. The road to the self proves impossible to chart except by detour. No quintessential self seems even to exist except by way of the multiplication of figures.

This problematic of the self and its language, moreover, finally emerges as a problematic of language itself. The drive to move beyond figures toward a self is equally a drive beyond language as such, an effort to evade what the Unnamable calls "the fatal leaning towards expressiveness" (*U*, p. 390). "I'll speak of me when I speak no more," the Unnamable announces (p. 392). "Let us be lucid for once, nothing else but what happens to me, I've shut my doors against them, perhaps that's how I'll find silence and peace at last" (pp. 390–91). "Me, utter me, in the same foul breath as my creatures? Say of me that I see this, feel that. . . . Yes, I will say it, of me alone. Impassive, still, mute" (p. 300). This longing for silence, for a self "impassive, still, mute," and for muteness as the ultimate expression of self, repeatedly marks Beckett's texts, inscribed in their very rhythm of utterance. "Now I'm haunted, let them go, one by one, let the last desert me and leave me empty, empty and silent," *Texts for Nothing* declares ("Text 5," p. 98). And the Unnamable speaks of a "true silence," a "real silence," "the one I'll never have to break any more, . . . the one I have tried to earn . . . the real silence at last, that gives me the right to be done with speech, done with listening, done with hearing" (p. 393), which some have rushed to identify with the mystical silence of apophasis and the union with truth beyond speech that such mystical silence asserts.

And yet, this movement toward the suppression of figures and silencing of language ultimately takes place in Beckett as a double impossibility: the impossibility of accomplishing it, and the emptiness of attempting to do so. It is impossible to accomplish, and not only because within the very act of utterance—even an utterance that attempts to be self-escaping and self-effacing—there is an inescapable multiplicity that compromises the unitary, ineffable self. This is an objection that the apophatic tradition would no less insist upon, and is one basis of that tradition's hostility to language. Rather, it is impossible because outside of such multiplicity there is in fact no self at all. This in Beckett becomes a point of grammar. Beckett repeatedly plays with the grammar of selfhood, with selfhood as itself a grammar. "Where would I go, if I could go, who would I be, if I could be, what would I say, who says this, saying it's me?" he asks at the outset of Texts for Nothing ("Text 4," p. 91). The "me" in the very act of speaking reflects on itself and discovers itself to be not singular, but multiple—"the same old stranger as ever," Texts for Nothing continues, "for whom alone accusative I exist" ("Text 4," p. 91). Indeed, Beckett characteristically treats his "I"s and "me"s not as personal pronouns but as objects in structures that always already imply self-multiplication. "It's they murmur my name, speak to me of me, speak of a me" ("Text 5," p. 98). "But that other who is me . . . because of whom I'm here. . . . It's as him I must disguise myself" (Text 8," p. 113). "If at least he would dignify me with the third person, like his other figments, not he, he'll be satisfied with nothing less than me for his me" ("Text 4," p. 92). "I'm alone, that's where I am, where I was then, where I've always been—it's from them I speak to myself" ("Text 11," p. 130). As the Unnamable sums up, "Someone says you, it's the fault of the pronouns" (p. 404). Beckett seems to be examining pronouns

rather than merely employing them, probing their functions and
dimensions, how they mean and the meanings they imply, how
they enmesh the self that would evade them:

> It's I who am doing this to me, I who am talking to me about
> me. You begin again. . . . there's someone there, someone
> talking to you, about you, about him, then a second, then a
> third . . . these figures just to give you an idea, talking to
> you, about you, about them, . . . then they depart . . . they
> were never there, there was never anyone but you . . . there
> was never anyone—anyone but me, anything but me, talk-
> ing to me of me. . . . I'll go on, without anyone, without
> anything, but me, but my voice." (U, pp. 394–95)

On the one hand, the insistence that it is indeed only "me"
who is talking, who is; on the other, this "me" at once inevitably
finds itself doubled: "talking to me about me." And the double
becomes at once another: "You begin again," and then another:
"someone talking to you." Instead of a self uttering its solitary
self, it finds itself surrounded by "figures," both in the sense of
multiple numbers, a "second" and "third," and in the sense of
multiple persons: I, me, you, someone, him, them. And the more
this self attempts not to be implicated by its figures, the more it
cannot but help keep producing them, so that even its retraction
only introduces another pronoun set—"anyone," "anything,"
ending with a "me" and a "voice" that must inevitably again
reproduce itself into multiplicity.

But the attempt at reduction to the pure "I" is not only, in its
very act, self-contradictory. It is also self-defeating, and attempting it is therefore empty. For the effort to strip away all figures to
arrive at a true self finally arrives not at the self in its truth but at
no self, at nothing, not as a figure for a superessential fullness,
but simply as a void. Having divested the self of everything, every
figment, every figure and voice, one finds no center, no unity;
divesting the self of everything one indeed is left with nothing at
all, no self at all. "Let them be gone now, them and all the others,
. . . there, now there is no one here but me . . . only I and this
black void have ever been . . . all is silent. . . . Nothing then but
me—of which I know nothing" (U, p. 304). The dream of unity,

of a "One alone" as the Unnamable calls it—evoking a Neoplatonist, or even an Augustinian formula?—is a "one who, having
nothing human, has nothing else, has nothing, is nothing . . . who
seems the truest possession, because the most unchanging, . . .
the one ignorant of himself and silent, ignorant of his silence and
silent, who could not be and gave up trying" (pp. 346–47). As in
Schopenhauer, so in Beckett, the effort to know and see ourselves
as a "self-existing unity"

> is by no means possible, for as soon as we turn into our-
> selves to make the attempt, and seek for once to know our-
> selves fully by means of introspective reflection, we are lost
> in a bottomless void. . . . And whereas we desire to compre-
> hend ourselves, we find, with a shudder, nothing but a
> vanishing spectre.[32]

In Beckett, the call for "no more denials . . . no more phrases,"
the concession to be "dupes of time and tense until its done and
the voices cease" ("Text 3," p. 85), leads ultimately not to the
discovery of self beyond evasion, but to the evasion of self. As
Beckett concisely puts it, "Every day a little purer, a little deader"
("Text 5," p. 113).

In Beckett, this drive to nothingness is a genuine impulse,
registered in a steady pressure of apophatic and apotropic modes.
Yet Beckett, in using these modes, ultimately takes the apophatic
at its word. For, if he follows its way toward the nothing, in him
the nothing remains exactly that: not a fullness, an ultimate being
beyond being, but a void; not a silence as plenum beyond language, but as linguistic failure; not an unnaming as ultimate
name, but as a namelessness that truly evades representation, that
represents nothing. "I'm in words, made of words," he writes,
"nothing else," but then continues, "yes, something else, something quite different, a wordless thing in an empty place, a hard
shut dry cold black place, where nothing stirs, nothing speaks"
(U, p. 386). This latter negation—in which "something" itself
becomes a denial of anything—is a genuine alternative; but it is
so as a movement not toward linguistic self-transcendence, but
toward a self-annulling language. Beckett's works then become
no more than linguistic antinomianism, a multiplication of lan-

guage that asserts a wordless nothing to which Beckett gives no
other name.

But, I would argue, Beckett's own path of negation finally
unmasks itself, and in so doing proves fecund. "Name, no, nothing is nameable, tell, no, nothing can be told, what then," he asks.
His movement into silence constantly impels his texts into further utterance. His negations may imply unstated but evoked
alternatives and paradigms that are thus negatively stated nonetheless. His meticulous language results in a rhetoric so elaborate
as to insist upon itself in a gesture that is anything but self-
effacing. And, each denial of figure itself constitutes an assertion,
a voice that again and again reemerges to reflect on itself, in an
incessant and enduring act of rebirth. His evasions of figure thus
constantly prove self-evasive. Beckett's treatment of the apophatic tradition remains ironic and nihilistic, presenting its paradoxically plethoric nothingness as in fact a void. His own apotropic modes, in contrast, convert nothingness into a fertile source
of continuous imaginative effort. Figuration turned against itself
ever turns back toward itself, so that in the end what emerges is
not the negation of figures but their affirmation as inescapable, in
a positive necessity. What Beckett finally offers then is a potent
defense of figures, of language, as the medium in which, against
and through all negation, we go on. By way of it, as he writes in
an echo of Dante that for once seems fully resonant, we are able
"to pass out, and see the beauty of the skies, and see the stars
again" ("Text 9," p. 121).


## Notes

1. Stanley Cavell, "Ending the Waiting Game," in Cavell, *Must We Mean What
We Say?* (Cambridge: Cambridge University Press, 1976), p. 120.
2. Samuel Beckett, *Fizzles* (New York: Grove Press, 1976), p. 8. Hereafter cited
as "Fizzles," followed by text number and page number(s).
3. Samuel Beckett, *The Lost Ones* (New York: Grove Press, 1972), pp. 13–14.
Hereafter cited in the text as *LO*, followed by page number(s).
4. Hugh Kenner, *Samuel Beckett* (Berkeley: University of California Press,
1961), p. 125.
5. Samuel Beckett, *Company* (New York: Grove Press, 1980), p. 50. Hereafter
cited in the text as *C*, followed by page number(s).
6. Samuel Beckett, "Imagination Dead Imagine," "Ping," and "Enough," in

*First Love and Other Shorts* (New York: Grove Press, 1974), hereafter cited in the text as IDI, P, and E, followed by page number(s); "All Strange Away," in *Rockaby and Other Short Pieces* (New York: Grove Press, 1981), hereafter cited in the text as ASA, followed by page number(s); *Ill Seen Ill Said* (New York: Grove Press, 1981), hereafter cited in the text as ISIS, followed by page number(s).

7. René Descartes, *Discourse on Method and Meditations*, trans. Lawrence Y. Lafleur (New York: Bobbs-Merrill, 1960), pp. 87–88.

8. Jacques Derrida, "White Mythology: Metaphor in the Text of Philosophy," in Derrida, *Margins of Philosophy*, trans. Alan Bass (Brighton: Harvester Press, 1982), pp. 219, 226–27.

9. Cited and discussed by Wesley Trimpi, *Muses of One Mind: The Literary Analysis of Experience and Its Continuity* (Princeton, N.J.: Princeton University Press, 1983), pp. 37–38.

10. See Jacob Klein's discussion of these Platonic concepts in *Greek Mathematical Thought and the Origin of Algebra* (Cambridge, Mass.: MIT Press, 1968), pp. 22–23, 50–51, 72–74.

11. St. Augustine, *Confessions*, trans. Richard Sidney Pine-Coffin (Harmondsworth, Eng.: Penguin, 1961), book 10, ch. 12, p. 219.

12. Descartes, *Discourse on Method and Meditations*, pp. 88–89.

13. Klein, *Greek Mathematical Thought*, pp. 198–200. Compare Anthony Kenny, "Descartes on Ideas," *Descartes: A Collection of Critical Essays*, ed. W. Doney (New York, Anchor Books, 1967), pp. 233–34.

14. Samuel Beckett, *Stories and Texts for Nothing* (New York: Grove Press, 1967), "Text 10," p. 124. Hereafter cited as "Text" followed by story and page number(s).

15. Samuel Beckett, *Murphy* (New York: Grove Press, 1957), p. 5. Hereafter cited in the text as M followed by page number(s).

16. Kenner, *Samuel Beckett*, p. 32

17. Wolfgang Iser, "The Pattern of Negativity in Beckett's Prose," *The Georgia Review* (1974), 29 (3):2.

18. Wolfgang Iser, *The Implied Reader* (Baltimore, Md.: Johns Hopkins University Press, 1974), p. 257.

19. Iser, "Pattern of Negativity," p. 11

20. Iser, *Implied Reader*, p. 267.

21. Samuel Beckett, *The Unnamable*, in Beckett, *Three Novels* (New York: Grove Press, 1955), p. 326. Hereafter cited in the text as U, followed by page number(s).

22. Derrida, "White Mythology," pp. 41, 48–49.

23. See Trimpi, *Muses of One Mind* pp. 107, 199, 210.

24. See Trimpi, *Muses*, pp. 182–83.

25. Cited and discussed by Harry Wolfson, *Studies in the Philosophy of Religion* (Cambridge, Mass.: Harvard University Press, 1979), 1:125, 116, 120.

26. See A. H. Armstrong, *The Architecture of the Intelligible World in the Philosophy of Plotinus* (Amsterdam; Adolf M. Hakkert, 1976), p. 14.

27. See Wolfson, *Studies in the Philosophy of Religion*, pp. 146–47.

28. See J. Patrick Atherton, "The Neoplatonic One and the Trinitarian Arche," in R. Baine Harris, ed., *The Significance of Neoplatonism* (Norfolk, Va.: Old Dominion University, 1976), p. 178.

29. Etienne Gilson, *Being and Some Philosophers* (Toronto: Pontifical Institute of Medieval Studies, 1952), pp. 32–34.

30. Pseudo-Dionysius, *Mystical Theology*, trans. Alan Watts (Sausolita, Calif.:
The Society for Comparative Philosophy, 1971), pp. 27–28.

31. St. Augustine, *Confessions*, book 11, chapters 6–7, pp. 258–59.

32. Arthur Schopenhauer, *The World as Will and Idea*, trans. R. B. Haldane
and J. Kemp (London: Kegan Paul, Trench, Trubane, 1883), 1:358.

# PROLIFERATING

# 7

# ON THE NEGATIVITY OF MODERN POETRY: FRIEDRICH, BAUDELAIRE, AND THE CRITICAL TRADITION
## Jonathan Culler

THE TITLE of this volume calls our attention to a major aspect of modern literature, or at least to a major aspect of reflection on modern literature. Critical opinion seems to concede that what for Flaubert was only a dream, the prospect of "un livre sur rien," has been amply realized, in prose and in poetry. A primary document in a consideration of these issues would be Hugo Friedrich's influential book, *Die Struktur der modernen Lyrik*, published in 1956, whose analytical enterprise begins with the following remarks:

> In attempting to understand modern poetry, we are faced with the task of finding descriptive categories. We cannot sidestep the fact (on which all critics concur) that negative categories predominate. However—and this makes all the difference—these negative categories are definitional, not pejorative. They are, in fact, applied as a result of the historical process by which modern poetry has departed from older literature.[1]

Deformation, depersonalization, obscurity, dehumanization, incongruency, dissonance, and empty ideality are a few of his negative categories; nor are these simply the imposition of a critic finally unsympathetic to modern literature. The key terms from German, French, Spanish, and English writings on modern poetry, he suggests, are largely negative ones: "disorientation, disintegration of the familiar, loss of order, incoherence, fragmentation, reversibility, additive style, depoeticized poetry, bolts of annihilation, strident imagery, brutal abruptness, dislocation, astigmatism, alienation" (pp. 8–9). As Dámaso Alonso wrote in 1932, "At the moment we have no choice but to apply negative terminology to our art" (p. 9).

What are the consequences of this orientation: the inclination to discuss modern literature, specifically modern poetry, in negative categories? To explore this question, one might look particularly at the critical tradition of interpreting Baudelaire, since for Friedrich and others Baudelaire is taken as exemplary—as the founder of that poetry which must be described with negative categories. Les Fleurs du Mal is the pivot on which the lyric turns toward the twentieth century. T. S. Eliot called Baudelaire "the greatest example of modern poetry in any language," and Marcel Raymond's well-known title, De Baudelaire au surréalisme, places him at the beginning of the trajectory of modern French poetry. Friedrich, for his part, concludes that "twentieth century verse has brought us almost nothing fundamentally new, no matter how fine some of the poets may be" (p. 107).

What is it that makes Baudelaire the beginning of this line? The negative quality most often adduced is dissonance. Baudelaire himself calls Les Fleurs du Mal "a dissonant product of the muses of the terminal era," and one of the best discussions of his work is Sandro Genovali's Baudelaire, o della dissonanza. Erich Auerbach, in "The Aesthetic Dignity of Les Fleurs du Mal," identifies Baudelaire's modernity with the fact that "he was the first to treat as sublime matters which seemed by nature unsuited to such treatment. . . . He wrote in the grand style about paralyzing anxiety, panic at the hopeless entanglement of our lives, total collapse."[2] Baudelaire's catachreses—"La Mort, planant comme un soleil nouveau," or "Quand le ciel bas et lourd pèse comme un couvercle"—drew new visionary power from unusual combinations, and these dissonances seemed "the most authentic expression both of the inner anarchy of the age and of a still hidden order that was just beginning to dawn."[3] For Friedrich, "Baudelaire's . . . most significant contribution to the genesis of

modern poetry" is a dissonant or destructive imagination: "Elle
décompose toute la création," as Baudelaire puts it in the "Salon
de 1859."[4] The modernity of this account, says Friedrich, "consists of its placing at the beginning of the artistic act an analysis,
a decomposition, a destructive process" (p. 36).

The two main techniques and negative categories are, first, a
process of *Entrealisierung*, whereby imagination transforms reality and makes it unreal. Modern poetry, according to Friedrich, is
characterized by the "dictatorial imagination," enemy of the reality, which imposes a transformation or destruction of the world.
"Reality, dismembered or torn to shreds by the power of imagination, becomes, in the poem, a landscape of ruins. Forced un-
realities lie above it" (p. 169). Second, there is *Entpersönlichung*:
"Baudelaire sparked off the depersonalization of modern poetry"
(p. 20):

> Baudelaire justifies poetry for being able to neutralize the
> personal heart. He gropes along; his ideas are often clouded
> by older ones. And yet we can recognize the historical ne-
> cessity of the future development, from the neutralization of
> the person to the dehumanization of the lyrical persona (the
> "I"). Baudelaire introduced the depersonalization which
> T. S. Eliot and other poets later viewed as a requirement for
> the precision and validity of versecraft. (p. 21)

This may sound rather strange, since when we think of Baudelairian lyrics we are likely to recall what seem above all distinctive,
first-person lyrical voices:

> "Andromaque, je pense à vous. . . ."
> "Je suis la plaie et le couteau."
> "O toi que j'eusse aimée, ô toi qui le savais!"
> "Mon enfant, ma soeur, / Songe à la douceur."

Or, from the poem that will here serve as primary example and
which certainly offers dramatic utterance:

> J'ai plus de souvenirs que si j'avais mille ans.
>
> Un gros meuble à tiroirs encombré de bilans,
> De vers, de billets doux, de procès, de romances,
> Avec de lourds cheveux roulés dans des quittances,

Cache moins de secrets que mon triste cerveau.
C'est une pyramide, un immense caveau,
Qui contient plus de morts que la fosse commune.
—Je suis un cimetière abhorré de la lune,
Où comme des remords se traînent de longs vers
Qui s'acharnent toujours sur mes morts les plus chers.
Je suis un vieux boudoir plein de roses fanées,
Où gît tout un fouillis de modes surannées,
Où les pastels plaintifs et les pâles Boucher,
Seuls, respirent l'odeur d'un flacon débouché.

Rien n'égale en longueur les boiteuses journées.
Quand sous les lourds flocons de neigeuses années
L'ennui, fruit de la morne incuriosité,
Prend les proportions de l'immortalité.
—Désormais tu n'es plus, ô matière vivante!
Qu'un granit entouré d'une vague épouvante,
Assoupi dans le fond d'un Sahara brumeux;
Un vieux sphinx ignoré du monde insoucieux,
Oublié sur la carte, et dont l'humeur farouche
Ne chante qu'aux rayons du soleil qui se couche.

This poem, the second "Spleen" from *Les Fleurs du Mal*, undoubtedly illustrates many of Friedrich's negative terms: dehumanization of the *matière vivante*, incongruency of self as *boudoir*, disintegration of the familiar into dead matter, fragmentation, additive style, brutal abruptness, strident imagery, alienation, possibly even "bolts of annihilation" *(Zerstörungsblitze)*. Its thematic representations are negative: the experience of loss; the mind as a cave or cemetery full of the dead, or as drawer full of what is faded or outmoded, entirely subordinated to disproportionate *ennui*; living matter transformed into a piece of rock which, to make matters worse, is forgotten and ignored.

The poem thematizes a process of depersonalization, as *ennui* blots out possibilities of interest and distinctiveness and as living matter is identified henceforth with a forgotten monument. But nevertheless the poem seems to proffer a vivid speaking voice, and depersonalization is evoked in an act of self-address—"Désormais tu n'es plus, ô matière vivante!"—that is not out of keeping with the self-aggrandizing, self-constituting exclamations that preceded it: "Je suis un cimetière abhorré de la lune." In fact, the depersonalization that Friedrich and others have in mind comes not from avoiding the idea of person or failing to evoke distinctive persons but rather from this description of depersonalization and also, as Auerbach explains, from the fact that "this poet, whose character and life were so strange, expressed the naked, concrete existence of an epoch. For his style was not based on his personal situation and his personal needs; it became apparent that his extreme personality embodied a far more universal situation and a far more universal need."[5] In Friedrich's terms, "the lyrical word no longer derives from a fusion of the poetic persona and an empirical person" (p. 36). Unlike Victor Hugo, for instance, Baudelaire does not date his poems so as to relate them to biographical events, and it takes an effort by critics to put them back into biographical contexts. We needn't imagine a biographically defined situation for the speakers of most of the *Fleurs du Mal*: certainly "Spleen" II requires no such move and seems even to gain force from the lack of specific motivation, from its lack of association with any particularly oppressive memories from which the poet might have suffered. There is a neutralization of the person in the sense that, Friedrich says, "the poet pays scant heed to his empirical ego when he writes his verses. He writes out of himself only insofar as he considers himself a sufferer of modernity" (p. 37). That sufferer, his response to the modern predicament, becomes the object of critical analysis.

We can already see in outline here one paradoxical result of this negative category. Emphasis on depersonalization, while it turns critics away from the tawdry and oppressive conditions of Baudelaire's life, leads to concentration on the poems as representations of consciousness and hence as embodiments of a modern mode of consciousness. Identifying the distinctiveness and modernity of Baudelaire's lyrics with the distinctive character of "modern consciousness," critics discuss the poems by working to elucidate the state of mind of a dramatized speaker. Depersonalization, instead of eliminating the category of person, leads to the construction and explication of a speaker. Indeed, one striking feature of Friedrich's negative categories is that while they appear to refer to stylistic procedures, to poetic techniques, and above all to the disruption of expectations, in fact they easily come to denote modes or qualities of consciousness and promote discussion of Baudelaire as a quintessentially modern consciousness. Paul Verlaine may have said it first: "la profonde originalité de Charles Baudelaire est, à mon avis, de représenter puissamment et essentiellement l'homme moderne. . . . Aussi, selon moi, l'historien futur de notre époque devra feuilleter attentivement et religieusement ce livre, qui est la quintessence et comme la concentration extrême de tout un élément de ce siècle."[6] Whether Baudelaire embodies or portrays modern man—and there is a crucial ambiguity in Verlaine's discussion—his poetry is seen as exemplary of modern experience, of the possibility of experiencing or dealing with what we have come to call the modern world. The ease of passing from what is portrayed to what is embodied may be one factor contributing to Baudelaire's centrality.

I shall return in the last part of this paper to questions about the distinctive consciousness embodied in modern poetry; I want here to note simply that the predominance of negative categories in describing the experience of consciousness portrayed in these poems—loss, absence, destruction, alienation, banality, *ennui,* fragmentation, disintegration—leads to an association of value with operations of consciousness or the imagination, which endow this "landscape of ruins" with an aura of mystery, or which move toward self-awareness in their condition of desolation.

What is striking in discussions of Baudelaire is the way in which the choice of Baudelaire as the founder of the modern lyric goes with an emphasis on the lyric as the embodiment of a depersonalized consciousness and the association of value with operations of consciousness itself, such as *Entrealisierung,* self-consciousness, or, in Hans Robert Jauss, to whom we shall come later, remembrance. The paradigm thus established treats the modern lyric not as patterning of words or as expression of truths (even particular modern truths), but as dramatization of consciousness attempting to engage the world.

One reason Baudelaire has been invested with such importance in accounts of the modern lyric (surprising importance, really, given his relative conservatism in matters of poetic form) is that his poems are frequently first-person portrayals of a speaker reflecting on or articulating his condition—so they make it plausible to think of lyric as the depiction of consciousness—but the notion of depersonalization enables critics to draw from these poems a general model of modern poetry, which can fit even poems that do not have clearly dramatized speakers. Baudelaire gives us distinctive speakers—so lyric can be associated with the representation of consciousness—yet sufficiently depersonalized that speakers need not be thought of as the poet but as instances of a generalized modern consciousness, or even as instances of the processes of sense making. Thus we obtain a single powerful paradigm, as in Friedrich's contention that "this new outlook touched off modern poetry" (p. 20) and that "twentieth century poets have brought us nothing new" (p. 107).

When this model of the poem as dramatized consciousness of a speaker was joined to the Anglo-American New Criticism's insistence on separating speaker from poet, the way was open to treat all lyrics, in effect, as dramatic monologues. In Anglo-American criticism at least this has become the most influential view of lyric, supplanting the older view of the lyric as a brief poem in which the poet intensely proclaimed his or her feelings. Pedagogical handbooks which once had promoted lyric as the expression of the author's most intense feelings had, by the postwar years, come to make it a basic principle, in the words of Laurence Perrine's popular textbook, *Sound and Sense*, "to assume always that the speaker is someone other than the poet himself."[7] Students are taught that the task of interpreting lyrics involves working out what sort of person is speaking, in what tone, and with what attitudes, and what sort of drama of consciousness develops.

To interpret a poem as a lyric, by this model, is to attempt to identify with an act of consciousness on the part of an imagined speaker. The model focuses attention on speakers and consciousness, even in spare imagist poems which may aspire to direct portrayal of the thing itself. Interpreting Pound's "In a Station of the Metro"—

> The apparition of these faces in the crowd;
> Petals on a wet black bough.

—critics imagine a person seeing the faces and making a connection expressed in the natural image, and they thus take the poem to be about the imagination's ability to transform reality and confer on it values associated with trees and flowers more than with mass transport. Imagist poems which might seem to consist of discrete observations and aspire to objectivity are, by this model of the lyric, made subjective, as interpretation inexorably posits a speaker and a consciousness and interprets their images as products of what Friedrich calls the dictatorial imagination: imagination which, as it makes unreal, endows the objects of perception with mystery and empty ideality.

The model of the modern lyric, which focuses on the drama of consciousness of a depersonalized speaker, has provided a powerful strategy for interpreting even the most refractory poems: the most bizarre and disconnected images can be read as signs of alienation and anomie or of a breakdown of mental processes brought on by the experience in question. When Friedrich declares that twentieth-century verse has brought us almost nothing new, this is perhaps as much a self-fulfilling prophecy as an empirical observation. Since a linguistic sequence seems to imply a speaker or at least a consciousness, this recourse to a depersonalized consciousness is always possible. "No matter how enigmatic or arbitrary modern poetry may become," Friedrich declares, "it is always recognizable in its structure" (p. 140) —a structure established historically by Baudelaire's poetic project.

This structure gives us a depersonalized subjectivity transforming reality by acts of consciousness. We have lost the old presumptions of lyric sincerity and the figure of the inspired or accursed poet, but, as Herbert Tucker remarks, "the new dogma took (and in my teaching experience it takes still) with such ease that it is worth asking why it did (and does)."[8] What this structure does is promote the notion of an autonomous or originary subjectivity by presuming that language must come from and should be explained by a consciousness. Tucker speaks of "that late ceremony of critical innocence, the readerly imagination of a self," and of "the thirst for intersubjective confirmation of the self, which has made the overhearing of a persona our principal means of understanding a poem."[9] He is thinking of the way in which, when looking at a piece of language, by imagining a self instantiated in the language we establish a specular relation that works to confirm for us the autonomy and freedom of the subject we consider ourselves to be.

I have been proposing a link between the use of negative categories, particularly depersonalization, to describe modern poetry and this model of the lyric, which has been immensely powerful but also reductive. Negative categories in effect empty the lyric of everything except the movement of consciousness. Ironically, the model's link with depersonalization (along with other negative categories that associate value with operations of consciousness) may enable it to impose all the more imperiously the requirement to explain details by relating them to the consciousness of a speaker. This model makes it difficult to deal pertinently and convincingly with aspects of poems that cannot easily be explained by reference to a consciousness: sound patterns, typographic arrangements, intertextual relations. Intertextual echoes, for instance, must be translated into attitudes. We are enjoined by this model to attend to sound patterning when it can be seen as elucidating the attitude of the speaker and to interpret puns as wit, instead of exploring verbal echoes or word play without reference to a principle of consciousness. It is as though in operatic arias one were supposed to attend only to that which contributed to understanding of a character. In sum, negative categories in the critical tradition may have exerted a more constraining influence than we imagine and contributed to an ideology of lyric and of self that systematically recuperates negativity. They describe movements that are certainly identifiable in the poems, especially the poems of Baudelaire, but they produce a general model which obscures the aspects of the poems that resist the typical modes of recuperation.

One might approach this problem from another angle by returning to the account of the poetic imagination as *Entrealisierung*, a making unreal. Friedrich writes that Baudelaire used the term *modernity*

to express the modern artist's special ability to look at the
desert of a metropolis and not merely see the decline of
mankind but also sense a mysterious beauty hitherto undis-
covered. This was Baudelaire's own problem: how was poetry possible in our commercialized, and technologized civilization? His verse points out the way, and his prose makes
an exhaustive study of it. The road leads as far as possible
from the banality of real life to a zone of mystery, but in
such a way that the subject matter found in civilized reality
is brought into this zone and thus becomes poetically viable.
This new outlook touched off modern poetry, creating its
corrosive but magical substance. (p. 35)

At stake in the interpretation of Baudelaire's lyrics, then, is the
question of how one can experience or come to terms with the
modern world, and poetic consciousness is seen as the solution
—albeit a desperate one, requiring a passage through negativity.
The poetic imagination is destructive, making unreal what it
touches, as happens to memories and everything else in the second "Spleen": the body itself becomes "un granit entouré d'une
vague épouvante." The transformations of poetic imagery generate mystery—an "absolute mysteriousness," Friedrich calls it, in
contrast to specific transcendental values of various religions or
spiritual systems. One might think of the sinister playing cards or
lidlike sky of other "Spleen" poems, or of the old women of "Les
petites vieilles" or old men of "Les sept vieillards": grotesque
and haunting figures that are endowed with an uncanny power.
Friedrich speaks of images devised to overcome reality by endowing it with mystery as the "attempt of a modern soul, trapped in
a technologized, imperialistic, commercial era, to preserve its
own freedom" (pp. 165–66).[10] Even if one is dubious about that
particular characterization, the structure is conspicuous: the negation of particulars brings together the disparate, unintegrated
aspects of modern experience—people, objects, situations, feelings—into a single category governed by an empty transcendental term: mysteriousness, magic, empty ideality. So doing, it produces a situation in which there is only a single category, whose
sign, positive or negative, can be made to shift with much greater
ease than that of the myriad objects, persons, or experiences. The

negatives have the effect of reducing the heterogeneity of these experiences, enabling the diverse elements to be assembled, as all the memories in "Spleen" are brought together as junk in the boudoir or indistinguishable corpses in the cemetery. They become instances of a negative category which can then be recuperated by focus on the consciousness of or representation of alienation itself. In Friedrich the strategy is clear: "Baudelaire's conception of modernity goes further. It is dissonant and turns the negative into something fascinating. Poverty, decay, evil, the nocturnal, and the artificial exert an attraction that has to be perceived poetically. They contain secrets that guide poetry on to new paths. In the refuse of urban centers, Baudelaire smells a mystery, which his poetry depicts as a phosphorescent shimmer" (p. 25).

The negative categories are the key to this redemptive movement, as a unifying device that makes the city something to which one can attribute a phosphorescent shimmer. The process here is similar to what Kant calls the mathematical sublime: when consciousness is confronted with a mass of materials that it cannot take in, the cognitive overload produces a blockage, a "checking of the vital powers," an experience of being overwhelmed. But this focusing of the mind on its inability to comprehend—a negative experience—produces a positive result: the mind "sinks back into itself," exultant at its own confrontation with excess, with the blocking agent. Neil Hertz describes this structure in The End of the Line as one where in fact "the wish is for a moment of blockage, when an indefinite and disarrayed sequence is resolved (at whatever sacrifice) into a one-to-one confrontation, when numerical excess can be converted into that supererogatory identification with the blocking agent that is the guarantor of the self's own integrity as an agent." "Although the moment of blockage might have been rendered as one of utter self-loss, it was, even before its recuperation as sublime exaltation, a confirmation of the unitary status of the self."[11]

We can see this recuperative process in the movement of "Spleen" II, which begins with the predicament of a subject overwhelmed by, unable to find itself in, an excess of memories:

J'ai plus de souvenirs que si j'avais mille ans.

Un gros meuble à tiroirs encombré de bilans,
De vers, de billets doux, de procès, de romances,
Avec de lourds cheveux roulés dans des quittances,
Cache moins de secrets que mon triste cerveau.
C'est une pyramide, un immense caveau,
Qui contient plus de morts que la fosse commune.
—Je suis un cimetière abhorré de la lune,
Où comme des remords se traînent de longs vers
Qui s'acharnent toujours sur mes morts les plus chers.
Je suis un vieux boudoir plein de roses fanées,
Où gît tout un fouillis de modes surannées,
Où les pastels plaintifs et les pâles Boucher,
Seuls, respirent l'odeur d'un flacon débouché.

These memories, or secrets, as the following lines call them,
characterizing their heterogeneity by comparison with the contents of a huge desk—registers or balance sheets, verses, love
letters, legal papers, romances, locks of hair wrapped in receipts
—are a mass of writings of different sorts which could be thought
of as richness but is experienced as excessive or oppressive,
unmasterable by the subject. The key operation is the introduction of negative categories that transform this heterogeneous series of texts into equivalent instances of an absence of life: corpses.
The mind is a cave "qui contient plus de morts que la fosse
commune." The introduction of the moon said to abhor the cemetery that is the speaker makes this seem a more awful condition,
masking the transformation of the indefinite and heterogeneous
series of memories, secrets, texts, into simply les "morts de la
fosse commune" or, in the next few lines, to what is outmoded
and gives off an odor—something that might be compared to
Friedrich's phosphorescent glimmer.

The movement here is one of self-loss: as the memories become
dead, ennui takes over—"prend les proportions de l'immortalité."
The self becomes, as it claims in a moment of self-address, a
lifeless object, "un granit entouré d'une vague épouvante." As the
cemetery is abhorred by the moon, the sphinx is ignored by the
world, lost in a desert:

Rien n'égale en longueur les boiteuses journées.
Quand sous les lourds flocons de neigeuses années
L'ennui, fruit de la morne incuriosité,
Prend les proportions de l'immortalité.
—Désormais tu n'es plus, ô matière vivante!
Qu'un granit entouré d'une vague épouvante,
Assoupi dans le fond d'un Sahara brumeux;
Un vieux sphinx ignoré du monde insoucieux,
Oublié sur la carte, et dont l'humeur farouche
Ne chante qu'aux rayons du soleil qui se couche.

Note what has happened, though: through the negative categories of death, ennui, and now dead matter, the proliferation of memories and writings that posed the original problem has been resolved into a single object, the sphinx. As Hertz suggested, "numerical excess can be converted into the supererogatory identification with the blocking agent that is the guarantor of the self's own integrity as an agent."

The identification with the sphinx is presented, of course, as tragedy, not triumph: the sphinx is ignored, forgotten, and its ill humor sings only to the rays of the setting sun. But once the excess of heterogeneous materials is resolved into a single figure through negative categories, there is potential for reversal or recuperation. The problem has been altered and simplified. No longer is it a question of what becomes of the self among this excess of discourses and experiences which cannot be mastered or integrated—a condition more frustrating, even ridiculous, than tragic. The problem is now focused on a figure in which more pathos is invested—the lurid figure of a sphinx forgotten in a desert, singing to the setting sun—and which is open to recuperation, as we shall shortly see.

Here and elsewhere, negative categories bring together the heterogeneous in such a vacant or deprived condition that positive recuperation becomes possible. The positive counterpart of the negative goes by various names in the tradition, including "a mysterious beauty" and "a phosphorescent shimmer." Walter Benjamin's increasingly influential discussion of Baudelaire as sufferer of modernity speaks of a "conciliatory gleam." Benjamin links Baudelaire's exemplary modernity with the fact that he wrote as one for whom urban experience had become the norm. "With Baudelaire, Paris for the first time becomes the subject of lyrical poetry. This poetry is no local folklore [which might be merely heterogeneous]: the allegorist's gaze which falls upon the city is rather the gaze of alienated man. It is the gaze of the flaneur, whose way of living still bestowed a conciliatory gleam over the growing destitution of men in the great city." [12]

This turn is taken further in essays on Baudelaire by Hans Robert Jauss, whose version of the conciliatory gleam is called "remembrance." In "Le Cygne" "the world appears as a chaotic, smashed 'forme d'une ville,' as the disorderly, desolate, burial ground of a vanished past into whose dead silence the banal noise of the beginning working day all of a sudden blares." [13] Here no "higher and more beautiful reality" reveals itself "to confer meaning on the alien 'landscape of ennui.' " But, Jauss writes,

> to demonstrate the dissonance between spleen and ideal, the reified chaos of the metropolis and the worldless exile of the mythical swan is not Baudelaire's ultimate object. From the ruins of the familiar nature of old Paris, his poem gives rise to a new counterworld of the beautiful. . . . there takes place a retransformation of the world of objects which has become alien and frozen in allegory. But now it is only remembrance from which the counterimage of the new and the beautiful arises in a solemn procession of evocations. The harmonizing and idealizing power of remembrance is the newly discovered aesthetic capacity which can replace the extinct correspondence of soul and timeless nature by the coincidence of present existence and prehistory, modernity and antiquity, historical now and mythical past. [14]

In this account, the various negatives of "Le Cygne" work in effect to prepare the way for a transformation, above all a change of value, brought about by remembrance. The last stanza of the poem describes Remembrance blowing its horn:

> Ainsi dans la forêt où mon esprit s'exile
> Un vieux Souvenir sonne à plein souffle du cor.

This links remembrance both to the possibility of rescue and to poetic destiny, but the poem actually ends on a different note, with *thought* beginning to enumerate figures of abandonment:

> Je pense aux matelots oubliés dans une île,
> Aux captifs, aux vaincus! . . . à bien d'autres encor!

Here, where the mind may be seen as running obsessively over a series of particulars, one might be suspicious of claims about a radical transformation. But the role of negative categories, it is clear, would be to bring items in this series together as, simply, "loss," which can be remembered.

As if recognizing a problem about remembrance, Jauss goes on to note that while

> the retransformation of the estranged reality into a new world of the beautiful frequently occurs in the medium of remembrance, as in "Le Cygne," . . . it is not invariably tied to [this]. In the second "Spleen" poem, for example, it is remembrance which, in a gradual intensification of the images of petrified recollection, remains the medium of estrangement until the very end, and the final image [un vieux sphinx ignoré] seems to put its seal on the calamitous process (as the allegory of a being no one remembers and that therefore must remain eternally unredeemed).[15]

Yet, he continues,

> it is precisely in the ambivalence of this final image that the switch takes place from which the unreal counterworld of the beautiful emerges and transfigures from the end what had first been evoked only under the aspect of "Spleen." . . . The forgotten Sphinx sings as the sun sets and thus transforms the melancholy landscape of the "Spleen" at the end into the bizarre beauty of a pure sound that detaches itself from its source and is meant for no one.

Here the problem we are studying emerges clearly. In Jauss' account the poem "Spleen" dramatizes the negativity of modern poetry and the aesthetic solution. Spleen, he writes, "is the experience and poetic objectification" of the loss of *world*, "the destruction of the certainty our senses derive from their spatial and temporal experience." It represents rather than succumbs to this predicament, and thus represents the overcoming of spleen through its poetic representation.

Cynthia Chase has noted that the plight Jauss discovers in the poem is none other than the condition his aesthetics of reception is designed to solve. Conventional literary history, a mass of historical data, must be replaced by a history of successive under-standings. The opening stanza of the poem shows the lyric "I" futilely seeking an identity in the collected memories of the past, which appear as things emptied of meaning—a reification which finally affects the subject itself, as it becomes, like its objects, unknowable.[16] (The same fate awaits the critic who tries to do literary history without an aesthetics of reception.) In the final stanza, however, it is the reflexive dialogue—dialogue of the divided subject with itself in the apostrophe—that brings on the emergence of a figure able to represent its own coming into being: the sphinx which, according to Jauss, sings "nothing other than the poem entitled 'Spleen.' " The sphinx who sings the poem in which he appears represents for Jauss a modern "poetry of po-etry" and provides confirmation of the possibility of an authentic aesthetic experience in the face of the alienations of modernity, through the emergence of modern allegory as the form that can represent its own coming into being.

Yet, as Chase notes, if we actually try to read "Spleen" as though it were sung by the sphinx, we grind to a halt with the first line. Jauss asks rhetorically, "For who may say with greater right than the sphinx, 'J'ai plus de souvenirs que si j'avais mille ans'?"[17] But since the sphinx is more than a thousand years old, it is scarcely surprising that he should have more memories: if said by the sphinx the verse entirely loses its poetic effect and becomes flatly a matter of fact statement—quite incompatible with its resonance as the predicament of a subject already bur-dened with more memories than an antiquity. It can hardly be the case, then, as Jauss maintains, that "what the sphinx sings is nothing other than the poem 'Spleen.' " On the contrary, ex-pressed by the sphinx, "Spleen" cannot begin as a poem. Far from returning us at its end to its poetic origin, Spleen reveals an incompatibility between the emergence of the poem and the expression of the allegorical figure and leaves us with a song whose status and impact are decidedly uncertain: notes directed toward a light about to be extinguished.

In a discussion of Jauss' article, Paul de Man emphasizes that the sphinx is described as "oublié sur la carte," which can mean "on the map but forgotten" as well as "left off the map." We have a written-down sphinx exemplifying the connection between writing and forgetting, linking the act of inscription not with remembrance but with obliteration, and thus questioning Jauss' confidence that "the allegorical intention, pursued to the utmost of rigor mortis can still reverse this extreme alienation into an appearance of the beautiful." The sphinx's song, de Man notes, "is not the sublimation but the forgetting, by inscription, of terror, the dismemberment of the aesthetic whole into the unpredictable play of the letter."[18]

Even if we are not wholly convinced by de Man's brief remarks, they do help us to note a contrast between two sorts of negativity, which are already identifiable in Hertz's description of scenarios of the sublime. On the one hand there is the negativity of what de Man here calls the unpredictable play of the letter, or inscription, and elsewhere the materiality of language: the negativity of proliferation, of indefinite series, and of whatever gets misread, anthropomorphized, by lyrics and lyrical reading. On the other hand, there is in the critical tradition, by contrast, the negativity of categories that reduce heterogeneity to prepare for aesthetic recuperation, the negativity that assembles or resolves, in scenarios of selves confirming their own integrity.

The first negativity, which does not appear as such, de Man has taught us to see as what gets misread by aestheticizing interpretations of poems. Quite possibly related to the Platonic *khora* that Derrida mentions in "How to Avoid Speaking," it is difficult to illustrate and discuss, except by contrast with the second, the reductive and integrative sort which prepares the way for recuperation and which takes various forms in discussions of modern literature and criticism. An extreme example of such a use of the negative, which differs substantially from the moves of Friedrich and Jauss but represents a particularly fine instance of the recuperative impulse, comes in Gerald Bruns' *Modern Poetry and the Idea of Language* where, working from the idea of the negative power of language, word as negation of the thing, he infers the power of a literary language to negate language and to function as

silence: "by his silence man may return himself to the world of
things, establish himself once more (in Heidegger's formula) as
'being-in-the-world,' which is to say that through his silence he
may once more establish himself in the immediate presence of
the world." [19] "What Blanchot means," he writes—a necessary
formulation, since Blanchot does not exactly say this—

> is that to speak and yet to say nothing is a way of allowing
> language to maintain the *plenum*; and this is to say that a
> literary use of language, as it approaches the condition of
> negative discourse—a discourse which disrupts or reverses
> the act of signification—is a way of holding the world in
> being against the annihilation that takes place in man's or-
> dinary utterances. Understood in this way, the poet does
> indeed become a kind of Orpheus, a poet of the earth, whose
> song shields the world against the void into which ordinary
> speech casts it. [20]

I cite this passage with its powerful appeal to the consolations
of the negative in order to pose the question of the role of negative
categories in the discussion of literature. What is accomplished
by the scenarios in which the negative is enlisted? And what in
literary works is transformed or repressed by the use of these
categories? The passage from Bruns is an extreme example—the
work becomes silence, everything in it neutralized—but it alerts
us to similar, less radical eliminations in other uses of the negative.

In focusing on negative categories in the critical tradition—the
role of depersonalization in solidifying the model of the poem as
drama of consciousness and the role of *Entrealisierung* in preparing a process of recuperation—I do not mean to suggest that
literary works themselves do not insistently use negative categories or thematize the processes that the critical and interpretive
discourses describe. Baudelairian examples amply illustrate that
they do. The question to be asked, then, may bear on the difference between categories used or processes thematized in the poems
and the critical discourse's adoption of these processes as general
models of what modern poetry achieves. What is the importance
or status of that difference, how does it work, and what is the

status of the elements in the poems that seem to resist these processes of negative totalization?

Hertz speaks of the way in which an indefinite and disarrayed sequence is resolved into a lurid but simple confrontation. There is something consoling in the highly dramatized conditions of deprivation — "Je suis un cimetière abhorré de la lune" or "Désormais tu n'es plus, O matière vivante / Qu'un granit entouré d'une vague épouvante" — consolations linked to the solidity of an isolated self. Those negative totalizations offer escape from the more banal and unsettling predicament of confronting an endless series of memories that cannot be integrated or — to move from the situation of the speaker to that of the reader — of coming upon potential patterns, hearing echoes, without being able to decide whether they signify or not. In the case of "Spleen" II, for example, we might contrast Jauss' confidence that the sphinx sings the song entitled "Spleen" and thus reverses this extreme alienation into the appearance of the beautiful, with the nagging memory — a souvenir from the gros meuble à tiroirs of a cerveau — that it was not the sphinx but the statue of Memnon that sang, and that it sang to the rising rather than the setting sun. But is this relevant to the poem?

This sort of problem, which has none of the pathos or lurid excitement of the negative conditions dramatized, is a banal instance of the problems of signification that negative scenarios evade.

## Notes

1. Hugo Friedrich, Die Struktur der modernen Lyrik (Hamburg: Rowohlt, 1956). See the English translation, The Structure of Modern Poetry, trans. Joachim Neugroschel (Evanston: Northwestern University Press, 1974), p. 7. Further quotations, from the English translation, will be cited by page numbers in the text.

2. Erich Auerbach, "The Aesthetic Dignity of Les Fleurs du Mal," in Henri Peyre, ed., Baudelaire (Englewood Cliffs, N.J.: Prentice Hall, 1962), p. 154.

3. Ibid., p. 168.

4. Charles Baudelaire, Oeuvres complètes, ed. Yves Gerard Le Dantec and Claude Pichois (Paris: Gallimard, 1961), p. 1037.

5. Auerbach, "Aesthetic Dignity," p. 168.

6. Paul Verlaine, "Charles Baudelaire," in Verlaine, Oeuvres en prose complètes, ed. Jacques Borel (Paris: Gallimard, 1972), pp. 599–600.

7. Laurence Perrine, *Sound and Sense* (New York: 1963), p. 21. For discussion, see Herbert Tucker, "Dramatic Monologue and the Overhearing of Lyric," in C. Hosek and P. Parker, *Lyric Poetry: Beyond New Criticism* (Ithaca: Cornell University Press, 1985).

8. *Ibid.*, p. 239.

9. *Ibid.*, p. 242.

10. In Baudelaire the operation of consciousness and the imagination is sometimes presented as an exercise of freedom, but it also appears frequently as entrapment, as in "Voyage à Cythère" ("J'avais, comme en un suaire épais, / Le coeur enseveli dans cette allégorie") or "Alchimie de la douleur" ("Dans le suaire des nuages, / Je découvre un cadavre cher"). It would be rash to assume that acts of consciousness are a form of freedom.

11. Neil Hertz, *The End of the Line* (New York: Columbia University Press, 1986), p. 53.

12. Walter Benjamin, *Charles Baudelaire: A Lyric Poet in the Age of High Capitalism* (London: New Left Books, 1973), p. 170.

13. Hans Robert Jauss, "On the 'Structural Unity' of Older and Modern Lyric Poetry," in Jauss, *Aesthetic Experience and Literary Hermeneutics*, trans. Michael Shaw (Minneapolis: University of Minnesota Press, 1982), p. 249.

14. Hans Robert Jauss, "Sketch of a Theory and History of Aesthetic Experience," in Jauss, *Aesthetic Experience and Literary Hermeneutics*, p. 84. In this passage he is extrapolating from remarks on Baudelaire's "Le Cygne."

15. Jauss, "On the 'Structural Unity' of Older and Modern Lyric Poetry," pp. 252–53.

16. Cynthia Chase, "How Baudelaire Changed the Subject," unpublished ms.

17. Hans Robert Jauss, "The Poetic Text Within the Change of the Horizons of Reading," in Jauss, *Toward an Aesthetics of Reception* (Minneapolis: University of Minnesota Press, 1982), p. 169.

18. Paul de Man, Introduction to Jauss, *Toward an Aesthetics of Reception*, p. xxv.

19. Gerald Bruns, *Modern Poetry and the Idea of Language* (New Haven, Conn.: Yale University Press, 1974), p. 200.

20. *Ibid.*, p. 201.

# 8

# PATTERNS OF NEGATIVITY IN PAUL CELAN'S "THE TRUMPET PLACE"

## Stéphane Moses

### Translated by Ken Frieden

| DIE POSAUNENSTELLE | THE TRUMPET PLACE |
|---|---|
| tief im glühenden | deep in the glowing |
| Leertext, | empty-text, |
| in Fackelhöhe | at torch-height, |
| im Zeitloch: | in the time-hole: |
| | |
| hör dich ein | listen in |
| mit dem Mund. | with the mouth. |

IN OCTOBER 1969, Paul Celan traveled to Israel for about two weeks, staying a few days in Jerusalem. Upon his return to Paris, he wrote a series of nineteen poems inspired by this journey. The poems were published in 1976, six years after Celan's death, as the central part of the collection called *Zeitgehöft*.[1] Some of these poems directly evoke the city of Jerusalem, its streets, neighborhoods, and monuments. Others, like "Die Posaunenstelle," do not refer, in the body of the text, to any definite site. But by the very fact of their presence in the cycle of Jerusalem poems—or by the light that emanates from the contiguous poems, which do refer to the physical reality of the city—these poems also lead back, in a more or less allusive manner, to an ensemble of themes and associations which gravitate around the same experience: the poet's encounter with Jerusalem.

Like many other texts from the last period of Celan's work, "Die Posaunenstelle" is characterized by extreme concision. It

consists of only seven lines, divided both typographically and
syntactically into two stanzas of unequal length, the first of five
and the second of two lines. Each stanza consists of one single
phrase. These phrases are rigorously contrasted to each other by
their grammatical structure: the first possesses a subject ("die
Posaunenstelle") but no verb, while the second possesses a verb
("hör dich ein") but no explicit subject. Nonetheless, these absent
grammatical forms refer to implied signifiers. The first phrase
implies the verb of being (or any other verb indicating position);
the second phrase alludes to the speaker himself, the (implicit)
subject of the utterance. However, the absence of a verb in the
first stanza and of a subject in the second has eminent semantic
import. If the positional mode of "the trumpet place" is not
precisely stated, this is because the entire stanza constructs a
different type of space, a decentered space where the coordinates
of the customary typology have lost their meaning. In the same
way, the injunctive proposition that constitutes the second stanza
has no subject, because the subject—which is at the same time
the speaker of the poem himself—is not given *before* the injunction, but constitutes itself precisely through it. The poem "Die
Posaunenstelle" is not the speech of an identifiable subject, existing in some way prior to the poetic utterance; on the contrary, it
is the act through which this subject seeks and perhaps finds
itself. Likewise, the poem does not describe a site that exists
outside of it, but is itself the search for this site, the projection
"in the . . . empty-text" of another type of space, where this very
site, which is "the trumpet place," could be situated.

The opposition between the two stanzas is not only syntactic.
One also finds it at the lexical, morphological, and rhythmic
levels. Whereas the first stanza includes four substantives out of
a total of ten words, the second has only one in six words. But it
is even more striking that the four substantives of the first stanza
are compounds, whether of two nouns ("Posaunen/stelle," "Fackel/
höhe," "Zeit/loch") or of an adjective and a noun ("Leer/text").
These four substantives are neologisms, while the single substantive in the second stanza consisting of a single component—the
word "mouth"—is a term of common usage. In addition, the four
compounds in the first stanza are constructed on the same seman-

tic scheme: the conjunction of a term designating an object ("Posaunen," "Text," "Fackel") or one of the dimensions in which the objects are perceived ("Zeit"), and of a term relating to space and its topology ("stelle," "Leer," "höhe," "loch"). Contrastingly, the mouth is an organ that is situated *in* space (in the body)—it has a place (like the "trumpet place"), a height (like the "torch-height")—but at the same time it *is* its own place: "empty," "hole." As if the space that is created in the first stanza—with its reference to "trumpets" and to "text," to "torches" and to "time" —would be absorbed or (more precisely) inspired into the cavity of the mouth at the end of the poem:

> hör dich ein      listen in
> mit dem Mund.    with the mouth.

The space that the first stanza constructs, the place that is created there, reveals a tension between profundity and height, between plunging to the bottom of a hole and ascending toward a summit. This space is oriented vertically—without reference to extension, to the horizontal dimension. The threefold repetition of the preposition *in/im* at once hollows out the trumpet place and elevates it:

> tief im glühenden     deep in the glowing
> Leertext                  empty-text,
> in Fackelhöhe        at torch-height,
> im Zeitloch:           in the time-hole:

However, this space does not (or does not only) refer to a landscape, since the terms that sketch its contours—"deep," "empty," "hole," "height," "torch"—are contrasted by two abstract nouns. "Text" and "time" seem to qualify "the trumpet place" as a place without physical reality, and its spatial coordinates as simple metaphors. But this tension between the concrete and the abstract already characterizes the word *Stelle*, which at once signifies a position in space and a passage in a book or in a musical score. This ambiguity originates in the etymology of *Stelle*, which in effect derives from *stehen:* to stand, to occupy a point in space. But *stehen* also means to stop or interrupt, to mark a pause. "Die Posaunenstelle" could then signify, simultaneously, "the place in space where the trumpets have sounded," "the passage of a text in which trumpets are evoked," or "the place in a musical score where trumpets are sounding." But more generally, "Die Posaunenstelle" would also refer to a halt, an interruption, a caesura, like the one that is alluded to in expressions such as "empty-text" or "time-hole"; but this very caesura would allow something else to occur, perhaps that "pause for the breath" *(Atempause)* of which Celan speaks in "The Meridian": when the process of breathing stops, when respiration is interrupted, a place is made vacant for a new inspiration; in the same way, the very moment where trumpets stop blowing is precisely the one that permits them to sound anew.

THE WORD *Posaune* derives from the Latin *bucina* (from *bos* = ox and *canere* = to sing), which seems to have designated an ancient Roman trumpet in the form of a bull's horn. The term was introduced into the German language by Luther, as a translation of the Hebrew word *Shofar*, a wind instrument made from a ram's horn. Thus, for instance, in Isaiah 27:13:

> Zu der Zeit wird man mit einer grossen Posaune blasen; so werden kommen die Verlorenen im Lande Assur und die Verstossenen im Lande Aegypten und werden den Herrn anbeten auf dem heiligen Berge in Jerusalem.

> (And it shall come to pass on that day, that a great Shofar shall be blown, and they shall come who were lost in the land of Ashur, and the outcasts in the land of Egypt, and shall worship the Lord on the holy mountain in Jerusalem.)

But the first occurrence of the word *Shofar* = *Posaune* in the Bible appears at the moment of the Revelation on Sinai. The text of the Ten Commandments is, in fact, preceded and followed by two descriptive passages that evoke God's "descent" to Mount Sinai. This theophany is marked above all by lightning and by the sounds of the Shofar, in Exodus 19:16–19:

> Als nun der dritte Tag kam und es Morgen war, da erhob sich ein Donnern und Blitzen und eine dicke Wolke auf dem Berge und ein Ton einer sehr starken Posaune; das ganze Volk aber, das im Lager war, erschrak. Und Moses führte das

Volk aus dem Lager Gott entgegen, und es trat unten an den
Berg. Der ganze Berg Sinai aber rauchte, darum dass der
Herr herab auf den Berg fuhr mit Feuer; und sein Rauch ging
auf wie ein Rauch vom Ofen, dass der ganze Berg sehr bebte.
Und der Posaune Ton ward immer stärker. Moses redete,
und Gott antwortete ihm laut.

(And it came to pass on the third day, in the morning, that
there was thundering and lightning, and a thick cloud upon
the mountain, and the sound of a Shofar exceeding loud; so
that all the people in the camp trembled. And Moses brought
the people out of the camp to meet with God; and they stood
at the foot of the mountain. And Mount Sinai smoked in
every part, because the Lord descended upon it in fire: and
the smoke of it ascended like the smoke of a furnace, and
the whole mountain quaked greatly. And then the voice of
the Shofar sounded louder and louder; Moses spoke and
God answered him with a voice.)

Some verses later, just after the Ten Commandments, the same
description is taken up again, but here the Hebrew text gives a
new detail: to the "voice" of thunder and the sounding of the
Shofar it now adds the glimmer of torches (*lapidim*, in Hebrew).
Luther understands this word metaphorically and translates it as
*Blitz* (lightning). But Buber and Rosenzweig's Bible gives a more
literal translation of this passage in the 1954 edition:

Alles Volk aber, sie sahn
das Donnerschallen,
das Fackelngeleucht,
den Schall der Posaune,
den rauchenden Berg,
das Volk sah,
sie schwankten,
standen von fern. (Exodus 20:15)

(And all the people saw the
voices, the torchlight, the voice
of the Shofar, the smoking
mountain: and the people saw
and were shaken, and stood far
away.)

In Celan's poem, the word *Posaune* appears in the same semantic
context as in the biblical episode of the Revelation on Sinai. Both
the contiguity of the trumpet and the torches, as well as their
topographical relationship, are identical. In the biblical text, the
glimmering of the torches issues from the heights of the mountain, the very place from which the Shofar resounds. So too in
Celan's poem:

Die Posaunenstelle          The trumpet place

. . . . . . . . . . . . . . .          . . . . . . . . . . . . . .

in Fackelhöhe              at torch-height

The visual images that evoke flames in the biblical text ("Blitz"/
"lightning," "Feuer"/"fire," "Geleucht"/"lightning") are recalled
by Celan in the present participle "glühenden." This word, however, does not relate to the height where the torches are located
("in Fackelhöhe"), but to the depth of the "empty-text":

tief im glühenden          deep in the glowing
Leertext                  empty-text

Hence the burning and glowing are at once situated above ("at
torch-height") and below ("deep in the glowing / empty-text"), at
the heights and in the depths. Moreover, the syntactic structure
of the phrase ("deep in the glowing / empty-text, / at torch-
height") seems to suggest that in this context depth and height
are not two distinct dimensions, but rather refer to each other,
perhaps in the way that the sky is reflected in the sea.

Or the reference may operate in accordance with the thought
that Celan expresses in "The Meridian," when he comments on a
sentence in Georg Büchner's story *Lenz* (1839): "For one who
walks on his head," says Celan, "the sky is an abyss beneath
him." Like the glowing text itself, "the trumpet place" is at once
situated "at torch-height" and "deep in the glowing / empty text,"
"in the time-hole." At the beginning of Büchner's story, the narrator describes Lenz's long walk through the forests of Les Vosges,
and depicts the first signs of his madness: "Yet at times he felt
uncomfortable that he could not walk on his head." In "The
Meridian" Celan makes Lenz into the prototype of the poet, a

man who has freed his vision from the stereotypes of ordinary
perception and thus sees the world topsy-turvy. But the price that
the poet must pay for this liberation, for this reversal of the laws
of perception, is the agony of seeing the sky below him, as an
abyss that opens beneath his feet.[2]

Throughout the biblical narrative of the Sinaitic Revelation, in
contrast, height and depth are sharply contrasted as the opposed
poles of a sacred topography. Of course, between these two poles
a continual circulation is established: Moses, the intermediary
between the sky and the earth, between God and the people,
repeatedly ascends and descends from the sacred mountain: "And
Moses went up to God" (Exodus 19:3); "And Moses came and
called the elders of the people" (19:7); "And Moses reported the
words of the people to the Lord" (19:8); "And Moses went down
from the mountain to the people" (19:14); "And the Lord called
Moses to the top of the mountain, and Moses went up" (19:20);
"And the Lord said to Moses: Go down and testify before the
people" (19:21); "And the Lord said to him: Go, descend, and
you shall come up, you and Aaron with you" (19:24); "And
Moses came down to the people" (19:25). But this circulation of
sense, this coming and going between above and below, does not
relate to Moses alone. God Himself "descends" to Mount Sinai:
"For on the third day the Lord will come down to Mount Sinai in
the sight of all the people" (19:11); "And all of Mount Sinai was
covered in smoke because the Lord had descended upon it in fire,
and the smoke rose up like the smoke of a furnace" (19:18); "And
the Lord descended upon Mount Sinai, on the top of the mountain" (19:20). As for the people, who are expressly forbidden to
climb the mountain (19:12–13, 15, 21–24), the text says that
"they assembled *at the foot* of the mountain" (19:17). The two
poles that define the space of Revelation thus remain clearly
distinct: the summit of the mountain (toward which God descends and Moses ascends) is contrasted to its base, where the
people camp. In the biblical text the distinction between high and
low creates a sacred space in which sense "descends," as if by
emanation, from God to men.

In Celan's poem this distinction is both maintained and abol-
ished: topologically, the dimension of height ("at torch-height")

is opposed to the dimension of depth ("deep in the glowing / empty-text," in "the time-hole"). But at the same time, the high and the low seem to vacillate. The Shofar sounds and the torches glow in "the empty-text," in "the time-hole," as if the experience transmitted here, from the poet to the reader, were that of someone who in effect "walked on his head," so that "the sky [is] an abyss beneath him."

IN THE biblical text the theophany on Sinai marks a moment of pause in the unfolding of the narrative. Description takes the place of narration, just as on the level of *fabula* (that is, of narrated events), the divine Revelation interrupts the people's wanderings in the desert. This stopping point in space corresponds to a stopping of time: the three days that precede the Revelation proper are first defined by God Himself (Exodus 19:10), and then by Moses, as an entity of sacred time. Revelation is separated from the unfolding of profane time, just as—during this period of three days—the space surrounding Mount Sinai appears as a sacred space. This cutting of space and rupture of time delimit a different kind of reality, through which absolute otherness can manifest itself. The biblical narrative itself thus tells us that interruption (or caesura) is the very condition for the constituting of sense: it is in the absence of narrative ("in the . . . empty-text") and the stopping of time ("in the time-hole") that divine speech may be heard. The "empty-text" and "time-hole" thus repeat, in Celan's poem, the suspension of space and time which, in the Bible, is the condition of Revelation.

But in Celan's poem an even more radical negativity is at the origin of the experience of Revelation. Here the suspension of the real and the rupture of continuity in space and time are not merely the conditions that permit human beings to receive divine speech and allow the harmonious procession of the transcendent wisdom from above to below. In Celan's poem, the Shofar—as a metonymy of Revelation—is located at the very bottom of the abyss. There, and not on the mountain's summit, its sounding makes itself heard; the height where the torches of Revelation glow appears at the bottom of this abyss:

| | |
|---|---|
| tief im glühenden | deep in the glowing |
| Leertext, | empty-text, |
| in Fackelhöhe, | at torch-height, |
| im Zeitloch | in the time-hole |

The Shofar's place would thus be far below, at the bottom of a text, in the rupturing of time. But this depth is also the place where the speaker of the poem can physically hear the sound, even if this perception passes, not only through the ear, but also through the mouth:

| | |
|---|---|
| hör dich ein | listen in |
| mit dem Mund | with the mouth |

If the Bible is indeed the "text" that is alluded to here, then the speaker would identify with the situation of the people, standing at the foot of Sinai. But this very identification would imply that the people drew the sounds of the Shofar, in some mysterious way, from the depths of their own mystical experience. The one who hears the sound of the Shofar is at the same time the one who blows, as if there were no other way to hear the sounds from above than to produce them oneself. In this sense Celan's poem, while referring to the biblical text, would radically reverse its traditional sense: in Celan's poem, Revelation is no longer an event that arrives from outside, descending from "above" to "be-low," so that man can be content to register it passively. On the contrary, as a being both speaking and listening, it is the speaker of the poem who engenders the blowing and who receives its echo in return.

From this point, another dimension of the poem seems to open up. The injunctive form of the last phrase, where the speaker in some way speaks to himself, shifts the poem from the level of *story* to that of *discourse*, that is to say from impersonal language to personal speech. The impersonal utterance of the first stanza is followed by an act of enunciation which implies the concrete presence of a subject situated *hic et nunc*, at a point in space and in a moment of time. Inscribed in the physical reality of the world, the speaking and listening subject attests to the fact that

for him "the trumpet place" designates not only the passage
where the word *Shofar* appears in a text, but also the point in
space where he physically perceives the sounding of the Shofar.
Six years before he wrote "Die Posaunenstelle," Celan had evoked
the Shofar in a poem of his book *Die Niemandsrose:*

—*Tekiah!*
wie ein Posaunenschall über Nächte hinweg in den Tag.

(—*Tekiah!*
like a trumpet blast across the nights into day.)[3]

*Tekiah,* the Hebrew word that signifies a prolonged sounding of a
wind instrument, designates in particular one of the three basic
sounds that compose the sounding of the Shofar in the Jewish
ritual of the New Year. In the poem just cited this term refers, by
metonymy, to the single occurrence in the cycle of the Jewish
liturgical year, when those who pray together, finding themselves
in the same situation as the people at the foot of Sinai, experience
the sounding of the Shofar. "The trumpet place" would then be
the moment of hearing the Shofar, the instant when, in the unfolding of the New Year's liturgy, the recitation of prayer is interrupted so that the sounding of the Shofar may be produced. "In
the . . . empty-text," in the gap of speech, in the pause of signification, the pure phonic essence of voice is heard in its originary
violence: a rasping of the breath which, beyond speech, nevertheless makes all speech possible. But this caesura of speech (in the
ongoing process of the liturgy) is itself the reflection or the repetition of a more general caesura of time, of a break through which
a radical otherness can manifest itself. Here the "time-hole" would
indicate the suspension of profane time for the sake of another
experience, that of the festival ritual. These are the same blanks
of time that Walter Benjamin, in his essay on Baudelaire, defines
as the precondition of authentic experience:

Chronology, which imposes its regularity upon duration,
cannot eliminate dissimilar, extraordinary fragments. To have
combined the recognition of a quality with the measurement
of quantity was the work of calendars, which, as it were, left
blank spaces of recollection, in the form of holidays.[4]

In the Jewish liturgical calendar, the New Year—like the other holidays, but in a more radical manner—stops time in order to let it begin anew. At the heart of this interruption of time, in the emptiness of an emptiness, the poem's subject calls upon himself to listen. But the sounding of the Shofar, on the day of the New Year, yields its meaning only against the horizon of the liturgical text which it interrupts; in turn, this text refers in multiple directions, and attests to the symbolic wealth of the Shofar ritual. Among the many meanings suggested by the New Year's liturgy, one refers directly to the episode of the Revelation at Sinai. In the third part of the Mussaf prayer, traditionally called *Shofarot* (*Shofars*), one finds the following passage:

> You revealed Yourself to Your people amid the cloud of Your glory, to speak to them. From heaven You caused them to hear Your voice, and revealed Yourself to them in clouds of purity. The whole world shook at Your presence, and the creatures of the beginning trembled before You. When You revealed Yourself, our King, on Mount Sinai, to teach Your people the law and the commandments, You made them hear the majesty of Your voice and Your holy work from amid flames of fire. With thunder and lightning you revealed Yourself to them, and in the voice of the Shofar You appeared to them, as it is written in Your Law: "And it came to pass on the third day, in the morning, that there was thundering and lightning, and a thick cloud upon the mountain, and the sound of a Shofar exceeding loud; so that all the people in the camp trembled." And it is said, "And the voice of the Shofar sounded louder and louder; Moses speaks, and God answers him with a voice." It is also said, "And all the people see the voices, the torches [lapidim], and the voice of the Shofar, and the smoking mountain; and the people saw and were shaken and stood far away."

This text is a montage of biblical citations and independent liturgical passages: the verses immediately preceding and following the Ten Commandments (Exodus 19:16, 19; 20:15) are introduced by a paragraph which, like the biblical verses themselves, emphasizes the correlation between auditory and visual perceptions in the experience at Sinai. The "flames of fire" and the "lightning" are associated with the "voices" and the sounding of the Shofar, just as in the voice that follows the Ten Commandments, "voices" are linked to "torches." If Celan's poem evokes a direct experience, as the last two verses suggest, it could be at once the acoustic experience of the Shofar's sounds ("hör dich ein / mit dem Mund") and the reading of the Mussaf prayer, which cites the biblical text on the sounding of the Shofar at the moment of the Revelation on Sinai:

| | |
|---|---|
| Die Posaunenstelle | The trumpet place |
| tief im glühenden | deep in the glowing |
| Leertext | empty-text, |
| in Fackelhöhe, | at torch-height, |
| im Zeitloch: | in the time-hole: |

In the New Year's liturgy, indeed, the blowing of the Shofar immediately follows the reading of the passage from the Mussaf prayer. The ritual unfolds on three parallel levels: the reading of the biblical text, the quotation of it within the text of the prayer, and the actual sounding of the Shofar. More precisely, these three levels relate to each other as do three concentric circles: the text of the prayer cites the biblical text which describes the sounding of the Shofar. As the quotation of a quotation, the sounding of the Shofar has its place "deep in the glowing/empty-text." But although this sounding seems to be separated from the speaker by the unfathomable distance hollowed out by a double remove, it comes to him as the most immediate experience, as a palpable reality that inscribes itself directly on his body:

| | |
|---|---|
| hör dich ein | listen in |
| mit dem Mund. | with the mouth. |

Between the speaker and "the trumpet place," the poem establishes a relationship consisting at once of unsoundable distance and extreme nearness. As in the perception of ambiguous, so-called "metastable" visual forms, the effect that impresses itself on the reader depends on the form (or in this case, the signifier) on which he fixes his attention. If emphasis is placed on the word "text," and if the central referent of the poem (the reality of which it speaks) is consequently the (biblical and liturgical) text, then the Shofar will be, in turn, nothing more than a remote word in the depths of the text. If emphasis is placed on the word "mouth," however, then the Shofar will be perceived in all its materiality, close to bodily experience; in this case, the word "Leertext" should not be understood as the emptiness of the text, the abyss at the bottom of which the word *Shofar* is buried, but as the "empty-text," that is to say the interruption in the text, that specific moment when prayer stops and the Shofar is blown. One could even go further and say that the word "empty-text" may designate the whole of the prayer. In that case, the speaker of the poem would be someone for whom the Hebrew text has lost its meaning; he may understand the words, but not the religious (or mythical) realities to which the words refer.

AS A material object, the Shofar has three distinct parts: the mouthpiece, the body of the instrument, and its bell. Celan's poem has the same structure, so that one may be tempted to see its linguistic structure as a reflection of the Shofar's material form. To a certain extent, then, the poem "Die Posaunenstelle" could be seen as an analogon of the object it evokes, as an "object-poem." It is framed between two substantives that designate objects—trumpets, the mouth—and delimit its formal space. In addition, the last word of the poem (the mouth) refers metonymically to one of the parts of the instrument denoted by the first word (trumpet), such that the poem's limits seem to be that of the instrument itself. Between these two extremities, the threefold repetition of the preposition *im/ in/ im*—the effect of which is reinforced by the accumulation of words denoting depth and emptiness ("tief," "Leer," "Loch")—sketches an emptied form, a hollow that links the two endpoints of the instrument. The same effect is produced on the phonological level by the distribution of vowels and consonants: the first and the last verses are characterized by the presence of rounded vowels ("Posaune," "Mund"). This effect is underscored in the last verse by the threefold repetition of the labial consonant m ("mit dem Mund"), whereas the middle verses are marked by the frequency of closed vowels ("glühenden," "höhe") and palatal and dental consonants ("glühend," "Leertext," "Zeitloch"). In addition, the threefold recur-

rence of *h*—"glühenden," "Fackelhöhe"—creates an effect of
aspiration, like that of the air passing through a tube. In the last
two verses, the breath that blows through the poem is relayed one
last time by the *h* of "hör dich ein," just before being exhaled in
two successive staccato sequences of three syllables:

hör dích eín        listen in

mít dém Múnd.    with the mouth.

Each of the three words in each of these last two verses is mono-
syllabic, thus reproducing in an almost mimetic manner the staccato rhythm (*Sh'varim,* in Hebrew) of one of the Shofar's soundings.

In the Jewish mystical tradition, the Shofar, as instrument of
Revelation, refers by metonymy to the structure of Revelation
itself. Its three parts designate the three steps of the process of
emanation by which divine Wisdom flows into the world. The
mouthpiece corresponds to the origin of the divine breath; the
body of the instrument corresponds to the process by which this
breath descends into the lower worlds; and the bell corresponds
to the transformation of breath into voice, that is, into an articulate series of sounds. At the same time, this mystical process
refers to the anthropological or organic transformation of ambient
air into human voice (as the physiological basis of speech). According to the logic of Jewish mysticism, this relation should not
be understood as metaphorical, but as properly metonymic. The
production of the human voice is not an image of Revelation, but
rather, on the level of human experience, it is Revelation itself.
Therefore, Celan's poem does not merely *represent* the image of
the Shofar. Even if such a representation is, in some way, inscribed in the linguistic structure of the text, the poem achieves
much more: it sets breathing in motion, and actualizes the process by which physical breath is transformed into human voice.

IN A letter to Walter Benjamin written during the summer of 1934,
Gershom Scholem observes that the world depicted in Kafka's
novels expresses "the Nothingness of Revelation."[5] What Scho-

lem means is that in our age of radical secularization the religious idea of Revelation, as it appears in the Bible, and as it has been accepted by Jewish tradition, seems to have lost all signification. Nevertheless, it has not totally faded away, and still constitutes —precisely through its absence—the background of some of the most characteristic intellectual trends of our time. It could be argued, indeed, that the preoccupation with negativity that is so typical of the philosophical and literary climate of the twentieth century points to the basic change of cultural paradigm which has been taking place in Western civilization since the Enlightenment. Through this ongoing process of secularization the fundamental religious categories transmitted by the Judeo-Christian tradition (such as Creation, Revelation, and Redemption) have become meaningless. But their very absence has opened a void which constitutes, in some way, the space in which modernity unfolds. For Scholem, this absence is exhibited in Kafka's work through linguistic and poetic forms of negativity.

In analyzing Celan's poem, I have tried to discover in it the structure of this "Nothingness of Revelation." The "text" to which the poem refers—whether it is the biblical story of Revelation or the Jewish prayer that quotes that story—appears to the speaker of the poem as an "empty" one; its original religious meaning no longer exists for him. But at the same time, the evocation of the Shofar in the semantic context of the biblical story and of its reduplication in the text of the prayer—as well as in the physical presence of the Shofar's sound—are reinterpreted as metonymies of poetic revelation, where the breath of inspiration ("hör dich ein") is transformed into a sequence of words exhaled through the poet's mouth ("mit dem Mund").

## Notes

1. Paul Celan, *Zeitgehöft: Späte Gedichte aus dem Nachlass* (Frankfurt am Main: Suhrkamp, 1976).

2. Paul Celan, *Der Meridian: Rede anlässlich der Verleihung des Georg-Büchner-Preises* (1961), in *Paul Celan: Gesammelte Werke* (Frankfurt am Main: Suhrkamp, 1983), 3:197.

3. The poem is "Es ist alles anders": Paul Celan, *Die Niemandsrose* (Frankfurt am Main: Suhrkamp, 1963).

# 9

# THE DISCOURSE
# OF A FIGURE:
# BLAKE'S "SPEAK SILENCE"
# IN LITERARY HISTORY
## Geoffrey H. Hartman

novum sidus addas
(Virgil, *Georgics*, 1:32)

IN BLAKE'S early "To the Evening Star"* there is a complexity
centering on "the metrical contract."[1] The poem is a sonnet in
blank verse and evokes, therefore, an ancient liberty recovered
from the bondage of rhyme, as Milton phrased it. But what ancient source of liberty does it allude to in so stylized a fashion? Is
it the classics, against which Blake will later fulminate in his
prefatory note to *Milton*? The title "To the Evening Star" could
point to the Greek Anthology: schoolboys did "versions" of a
Greek lyric about the evening star attributed to Bion or Moschus.
Or does Blake wish us to remember the poetical portions of
Hebrew Scripture? The opening poem of *Poetical Sketches*, "To
Spring," also in blank verse, echoes the Psalms and Song of
Songs.

There is no decisive clue. *Poetical Sketches*, as a whole, is the
workbook of a young poet. It elaborates, takes fire from, a subject
matter popular in the second half of the eighteenth century. So it
also contains native materials: ballads, songs, imitations of Spenser and Shakespeare, and it begins with a series of poems on the

* *Editors' note:* For the reader's convenience "To the Evening Star" is printed at
the end of this essay.

seasons. There is no sure evidence that Blake, at this point, was dividing up the muse into ideological and oppositional parts. The type of ancient liberty recovered cannot be exclusively typified as Hebrew or Classical or Nativist. Blake is eclectic; or he is syncretic in the sense of finding a metrical and thematic emblem that fuses these traditions. What is important is the linkage of poetry, or of the poetical genius, to a certain style, which may not be literally of the East, but has the Eastern pizzazz.

The historical question is made more interesting by comparing Blake's sonnet not only to other small poems on the evening star but to the one great English ode deriving from the same genre, and which had already transformed it: Collins' "To Evening" (the evening star appears formally in line 21). At first glance Collins has changed a Greek minor poem, an eidyllion, into an elaborate pseudo-Pindaric and Orientalizing ode. Yet whatever deceptions may be enacted on the level of style, the theme is focused on a poetics that would suit the West, its cooler and more temperate climate. The evening country or *Abendland*, while not identified exclusively as England, certainly includes that "western isle" and evokes a new magic of representation. A new music too, for meter is again of special interest. Though a quasi-divinity is addressed in Oriental fashion, the strophic form is not irregular Pindaric but a linked series of Horatian stanzas. Through Collins' "evening ear" a Greek or Eastern style blends with silver Latinity. And rhythmically there are no sudden transitions of mood or tempo: we approach night by the softest, most circumcuitous steps that imitate the descent of a "gradual, dusky veil." Collins' "Musing Slow" takes twenty processual verses to complete itself.

It is startlingly different, then, from Blake's lyric, and what affinity exists merely underlines the difference. Both poems, Blake's and Collins', are unrhymed; both have evening as their theme; and both have an extraordinary sense of meter and verbal music. Blake's verses, however, are without iffiness and hesitation. The "Thou" with which he begins is as intimate as it is lofty. Whereas Collins, in his exquisitely indirect form of address, and taking full advantage of the longer lyric form, delays the "Now" until the ninth and again the fifteenth line, Blake hits us with it in the very next verse. "Thou . . . Now." So intense, so frontal, is Blake's apostrophe that an illusion is created of rhyme moving from an end to an initial position.

Is it evening, then, that Blake has described? The first three lines leave an impression almost the reverse of that of Collins' veiling muse. The succession of the evening star to the sun is not a carefully graded movement from one power source to another: it is one torch lighting another, a contagion of fire. The evening star does not appear to be a lesser light at all but a sun risen upon the sun. "Now, while the sun rests on the mountains, light / Thy bright torch of love; thy radiant crown / Put on." The theme is evening, but Blake's poetical energy has transformed it into an emblem of dawn.

The new and milder tonality entering after line 3, "smile upon our evening bed," "wash the dusk with silver," is only incipiently a diminishment. For, as we move away from a sun displaced by the star's new and equal energy, we come upon the very center of the poem, on the strongest, most startling figure of speech Blake allows himself: "speak silence with thy glimmering eyes."

"Glimmering" retains the theme of evening light; but the force of the figure lies in the paradox "speak silence." This directs our attention to the creative, the logos-power of voice, so clearly in the poem from its first words, "Thou . . . Now," with their imperative, even imperious manner of speaking. It also directs us to something negative, "silence," that replaces voice as surely as the evening star the sun. What is the status of that "silence"?

The only East-West motion in Blake, comparable to Collins' Hesperian or twilight drift, is this displacement of heliocentric by logocentric. Despite mimetic tremors as twilight is evoked, this change is not seen as a loss but as a disclosure. Helios or light is subsumed by logos or voice as the procession from east to west reaches a new East, a new orientation. The remarkable figure "speak silence" intimates presence, not absence; even on the mimetic level, silence is a sign of love, of the presence of creatures to each other.

Yet Blake's climactic figure *is* followed by one precarious moment: "Soon, full soon / Dost thou withdraw. . . ." The star's withdrawal brings a short, stylized pause in which "wolf" and "lion" emerge from within the dark: creatures made, as it were, *of* the dark, and whose "glare" is a demonic equivalent of the light described in the previous lines. We approach here a dangerous phase close to power vacuum and mysterious void. Collins' "To Evening" never reaches nightfall; it proceeds so evenly that it stops short of a decisive *nox ruat*. The silence evoked by Blake's poem is now traversed by something akin to nightmare, a hollow and hellish state.

How do we interpret this "forest of the night," a void that fills up so fast with demonic shapes? Those familiar with later Blake may be alerted to his polemic against the idea of a creation *ex nihilo*, of a time when there was Nothing—an idea that according to one of his pronouncements causes the mind to become the habitation of unbelieving demons.[2]

The present poem, however, does not allow us to interpret the strange vacuum except in one respect. The phrase "Soon, full soon," is ambiguous: its obvious sense is "Soon, very soon," that is, too soon; but a second, simultaneous meaning is "being soon full, thou dost withdraw." This quick fullness, this rapid emergence and maturing, belong to the thematics of the evening star; and in a poet like Rilke is explicitly related to the swiftness with which love comes to birth and dies. At certain times of the year no sooner has the evening star risen over the horizon than it sets. In Blake's sonnet fullness is an attribute of star rather than moon; the moon, in "Soon, full soon," is present only as a spectral rime.

The "then" of line 11, therefore, which anticipates the next stage, does not point to a rising moon. There is no other light to take over. Blake's poem remains within the star's sphere of influence, whether by a constraint coming from the genre, or whether Blake modifies the Night Piece sequence in *Paradise Lost* (book 4, ll. 598–609) that presents the progression sunset, evening star, moon, as hierarchical and climactic:

> Now came still Ev'ning on, and Twilight gray
> Had in her sober Livery all things clad;
> Silence accompanied, for Beast and Bird,
> They to thir grassy Couch, these to thir Nests
> Were slunk, all but the wakeful Nightingale;

> She all night long her amorous descant sung;
> Silence was pleas'd: now glow'd the Firmament
> With living Sapphires: Hesperus that led
> The starry Host, rode brightest, till the Moon
> Rising in clouded Majesty, at length
> Apparent Queen unveil'd her peerless light,
> And o'er the dark her Silver Mantle threw.

Instead of a supervening, majestic moon, Blake offers a musical reprise: 'that fine rhythmic coda, "The fleeces of our flocks are cover'd with / Thy sacred dew: protect them with thine influence." "Influence" is used with the elegant ease of a poet who knows his classical clichés. Starlight and inspiration fall from the heavens, and remain on earth as evanescent dewdrops. From a very strong, imperious beginning, we have modulated, after all, into a final petitionary phase, impressive in its stabilizing rhythm and its ability to produce the proper word that effects closure and absorbs without canceling the darkling moment.

WHAT I have shown so far is that the difficulty of undoing hierarchy settles into the very frame of Blake's verses. The poem is about "stellar junk," as Wallace Stevens might have said. A notion of Oriental sublimity is maintained whose symbols or idols are in the heavens, so that the movement toward human affairs must seem to be descendental. Hierarchy, moreover, is associated with an intimation of procreative sleep, protection and peace. The heavenly marriage or coronation that begins the poem and averts the darkling moment is necessary to its pastoral ending, which revives a religious commonplace: "We are Thy flock." "Speak silence" remains a command, or the wishful demand for a command that would order all things this way. A nonbenevolent reader could see it as enjoining absolute obedience rather than describing the wordless effect of soothing light, or the understanding eyes of a person in love. The climate of harmony still rests on the possibility of a commanding word, which fills the air with silver or silence.

Why are the poet's eyes in the heavens, among the stars? Why that traditional *sursum cordis* or upward gaze? And must he find his voice also there, that is, an outmoded thesaurus of dictions that may strike the reader as pseudosublime? Blake is not Wordsworth; from the beginning he magnifies a Poetic Diction Wordsworth found offensive and wished to clean out. Yet we know that Blake was no less egalitarian, and perhaps more of a revolutionary, than the somewhat younger Wordsworth. I am not saying that Wordsworth did not have his own problem with the inherence of language in notions of hierarchy; but he did achieve for a time, and in a way that we recognize as innovative, a style that changed the course of poetry by appearing to be "natural," in the sense of creating the appearance of a humanizing dialogue between ourselves and our fellow creatures.

We do not feel the conflictual attitude toward hierarchy I have described, precisely because Blake's code is so exquisitely artificial, or because this small recovered genre, close to pastoral, overrides the sentiment of hierarchy by evoking a more terrible alternative: the "Nothing" that will threaten and animate his later poems, and which only absolute presence exorcizes. The line-end pauses gather, as it were, into a thematized darker pause which escapes the evening star's power. That space of time (ll. 8–11) cannot be assigned to another deity; it can only be *closed off* by a ritual and rhythmic coda.

In Blake's longer poems closure becomes as indefinite as in dreams or dream interpretation. A haunting sense of space constantly draws imagination into a vortex that feeds on itself without ever filling up. Blake blames "Natural Religion," intensified by Newtonian science, for imposing the image of space as a vacuum that cannot be filled—and science fiction with its endless, elaborating "Star Wars" is teaching us that lesson once again. Those star wars have already taken place in Blake. He knew better than our modern makers that space, inner or outer, was not to be domesticated by mighty machines and droll animals with synthesized voices. They merely replicate the fear they seek to allay. The dream of reason engenders *ex nihilo* monsters, or a theogony Blake labels "unprolific."

*The Book of Urizen* is his simplest effort to parody the genesis of Something out of a hypostatized Nothing:

.   .   .

> Some [of the Elohim] said
> "It is Urizen." But unknown, abstracted,
> Brooding secret, the dark power hid.

The mock-darkness of the name Urizen—it suggests horizon (boundary), Your Reason, and Your Risen—defeats the attempt to limit by speech the "shadow of horror . . . risen / In Eternity." Speech cannot displace vacuity with a firmament of its own. "The silence of those infinite spaces frightens me," Pascal said; from this perspective Blake's "speak silence" is an extraordinary gesture to humanize the inhuman ("abominable") void. By the figure "speak silence" he keys his entire poetic quest: the silence or darkness that has bred Urizen, or mystery-religion, is contradicted by a virtue implicit in poetic naming.

Yet the declarative "It is Urizen," obscured by the opacity (however playful) of the actual name, cannot be distinguished as a speech-act from "speak silence." In the first case, *coeli enarrent* quite literally; in the second, the heavens are ordered to speak. Both acts involve personification as an error basic to figurative language. The human voice, projecting speech into or onto a vacuum, involuntarily alienates itself and becomes sublime. The error has even penetrated the Bible and Milton, according to Blake. Blake's "Now," opening the second line of "To the Evening Star," is already charged with something urgent and nervous that alerts us to the horror of emptiness he ascribes to a faulty, ex-nihilating imagination. His sonnet anticipates the later quest for a figurative language that is figurative *and* not in error. Blake's Prophetic Books are on the way to that language. They argue that Scripture and Milton shadow forth something anterior: a once and future writing which undoes "the False Tongue! vegetated / Beneath your land of shadows" (*Milton*). Blake cleaves to the sublime diction of "The heavens declare the glory of God" in order not to drift further into those shadows. When he writes "The sky is an immortal tent builded by the Sons of Los" (*Milton*), he substitutes for creation *ex nihilo* an image of collective, gigantic labor still attached to earth. The line signals a human yet sublime, that is, unaccommodated, imagination.

. . .

AS A methodological device the virtue of this early, minor lyric is considerable. It raises the issue of the massiveness of *Milton, Jerusalem, Vala,* that one greater poem Blake was always rewriting. His multimembered epics convey an effect of what Dr. Johnson called sublimity by aggregation; and it is hard not to decompose them into lyric parts or passages. Their narrative thrust, which is as stylized and repetitive as the Book of Revelations, culminates in "Times are ended!" *(Night the Ninth),* yet intimates an indefinite series of catastrophes. In what poetic universe does "To the Evening Star," which one can hold in the palm of one's mind, equal Blake's "March of long resounding strong heroic verse" and its assault on the "Auricular Nerves"? Moreover, and this is a strictly parallel question, are there not features within this poem, however short, that challenge *its* perfection of form, *its* superstructure, in the same way as its own qualities of closure and genre can be marshaled against the hugeness of Blake's redundant and terrific scribbles?

I must admit that the way narrative collapses, or poetry condenses itself, has always fascinated me. I don't mean to devalue narrative and I certainly don't wish to suggest that there exists a quintessential aesthetic moment. At issue is the relevance of genre to reading, or *reading aright.* Reading cannot proceed without the conventions that govern genre and make it one of the more stable entities on the literary scene. Yet reading, while it contains a phase of "reading aright," also, as the archaism suggests, points to the fact that only a moment of pure anteriority could ground such rightness. To read Blake aright is to honor the insistence in him of a quest for an original language. Almost each place or state tries for a recovery; and one suspects that the poet's attraction to the apocalyptic cycles in the Book of Revelations is that they allow everything to begin again. Temporality is pure repetition: endless, serial verse turning toward a final state which might restore all things to their proper verbal and physical identity. The language spawned, or the writing-energy disseminated, by climactic episodes bursting like competitive fireworks, is remarkably self-subverting, not only because we know that there is no promised end but because the extraordinary textual surface they so massively create overshadows whatever sense their sequence has—a sense always less impressive than the continuous linguistic energy laboring, as in *Vala*, to purge yet fill Nine Nights that must dawn into "All human forms identified."

In what way, we might ask, thinking of Paul de Man, is Blake's rhetoric of apocalypse a rhetoric of temporality? Though Blake insists that poetry is vision, not allegory, how de Man describes allegory, after Walter Benjamin, fits the frustration, now mortifying and now productive, that impels the unwieldy longer poems. Yet what should interest us at this point is not another deconstructive conquest. We should evaluate the role of historical concepts in Blake, as in Hölderlin and Hegel, even if such concepts, which include that of genre, remain in the service of visionary schemes. Precisely because these concepts belong to the superstructure of poetry, they incisively raise the question of hierarchy and the persistence of a discourse of sublimity in writers whose temperament, sometimes even programmatically expressed, is revolutionary, not only in politics but in and through language. The rough and stubborn basement of English—the expression is Blake's own—is not superseded by the generic sublimity of his visionary drive; rather, it keeps reinstating linguistic particulars, fluid puns, and an often moving montage of tones, from mild to terrific.

IN TERMS of the starry code we have been deciphering, "speak silence with thy glimmering eyes" is an ingenious variant of "speak light," or "speak, light." The divine word—"A Voice to Light gave Being" (Wordsworth)—evokes in this instance a scene of love and rest that allows the softer passions to enter. It is as if Blake were gendering, engendering, "Eve" in his own way. Light becomes delight, "My shadow of delight," as he (fondly, one supposes) called his wife. One of the names of the evening star is Venus. It is difficult not to see a cliché behind the sublime trope. If the logos spoke and light was, it is also in the speaking eyes of lovers: "Drink to me also with thine eyes."

So our attempt to catch the resonances of this adolescent lyric may only result in demystifying its art. Yet demystification had already occurred, as Blake's "To the Muses," in the same collection, suggests. "The sound is forc'd, the notes are few!" Blake's

project is powered rather than subverted by a supposed eighteenth-century trivialization of poetry: he is the most unmystical
of mystics who takes the fallen or overdomesticated figures of a
residually sublime verse and gives them a restorative setting.

The question of speech for Blake—of true, communicative,
vehicular speech—was linked to the return "of the Poetic Genius
which is everywhere call'd the Spirit of Prophecy." This did not
always mean sounding off as if London were Jerusalem and Blake
Jeremiah. It meant reversing the decline of poetry by an effort to
"Awake the Dawn" (Psalm 108): the dawn of a new era of verse
and social prophecy, but also of a hyperbolic art associated with
the East, particularly with the Hebrew Bible.

We should remember that neoclassical verse was always adapting the exotic menagerie of Oriental expressions to the proportions of the English home, in which strangely shaped teapots
crowned rococo tables with crazy feet. ("And did those feet in
ancient time. . . ?") Blake's extravagance, especially in the long
poems, rejects a frozen nostalgia, parodied so exquisitely by Pope
("This casket India's glowing gems unlocks, / And all Arabia
breathes from yonder box"). That nostalgia placed sublimity and
beauty in the East. Blake's style reverses that proposition: the East
is wherever poetry is.

Blake's mock-Asiatic or archaizing style makes sense. Its reviv-
alist energy restores fallen figures to their splendor. Yet even as
we discover their transfigured conventional base (the logos, or
"Venus," or the theme of a recession of poetry) something is not
accounted for. One has to come to terms with the excess of trope
over topos, of motif over motivation. The figures are not subsumed by the discourse they provoke, and which frames them
into intelligibility.

Yet poetry does speak them, or make them perceptible; and
there is no reason to value their negative, excessive aspect over
the frame provided by poet or interpreter. What we must mini-
mally do is honor Blake's contention that in poetry as in perception we have given up too much. His lyric produces a tension
within the very idea of representation, so that perception approaches vision; rather, vision claims back its eyes. "If the doors

of perception were cleansed, everything would appear to man as it is, infinite" (*The Marriage of Heaven and Hell*).

Talking of eyes, that commanding figure "speak silence" could evoke the *ut pictura poesis* doctrine, which holds that a poem is like a picture, but one that speaks. An attractive cliché suggests itself that attaches this poem to an issue in poetics. Lend words to the mute medium of painting, Blake may be saying; capture the picture. Though a star is addressed, it is really the eyes that are addressed—the eyes of a star that appear as our own begin to be curtained.

If the *pictura poesis* theme evokes the representational power of poetry, the starry eye theme points to the pressure of vision on perception as sleep approaches. Yet at the very onset of such vision, that is, on the verge of sleep, Blake pauses. That pause coincides with the break in verse 10. Perhaps he does not wish to close his eyes in order to see? Must vision be a compensation involved in a calculus of loss and gain? He has gone from light to light; the poem as a whole, like many of the later Songs of Innocence, is a charm against night. For the night-eyes he needs are and are not eyes opened as in fear by the dream image of wolf and lion. Blake cannot neglect them, though they belong to the dark, for so much in his poetry will glare at us that way. He has no choice but to see with those spectral eyes; and when he finally dismisses the nightmarish style of his own Prophetic Books as a "delusive phantom," it has taken him Nine Nights and four thousand verses to do so. At the end of the *Four Zoas* he envisions night *with* day instead of *against* day:[3] "Man walks forth . . . His eyes behold the Angelic spheres arising night & day / The stars consumd like a lamp blown out & in their stead behold / The Expanding Eyes of Man behold . . . ." The first part of "To the Evening Star" is a song of innocence suggestive of expanding, vigilant eyes that do not need the dark light of dream vision.

WHAT IS excessive, you may feel by now, is not Blake's figures but my effort to gain intellectual control over them. These marvelous linguistic accidents, do they really fit into a discursive structure? Why not be satisfied to describe the poem as a series of images strung together musically, and by means of a strong central personification? The images, traditional or not, have an aura we could then ascribe to "pure poetry"—a notion that is far from silly. Valéry gave it serious play, and Benjamin analyzed the difficulty of aura in an age where images are mechanically reproduced rather than spontaneously repeated. Since we know that Blake's project was to recover their Adamic resemblance—anterior not only to eighteenth-century trivialization but even to Milton and the Bible—we could place that project into a sociopolitical context and consider Blake a fighter for aura against mechanical image, word, and page.

I want to conclude in a less speculative manner. Even though Blake thinks that he is closer to the Bible than the Bible, that book is as far East as he textually gets. His poetry always looks *through* Scripture. If "speak silence" has a matrix in eighteenth-century *ut pictura poesis* doctrine and its encouragement of picturesque personification, it has a more significant matrix in the Bible.

I come back to Psalm 19, the *locus classicus* of all sky poems: "The heavens declare the glory of God." The psalm's second verse expands that declaring into a cosmic conversation: "Day unto day uttereth speech, and night unto night showeth knowledge." But the psalm's third verse has been a puzzle to commentators. It reads, verbatim: "No speech nor language, their voice is not heard." The King James Bible glosses over the apparent retraction or contradiction by amending a supposed ellipsis: "*There is* no speech nor language *where* their voice is not heard." This remedial move harmonizes with the psalm's fourth verse: "Their line is gone out through all the earth, and their words to the end of the world. . . ."

It is not possible (we can imagine the translators saying) that the Author of Scripture should be putting his own way of speaking in doubt and cautioning us that his figures are merely figures. They would surely have approved of Blake's proverb: "If the Sun & Moon should doubt / Theyd immediately Go out." Their solution was to posit and then fill a lexical space. Blake's solution takes a more daring form of this filling up. His "speak silence" represents the verbatim meaning of verse 3 together with this energetic intervention of the translators. A silence (lacuna) in the verse compels them to speak that silence—that is, to restore the sublime figure of sky or cosmos confessing God's glory.

Thomson, author of The Seasons, a famous series of nature descriptions that prompt the opening lyrics of Blake's Poetical Sketches, ventures his own variation of "speak silence" in a hymn added to his poem: "Come, then, expressive Silence, muse His Praise." The need for "expressive Silence" was the greater because of Newton's challenge to the Muse. He saw, Thomson writes of Newton, "The Whole in silent harmony revolve."[4] The untuned, silent sky was restored by Newton to a kind of harmony —that holistic vision of cosmic space Newtonian science aspired to. We recall at this point that Blake conducted a fierce and stupid yet morally exhilarating polemic against Newton: "May God us keep / From Single vision and Newtons sleep!" It was always for him Newton against Milton, or Milton against the Newton in Milton.

"Speak silence" captures in a single but far from sleeping phrase this Blakean polemic. For the line does not actually read "speak silence" but, unedited, "speak si[l]ence."[5] The missing l allows us, obliges us, to fill a silence, to pronounce a silent letter, and in two ways rather than a single way. If the missing letter is indeed l, Blake is playing a joke on us, by silencing performatively that l—just as linguistic process has made both the l and the p unvoiced in the word psalm.

This jocular performative makes good sense: it reminds us of the linguistic basis of all figuration, it brings us from the sky down to earth and to the stubborn basement of English as a system of signs, riddling rather than readable. It thus throws a doubt, after all—though a high-spirited one—on the skyey symbolism Blake is refusing to give up. But the phrase in its unedited version could also be construed as "speak s[c]ience."[6] In that form it would allude to the knowledge (natural philosophy) or the religion (natural theology) that science draws from the stars, but which Blake's poetry overgoes.[7] Blake makes a claim here for a science (a mode of representation) that belongs to poetic perception as such, and does not presuppose a Newtonian or biblical power vacuum in which creation supposedly took place. His

## TO THE EVENING STAR

Thou fair-hair'd angel of the evening,
Now, while the sun rests on the mountains, light
Thy bright torch of love; thy radiant crown
Put on, and smile upon our evening bed!
Smile on our loves; and, while thou drawest the
Blue curtains of the sky, scatter thy silver dew
On every flower that shuts its sweet eyes
In timely sleep. Let thy west wind sleep on
The lake; speak si[l]ence with thy glimmering eyes,
And wash the dusk with silver. Soon, full soon,
Dost thou withdraw; then the wolf rages wide,
And the lion glares thro' the dun forest:
The fleeces of our flocks are cover'd with
Thy sacred dew: protect them with thine influence.

## Notes

1. For the concept of such a contract between writer and reader, see John Hollander, *Vision and Resonance: Two Senses of Poetic Form* (New York: Oxford University Press, 1975).

2. "Many suppose that before *[Adam]* (the Creation) All was Solitude & Chaos This is the most pernicious Idea that can enter the Mind as it takes away all sublimity from the Bible & Limits All Existence to Creation & to Chaos To the Time & Space fixed by the Corporeal Vegetative Eye & leaves the Man who entertains such an Idea the habitation of Unbelieving Demons"; from Blake's Catalogue of Pictures for the Year 1810, *The Poetry and Prose of William Blake*, ed. David V. Erdman (Garden City, N.Y.: Doubleday, 1965) p. 552. All Blake quotations are from this edition.

3. That the evening star is also the morning star helps this perspective.

4. Shelley will write in *The Daemon of the World* (ll. 247–52): "The circling systems formed / A wilderness of harmony. / Each with undeviating aim / In eloquent silence through the depths of space / pursued its wondrous way."

5. See the definitive edition of Erdman (cited above).

6. The Biblia Vulgata renders "knowledge" as "scientia" in Psalm 19's second verse: "nox nocti indicat scientiam."

7. The *locus classicus* for this science or supplementation is a "Lucretian" moment in Virgil's *Georgics* (2:478ff): "Teach me [O Muses] to know the paths of the stars in heaven," etc., which modulates into a less glamorous theme, that of love of rivers and woods. The poems on the seasons with which the *Poetical Sketches* open derive from the "Georgic" tradition mediated by Thomson. In this spirit Blake's poem discloses "a new sign in the Zodiac" (*Georgics*, book 1, l. 32).

# 10

# UNDER THE SIGN OF LOSS: A READING OF FAULKNER'S *THE SOUND AND THE FURY*
## Shlomith Rimmon-Kenan

"THE SPOON came back to my mouth"; "The spoon came up"; "the bowl went away" (p. 30); "the flowers came back" (p. 55); "the candles went away" (p. 57); "A long piece of wire came across my shoulder. I went to the door, and then the fire went away" (p. 57); "the cushion went away. . . . Then the cushion came back" (p. 63).[1] Syntactically, these examples (and many others) are characterized by the use of inanimate objects as subjects of active verbs and the deletion of the human agent who (we assume on the basis of conventional reality models) must perform the action. In the spirit of Leo Spitzer, I would like to suggest that such a use of language, seeming to give objects an independent existence, dissociating the doer from the deed and disintegrating the causal chain, is a miniature reflection of the fragmentation that dominates Benjy's physical and psychic makeup as well as the structure of his section of the novel.

Nor is this the only form of fragmentation in Benjy's section. With Spitzer again in mind, consider the following sentences: "her hand went away" (p. 17); "a head came out" (p. 57); "I ate some cake. Luster's hand came and took another piece" (*ibid.*); "Mother's hand came into the firelight. Her rings jumped on Caddy's back" (p. 61); "My hand jerked back. . . . My voice was going loud every time. . . . My hand was trying to go to my mouth" (p. 59). By isolating parts from the whole, the language expresses Benjy's defective perception of the totality of both other people and himself; a state of affairs that—according to Lacan—

characterizes a lack of subjecthood. In his almost mythical account of the "mirror stage," Lacan conceives of the formation of
identity in three stages: recognition of the other, recognition of
the other as self, and recognition of the other as self but other. A
mirror stage gone wrong causes a partial identification which
Lacan calls *le corps morcelé*.[2] Benjy's perception is not only at
the level of "the body in pieces," but also distorts mirror images.
Thus he repeatedly fails to grasp the sameness and difference
between the image in the mirror and the person or object outside
it: "There was another fire in the mirror" (p. 61); "The fire went
out of the mirror" (p. 61); "Caddy and Jason were fighting in the
mirror and Father put me down and went into the mirror and
fought too" (p. 64); "He [Jason] rolled into the corner, out of the
mirror. Father brought Caddy to the fire. They were all out of the
mirror. Only the fire was in it. Like the fire was in a door" (p. 64).

True, Benjy's failure to see the reflection in the mirror as different from but also identical to what it reflects concerns other
people and objects, not himself. But this failure seems to me to
entail a failure in establishing an identity of the self, for it is in
others that the infant first sees an image of a totality and only
later, in the mirror stage, in himself. The others are, in a sense,
the first mirror available to an infant. An unintegrated vision of
them in the mirror therefore seems to imply an unintegrated
image of the self, and Benjy's use of synecdoches for both others
and the self would seem to confirm this. Indeed, the image of the
"body in pieces" is clinched in *The Sound and the Fury* by
Benjy's physical dismemberment through castration (pp. 53–54,
71, 225) as well as by the textual dismemberment of his narrative
as a result of the frequent temporal shifts which break the totality
into fragments.

Benjy's physical castration not only reflects his psychic fragmentation (or lack) but also represents the loss (death?) of something he once had. Jason retrospectively muses upon Benjy's loss
of that which he hardly knew he had: "I often wondered what
he'd be thinking about, down there at the gate, watching the girls
going home from school, trying to want something he couldn't
even remember he didn't and couldn't want any longer" (p. 255).
Loss, I think, is as central to Benjy's narrative as the congenital

lack manifested by the fragmentation discussed so far. Indeed, a reexamination of the opening quotations will show that while their syntax enacts fragmentation, their lexis, concerned as it is with going and coming (e.g., "the spoon came up," "the bowl went away"), emphasizes the experience of loss and attempts at retrieval.

Within a narrative present which unfolds fragments of Benjy's wandering with Luster in search of a lost quarter, Benjy's memory moves back and forth among various experiences of loss: loss of people who die—Damuddy, Quentin, Mr. Compson, Roskus; loss of the mother who in a sense dies long before her actual death, being constantly ill, confined to her room, protecting herself against contact with her children; and above all, loss of Caddy.

Caddy becomes a mother substitute for Benjy, who is emotionally rejected by his real mother: "You don't need to bother with him," she says to Mrs. Compson, "I like to take care of him. Don't I, Benjy" (p. 63). She is also associated with the natural elements —the trees, the leaves, the rain—with which Benjy, the Natural, has a special affinity. Benjy's dyadic unity with this sister-mother-nature is disturbed by intrusions of which he becomes aware in flashes, fragmented episodes, the implications of which he intuits without understanding. First, there is Caddy's use of perfume which—for Benjy—contaminates her with an alien, artificial element, causing him to cry and shrink from physical contact with her. Only when she washes the perfume away with water does the real Caddy return, smelling like trees once more (p. 44). Though Benjy has no words to express this sensation of separation and reunion, Caddy guesses the meaning of the episode for him: "Did you find Caddy again. . . . Did you think Caddy had run away. . . . Caddy's not going away" (p. 44).

The perfume episode is followed in the text by another separation scene, the contiguity between the two emphasizing their similarity as two versions of loss. Upon reaching his thirteenth birthday, Benjy has to start sleeping alone: "You a big boy," Dilsey explains to him, "Caddy tired sleeping with you" (p. 46).

Benjy's encounter with Caddy and Charlie in the swing is the next stage in the drama, explicitly introducing a separating third party, which was only implicit in the perfume scene (somebody

—probably a man—must have given her the perfume, though it is not clear whether Benjy is capable of establishing such a causal connection). Benjy instinctively holds on to Caddy's dress (a metonymy of her femininity) and tries to pull her away. As in the earlier scenes, the reunion occurs when Caddy expels the intrusive element, by washing her mouth at the sink and, thus purified, once more smells like trees.

From the use of perfume to a kiss on the swing to the actual loss of virginity: a progression in Caddy's relations with men and an intensification of Benjy's sensation of losing his sister. This time it is she who shrinks from physical contact with Benjy. He cries and pulls at her dress as before, but there is no brother-sister reunion in this scene.

The absence of reunion is even stronger in the scene of Caddy's wedding. Here, the recurrent tree image is used negatively: "and Caddy put her arms around me, and her shining veil, and I couldn't smell trees any more and I began to cry" (p. 43). The textual sequence emphasizes the irreversibility of the wedding scene by making Benjy's memories of it alternate with his recollections of Damuddy's death, implicitly equating the two.[3]

But Benjy does not accept this finality. Just as in the earlier episodes of partial loss he tried to prevent separation by clutching at Caddy's dress, so after the wedding he tries to recapture her by clinging to metonymies and synecdoches. He is riveted to the gate through which Caddy has disappeared, as if his proximity to this inanimate object could bring her back. Here we can rely on T. P.'s explanation: "You can't do no good looking through the gate, . . . Miss Caddy done gone long ways away. Done got married and left you. You can't do no good, holding to the gate and crying. She can't hear you. . . . He think if he down to the gate, Miss Caddy come back" (p. 52).[4] And the only thing that can calm him is Caddy's slipper, which becomes a kind of fetish for him (e.g., pp. 60, 70). His pitiful attempt at recuperation is thus characteristically a form of fragmentation: the slipper, a part of the whole, comes to replace the whole. Ironically, this is Caddy's *wedding* slipper, hence an object associated with the scene of separation and incapable of becoming an agent of recuperation.

Moreover, as Matthews points out, the problem with the objects Benjy fixes on is that "they are just barely separated from the body of the beloved" (p. 67) and therefore cannot reappropriate the lost presence on a different level. Nor is Benjy capable of regaining the lost Caddy at the level of language. Charlie realizes how limited Benjy is because he "can't talk" (p. 49); Caddy intuits his need to resort to body language—clinging, bellowing, etc.—instead of words: "And you were trying to tell Caddy and you couldn't tell her" (p. 44); and in the sexual assault on the Burgess girl Benjy himself experiences most powerfully the frustration of having no access to language:

> I was trying to say, and I caught her, trying to say, and she screamed and I was trying to say and trying and the bright shapes began to stop and I tried to get out. (pp. 53–54)

Not only is Benjy, as Matthews writes, barred from "the more consoling, more dangerous powers of speech" (p. 64), but his action-language dooms him to castration, and—if Matthews is right in seeing the assault on the girl as an attempt to recapture Caddy (p. 72)—the scene only repeats the initial loss, thereby emphasizing the hopelessness of repossession.

The hopelessness of repossession is not confined to Benjy's part of *The Sound and the Fury*. Throughout the novel, Faulkner explores lack, loss, and the failure to fill the vacuum, whether through object substitution or through language. An examination of the ways in which other characters experience the same predicament will occupy the remainder of this paper.

A BROTHER's loss of Caddy through Caddy's loss of virginity is even more central in Quentin's section than it is in Benjy's. The actual loss of virginity and related events are recalled six times in Benjy's section (only two of which refer to the defloration scene itself), and Caddy's wedding five times.[5] In Quentin's section, on the other hand, Caddy's loss of virginity is mentioned forty times (as well as three additional related events); the eve of her wedding twenty-three times; and the wedding itself, six. There seems to be no doubt that this is the central obsession in Quentin's mind. I would like to suggest, however, that this obsession screens a more central one, of which it is the inverted mirror, namely

Quentin's inability to lose his own virginity. It is this inability
that compels him to reproduce, both in the narrative present and
in memories of the past, scenes of impotent competitions with
various "sister stealers," and these repetitions, providing no mastery, reinforce the sense of inescapable entrapment. What he does
finally lose is not his virginity but, tragically, his life.

That men are more preoccupied with their own virginity than
women are with theirs is asserted by Mr. Compson in one of his
generalizations: "In the South you are ashamed of being a virgin.
Boys. Men. They lie about it. Because it means less to women,
Father said. He said it was men invented virginity, not women"
(p. 75). That Quentin's particular preoccupation with this is aggravated by his sister's loss of virginity is suggested both by
Caddy and by Quentin himself. "You've never done that have
you," Caddy asks (p. 137). And in the conversation with Mr.
Compson, Quentin says: "Why couldn't it have been me and not
her who is unvirgin" (p. 75).

Quentin's inability to either lose or accept his virginity generates two opposed fantasies: the fantasy of self-castration and the
fantasy of incest:

> Versh told me about a man mutilated himself. He went into
> the woods and did it with a razor, sitting in a ditch. A
> broken razor flinging them backward over his shoulder the
> same motion complete the jerked skein of blood backward
> not looping. But that's not it. It's not not having them. It's
> never to have had them then I could say O That That's
> Chinese I don't know Chinese. (p. 107)

While Benjy's castration was cruelly imposed upon him, Quentin
contemplates a self-inflicted castration, but soon realizes that
losing is not good enough, because—I suppose—a memory of
desire, or of the lost potential, might linger. Indeed, the lingering
of desire leads him to fantasize the opposite scenario: not only
will he lose his virginity like Caddy, but he will lose it with her:
"I have committed incest I said Father it was I it was not Dalton
Ames" (p. 76), and to Caddy herself: "You thought it was them
but it was me" (p. 135).[6] He also urges Caddy to escape with him

on his school money (pp. 114, 137), thus casting himself in the role of a husband of sorts.

But Caddy does not run away with him. She escapes on her own, and her loss of virginity is forever associated in his mind with her disappearance: "one minute she was standing in the door" (pp. 76, 83, 86, 114, 137, and elsewhere). For Quentin, as for Benjy, there is no recuperation, only reproduction, repetition of Caddy's loss, and his loss of her.

The effect of repetition is created by analogies among various love scenes. Taking these in their chronological story-order, we begin with the episode between Quentin and Natalie which, though undated, seems to precede Caddy's loss of virginity and Quentin's jealousy of her lovers.[7] This scene of "dancing sitting down" (p. 123) becomes analogous to various encounters between Quentin and Caddy, thus making Quentin's failed sexual attempt with Natalie an anticipation of his relations with Caddy. Natalie is far from keen, but Quentin persists: "She turned her back. I went around in front of her" (p. 125), exactly as he does with Caddy: "I got in front of her again" (p. 140). In spite of Quentin's persistence, both women remain unyielding and Quentin retains his virginity. Slapping takes place with both women and is similarly described in the narrative, although an interesting reversal occurs: while Natalie hits Quentin—"her fingers going into my face" (p. 125)—it is Quentin who slaps Caddy—"red print of my hand coming up through her face" (p. 122)—for kissing a boy. Water is another link between the Quentin-Natalie and the Quentin-Caddy scenes. Just as Quentin and Natalie get soaked by rain, so Quentin tries to make love to Caddy when he finds her drenched from floating in the water.[8]

For a moment in the linear reading the analogy between Natalie and Caddy seems to become a full interchangeability. Here is the quotation from the Natalie scene:

> It was raining we could hear it on the roof, sighing through
> the high sweet emptiness of the barn.
> > There? touching her
> > Not there

There? not raining hard but we couldn't hear anything
but the roof and as if it was my blood or her blood
   She pushed me down the ladder and ran off and left me
Caddy did .
   Was it there it hurt you when Caddy did ran off was it
there (p. 123)

A few lines later it transpires (to the extent that anything transpires in this purposefully confusing text) that, seeing Quentin
with Natalie, Caddy tried to interfere, pushing Natalie down the
ladder, but for a fleeting moment it seems as if Quentin is describing a scene in which Natalie or Caddy—a kind of strange composite of both—pushed him down the ladder.

   If Caddy did intervene between Quentin and Natalie, then a
triangular relationship is present from the start, though here it is
the reverse of the recurrent situation where Quentin is the one
who comes between his sister and a lover. Several motifs are
repeated in the different triangles, the basic configuration being
set up by the Caddy–Dalton Ames–Quentin scene: a physical
fight, though in this particular case Quentin faints "like a girl" (p.
147) without even giving Ames the chance of hitting him back;
Quentin's persistent question, "did you ever have a sister did
you" (to which Ames answers, "no but they are all bitches," p.
145); and the contrast between Quentin's tragic view of Caddy's
loss of virginity and her lover's indifference to it (and often to
Caddy herself). Here is Dalton Ames: "listen no good taking it so
hard its not your fault kid it would have been some other fellow"
(p. 145).

   Unlike the fight with Ames, the contest with Herbert is verbal,
not physical, but a suggestion of physical violence hovers through
the image of shooting: "Quentin has shot Herbert he shot his
voice through the floor of Caddy's room" (p. 98). Although Herbert does express passion for Caddy, together with jealousy of
Quentin, whom he never imagined to be a brother ("she couldn't
have talked about you any more if you'd been the only man in the
world husband wouldn't have been in it" [p. 100]), like Ames he
shows complete indifference to the question of her virginity: "of
course a young fellow like you would consider a thing of that sort

a lot more serious than you will in five years. . . . I wasn't the first or the last" (p. 100).

If Ames and Herbert are part of Quentin's memories of the past, Julio belongs to the narrative present. Unlike Ames, Julio does have a sister, the little Italian girl whom Quentin, having Caddy on his mind, also calls "sister" ever since their first meeting in the bakery. And unlike Ames and Herbert, Julio does care about the question of honor. Thus he accuses Quentin of stealing his sister (p. 127), and there follows a physical quarrel in which—unlike Ames—Julio does hit Quentin.

Immediately after the physical altercation with Julio, there is a violent scene with Gerald who, diametrically opposed to Quentin, keeps boasting of his success with women and his indifference to them (e.g., p. 151). As with Ames, Quentin asks Gerald the poignant question, "Did you ever have a sister? did you" (p. 151)—"sister" becoming at this point a compound of Caddy and the little Italian girl—and when Gerald, like Ames, answers in the negative, Quentin hits him. This time, as with Julio, Quentin does get "bloodied up" (p. 150)—like a woman losing her virginity?—as a result.

The analogies between the scenes and the sense of repetition they generate are apparent even in the story-order I have reconstructed from the novel. But the text does not unfold in this chronological manner, and the temporally disjointed textual continuum increases the effect of sameness through a contiguity between analogous episodes. Thus the alternation between the walk with the Italian girl in the narrative present and Quentin's memories of the love scene with Natalie as well as of his attempt to seduce Caddy (pp. 122–23) superimposes the three women, suggesting an endless recurrence of the same. A parallel superimposition of the men is created by the sequence between the quarrel with Julio in the narrative present and memories of the scene with Dalton Ames in the past (pp. 135–47), as well as by the contiguity between Quentin's present thoughts about Gerald's treatment of women and the evocation of Dalton Ames and the loss of virginity, then of Herbert and the wedding eve (p. 98). Seemingly opposed to these is the alternation between Quentin's

walk with the Italian girl and his memories of Caddy's loss of
virginity and of the eve of her wedding. Here there seems to be a
contrast between the past in which he desperately clung to Caddy,
who pushed him away (p. 123), and the present, in which he
gives the little girl a quarter and tries to get rid of her (p. 122).
Such a reversal of roles could suggest a mastery of a traumatic
experience: he who was rejected by Caddy now rejects the little
girl. But behind this apparent contrast in Quentin's position there
is a latent similarity: even after parting from the girl, Quentin
does not really go away; he keeps watching her every movement
and then rejoins her until they are separated by Julio.

Perhaps strongest in its effect of superimposition is the sequence between memories of Quentin's scene with Caddy after
his quarrel with Ames and the narration of the aftermath of the
fight with Gerald in the narrative present, this scene itself following the altercation with Julio. Untypically, there is no typographical demarcation of a temporal shift here, nor is there a transition
between the episodes. Moreover, the pronoun "it" can refer ana-
phorically to the scene with Caddy and cataphorically to what
first seems the fight with Julio and is then revealed to be the
episode with Gerald:

> her [Caddy's] blood surged steadily beating and beating
> against my hand
>   It kept on running for a long time, but my face felt cold
> and sort of dead, and my eye, and the cut place on my finger
> was smarting again. I could hear Shreve working the pump.
> (p. 149)

The "it" first seems to refer to Caddy's surging blood and only
subsequently—through the mention of Shreve—do we realize
that the pronoun refers to Quentin's blood, spilt by Gerald. Ames,
whose name made Caddy's blood beat in her throat, Julio, who
seems to be the cause of Quentin's injury, and Gerald, who actually is, are all superimposed in this segment.

In such superimpositions sameness overrides difference, providing no mastery or recuperation, inevitably leading to death.[9]
Interestingly, virginity and death are linked in The Sound and
the Fury not only through repetition. Mr. Compson says that

virginity, like death, is "only a state in which others are left" (p. 75), a comment invested with poignant irony in retrospect, when we know that Quentin is indeed left in both. Virginity, to Mr. Compson, is no more than a word: "It's nature is hurting you not Caddy and I said That's just words and he said So is virginity" (p. 107). Death, to Quentin, is similarly reduced to language: "And then I'll not be. The peacefullest words. Peacefullest words. *Non fui. Sum. Fui. Non sum*" (p. 157).[10] Although Quentin's intention may not be reductive, his language does in fact reduce death to words and—moreover—Latin, bygone words. It is again Mr. Compson who links such reductions to the iterative nature of language and, consequently, of human experience: "On the instant when we come to realize that," he says, "tragedy is second hand" (p. 107).

The loss of virginity, like its retention, is associated with death, both in Caddy's "I die for him [Ames] over and over again every time this goes" (p. 137) and in Quentin's attempt to seduce Caddy, where the knife has both sexual and morbid overtones (p. 138).[11] Characteristically, Caddy loses her virginity and "dies" in a life embrace, whereas Quentin's incapacity to lose his, tragically culminates in the most overwhelming loss of all—the surrender of his life to "Little Sister Death" (p. 73).

ONE QUENTIN commits suicide and another Quentin—a girl, named after him—comes to life in the Compson family. Born under the sign of loss, she seems to serve as a substitute for her absent mother and dead uncle, but her life becomes a repetition—not a recuperation—of theirs.

Quentin's parents are absent from the start. Her father's identity is known to no one, not even her promiscuous mother (pp. 107, 177, 199, 233), and the mother—having been cast away by her husband as well as by her own mother—has to let the latter (herself an "absent" character) take care of the baby. Quentin's name is that of a dead person, and her mother's name is supposedly dead to her: "She must never even learn that name," says Mrs. Compson, "If she could grow up never to know that she had a mother, I would thank God" (p. 179). Quentin's contact with the absent Caddy is limited to the checks that she needs to receive for her own purposes but which are no substitute for a mother's love: "Dilsey, I want my mother," she says at a particulary difficult juncture with Jason (p. 167). Not only is money an inadequate compensation for the mother's absence, but this compensation itself does not always reach Quentin, finding its way to Jason's safe, after being deceitfully given to his mother to burn as an expression of her pride.

For Quentin, then, as for her uncle, there is no real recuperation of the lost object. Instead, as with her uncle (though perhaps less strongly), her life becomes a repetition—expressed in the text by analogies—of the lives of both the absent Caddy and the dead Quentin. Like Caddy, Quentin sits with her lover in the swing, an analogy emphasized by the textual sequence in Benjy's section (p. 48). Nor is this an isolated incident. Quentin, characterized by Jason as "running about the streets with every drummer that comes to town" (p. 205), proves to be as promiscuous as her mother. Drawing this analogy between mother and daughter, Jason recalls a specific incident in Caddy's youth in which Mrs. Compson's behavior already betrays the same whining impotence that will be evident in her attitude to Quentin:

> I says, because how the hell can I do anything right with that damn family and her [Mrs. Compson] not making any effort to control her [Quentin] nor any of them, like that time she happened to see one of them kissing Caddy and all the next day she went around the house in a black dress and a veil and even Father couldn't get her to say a word except crying and saying her little daughter was dead. (p. 105)

And the analogy between Caddy's disappearance and Quentin's elopement is underscored by Benjy's constant bellowing on both occasions.

But Quentin does not only resemble her mother; to Mrs. Compson, at least, she also recalls her uncle: "Like uncle, like niece. Or mother. I don't know which would be worse. I don't seem to care" (p. 266), and: "But she has inherited all the headstrong traits. Quentin's too. I thought at the time with the heritage she would already have, to give her that name, too. Sometimes I think she is the judgment of Caddy and Quentin upon me" (p. 232). The analogy becomes particularly strong in Mrs. Compson's mind when her granddaughter elopes with her lover: "Find the note. . . . Quentin left a note when he did it. . . . I knew the minute they named her Quentin this would happen" (p. 251). But "this" does not happen. Unlike her uncle, Quentin does not commit suicide, and however miserable her life with (or without) her latest lover may prove to be, she has at least opted for life and for an escape from the kind of repetition imposed on her at home. Perhaps she has only substituted one form of repetition for another, but this can be no more than speculation, since the novel does not follow Quentin into her future.

QUENTIN'S ESCAPE with the "stolen" money, and—in fact—Quentin herself, is for Jason the symbol of what he considers the central loss in his life:

> Of his niece he did not think at all, nor of the arbitrary valuation of the money. Neither of them had had entity or individuality for him for ten years; together they merely symbolized the job in the bank of which he had been deprived before he ever got it. (p. 271)

The job in the bank is the one Herbert promised Jason while courting Caddy, a job lost as soon as Herbert cast Caddy away for being pregnant with Quentin, somebody else's child. Thus the loss of Caddy (for whom Jason, unlike his brothers, had no particular love)[12] entails the loss of the job but also, ironically, the presence of Quentin. For the loss of a job involving money, Jason tries to compensate by playing with money on the stock exchange and, more specifically, by stealing the money intended for Quentin, the symbol of his loss. This explains his rage when he is robbed of the money he himself stole for that purpose: "But to have been robbed of that which was to have compensated him for the lost job, which he had acquired through so much effort and risk, by the very symbol of the lost job itself, and worst of all, by a bitch of a girl" (p. 272). The analogy between Jason's dealings with the stock exchange and his chasing of Quentin is emphasized by their alternation in the text continuum (e.g., p. 209) as well as by his fury when both seem to deceive him. Thus, Jason responds to loss by resorting to the language of money, but he fails in his financial affairs just as he fails in finding Quentin and in securing the desired job.

It seems to me, however, that behind the loss which Jason sees as governing his life, there is a more fundamental lack which leads both to the hoarding of money and to the persecution of Quentin: a lack of human warmth and of sexual potency. "You's a cold man, Jason, if man you is," says Dilsey, "I thank de Lawd I got mo heart dan dat, even ef hit is black" (p. 187). And Caddy: "You never had a drop of warm blood in you" (p. 227). Thus, for example, he prefers burning two free tickets to the show rather than give one of them to Luster who is craving to go (p. 227). Sexuality is connected in his imagination either with filth or with money. Thus he visualizes Quentin with her lover in terms that recall Iago's description of Othello and Desdemona "making the beast with two backs" (I,i,l.115). Of course, Quentin is no Desdemona, but Jason's thoughts about her love-making tell us at least as much about him as about her: "I'm afraid all the time I'll run into them right in the middle of the street or under a wagon on the square, like a couple of dogs" (p. 234). His own "love-life" is confined to his "commercial" relationship with his whore Lorraine, where money compensates for the absence of feeling and bribes the other into expecting nothing beyond the limited time of "togetherness." Proudly, Jason formulates the principle behind his behaviour with women: "I never promise a woman anything nor let her know what I'm going to give her. That's the only way to manage them" (p. 174). Somewhat less proudly, he recalls Lorraine in the middle of his outrage about Quentin and the robbery:

> "I'll think of something else" he said, so he thought about Lorraine. He imagined himself in bed with her, only he was just lying beside her, pleading with her to help him. (p. 272)

Dilsey's comment about his being a cold man "if man you is" (p. 187) here seems to take the overtone of impotence. And it is this

possibly impotent man who considers dismemberment the only
cure for female desire, at least in his own family:

> Well, like I say they never started soon enough with their
> cutting and they quit too quick: I know at least two more
> that needed something like that, and one of them not over a
> mile away, either. (p. 234)

Thus if Benjy's castration was cruelly imposed upon him, and
his brother Quentin contemplated self-castration, Jason wishes
castration on others and needs none himself, having no desire to
truncate. Quentin's wishful-sad rumination becomes an adequate
characterization of Jason: "It's not not having them. It's never to
have had them then I could say O That That's Chinese I don't
know Chinese" (p. 107). Jason, I believe, is the man who does not
know "Chinese" and who, unlike Benjy, cannot even try "to want
something he didn't and couldn't even remember he didn't and
couldn't want any longer" (p. 225). Money is his way of compen-
sating for the fundamental lack he is unconscious of as well as
for the loss he consciously dwells upon. "Watching pennies,"
says Mr. Compson to his son Quentin in a different context, "has
healed more scars than jesus" (p. 161). But despite Mr. Compson's cynicism, money has no power to heal Jason's loss (of the
job, i.e., of money), nor does it cure his more basic lack of humanity, and it is thus appropriately taken away from him. In a kind of
poetic justice, not having is punished by not having, a cruel
repetition, dramatizing the futility of Jason's career.

AND CADDY? Where is Caddy in all this? As in the novel itself,
there is no separate section devoted to her in my discussion, but
she emerges from the other sections both as a loser—of virginity,
of a husband, of a daughter—and as the symbol of loss in the
lives of the other characters. To our surprise, we learn from
Jason's monologue that this lost girl (in both senses of the word)
is not completely lost. The absent Caddy does occasionally return
to the house, no matter how stealthily and fleetingly—one such
occasion being precisely a scene of loss and bereavement: the
death of her father. This return, however, is characterized both by

its belatedness (the father is already dead, and reunion is therefore impossible) and by Caddy's exclusion from the family (she
has not even been informed of Mr. Compson's death, and during
the funeral she stands apart, concealing herself from the rest of
the family).

What is true of this scene is also true of Caddy's other returns.
Contact with her mother is completely severed, the latter not only
refusing to accept the lost Caddy again, but also denying herself
and the whole family the privilege of reappropriation at the level
of language by forbidding the mention of Caddy's name in the
house. Contact with her daughter is more tantalizing than real,
this being epitomized by the early—and only reported—scene of
Caddy catching a glimpse of baby Quentin through the window
of a rapidly moving horse-drawn carriage. Brother Quentin is no
longer alive and cannot benefit from Caddy's occasional returns,
and brother Benjy only increases his bellowing when he senses
Caddy's presence in the house. Indeed, Caddy's returns ironically
emphasize her absence rather than providing an opportunity for
her to regain her family and for the family to retrieve her.

AS WE have seen, the lives of the Compsons are shaped by loss:
loss through death (Damuddy, Mr. Compson, Quentin, Roskus);
disappearance (Caddy, Miss Quentin), or unavailability (Mrs.
Compson); loss inhibiting sexuality (Benjy's castration, Quentin's
inability to lose his virginity, Jason's impotence); and loss of
meaning within language (Benjy's incommunicative sounds,
Quentin's sophisticated reduction of experience to words, Jason's
substitution of communication by the language of money). Through
these lives, Faulkner explores not only the inevitability of loss
but also the hopelessness of attempts at recuperation: Benjy's
clinging to objects that ironically recreate the scene of separation;
Quentin's reproduction of his relations with Caddy in all other
interactions; and Jason's repetition of an initial lack by a final
loss.

The only exception to this "Compson devilment" is Dilsey, the
devoted black servant of the Compson family. On the day of Miss
Quentin's disappearance—which Mrs. Compson experiences as
a reproduction of Quentin's suicide, Benjy as a repetition of Cad-

dy's escape, and Jason as a re-presentation of all his losses—
Dilsey (who has had her own share of bereavement) is nevertheless filled with a sense of an ending far beyond personal deprivation. "I've seed de first en de last" and "I seed de beginning, and
now I see de ending" (p. 264), she says under the inspiration of
Reverend Shegog's Easter sermon. But Reverend Shegog's vision
goes beyond the ending to a new beginning: "I sees de darkness
en de death everlastin upon de generations. . . . I sees de resurrection en de light; sees de meek Jesus sayin Dey kilt Me that ye
shall live again" (p. 263). Ending, loss, is here transcended by
belief, but no less (perhaps more) by the voice of the speaker. In
sharp juxtaposition to Benjy's bellowing, referred to in this section as "the grave hopeless sound of all voiceless misery under
the sun" (p. 280), the preacher's voice is described as "sinking to
their hearts and speaking there again when it has ceased in fading
and cumulate echoes" (p. 261). The preacher's voice "consumed
him, until he was nothing and they were nothing and there was
not even a voice but instead their hearts were speaking to one
another in chanting measures beyond the need for words" (p.
261). Here for once there is language that goes beyond words, a
voice that transcends the vicious circle of loss and its repetitions,
and replaces separation by the unification of hearts.

But the novel does not end with this climactic scene. It ends
with Jason and Benjy: Jason hopelessly pursuing Miss Quentin
and unnecessarily injuring the man whom he suspected of knowing where she is; and Benjy going to the cemetery with Luster,
who—in a circular return to the first section—keeps taking objects (here the bottle, the flower) away from Benjy, then grudg-
ingly giving them back and, worse, reducing Benjy to a constant
whimper by changing the direction of the surrey. Calm returns
only in the last sentence, when Luster again goes in the well-
known direction, things are "each in its ordered place," and
Benjy sits with expressionless eyes and a broken flower.

Which vision is affirmed by the novel? The glimpse of a revelation transcending loss, or the sound and the fury that surrounds
this apocalyptic moment? I think the question cannot be answered in any definitive way: the vision, the voice beyond words,
the unification of hearts have a tremendous impact in the novel,

but the many experiences of loss, the voiceless and voiced agonies, are equally resounding. The two visions are interlocked in the novel in a complex undecidability, a reflection of the intertwining of misery and hope in human life.

## Notes

1. All references are to William Faulkner, *The Sound and the Fury* (Harmondsworth: Penguin Modern Classics, 1965).

2. See Jacques Lacan, *Ecrits I* (Paris: Seuil, 1966), pp. 89–97. See also Christine Brooke-Rose, "The Squirm of the True: A Structural Analysis of Henry James' *The Turn of the Screw*," *Poetics and Theory of Literature* (1976), 1(3):513–46, for a similar explication of Lacan's insight and a brilliant analysis of *The Turn of the Screw*.

3. Note that the opposite equation also emerges. The children, especially Caddy, think of the gathering preceding the funeral as a party (p. 41).

4. Jason later suggests that Benjy's clinging to the gate may be caused by a desire to see the girls coming from school, not only by his longing for Caddy. As Matthews shows, there may be an association in Benjy's mind between these girls and Caddy; see John T. Matthews, *The Play of Faulkner's Language* (Ithaca and London: Cornell University Press, 1982), p. 72. Further page references for Matthews will be cited in the text.

5. The numbers are based on Volpe's list of events, but I have also verified them myself. See Edmond Volpe, "Appendix: Chronology and Scene Shifts in Benjy's and Quentin's Sections," in Michael H. Cowan, ed. *Twentieth Century Interpretations of "The Sound and The Fury"* (Englewood Cliffs, N.J.: Prentice-Hall, 1968), pp. 103–8.

6. Note that Quentin's memories include a scene (or a fantasy) of his trying to make love to Caddy, a scene with a knife which is both an obvious phallic symbol and a harbinger of a suggested double death (p. 138). It is probably this scene that he then confesses (or imagines himself confessing) to his father. I shall discuss this episode later in connection with the Natalie scene.

7. See Volpe's list.

8. Water also links these scenes to the episode with the Italian girl within which these memories are inserted. Quentin and the girl get wet when the boys in the river splash water on them (pp. 125–26).

9. See also Sigmund Freud, *Beyond the Pleasure Principle* (New York: Norton, 1961), pp. 16, 30, 32.

10. Similar reductions to words occur in relation to desire (p. 109) and to Harvard University (p. 158).

11. See also John T. Irwin, *Doubling and Incest: Repetition and Revenge: A Speculative Reading of Faulkner* (Baltimore, Md.: Johns Hopkins University Press, 1975), p. 46.

12. Opposed to my view is Matthews' interesting, though not fully substantiated, interpretation of Jason's behavior as a displacement of his repressed desire for Caddy (pp. 92, 99).

# 11

# DISLOCATIONS: THE CRISIS OF ALLEGORY IN THE *ROMANCE OF THE ROSE*
## Jon Whitman

IN RECENT years it has become so customary to talk about crises in the designs of language that to call attention to a crisis seems almost to reassure us with a norm. In one sense, the problem I would like to consider here is a familiar crisis of this kind. It concerns the development of pressure in a literary work when its effort to coordinate one point of reference with another begins to break down. Expressed in such general terms, the problem of dislocations in the design of a text applies at least potentially to nearly any work or genre that seeks to correlate disparate materials while recognizing their diversity. The problem has a particular force, though, when it affects the technique of allegorical writing, which makes the interplay between one conceptual framework and another the very principle of its organization. If there is a text central to the development of that technique, it is the *Romance of the Rose*, not only the most prominent allegory, but the most influential vernacular work, of the Middle Ages.[1] At the same time, it is precisely this text that seems to me to end not by affirming close correlations between one order and another, but by calling them into question. With its increasing critique of its own conventions, I believe the *Rose* marks not only a culminating point in the development of one kind of allegory, but a point of no return. In this sense, perhaps the work presents not just one more instance of some "normal" crisis, but a decisive early exposé of the crisis of establishing norms themselves.

The tension in the poem is partly traceable to its divided

authorship. The first part of the work, written by Guillaume de Lorris in the early thirteenth century, suggests something of the artful ambience of Guillaume's Loire Valley. It evokes the dream of a love affair, framed by the dreamer's encounter with abstract figures in the enclosed garden of Delight, or Diversion ("Deduit"), and centered on an elusive rose. The second part of the work, written some forty years later by Jean de Meun, displays a sense of the intellectual restlessness of late thirteenth-century Paris. It broadly turns Guillaume's plot, which breaks off inconclusively, into a kind of pre-text for a series of intricate disquisitions on human behavior at large—from Reason's systematic analysis of different forms of love to the Old Woman's outspoken advocacy of "all females for all males, and all males for all females" ("toutes por touz et touz por toutes"; l. 13856). The affair itself finally advances only after its scope broadens into the comprehensive framework of Nature, who appears in her workshop of cosmic production and surveys the phenomena of the natural world. While acknowledging that some matters, like divine Incarnation, lie beyond her understanding—God, she points out, is a wondrous sphere with its center everywhere, its circumference nowhere (ll. 19099–102)—she laments that in the natural realm man alone deviates from her principles by failing to perpetuate the species. Consulting with Genius, the principle of natural generation and her "priest" (l. 16242), she asks him to excommunicate those who work against that goal and pardon those who work for it. Genius flies to the allies of love, urging them to consummate their natural desires and describing to them the rewards of heavenly paradise. The goddess Venus sets fire to the fortress enclosing the rose, and the lover, proceeding "like a good pilgrim" (conme bons pelerins; l. 21317), with his hard staff and sack, enters the "sanctuary" and plucks the rose. He awakes, and the poem ends.

The *Romance of the Rose* is a poem that points in several different directions, and its readers have frequently sought to formulate for it some principle of coherence. In the early fifteenth century, when the work stimulated a lively public debate, the interpretive controversy centered on the problem of its moral

orientation. One French intellectual protested that if the last existing copy were worth a thousand pounds, he would burn it;
another commended the work for its "most noble doctrine."[2] In
our own century, the discussion has tended to shift toward formal
and tonal questions, often with the aim of assessing the relation
between the two parts of the poem. Perhaps the most familiar
claim in this discussion is that Jean's part of the work satirizes
Guillaume's part, completing his story of refined loving by criti-
cizing or opposing it. This issue, however, has itself received
divided critical responses. One group of recent readers, emphasizing the "naturalistic" strain in Jean's work, has argued that
whatever its differences in style and scope from Guillaume's
section, it essentially endorses the love affair, even if it qualifies
it.[3] Another group has countered that Guillaume's work itself at
least indirectly condemns the affair, and that Jean's portion comically elaborates the outrage.[4] Each of these disparate reactions is
finally an effort to correlate the poem's sensual and spiritual
points of reference according to some orderly conceptual program.

If the attempt to find such correlations is understandable when
applied to an allegory, it seems limited when applied to a work
that openly tests the intelligibility of the very relationships on
which it appears to depend. Such a test, I think, distinguishes the
concluding movement of the *Romance of the Rose*, during which
the figure of Genius explicitly develops the earthly/heavenly nu-
ances underlying the poem at large into a systematic formulation.
Perhaps I should say the concluding movement of the composite
*Romance of the Rose*, since Guillaume apparently never com-
pleted his part—although this state of incompletion may itself be
a symptom of the problem that Jean later articulates. Genius'
speech, of course, is not the only part of Jean's work that contributes to his argument; I concentrate on it in part because the
narrator himself refers to it, the last major discourse of an allegorical character, as "the definitive sentence" (*la diffinitive san-
tance*; l. 19474), with its overtones of the Latin *sententia*, implying
not only the moral of the story, but the resolution, or *sententia*, of
a scholastic *disputatio*[5]—as if Genius were organizing the diverse

attitudes expressed earlier in the poem into logical form. The
more Genius develops that logic, though, the more inconclusive
the definition seems to become.

Something of the ambivalence in his performance appears from
the start, with his role as a priest promising absolution to the
forces of love. The strategy of giving this agent of natural generation a spiritual dimension had developed already in the twelfth-
century *Complaint of Nature* by Alan of Lille, but Jean noticeably
increases the pressures involved in such a maneuver. On the one
hand, he limits Genius' own status more strictly than Alan does
to the physical world; for example, the Genius of the *Rose* is
given a burning candle to excite his audience by a laughing
Venus, an alliance hardly available in the *Complaint of Nature*,
which distinguishes Genius' aspiration from Venus' delin-
quency.[6] On the other hand, Jean simultaneously elevates Genius'
sights more explicitly than Alan does to the celestial realm; in his
poem, Genius elaborately envisions the pleasures of paradise, a
realm so remote from the *Complaint of Nature* as to be scarcely
mentioned in it. More than one reader of the *Rose* has stressed
how Jean manipulates the values of speeches by playing them off
the contexts of speakers,[7] and it is a cunning move to assign the
discourse on paradise not to Reason, or some (here absent) figure
such as divine Grace, but to the spokesman of sexual reproduction. At the same time, it seems to me inadequate to treat this
juxtaposition either as incipient naturalism or as pious parody,
not because either of these strategies was unavailable in late
thirteenth-century Paris (in fact, both were current), but because
such a reading no sooner recognizes Jean's emphasis on the functional components of meaning than it reduces those functions to
fixed systems. The principal effect of Jean's *Romance of the Rose*,
I believe, is that in mixing an erotic plot with a cosmic program,
it makes each a reference point from which to evaluate the other,
while turning the issue of their relationship from a question of
establishing categories toward a question of assessing the conditions in which comparisons take place. Perhaps I could elaborate
on this process first by examining some selections from the text;
then by considering briefly certain similar tendencies in the phi-

losophy of Jean's period; and finally by offering a few thoughts
about the general implications of these developments.

Although Genius' extended address resists brief quotation, three
passages in it seem to me to provide some sense of its overall
tendencies. All three concern the crucial relation between the
earthly and heavenly realms, and they provide a convenient way
to consider what might be called three different modes of transition between the two realms—modes of acting, knowing, and
speaking—although these modes of course overlap. The first passage concentrates on the kind of activity that offers a way to
heaven:

> Fight against the vices that Nature, our mistress, came to tell
> me about today at my mass. . . . You will find twenty-six of
> them, more harmful than you think. . . . The lovely *Romance
> of the Rose* explains them to you quite briefly; please look at
> them there so that you may better guard against them.
>
> *Think of leading a good life; let each man embrace his
> beloved,* and may each woman embrace her lover and kiss
> and feast and comfort him. If you love each other loyally
> *you should never be blamed* for doing so. And when you
> have played enough, as I have recommended to you here,
> *think of confessing yourselves well, in order to do good and
> avoid evil,* and call upon the heavenly God whom Nature
> calls her master. He will save you in the end. . . .[8]

The problem with this advice is that each time the text seems
to specify an appropriate action, a new context qualifies or undermines the specification. A case in point is the word "good" *(bone)*
at the start of the second paragraph: "Think of leading a good
life." The preceding sentences speak of the vices Nature has
mentioned to Genius, and since this list of over twenty vices
earlier in the text (ll. 19195–204) mainly details categories of
moral wrongdoing—it includes pride, cruelty, covetousness, and
the like—the word "good" here seems to refer to pious behavior.
But the phrase immediately afterward, "let each man embrace his
beloved," suddenly transforms the gloss on the word "good,"
referring it to sensual pleasure. And no sooner does that adjust-

ment encourage us to transfer comfortably the spiritual "good"
into the sexual one than a new phrase—"think of confessing
yourselves well, in order to do good and avoid evil"—tends to
reverse that reversal, by allying the good with the pious act of
confession. On the other hand, the meaning of "confession" itself
oscillates the more it is scrutinized. If, in its immediate context,
it seems to specify a religious act, renouncing the sensual "play"
at the start of the sentence, the preceding sentence nonetheless
indicates that such play is not blameworthy ("you should never
be blamed"), but commendable, and thus hardly confessable. The
play of this language, if I can use the expression, recalls the
problem posed (before the excerpt quoted here) by Nature's original instruction to Genius to pardon those who "know fully how
to confess their sins" (l. 19368)—where it is unclear whether
"sins" refers to generative activity or generative inactivity, and
therefore whether "confession" is a corrective to the sensual life
or a coordinate of it—even a renaming of the very sexual play
that seems at times in this excerpt to be renounced. Such displacements and replacements of meaning perhaps suggest how
limited is the normal critical appeal to categories like "parody"
and "irony" with regard to the Romance of the Rose. For although
those procedures contribute to Jean's technique, he makes terms
change in valence according to their different locations in the text
as actions change in value according to their different reference
points in the world. The reference points themselves are conventional; Genius, no less than any preacher, acknowledges an earth
and a heaven. What remains uncertain from his sermon is whether
a person reaches heaven by means of earthly activity or in spite
of it. In this respect, the twists and turns of his language expose
not only his own comic limitations, but the serious dilemmas in
any definition of the "good life."

Such dilemmas intensify when Genius tries to describe the
other world that awaits those who act according to instructions
in this one. He seeks, understandably, to direct his listeners'
thoughts to heaven, and thus to transport them, in effect, not only
in the mode of acting, but in the mode of knowing. This second,
overlapping operation begins in earnest with his assurance:

And if you preach in this way, upon my word and my promise, *provided that the deeds accord with the discourse,* you will never be prevented from entering *the park of the lovely field, where the son of the Virgin, the ewe in all her white fleece, leads his flock with him, leaping over the grass.* They follow after him . . . the little white ewes, *good-na-tured and open animals, that graze and eat the young grass and the flowers* which spring up there. But know that they have a pasture of such a wondrous nature that *the delightful little flowers* which spring up there fresh and clean, all in their spring maidenhood, *are as young, are as new, as stars glistening through the green grass in the morning dew.* . . . I tell you too that no matter how much of the grass and the flowers the little sheep can nibble and eat, for they will always want to eat them, they can never eat as much as they will always see spring up again. I tell you further, and *do not take it as a fable,* that they do not at all decay no matter how much the sheep graze on them. *And their pastures cost the sheep nothing, for their skins are not sold at the end.* . . . But certainly, whatever I say, I do not at all doubt that *the good shepherd, who leads them grazing before him, may be clothed in their wool;* but he neither skins them nor plucks from them anything that costs them the price of one feather. . . .[9]

These and similar descriptions, which incidentally have re-ceived high critical praise,[10] seem to me to expose three related problems in the effort to conceive a higher world. First, the more the account exploits the images upon which it depends, the more the images take on a disturbing life of their own. It may be true that a host of biblical and liturgical sources treat the blessed as a "flock," but to pursue the consequences, by depicting these "good-natured . . . animals" and their grazing patterns, finally leads more to a pasture than to a paradise. If Genius' own preoccupation with the natural realm makes him particularly liable to this di-lemma, his description nonetheless exposes the more general problem of a conceptual vehicle that keeps turning into the tenor itself. Second, by a closely related process, the tendency to objec-tify images begins to produce new, diverting objects of interest in turn. The pasture no sooner appears, for example, than it prompts speculation about the economics of heavenly sheep farming (near the end of the excerpt: "their pastures cost the sheep nothing, for their skins are not sold at the end"). Even to deny the economic question here involves posing it; in effect, the very effort to determine a spiritual point of reference finally overdetermines it, and thus produces the difficulties it wishes to avoid. Third, and more broadly, the categories applied to the heavenly park originate in an earthly framework to which they necessarily return in the end. This turnabout dominates Genius' account, whether in a harshly reductive form, as in the passage almost at the end of the excerpt where the "good shepherd" himself has an interest in wool clothing ("the good shepherd . . . may be clothed in their wool"), or in a subtler, more intricate pattern, as in the passage near the middle where the paradisal flowers are as bright as the stars shining in the dew of a lovely—but terrestrial—dawn ("as stars glistening through the green grass in the morning dew"). For all Genius' enthusiasm, his exposition repeatedly shows that the very effort to know the other world tends to interpose the categories of this world, and thus that conceptual turns of this kind are constantly liable to end by turning in upon themselves.

Such a liability might seem only to confirm the conventional argument that it is not possible accurately to conceive the realm of the absolute. But Genius' speech finally poses the more radical problem of how that limitation affects the realm of the relative. For the whole point of his discourse is to show how one world relates to the other, and insofar as no convincing transaction between the two can take place either in acting or in knowing, the disparity calls into question the very notion of a relative or comparative value for this world. Such a consequence is particularly unsettling for an allegory that makes the resemblance between the earthly and heavenly worlds its very basis of operation. In the end, the problem of correlation thus applies also to the mode of speaking to which the poem itself belongs.

Genius' most self-conscious engagement with this third, overlapping issue begins with the following passage, which turns the relationships underlying the allegory at large into an explicit, formal comparison:

> *Anyone who wanted to make a comparison between the*
> *beautiful square garden,* closed with the little barred wicket,
> where this lover saw the carol where Diversion dances with
> his people, *and this beautiful park* that I am describing, as
> strikingly beautiful as one could wish it, would make a very
> great mistake if he did not *make the comparison as one*
> *would between the truth and a fable.*

As much as this assessment devalues the garden of love, it allows
at least the possibility of some useful relationship between the
garden and the park. The same word "beautiful," after all, applies
to each; the question turns on whether there is a genuine relationship between the beauty of a fable and the beauty of truth. The
next sentence uncompromisingly takes away that prospect:

> For anyone who was inside this park or who only cast his
> eye within would safely dare to swear that *the garden was*
> *nothing ("neanz") with respect to this enclosure.*[11]

Such an extreme reduction of the garden to nothingness undermines the very possibility of a true proportion, a ratio, between it
and the park. And as the speech has just implicated the assessment of the garden with the assessment of fables, it implicitly
calls into question the rationale of the allegory itself. It is no
wonder that Genius stresses that he wants to end the story quickly.
"What do you want me to tell you?" he continues in the following
lines. We will "pass over" the items associated with the garden
"in a few words" (ll. 20268–72).

In fact, he requires more than a few words. His reductive
strategy consists rather in elaborately excluding not only the earthly
garden, but level after level of the universe ("hell," "earth," "sea,"
"air," "fire," "stars," "all . . . shut out"; ll. 20275–304), from the
premises of the park, and then in enumerating principal features
of the garden only to oppose them with their celestial counterparts in the park—about which, he nonetheless admits, he cannot
speak "properly" (*propremant*; l. 20344). The "beautiful," life-
giving fountain in the heavenly park, he announces, is "not" the
death-giving fountain of Narcissus in the garden, which in fact is
not "clear," as the lover claims, but "ugly" (ll. 20356–408). The

fable of the whole allegory, it turns out, is only a lie, and not even
a beautiful one, at that.

Such a conclusion tends to undermine the very possibilities of
figurative discourse. The dreamer of Guillaume de Lorris had
spoken of the earthly garden itself as a nearly spiritual place.
"And believe me," he recalled about his initial reactions to that
scene, "I thought I was truly in the earthly paradise. The place
was so delightful that it seemed to be spiritual."[12] The close
rapport here between the conditions of the dreamer and the realm
of the spirit is reinforced in the complementary format of the
original couplets: "je cuidai estre . . . em paradis terrestre"; "delitables . . . esperitables." It is true that Guillaume qualifies the
imaginative transfer by calling attention to the element of subjectivity ("I thought" I was in paradise) and the influence of appearances ("it seemed" to be spiritual), as well as by later developments in the dream. Jean, however, gives such moral and
psychological disjunctions a metaphysical foundation. By the end
of Genius' speech, he has reduced the sensual world to a condition of negation, thereby as it were dislocating the *locus amoenus*
of the garden, while reserving the spiritual world for a realm
beyond affirmation, by displacing even the "good shepherd" and
his "flock" from their proper reference points. He underlines this
dilemma by assigning the "definitive sentence" about it to a
character, Genius, who is himself radically divided in orientation. On the one hand, Genius is the principle of natural generation who spurs the forces of love toward sexual consummation.
On the other hand, in the very act of encouraging their drive,
Genius almost unwittingly undermines their position (and his
own), by showing how the way of the senses eludes the way of
the spirit to which it is supposed to lead. Genius and the forces
of love as a whole can hardly act, know, or speak effectively
without a worldly context, but they can hardly do so within such
a context, either.

The dilemma has its climax in the consummation scene at the
end of the poem, as the lover's sensual pursuit no sooner acquires
the pretense of a spiritual pilgrimage than loses it. Lifting the veil
that conceals the "relics" of the desired "sanctuary," the lover
inserts his pilgrim's staff and passes inside (ll. 21553–642). But

he has broken through the imagery in more ways than one; the imagery shifts and he scatters "a little seed" on the rosebud (ll. 21665–700), which by this time has become so palpable an object as to lose any clear relation with the spiritual flowers of the park, while simultaneously becoming so transparent a pretext for the sexual preoccupations of the garden as to lose any substantial sign of its imaginative integrity. In a sense, the consummation scene thus aggressively confirms the early troubadour anxiety that the very act of approaching the object of desire is liable to vitiate it. It is as if the elusive lady of the poem, who never appears in propria persona, could finally be possessed only by a self-imposition that betrays the absence at its heart. If I can put it this way, Jean de Meun relentlessly takes the "romance" out of the Romance of the Rose. In the end, it is not only the dream of a rose from which the dreamer awakens; it is the dream of relationships called allegory.

If the Romance of the Rose marks a crisis in the design of allegory, I do not think it exactly "produces" that crisis or causes the deep changes in allegorical writing in the following generations. It seems to me rather to participate in a larger intellectual controversy that acquires new intensity by the late thirteenth century, the problem of formulating the relation between the created and divine worlds. In a sense, of course, this problem is central to any Christian philosophy, and its treatment in the late thirteenth century alone has received a host of systematic studies.[13] I do not want to discuss in detail any of the intricate approaches to this problem in late thirteenth-century scholastic thought, which in any case concentrates more strictly on the relation between creature and Creator than on the relation between the earthly and heavenly realms. Nor do I want to argue for specific influences between such analyses, including those of philosophers associated with the developing University of Paris, and Jean's work, although Jean did read widely in philosophic subjects and may well have been associated with the university.[14] At the same time, as far as I can tell, no one has seriously examined the broad interests shared by these analyses and the Rose, and it seems to me important to explore in this respect how a philosophic controversy converges with a poetic dilemma.

Among late thirteenth-century efforts to assess the relation between creatures and the Creator, perhaps the most rigorous critique comes from Thomas Aquinas, whose last writing dates from the same generation in which Jean composes his portion of the *Rose*. In Aquinas' treatment, as in other philosophic accounts, the analysis of possible connections between this world and God involves overlapping questions about the actual, or conceptual, or linguistic relations between them, so that his discussion of what can be predicated of both subjects involves—as it does in the *Rose*—arguments not only about modes of speaking, but also about modes of knowing and acting. For Aquinas, the effort to relate such disparate reference points by predicating the same terms of them, however, involves almost insuperable problems. On the one hand, Aquinas observes, it is not possible to apply the same words in the same sense—that is, univocally—to both creatures and God. Such a procedure would attribute not only the same terms, but the same conceptual and actual categories, to finite and infinite beings. On the other hand, if words could be predicated of both creatures and God only in completely different senses—that is, completely equivocally—not only would such a discord imply an inability to speak or reason about God; it would deny the actual order shared between his creation and him.[15] To try to formulate the relation between creation and Creator seems either to involve an illegitimate conflation of the two in language, knowledge, and actuality, or to register a radical dissociation between them.

It would be possible, of course, to try to coordinate these reference points by indicating a word, a concept, or a thing in order to specify what God is not. Aquinas endorses certain negative theological strategies of this kind, noting, for example, that it is appropriate to call God "infinite" because the term denies that he is finite.[16] For Aquinas, however, such a strategy has severe limits; as he stresses, "it will not tell us what God is in Himself."[17] Whatever its value in contrasting God and the world, then, or even in elaborately articulating God's distinction, it can hardly indicate a clear basis for comparing them. Something of its frustrations can perhaps be seen in the last of the passages discussed above from Genius' speech, where Genius directs attention to the heavenly park by excluding everything else, from hell to the stars —a strategy that leaves in limbo the earthly affair that he himself supports.

It might be argued that while such a negative procedure fails to specify what God is, a metaphorical strategy can at least provide an approximate sense of the divine. For his part, Aquinas deeply qualifies that claim. It is possible, he grants, for terms properly belonging to creatures, like the term "lion," to be transferred metaphorically to God (ST, I, q. 13, a. 6). But since the very definitions of such borrowed terms belong to creatures, not the Creator, they cannot finally pass beyond the creatural reference points in which they originate. Part of the importance of Aquinas' critique of metaphor lies in the rigor he demands of such trans- fers. By contrast, his more conservative contemporary, Bonaven- ture, more broadly, though still cautiously, defends the attribu- tion of terms like "lion" and "lamb" to God.[18] As later commentary on Aquinas has observed, in the Thomistic critique we cannot know clearly what metaphors mean when applied to God, unless we already know the element in God that legitimates the compar- ison. And in that case, there would be no need to resort to meta- phor in the first place. From this standpoint, metaphorical trans- fer presupposes the knowledge about God that it claims to reveal.[19] Aiming to provide a transition between one framework and an- other, it ends by reverting to its starting point. Such a turnabout dominates the second of the passages discussed above, where the more Genius elaborates the metaphors of paradisal "pasture," ethereal "flock," and spiritual "shepherd," the more the meta- phors betray their earthbound condition. If I can put it this way, the problem with this heavenly vision is not that the lion and the lamb will not live in harmony with each other; it is that even if they do, they will remain just a lion and a lamb.

Whatever the liabilities of both negative and metaphorical ef- forts to align creatures with the Creator, Aquinas himself does claim that it is possible to articulate a relation between them. The terms suited to this purpose are terms used "analogously" like "good," "wise," and the like, which apply to the world and God not in the same sense, that is, univocally, nor in completely different senses, that is, purely equivocally. A term like "good," for example, applies to both the world and God because creatures display in their own imperfect ways the goodness that is preeminently in their Creator. To say that "God is good," then, argues Aquinas, means that "*Whatever good we attribute to creatures pre-exists in God*, and in a higher way" (*ST*, I, q. 13, a. 2). Such expressions avoid a problem with negative terminology because they indicate a positive relation between the world and God. At the same time, they avoid a problem with metaphor because although we apprehend analogous terms like "good" only from a creatural viewpoint, the very "reality in the names," as Aquinas puts it, "belongs by priority in God."[20]

Whatever the appeal of this strategy, in one sense it begs the question, as Aquinas himself recognizes. Precisely because we understand analogous terms only by their application to creatures, not according to the "reality in the names," in the end these terms expose largely God's priority to the world, not the nature of the standard on which their relationship is based. Whatever authorizes such a relationship thereby eludes our own understanding. Nor does this elusiveness distinguish only the extreme case of an analogy between the world and God. As the extensive philosophic commentary that has developed around the problem of analogy has shown, it is difficult to specify any "common element" that clearly relates the diverse uses of a term like "good," as when we call a law a "good" law, and a robbery a "good" robbery. Even the attempt to make "good" mean "fulfilling its nature," it has been pointed out, tends to turn the word into simply an intensifier of the very objects the natures of which are disparate from the start.[21] The intricacies of this problem are far beyond any discussion of the *Romance of the Rose;* I want here only to stress that the problem itself deeply affects Genius' own discourse, as in the first excerpt above, which slips almost unawares from a "good" sensual life ("Think of leading a good life; let each man embrace his beloved") to a "good" pious life ("think of confessing yourselves well, in order to do good and avoid evil"), and eventually, in the second excerpt, to a "good" shepherd in heaven—or for that matter, in the third excerpt, from a "beautiful" garden to a "beautiful" park. If there is a relation among these disparate points of reference, it seems that the only way to clarify it would be to step outside the garden into the park itself, to see the "reality in the names," as Aquinas puts it, in which creatures participate. But Genius' whole speech repeatedly betrays the fact that he—and we—are always standing in the garden, that we belong inevitably to the very world we would like to judge.

Given an allegory that is constantly deferring the very transitions upon which it depends, it might be argued that the poem as a whole simply breaks down in the end. Such an argument, I think, would not fully describe either the *Rose*'s own method of operation or its importance for the technique of allegory at large. The *Romance of the Rose* seems to me rather to signal a shift in intellectual orientation, an effort to evaluate modes of acting, knowing, and speaking less by systems of correspondence than by contexts of application. At the same time, it seems to me to stress that such applications require continual reassessment, not exactly by recourse to an absolute standard that is only imperfectly accessible to us, but by an awareness of the limitations of our own conventions.[22] In a sense, the very shift in the function of "good" in the first excerpt calls attention to this need for reassessment, by exposing the tensions inside a single category of discourse. The problem is not that sexual and spiritual activity cannot each be "good"—that remains at least a possibility—but that the speaker himself is not fully aware of his own changing inflections, not fully assessing the categories he advances. Some sense of this need, I think, appears in Genius' amusing comment at the end of the first section of the excerpt, where he tries to explain what is not good by appealing to the very poem that includes his own speech. I would tell you about the vices, he claims, but the "*Romance of the Rose* explains them to you quite briefly; please look at them there so that you may better guard against them." Taken as a comment addressed to his audience within the poem, this instruction scarcely acknowledges that the "readers" are already participating in the realm of discourse they are supposed to consider. Yet insofar as every reader belongs to such a realm of discourse, the call to evaluate—here, in effect, to reread an earlier passage—suggests that every act of appraisal occurs only within a context that itself needs to be appraised. In this sense, the comment directs its readers at large less outside the hermeneutic circle than through it, toward an understanding of its own closures.

Such movements in the poem toward a critical awareness that escapes its characters seem to me to affect the conclusion of the work as a whole. When, in the second excerpt, Genius relentlessly objectifies his images of sheep and pasture, he declares toward the end of the excerpt: "do not take it as a fable"—a warning that by this point does not so much reinforce the terms of his story as call attention to his own objectifying tendencies. In the end, his insistent denial here of a fabulous mode both exposes the fable and suggests the need to reconsider its designs. In a sense, he almost formulates that need despite himself when, near the beginning of the same excerpt, he promises his allies access to the park "provided that the deeds accord with the discourse." If this phrase specifies a code of behavior for his audience, it also implies a chronic problem in his speech, its need to establish a suitable proportion between word and object. In a world where that proportion is not fixed, where the distinction between word and object tends either to narrow drastically, as in the objectified image of the "pasture," or to widen casually, as (elsewhere in Genius' speech) in the modulating figures of "plowing"—now used metaphorically (sexual activity; ll. 19513–52, 19610–705), now mythologically (the story of Cadmus; ll. 19706–20), now practically (the aftermath of the Golden Age; ll. 20089–92)—it at least remains possible to make that variation itself a measure of shifts in conceptual orientation, and thus to turn it into a standard for readjustment.

Such a possibility has its formal literary expression in the third excerpt, which explicitly evaluates terms which help to organize the poem at large. Anyone who was "inside" the heavenly park, claims Genius, "or who only cast his eye within would safely dare to swear that the garden was nothing with respect to this enclosure." If Genius himself is in no position to swear by that statement—he is the genius of another place, after all, the earthly garden—it is nonetheless significant that it is he who calls attention to the prospect of his own displacement. Given Genius' rather limited self-consciousness, perhaps it is better to say that the configuration of the poem itself dramatizes that prospect, not by abandoning its earthly and heavenly reference points, but by placing them here as a formal inset within the work, and thereby developing a perspective on its own operations. But then, that effort to reassess from the inside the conditions which authorize an argument, by playing judgments and counterjudgments off each other, distinguishes the turn of this allegory as a whole.

At the same time, the *Rose* seems to me more to point in this direction than to complete such a movement in its own right. It never really organizes this process of appraisal around a continuous consciousness that develops inside the text. Such a consciousness need not be a narrative "I," although perhaps it is significant that for most of Jean's portion of the poem the "I" completely disappears from the narrative foreground, displaced by a variety of characters whose prolonged speeches move the poem in conflicting directions. When the narrator returns to command the foreground in the consummation scene, he does so only with a precipitous drive dominated by impulsive shifts in speech, thought, and action. Even he, though, manages at times to suggest principles which inform the larger order of the work. Just before entering his erotic "sanctuary," he authorizes, highhandedly, the pursuit of women of various ages; "it is good to try everything." After all, "he who has not tried evil will hardly ever know anything of the good" (ll. 21521, 21532–34). As if to reflect half-consciously on the ambivalence of those categories, he continues: "Thus things go by contraries; the one is the gloss of the other. And if anyone wants to define the one, he must remember the other, or he will never, by any intention, assign a definition to it. For he who does not have an understanding of the two will never understand the difference between them, without which a definition that he may make cannot come to anything."[23] The argument is not remarkable in itself; it cites Aristotelian principles noted by a number of medieval scholastic philosophers, including Aquinas.[24] Its effect comes rather from its placement in the text, just as the allegory is about to close. It offers, as it were, the definition of formulating a definition, and it refers that process to an act of internal differentiation which itself qualifies, by the play of contraries, the narrator's own sexual pilgrimage. Perhaps the

need for reorientation implied by the passage appears most strikingly in its use of the term "gloss" to describe this process, as if
the end of the poem, like late medieval scholastic interpretation
at large, were shifting the notion of "glossing" a text from the
discovery of hidden levels of meaning to the exposition of logical
implications, from a figural emphasis to a dialectical one.[25] In
any case, perhaps the passage has a special value for a poem
marked by dislocations; no definition can "come to anything" (in
the idiom of the text, "come into place," *venir en place*) unless it
is placed in a context of differences that discloses its own parameters. Something of this play of differences, I think, distinguishes
Genius' own "definitive sentence," which no sooner takes a position than it exposes the limits of its own formulations, thereby
making the act of definition a basis for continual reassessment.

For his part, the narrator scarcely articulates this distinction
before he loses it, appropriating spiritual terms to their sexual
counterparts. It requires a subtler, Dantesque movement some
two generations later to coordinate the passage from one reference
point to another in the world with the conversion from one condition to another in the mind. Yet the *Divine Comedy* hardly
eases the dilemma of defining the connection between one such
framework and another. By implicating the changing status of an
object with the changing perception of a subject, the *Comedy*
poses the problem of distinguishing between the two that increasingly preoccupies allegorical writing, from the constantly shifting
dream visions of *Piers Plowman* later in the fourteenth century to
the modulation between outer and inner states in the *Faerie
Queene*. Already in Dante's generation, for that matter, the problem of organizing a world where analogies are breaking down
finds philosophic expression in the work of Ockham, who denies
a Thomistic analogy between finite and infinite being, arguing
that such a common element "stands only for the concept in the
mind."[26] But these later crises require discussions in their own
right, and even with respect to the *Rose* I have been able to
discuss here only a few passages.

In the speech that leads to Genius' "definitive sentence," Nature admits that she cannot really understand the divine sphere
that has its center everywhere, its circumference nowhere. If in

one sense this elusive formula exposes only the limits of the speaker, in another sense it implies the only relation finally available in this poem between the natural and divine realms. For in a work where modes of acting, knowing, and speaking are constantly being decentered, to explore the circumference offers at least the possibility of participating in the whole, a whole that can never be specified. In the end, the poem itself seems to suggest that such a whole is not exactly a circumscribed "place," but the ground on which normative positions are endlessly tested.[27] From this perspective, perhaps the *Romance of the Rose* not only displays the increasing dislocation of one world, but anticipates the gradual disclosure of another.

## Notes

1. Citations of the text refer to Félix Lecoy, ed., *Guillaume de Lorris et Jean de Meun: Le Roman de la Rose* (Paris: Honoré Champion, 1965–1970). My translations are based on *The Romance of the Rose by Guillaume de Lorris and Jean de Meun*, trans. Charles Dahlberg (Princeton, N.J.: Princeton University Press, 1971).

2. See John V. Fleming, *The "Roman de la Rose": A Study in Allegory and Iconography* (Princeton, N.J.: Princeton University Press, 1969), p. 47. Cf. Eric Hicks, ed., *Le débat sur Le Roman de la Rose* (Paris: Honoré Champion, 1977).

3. See, e.g., Gérard Paré, *Les idées et les lettres au XIIIe siècle: Le Roman de la Rose* (Montreal: Le Centre de Psychologie et Pédagogie, 1947), and Alan M. F. Gunn, *The Mirror of Love: A Reinterpretation of "The Romance of the Rose"* (1951; rpt. Lubbock: Texas Tech Press, 1952).

4. See, e.g., D. W. Robertson, Jr., *A Preface to Chaucer: Studies in Medieval Perspectives* (1962; rpt. Princeton, N.J.: Princeton University Press, 1970), pp. 91–104, 196–207, and Fleming, *The "Roman de la Rose."*

5. See Paré, *Les idées*, pp. 23–27; cf., however, Daniel Poirion, *Le Roman de la Rose* (Paris: Hatier, 1973), pp. 131–33, 142, 147–50, and my discussion below.

6. See George D. Economou, *The Goddess Natura in Medieval Literature* (Cambridge, Mass.: Harvard University Press, 1972), pp. 111–24, and Denise N. Baker, "The Priesthood of Genius: A Study of the Medieval Tradition," *Speculum* (1976), 51:284–86.

7. See especially Rosemond Tuve, *Allegorical Imagery: Some Mediaeval Books and Their Posterity* (1966; rpt. Princeton, N.J.: Princeton University Press, 1977), pp. 241–83.

8. The italics are mine in the second paragraph and in later excerpts from the *Rose*; see ll. 19836–67: ". . . contre les vices batailliez / que Nature, nostre mestresse, / me vint hui conter a ma messe. . . . / vos an trouveroiz .xxvi. / plus nuisanz que vos ne cuidiez. . . . / Assez briefmant les vos expose / li jolis Romanz de la Rose: / s'il vos plest, la les regardez / por ce que mieuz d'aus vos gardez. / Pansez de mener bone vie, / aut chascuns anbracier s'amie, / et son ami chascune

anbrace / et bese et festoie et solace. / Se leaumant vos antr'amez, / ja n'an devroiz
estre blamez. / Et quant assez avrez joué / si con je vos ai ci loué, / pansez de vos
bien confessier, / por bien fere et por mal lessier, / et reclamez le dieu celestre /
que Nature reclaime a mestre. / Cil en la fin vos secourra . . ."

9. See ll. 19901–68: "Et se vos ainsinc preeschiez, / ja ne seroiz anpeeschiez, /
selonc mon dit et mon acort, / mes que li fez au dit s'acort, / d'antrer ou parc du
champ joli, / ou les berbiz conduit o li, / saillant devant par les herbiz, / li filz de
la Vierge, berbiz / o toute sa blanche toison, / amprés cui . . . / . . . les berbietes
blanches, / bestes deboneres et franches, / qui l'erbete broutent et pessent, / et les
floretes qui la nessent. / Mes sachez qu'eus ont la pasture / de si merveilleuse
nature / que les delitables floretes / qui la nessent fresches et netes, / toutes en leur
printans puceles, / tant sunt jennes, tant sunt nouveles, / conme esteles reflam-
boianz / par les herbetes verdoianz / au matinet a la rousee . . . / Si vos di que les
berbietes / ne des herbes ne des floretes / ja mes tant brouter ne porront, / car
tourjorz brouter les vorront, / que tourjorz nes voient renestre, / tant les sachent
brouter ne pestre. / Plus vos di, nou tenez a fables, / qu'el ne sunt mie corrumpa-
bles, / conbien que les berbiz les broustent, / cui les pastures riens ne coustent, /
car leur piaus n'an sunt pas vandues / au darrenier . . . / Mes, san faille, que que
je die, / du bon pasteur ne dout je mie, / qui devant sai pestre les maine, / qu'il ne
soit vestuz de leur laine, / si nes despoille il ne ne plume / qui leur coust le pris
d'une plume . . ."

10. See C. S. Lewis, *The Allegory of Love: A Study in Medieval Tradition*
(1936; rpt. London: Oxford University Press, 1970), pp. 151–154; contrast Tuve,
*Allegorical Imagery*, pp. 275–78, to which I am particularly indebted.

11. For these selections, see ll. 20249–63: ". . . qui du biau jardin quarré / clos
au petit guichet barré, / ou cil amanz vit la querole / ou Deduiz o ses genz querole,
/ a ce biau parc que je devise, / tant par est biaus a grant devise, / fere vorroit
comparaison, / il feroit trop grant mespraison / s'il ne la fet tele ou semblable / con
il feroit de voir a fable. / Car qui dedanz ce parc seroit, / asseür jurer oseroit, / ou
meïst san plus l'ueill leanz, / qui li jardins seroit neanz / au re-
gart de ceste closture . . ."

12. See ll. 633–36: "et sachiez que je cuidai estre / por voir em paradis
terrestre: / tant estoit li leus delitables, / qu'i sembloit estre esperitables . . ."

13. Among many, see, e.g., George P. Klubertanz, *St. Thomas Aquinas on
Analogy: A Textual Analysis and Systematic Synthesis* (Chicago, Ill.: Loyola
University Press, 1960); Bernard Montagnes, *La doctrine de l'analogie de l'être
d'après saint Thomas d'Aquin* (Louvain and Paris: Publications Universitaires
and Béatrice-Nauwelaerts, 1963); and David Burrell, *Analogy and Philosophical
Language* (New Haven, Conn.: Yale University Press, 1973).

14. See Lecoy's text (cited in note 1), 1:viii–xi; and Dahlberg's translation
(also cited in note 1), p. 2.

15. See *Saint Thomas Aquinas: Summa Contra Gentiles, Book One: God*,
trans. Anton C. Pegis (1955; rpt. Notre Dame, Ind.: University of Notre Dame
Press, 1975), hereafter cited as SCG, I, 32–34; and *Summa Theologiae*, in Anton
C. Pegis, ed., *Basic Writings of Saint Thomas Aquinas* (New York: Random House,
1945), vol. 1 hereafter cited as ST, I, q. 13, a. 5.

16. See ST, I, q. 7, a. 1; q. 11, a. 3, ad 2 (reply to objection 2); Etienne Gilson,
*The Christian Philosophy of St. Thomas Aquinas*, trans. L. K. Shook (London:
Gollancz, 1957), p. 100; and Harry Austryn Wolfson, "St. Thomas on Divine

Attributes," in *Mélanges offerts à Étienne Gilson* (Toronto: Pontifical Institute of Mediaeval Studies, 1959), pp. 673–78.

17. See *SCG*, I, 14, and, here and below, Gilson, *Christian Philosophy*, pp. 96–110.

18. See John Francis Quinn, *The Historical Constitution of St. Bonaventure's Philosophy* (Toronto: Pontifical Institute of Mediaeval Studies, 1973), pp. 479–80.

19. See, e.g., Klubertanz, *St. Thomas Aquinas on Analogy*, pp. 81–83. For a revaluation of the role of metaphor in such contexts, see Burrell, *Analogy and Philosophical Language*, pp. 252–63, and my discussion below.

20. See *SCG*, I, 34 and 30; *ST*, I, q. 13, a. 3; q. 13, a. 5; q. 13, a. 6; and Gilson, *Christian Philosophy*, pp. 105–7. For diverse types of analogy in Aquinas, see note 13 above.

21. See Burrell, *Analogy and Philosophical Language*, pp. 10, 15–17, 226–27.

22. On related strategies and their development, see *ibid.*, pp. 215–67, and Wolfgang Iser, *The Act of Reading: A Theory of Aesthetic Response* (1978; rpt. Baltimore, Md.: Johns Hopkins University Press, 1984), pp. 180–231.

23. See ll. 21543–52: "Ainsinc va des contreres choses, / les unes sunt des autres gloses; / et qui l'une an veust defenir, / de l'autre li doit souvenir, / ou ja, par nule antancion, / n'i metra diffinicion; / car qui des .ii. n'a connoissance, / ja n'i connoistra differance, / san quoi ne peut venir en place / diffinicion que l'an face."

24. See Paré, *Les idées*, pp. 31–32; cf. *SCG*, I, 14.

25. For early movements in this direction, see my *Allegory: The Dynamics of an Ancient and Medieval Technique* (Oxford and Cambridge, Mass.: Clarendon Press and Harvard University Press, 1987), pp. 166–67, 180–92, 196–218, with the references in the notes.

26. See *Reportatio*, III, q. 8, in *Philosophical Writings: A Selection, William of Ockham*, trans. Philotheus Boehner (1957; rpt. Indianapolis, Ind.: Bobbs-Merrill, 1979), p. 125.

27. Cf. Burrell, *Analogy and Philosophical Language*, pp. 266–67.

# 12

# SOME WORDS IN GEORGE ELIOT: NULLIFY, NEUTRAL, NUMB, NUMBER
## Neil Hertz

LATE IN *Daniel Deronda* a new character is introduced, the last significant figure in George Eliot's fiction. Described when he first appears as "this shabby, foreign-looking, eager, and gesticulating man,"[1] he will later be referred to, in an oddly generic turn of phrase, as "the undesirable father" (p. 849). He is Lapidoth, a wheedling, gambling Jewish deadbeat, father of Mordecai-Ezra, Daniel's instructor in Judaism, and of Mirah, who will become Daniel's wife. Lapidoth figures in only four chapters of this long novel, but he figures memorably, as a tour de force of caricatural realism, and as the focus for some of the book's most astonishing language. I shall begin by looking at one particular scene, commenting on the peculiarities of its language, then go on to develop its resonances elsewhere in the novel.

The arrival of this undesirable father releases in Mordecai-Ezra an "outburst of feelings which for years he had borne in solitude and silence" (p. 848), a detailing of his father's crimes and character that prompts a fit of "hysterical crying" (p. 847) on the father's part and leaves the son "exhausted by the shock of his own irrepressible utterance" (p. 848). That is, the arrival of the father is, among other things, the occasion for one more of those scenes of morally impeccable denunciation that have punctuated George Eliot's fiction from the first—thoroughly gratifying scenes in which one character is licensed to verbally excoriate another. Her readers have always admired them and no doubt even come to expect them: Nanny, in "Amos Barton," giving the Countess

what for, Mrs. Poyser "having her say out" in *Adam Bede*, Will
Ladislaw lashing Rosamond Vincy in *Middlemarch* until "what
another nature felt in opposition to her own was . . . burnt and
bitten into her consciousness."[2]

These citations can serve to remind us of the energy and violence implicit in such scenes, even when (as is the case in *Adam
Bede*) they are presented lightheartedly, and of the ways in which
the narrative thematizes and figures that violence. The force that
propels anathematizing language across the airwaves from de-
nouncer to denounced is that of "irrepressible utterance," of
checked or suppressed feeling finally bursting its bonds; the impact it produces is that of inscription, of a burning or biting or
branding of its message—or perhaps only of its force—into the
consciousness of the listener. The satisfaction these scenes hold
out to George Eliot's readers is therefore double: it is blended of a
liberationist component, the relief inherent in speech after long
silence, and of a punitive one, the justified violence with which a
guilty party is made to receive an ineradicable mark. Some scenes
stress the satisfactions of utterance, some of marking; some bring
both into salience. A variation worth noting, in *Felix Holt*, elides
the moment of sadistic marking: Esther Lyons, that novel's hero-
ine, conquers her timidity to take the witness stand at Felix's trial
for murder. Her need for utterance is powerful and, as in Mordecai-Ezra's case, we learn that "the acting out of that strong impulse [exhausts] her energy,"[3] and, although Esther's words brand
nobody, they have their effects, and win a commuted sentence
for Felix. The fact of their impingement on the audience in the
courtroom is described in terms that acknowledge the force of
Esther's speaking while dissimulating any hint of violence: "You
made all the men wish what you wished," she is told, after the
trial.[4] Years later, the aggression latent in this moment reappears
at a crucial point in *Daniel Deronda*. Gwendolen, stifled, literally
silenced in her marriage to Grandcourt and driven to wishing her
husband dead, finally gets to watch him drown before her eyes:
"I saw my wish outside me" she reports, in horror (p. 761). She
is paying Esther Lyons' dues.

(And not just Esther's dues. Stepping back, we can note that
scenes of this sort play out, within the particular fiction of each

novel, and with varying degrees of explicitness, what is also the
allegory of a writer's dream, the dream of a hard-won accession
to language that is as innocent as it is forceful. They are scenes
that give dramatic form to, and offer a locally motivating context
—that is, a reassuringly unequivocal context—for, what Maurice
Blanchot has called *l'exigence de dire*, the necessity or demand
or exaction of utterance. I shall return to Blanchot, but for the
moment let us stick with Lapidoth, a horse, as I hope to show, of
a not entirely different color.)

Lapidoth's response to his son's words marks a slight departure from the pattern I've just described. Ezra's voice had indeed
affected him: we are told that it "touched a spring of hysterical
excitability" in him, that he "threw himself into a chair and cried
like a woman," but here the narrator adds a qualification:

> —and yet, strangely, while this hysterical crying was an
> inevitable reaction in him under the stress of his son's words,
> it was also a conscious resource in a difficulty; just as in
> early life, when he was a bright-faced curly young man, he
> had been used to avail himself of this subtly-poised physical
> susceptibility to turn the edge of resentment or disapproba-
> tion. (pp. 847–48)

This subtle poise, between inevitable reaction and conscious resource, between the hysterical and the histrionic, the womanly
and the crafty, has the effect of turning the edge or diverting the
force of the language bearing in on Lapidoth; it is his defense, the
weakness that is his particular strength. And, as we shall see, it is
verbally linked to his addictive gambling by way of another "poise,"
one the narrator has already referred to as "the habitual suspensive poise of the mind in actual or imaginary play" (p. 843). For
gambling, we discover in the concluding paragraphs of this chapter, is not just Lapidoth's vice, it is his essence, "the very tissue
of [his] consciousness," serving as a strong antidote to the effec-
tiveness of Ezra's language. Lying awake that night, Lapidoth goes
"back over old Continental hours at *Roulette*, reproducing the
method of his play and the chances that had frustrated it":

> These were the stronger visions of the night with Lapidoth,
> and not the worn frame of his ireful son uttering a terrible

judgment. Ezra did pass across the gaming-table, and his words were audible; but he passed like an insubstantial ghost, and his words had the heart eaten out of them by numbers and movements that seemed to make the very tissue of Lapidoth's consciousness. (p. 849)

If that last sentence is surprising, it may be because it seems to be composed of better language than Lapidoth is quite entitled to. A conflict, or a case of interference—between a partially awakened remorse and a deep, distracting preoccupation—is rendered in ways that don't so much blur the moral of the observation (that gambling is bad, that it warps the mind, hardens the heart) as redirect attention to epistemological and figural elements that have a pronounced oddity, even a dignity, of their own. It can't be good—it has to be a sign of Lapidoth's degradation—that his son's "words had the heart eaten out of them by numbers and movements that seemed to make the very tissue of [his] consciousness" but, on the other hand, how remarkable! There is the dense abstraction of the nouns, and there is the sudden shift from a readily visualizable image (a ghostly form passing across a roulette table) to metaphors that hold out the promise of imagery but resist visual resolution. For what would a tissue—or numbers, or movements—eating the heart out of words look like? like a mouth eating something? like a corrosive liquid eating into something? The figures are intelligible but strained, and all the more powerful for that.

The distortions of this language are signs of the struggle they gesture toward without quite miming, here named as a struggle of language and consciousness—the thrust of the son's moral language, the mysteriously passive aggression of the father's undesirable consciousness. And it is worth noting that in this passage— and for the first and only time in George Eliot's fiction—the stress is on the ineffectiveness of powerful moral language. Here it seems to have met its match. But what exactly is its match? To stay within the framework of plot and character, we could say that Lapidoth is incorrigible, that Ezra's words leave him unmarked, like water off a duck's back. But the sentence is saying something else, something that exceeds the character of Lapidoth or the drama of his encounter with his son's wrath. It is figuring not just a protective sheath but a counterforce, an instance that acts to neutralize or nullify Ezra's words, to hollow them out, to render them as insubstantial and ghostly as his image in his father's mind, and it is naming that force, in an enigmatic and peculiar idiom, as "numbers and movements" which somehow form a "tissue." What attacks Ezra's words would seem to be the surface on which those words impinge: it is as if paper were both receiving and corroding print, or as if a ground could both accept and invalidate a figure. "The imperious gambling desire within [Lapidoth]," we are told a few pages later, "carried on its activity through every other occupation, and made a continuous web of imagination that held all else in its meshes" (p. 858). George Eliot is seeking figures for the unrepresentable, just as Freud will when, in attempting to describe the death drive, he evokes a silent, colorless something which both sustains and erodes the erotic drives that tint it with their hues, rendering it as recognizable as it ever gets.[5] And indeed Eliot appears to be grappling with the same phenomena as Freud, that is with instances of compulsive repetition, the "narrow monotony of action" (p. 37) around the roulette wheel, orchestrated by a croupier whom the narrator likens to "an ingeniously constructed automaton" (p. 35).

What is this counterforce that resists representation, and what is to be gained by dwelling on these difficulties? That will be the burden of what follows. I spoke of the numbers and movements in Lapidoth's mind acting to "neutralize" or "nullify" the effects of his son's speech. I chose those verbs from a cluster of n-words salient in *Deronda*, words like *numbers* and its derivatives (*unnumbered*, for example), but also *numb* (with its derivatives *numbness*, *benumbing*, and the rhymes *dumb* and *dumbness*), *neutral*, *neutralize*, *neutrality*, *nullify*, *nullity*, *negative*, *nought*, and even, as we shall see, *nucleus*. But I also had in mind an apposite page in Blanchot, a page in which Blanchot is engaged with the difficulties of grasping, in language, that about language which he calls *le neutre*, a term sometimes translated as *the neuter*, when its relation to the grammatical category is being emphasized, or as *the neutral*, when the stress is placed on its affective, or affectless, connotations. The page occurs in the central—and longest—fragment of *Le pas au-delà*, a fragment beginning, not without an overtone of irony, "Nous pouvons toujours nous interroger sur le neutre":[6] "We can always interrogate ourselves about the neutral." "Lotsa luck!" would seem to be the unspoken reply to this proposal, and indeed Blanchot had had something to say, earlier in *Le pas au-delà*, about the entanglements of luck, gambling, writing, and the neutral. Here he is turning over the problem of naming the neutral, of locating it regionally within language, since it is carried by all language, as if—I'm translating now—"language 'in general' were neutral, since all forms and possibilities of affirmation and negation deploy themselves in language against a neutral ground [sur fond de neutre]." He goes on to describe *le neutre*—that expression— as "indicating, in the form of a noun, *une manière verbale de retenir l'exigence de dire*": here a translator must decide what to do with *retenir*—it must mean "a verbal means of *containing* the exigency of utterance," of putting on the brakes, of restraining it; but it must also mean "of holding onto it, of keeping it in mind, of reminding ourselves that there is this exigency, this pressure." What other names perform this function? Blanchot continues:

> The neutral: we think we have grasped it, if we invoke, randomly [au hasard] forms of passive action as marked and remarkable as those, precisely, of randomness [le hasard], more accurately of the aleatory, of the unconscious, of the trace or of play [le jeu]. And many other forms could be proposed, none of which would seem satisfactory: the *sacred* with respect to *god*, *absence* with respect to *presence*, *writing* (offered here as an un-exemplary example [as *an* example, not *the* privileged example]) with respect to *speech*, *the other* with respect to *the self* . . . *being* with respect to *existence*, *difference* with respect to the *One*.

The list could go on, Blanchot implies: the neutral could be found at play within each of these terms, rendering each of them that much more difficult to conceptualize, and eluding conceptualization "itself." Take, for example, *la chance* (luck), which, like *le hasard* and *le jeu* will concern us in *Deronda*. There is a fragment, earlier in *Le pas au-delà*, where Blanchot takes up the expression "I'm lucky" ("J'ai de la chance"), and takes it up *as an expression*,

as something just said by someone whom he then addresses,
turning on him as if to set him straight:

> "J'ai de la chance." A formula as forceful as it is shameless,
> for chance is that which dispossesses and disappropriates.
> Which—O gambler who pretends to speak in the name of
> the game—which would amount to saying [ce qui revien-
> drait à dire]: I possess that which dispossesses, since it is
> the very relation of dispossession. Which amounts to saying
> that there's no chance for chance, no chance for luck, and to
> saying that one's only chance [la seule chance] is in that
> anonymous relation which itself can't be called luck, or, if
> so, only that luck that never falls out [qui n'échoit pas],
> which is played on by—and which plays on—the neutral.[7]

The interest of this passage is not particularly in the propositions
it puts forward, propositions that are likely to stir little surprise
at a conference on absence and negation: we "know," in the way
that we know such things—that is, by hearing them said at con-
ferences like this one—that we don't "have" luck, hold it in our
grasp, that it is more accurate to say that it "has" us, etc., etc.
More interesting are the gestures with which these matters are
engaged, the apostrophe to the "shameless" gambler, the triple
stress on "ce qui revient à dire" ("which comes to saying")—as
though these paradoxes of agency, possession, and control must
be thought of as generators of skewed discourse, of formulas that
are never quite on the mark, hence requiring us to try again, but
also requiring us to conjure up interlocutors, for example, shameless gamblers at whom to aim our telling indictments. So Ezra, in
the grip of just such an *exigence de dire*, plays it out by addressing his father: "You have become a gambler," he pronounces, "and
where shame and conscience were, there sits an insatiable desire"
(p. 847).

What seems to me exemplary about this fragment of *Le pas au-
delà* is its offering us a rapid, condensed glimpse into the ongoing
genesis of the elements of fiction—of motivated speech, of characters, of conflict, of plot—seen as means of coming to terms
with what Blanchot likes to call not the workings but the unwork-

ings or undoings (not *oeuvres* but *désoeuvres*) of the neutral. Turning back to *Deronda*, I would propose that we see in the gambler Lapidoth one last casting up of the neutral, a character whose appearance toward the end of a long work of fiction (and a long career) can best be brought into focus by considering the similarly late appearance—in *Deronda* both more frequently and more tellingly than in any of the earlier novels—of words like *neutralize, nullify,* and *numb.* These terms are scattered throughout the novel, sometimes in contexts about which there is little to be said, elsewhere clustered at points of thematic interest and stress. I shall look at some instances of this, then return, finally, to the question of why Lapidoth appears when he does.

ABOUT HALFWAY through the novel, just before he will first meet Mordecai-Ezra, Daniel's hopes for his life, his dissatisfactions, and the reasons for his sense of *désoeuvrement* are presented in a long ruminative paragraph. It is a seemingly sluggish bit of narration, which accomplishes its forward movement by doubling back, again and again, to some of the same words and syntactical turns. What results is a series of echoing sentences, five of them, spaced fairly evenly over the two pages of text; I'll lift them out of the surrounding prose and cite them in sequence:

> His early-wakened sensibility and reflectiveness had developed into a many-sided sympathy, which threatened to hinder any persistent course of action. . . .

> His plenteous, flexible sympathy had ended by falling into one current with that reflective analysis which tends to neutralise sympathy.

> A too reflective and diffusive sympathy was in danger of paralysing in him that indignation against wrong and that selectness of fellowship which are the conditions of moral force. . . .

> . . . he did not attempt to hide from himself that he had fallen into a meditative numbness, and was gliding farther and farther away from [a] life of practically energetic sentiment. . . .

> He wanted some way of keeping emotion and its progeny of
> sentiments—which makes the savours of life—substantial
> and strong in the face of a reflectiveness that threatened to
> nullify all differences. (pp. 412–14)

One could claim that each of these sentences is saying something
slightly different, and that together they offer a carefully inflected
representation of Daniel's state of mind. But that wouldn't quite
account for the plangency with which the dangers of this neutralizing, numbing, nullifying force are evoked, nor for the drift of
the paragraph toward the most abstractedly conceived threat, that
of the nullification of all differences. The epistemological flavor
of the last of these sentences, along with the air of obsessiveness
that clings to the paragraph, suggest that the threats envisaged
here are directed at more than the moral fiber of an especially
sympathetic young Englishman. The pages invite a double reading. In their exploration of the paradoxical consequences of sym-
pathy and reflectiveness, they not only lay out the terms of Daniel's dilemma, they reflect back on a problem that can be seen
emerging in George Eliot's fiction up to this point, the problem of
what her critics have come to call her powers of "sympathetic
imagination." These powers had been most impressively displayed in *Middlemarch,* and most convincingly embodied—or
rather dis-embodied—in the shrewd and melancholy presiding
consciousness and narrative voice of that novel. In *Deronda,* George
Eliot experiments with relocating both that consciousness and its
voice within the framework of the novel in the figure of Daniel.
What would happen, she seems to be asking herself, if the *Middlemarch* narrator had to engage with the characters he had been
merely observing?

Her response to that question can be seen in the economy of
the novel's double plot. On the one hand, the gains in "moral
force" and "practically energetic sentiment" are played out in the
redemptive Jewish plot; on the other hand, Daniel's relations with
Gwendolen and Grandcourt allow us to calculate the price to be
paid for redemption. Between the two plots elaborate structural
analogies, as well as glancing links of figuration, complicate that
calculation, however, and tell still another story. Let me trace one

such complication and pursue its consequences for a reading of
*Deronda*.

We can pinpoint the moment when Daniel moves beyond reflectiveness into the scene he had been contemplating sympathet-
ically but distantly: it is the moment he is led to rescue Mirah, to
prevent her from drowning herself—the moment that initiates
the Jewish plot—and it is rendered precisely as the movement of
a neutral consciousness drawn into action. Daniel is depicted
rowing on the Thames at sunset, and poised in what I have called
elsewhere an end-of-the-line position,[8] contemplating an emblem
of self-reflection, the "double glow of the sky and the river,"
pausing "where he had a great breadth of water before him,
reflecting the . . . sky, while he himself was in shadow":

> for a long while he never turned his eyes from the view right
> in front of him. He was forgetting everything else in a half-
> speculative, half-involuntary identification of himself with
> the objects he was looking at, thinking how far it might be
> possible habitually to shift his centre till his own personal-
> ity would be no less outside him than the landscape,—
> when the sense of something moving on the bank opposite
> him . . . made him turn his glance thitherward. (pp. 229–30)
> 30)

Although the river scene is an attractive one, there are hints of
difficulty latent in that "double glow," and in the notation that
Daniel's acts of projective identification are "half-speculative,
half-involuntary." But whatever dangers lurk there are brushed
aside; Daniel is rescued from neutrality when he chances to fix
his attention on the single figure of Mirah preparing her "drown-
ing-shroud" and rows across to her.

But consider this complementary moment, another near-
drowning. It occurs during one of the searching conversations
between Daniel and Gwendolen, exchanges in which Daniel mimics
the diction and imagery of the *Middlemarch* narrator[9] in yet
another effort at rescue, only to be obliged to register the ineffectiveness of that language in alleviating Gwendolen's despair:

> He was under the baffling difficulty of discerning, that what
> he had been urging on her was thrown into the pallid dis-

tance of mere thought before the outburst of her habitual emotion. It was as if he saw her drowning while his limbs were bound. (p. 509)

If Daniel had been drawn to eliminate the distance between himself and Mirah in the earlier scene, here he is cast back into the position of the sympathetic but impotent observer, his urgent imperatives "thrown into the pallid distance of mere thought," that is, effectively neutralized by the force of Gwendolen's "outburst." But notice that what goes wrong here is not a function of the hero's speculative distance or of his lack of moral involvement: if *Middlemarch* language doesn't work, that failure can now be blamed on its coming up against a particularly resistant counterforce, in some ways like the "numbers and movements" that will oppose Ezra's strong words later in the novel. Here that malign power is generated not by gambling but by something equally "habitual," the emotion of compulsive fear or dread that drives Gwendolen to outbursts of this sort.

The comparison I've been sketching suggests two things. First, that there is a surreptitious structural relation between, on the one hand, the unavoidable (or call it innocent) "neutrality" inherent in narrative (for example, in the distance of a narrator's voice) and, on the other, the neutralizing power of the forms of compulsive repetition thematized in this novel in various ways (as gambling, hysterical dread, or the return of the repressed); and second, that this relation allows a series of displacements to occur in the figuring of "the neutral," displacements between "innocent" and "guilty" forms of neutrality, between problems that are unavoidable and thematizations of those problems in more or less lurid moral and psychological terms.

The n-words scattered about the novel make up a network along which these displacements may be tracked: invariably they lead to nodes of equivocation, points where elements of characterization or thematic motifs can be seen entangled with one another, often entangled in such a way that questions of agency, the basis for judgments of innocence and guilt—questions of what (or who) is active, what (or who) passive—are made to claim the reader's attention.

Consider the ways in which the novel lends itself to psycho-analytic readings: it is a commonplace that George Eliot had anticipated Freud—in her presentation of the urgencies of trans-ferential need as they shape Gwendolen's painful talks with Dan-iel, and, more compellingly still, in her exploration of repression and of the terrors associated with the return of repressed images and feelings. "Things repeat themselves in me so," Gwendolen says, shuddering, toward the end of the novel, "They come back —they will all come back" (p. 840). The explicitness and, at the same time, the subtlety with which these matters are dramatized makes it easy to ignore the variations in representational mode employed in a narrative that blends techniques of high realism with those of Gothic melodrama and of allegory. But the blend is there, and its effect is consistently to convert nuanced and pow-erful accounts of intrapsychic activity into allegorical encounters between persons. The repressions that elements in Gwendolen's experience undergo are presented convincingly as the work of her psyche, but they are also represented as suppressions, en-forced silences imposed on her by her husband, whose "benumb-ing effect" is compared to the "touch of a torpedo" (p. 477). One result is to enlarge the space within which Gwendolen's story unfolds, while keeping it no less claustrophobic: it is not just her wish but her dread that she sees outside herself, and, as her interior life is turned inside out, she reappears "within" it as a passive victim as well as a projecting agent.

Another result of this particular bit of allegorizing is the the-matic alignment of the numb with the dumb, of the suppression of feeling with the externally imposed inhibition of speech. Here Grandcourt comes to the fore as the agent of the neutral, appear-ing all the more frighteningly effective as a paralyser of others when at his most catatonically languorous himself. We read, at one point, of

> the languor of intention that came over Grandcourt, like a fit of diseased numbness, when an end seemed within easy reach: to desist then, when all expectation was to the con-trary, became another gratification of mere will, sublimely independent of definite motive. (p. 187)

This analysis offers a context for Grandcourt's "diseased numbness" in intersubjective struggles for power: his inertia is not a lack but a strategy for defeating the expectations of others, his want of motive an exercise of will. Words like "dominance" and "empire" and particularly "imperious" reappear in descriptions of Grandcourt's wooing, subduing, and silencing of Gwendolen. Her will "had seemed imperious" (p. 477) but it was no match for what is referred to as "the imperious spell" that Grandcourt exercised (p. 331). Mere will, then, with the emphasis on the "mere," becomes a mode of the neutral, and, in a telling juxtaposition, it is aligned with chance:

> The navvy waking from sleep and without malice heaving a stone to crush the life out of his still sleeping comrade, is understood to lack the trained motive which makes a character fairly calculable in its actions; but by a roundabout course even a gentleman may make of himself a chancy personage, raising an uncertainty as to what he may do next, which sadly spoils companionship. (p. 364)

But here an important equivocation develops. Grandcourt may be a "chancy personage" in the eyes of others, but he seems to know his own mind, to know what he wants. At least, so these citations would suggest; but the epigraph (p. 322) to one of the chapters concentrating on him complicates this picture: "How trace the why and wherefore in a mind reduced to the barrenness of a fastidious egoism," it begins, "in which all direct desires are dulled, and have dwindled from motives into a vacillating expectation of motives . . . ?"

Here Grandcourt would seem to be capable of raising "uncertainty as to what he may do next" in his own mind as well: a will of the degree of purity of his may no longer be quite in the possession of its owner. This at once makes Grandcourt a bit less villainous, though no less frightening, and it assimilates him to the gamblers in the novel: his vacillating expectation of motives is like the "habitual suspensive poise of the mind" the narrator will locate in Lapidoth:

> The gambling appetite is more absolutely dominant than bodily hunger, which can be neutralised by an emotional or

intellectual excitation; but the passion for watching chances —the habitual suspensive poise of the mind in actual or imaginary play—nullifies the susceptibility to other excitation. In its final, imperious stage, it seems the unjoyous dissipation of demons, seeking diversion on the burning marl of perdition. (p. 843)

A vacillation or a poise can be named as an "appetite" or "passion" to allow it to enter into calculations, quantifications of more or less "dominant" or "imperious" excitations, but—again, like the death drive—it is never properly named in that idiom, or in any particular idiom, Blanchot would remind us. How, after all, can an appetite be a poise? But it is precisely the migrations of this hard-to-lay-hold-of neutralizing force or appetite or poise or drive that I have been asking you to follow, as it shifts from Daniel to Gwendolen, from Gwendolen to Grandcourt, from Grandcourt to Lapidoth. In each case the elaboration of the novelist's language leads her, in her explorations of motive, to the point where motive is dispersed in equivocations, where agency is hard to distinguish from passivity, or from a poise that is at once suspensive and habitual. The threat of such dispersion prompts a consolidation of character in each case—as either redeemable (Daniel and, perhaps, Gwendolen) or dismissable (Grandcourt and Lapidoth)—and the neutralizing force moves on, until it has, with Lapidoth, exhausted the possibilities of embodiment in this particular fiction.

I have left to one side a character who, like Lapidoth, shows up late in the novel and, like him, departs rapidly. She is the unloving mother who serves as a complement to the undesirable father—Daniel's mother, the Princess Halm-Eberstein, who had abandoned him as a child in order to pursue her career as an operatic singer and actress, and who now summons him to learn of his Jewish birth and to turn over to him, against her will, documents that confirm him in his commitment to Zionism. The Princess takes her place in the series of characters I have been examining: she had, Daniel reminds her indignantly, "willed to annihilate" (p. 727) his Jewish identity and his links to the past. She is as numbing as Grandcourt, placing Daniel "under a ban of silence . . . an imperious prohibition of any tenderness" (p. 724);

she is as haunted by remorseful thoughts as is Gwendolen; she presents as unsettling a mix of sincerity and canny histrionic manipulation as does Lapidoth: indeed the language in which she is characterized mobilizes the entire thematics of neutrality, of uncertainty and equivocation that I have been tracing, draws it together and shapes it into a portrait in which many readers have recognized the lineaments of George Eliot herself, for the Princess is presented as an elderly, accomplished, and renowned mimetic artist:

> this woman's nature was one in which feeling—and all the more when it was tragic as well as real—immediately became matter for conscious representation: experience immediately passed into drama, and she acted her own emotions. . . . It would not be true to say that she felt less because of this double consciousness: she felt—that is, her mind went through—all the more, but with a difference: each nucleus of pain or pleasure had a deep atmosphere of the excitement or spiritual intoxication which at once exalts and deadens. (pp. 691–92)

I have written elsewhere of the ways in which the Princess's ejection from the novel functions to sustain its redemptive economy by translating questions of difference and of the representation of difference into a moral and psychological idiom that allows for their apparent resolution.[10] What remains to be said? What remains to be said is why the novel doesn't end right there, with a resonant *mise-en-abyme*, the neutral finally named as the irreducible distance between a novelist and her most explicit attempt to write herself into her fiction by grandly representing both her considerable powers of mimesis and the double consciousness that is the condition of her exercising those powers. Why isn't that enough?

We can begin to answer that by noticing the drift of those sentences as they work to come to terms with a residual difference. It is first formulated as the difference between real feeling and its conscious representation, between experience and drama, in the generic singular. It is then reformulated as double consciousness, only to have the "integrity" of that double consciousness further dispersed into an indefinite number of nuclei, atoms of experience characterized in the abstract idiom of their most common denominators as units of pain or pleasure, each surrounded by its own ambivalently exalting and deadening aura. It is only a short step from these almost undifferentiated nuclei to the numbers and movements that will make up the texture of Lapidoth's consciousness.

It is in this sense that we can take the language associated with Lapidoth as what remains to be said after the scapegoating of the Princess—that is, after an attempt to capture the writer's relation to writing in a specular relation has proved unsuccessful. Lapidoth cannot embody the neutral, even though at moments he can be made to pantomime its effects—for example, when he is shown "remaining silent but incessantly carrying on a dumb language of facial movement and gesticulation" (p. 852). But, more abstractly —and more tellingly because more abstractly—his consciousness can be reduced and dispersed into the plural sameness of the automatic movements of roulette (whose dynamics blurs the differences between the croupier, the players, and the wheel) and into the sameness of numbers that are not really numbers (not, that is, units of calculation) but numerals marking off otherwise identical segments of the roulette wheel, a final figure for the arbitrary marks without which no investments of any sort—not just no bets—would be conceivable.

## Notes

1. George Eliot, *Daniel Deronda*, ed. Barbara Hardy (Harmondsworth, England: Penguin, 1967), p. 807. Further page references will be given in the text.

2. George Eliot, *Middlemarch*, ed. W. J. Harvey (Harmondsworth, England: Penguin, 1965), p. 836. The language is echoed by the artist Klesmer: "Every word that Klesmer had said seemed to have been branded into her memory, as most words are which bring with them a new set of impressions and make an epoch for us" (p. 306).

3. *Felix Holt*, ed. Peter Coveney (Harmondsworth, England: Penguin, 1972), p. 589.

4. *Ibid.*

5. The allusion is to a passage in *Civilization and Its Discontents* in *The Standard Edition of the Complete Psychological Works of Sigmund Freud*, 24 vols., trans. James Strachey (London: Hogarth, 1953–1974), 21:120. I have discussed the language of this passage, and related figures, in "Freud and the Sand-

man," in *The End of the Line* (New York: Columbia University Press, 1985), especially pp. 100–102.

6. Maurice Blanchot, *Le pas au-delà* (Paris: Gallimard, 1973) pp. 101–7. See also Blanchot's *L'Ecriture du désastre* (Paris: Gallimard, 1980), which has been finely translated, by Ann Smock, as *The Writing of the Disaster* (Lincoln and London: University of Nebraska Press, 1986), in particular the entry on p. 37 of the translation: "Write in order that the negative and the neutral, in their always concealed difference—in the most dangerous of proximities—might recall to each other their respective specificity, the one working, the other un-working [l'un travaillant, l'autre désoeuvrant]."

7. Blanchot, *Le pas au-delà*, p. 41.

8. See the "Afterword" to *The End of the Line*, pp. 217–39, for a discussion of similar figures, in *Deronda* and elsewhere.

9. Compare Daniel's "Take your fear as a safeguard. It is like quickness of hearing. . . . Try to take hold of your sensibility, and use it as if it were a faculty, like vision" (p. 509) with these well-known (and representative) lines from chapter 20 of *Middlemarch*: "If we had a keen vision and feeling of all ordinary human life, it would be like hearing the grass grow and the squirrel's heart beat, and we should die of that roar which lies on the other side of silence. As it is, the quickest of us walk about well wadded with stupidity" (p. 226).

10. In the "Afterword" to *The End of the Line*, pp. 224–33.

# 13

# TRADITION IN THE SPACE OF NEGATIVITY
## Sanford Budick

MY AIM in this essay is to suggest some of the ways in which tradition was both bequeathed and inherited by neoclassical as well as classical writers. The focus of my discussion is a series of Greek, Latin, and English apostrophes, all of which are framed by certain recurring tropes of division and negation. Classical apostrophe is, I believe, a particularly fascinating object for an inquiry into the mechanisms of tradition. By its very nature, apostrophe deprives its contents of the temporal and spatial contexts that would make determinate description possible. Formally considered, it delimits areas of virtually *inaccessible* meaning within the worlds it inhabits. We may say, indeed, that according to most recognizable usages of the term *ontology*, these areas are ontologically discontinuous with the worlds from which they are cut out. Yet despite these delimitations, the tropes of division and negation, which constitute the settings of at least the particular apostrophes that I will discuss, condition and mitigate the inaccessibility of apostrophe's meanings in a special way. In these tropes a venue of transmission is created that shares many features of rhetorical division with apostrophe itself and that necessitates the subsequent bonding of individual apostrophes (and their contexts) with each other. In the final analysis, this interdependency constitutes a large part not only of the inheriting but also of the *willing* of tradition by classical and neoclassical writers.

In this *traditio,* or "handing on," meaning is precisely not viewed as being contained in a particular image or concept, but is reenacted as an interpretive drama that acknowledges and internalizes the very inaccessibility of meaning that apostrophe evokes. This drama is played out in the relationships between individuals and between texts. I will proceed, therefore, by re-creating some of the scenes in which classical and neoclassical apostrophes occur, attempting thereby to retrieve the structures of meaning that these writers perceived. The totality of their recourse to apostrophe and its special framing can, I believe, tell us a good deal about the classical forms of handing on.

The texts I will be discussing, in retrospective order, are 1. Pope's "Epistle to Oxford" (1721); 2. Dryden's elegy to Oldham (1684); 3. the apostrophe to Nisus and Euryalus in book 9, and some related passages in book 6, of the *Aeneid*; and 4. the apostrophes to Patroklos in book 16 of the *Iliad*.

## Filiations

Certain aspects of the interrelations among these texts have been pointed out before and are more or less well known. Not only, for example, are Virgil's stories of Nisus and Euryalus presented as a parallel to the Patrokleia, which brings about the major shift in the action of the *Iliad* by precipitating Achilles' fulfillment of his destiny, and not only does Dryden's elegy to Oldham turn on the simile of the race run by Nisus and Euryalus, but in the lines of Pope's "Epistle" that first describe Oxford's relation to Parnell, Pope invokes Dryden's elegy by overt allusion. "Pope echoed Dryden," as Tillotson says, "both echoing Virgil."[1] Taken together with the memorializing of a friendship inter-rupted by death, these filiations suggest separate attempts by Virgil, Dryden, and Pope to retrieve a species of literary relation-ship with at least one earlier poem. But the network of correspon-dences generated and deepened among these multiple parallel-isms is far greater than this, as we shall soon see. My aim is to understand how these filiations function. Do they point only to poetic modes held in common or do they also indicate the ways in which the poems bind themselves to each other—prospec-tively as well as *retrospectively*? Do the poems themselves, in other words, *make* the tradition in which we locate them histori-cally?

Although Dryden's elegy and Pope's "Epistle" have long been valued as two of the major achievements of English classicism, they are only infrequently discussed by critics and they are, I believe, unfamiliar to many readers. I will therefore begin by citing these poems whole:

## TO THE MEMORY OF MR. OLDHAM

> Farewel, too little and too lately known,
> Whom I began to think and call my own;
> For sure our Souls were near ally'd; and thine
> Cast in the same Poetick mould with mine.
> One common Note on either Lyre did strike,                5
> And Knaves and Fools we both abhorr'd alike;
> To the same Goal did both our Studies drive,
> The last set out the soonest did arrive.
> Thus *Nisus* fell upon the slippery place,
> While his young Friend perform'd and won the Race.        10
> O early ripe! to thy abundant store
> What could advancing Age have added more?
> It might (what Nature never gives the young)
> Have taught the numbers of thy native Tongue.
> But Satyr needs not those, and Wit will shine             15
> Through the harsh cadence of a rugged line.
> A noble Error, and but seldom made,
> When Poets are by too much force betray'd.
> Thy generous fruits, though gather'd ere their prime
> Still shew'd a quickness; and maturing time               20
> But mellows what we write to the dull sweets of Rime.
> Once more, hail and farewel; farewel thou young,
> But ah too short, *Marcellus* of our Tongue;
> Thy Brows with Ivy, and with Laurels bound;
> But Fate and gloomy Night encompass thee around.          25

## EPISTLE TO ROBERT EARL OF OXFORD,
## AND EARL MORTIMER

Such were the Notes, thy once-lov'd Poet sung,
'Till Death untimely stop'd his tuneful Tongue.
    Oh just beheld, and lost! admir'd, and mourn'd!
With softest Manners, gentlest Arts, adorn'd!
Blest in each Science, blest in ev'ry Strain!              5

Dear to the Muse, to HARLEY dear—in vain!
   For him, thou oft hast bid the World attend,
Fond to forget the Statesman in the Friend;
For *Swift* and him, despis'd the Farce of State,
The sober Follies of the Wise and Great;           10
Dextrous, the craving, fawning Crowd to quit,
And pleas'd to 'scape from Flattery to Wit.
   Absent or dead, still let a Friend be dear,
(A Sigh the Absent claims, the Dead a Tear)
Recall those Nights that clos'd thy toilsom Days,   15
Still hear thy *Parnell* in his living Lays:
Who careless, now, of Int'rest. Fame, or Fate,
Perhaps forgets that OXFORD e'er was Great;
Or deeming meanest what we greatest call,
Beholds thee glorious only in thy Fall.           20
   And sure if ought below the Seats Divine
Can touch Immortals, 'tis a Soul like thine:
A Soul supreme, in each hard Instance try'd,
Above all Pain, all Passion, and all Pride,
The Rage of Pow'r, the Blast of publick Breath,   25
The Lust of Lucre, and the Dread of Death.
   In vain to Desarts thy Retreat is made;
The Muse attends thee to the silent Shade:
'Tis hers, the brave Man's latest Steps to trace,
Re-judge his Acts, and dignify Disgrace.         30
When Int'rest calls off all her sneaking Train,
And all th' Oblig'd desert, and all the Vain;
She waits, or to the Scaffold, or the Cell,
When the last ling'ring Friend has bid farewel.
Ev'n now she shades thy Evening Walk with Bays,   35
(No Hireling she, no Prostitute to Praise)
Ev'n now, observant of the parting Ray,
Eyes the calm Sun-set of thy Various Day,
Thro' Fortune's Cloud One truly Great can see,
Nor fears to tell, that MORTIMER is He.[2]

These two poems about pairs of friends are themselves very
much a pair. Pope composed the "Epistle" soon after bringing his
translation of the *Iliad* to a triumphant conclusion. The project
had cost him six years of tremendous effort, the fruits of which,
he dearly hoped, were on the order of what Johnson would in fact

soon describe as "certainly the noblest version [translation] of poetry which the world has ever seen." Its publication, said Johnson, putting his finger directly on the *translatio studii*—the transposition of cultural riches and power—which lay at the heart of Pope's matter, was "one of the great events in the annals of learning."[3] The heroic pitch of Pope's exertions as translator of Homer contributed an important part of the epic identity he had created for himself in the shadow of the most acclaimed English translation of Virgil in the previous century: Dryden's *Aeneid*.

## The "Fall" of Harley

In the "Epistle to Oxford" Pope brings the parallelism between Dryden's and his own ambitions to a point of virtual convergence, even while bestowing on the very possibility of that convergence a remarkable depth of meaning. This depth of meaning is not restricted to the poem's activity of retrieving layers of accumulated influence in order to point toward the source of the tradition in which it stands. The poem also suggests, thematically and structurally, how the poet is absorbed into this tradition, and creates it, even as he writes.

Right at the beginning, Pope's poem announces its relation to Dryden's Virgilian apostrophe to a dead young friend, and it places its own apostrophes, to Oxford and his friend Parnell, in a context that alludes directly to the setting of Homer's apostrophes to Patroklos, the doomed friend of doomed Achilles. I will discuss these allusions to death and their fateful implications for Harley in a moment, but we can already say that in turning directly to the *Iliad* Pope capitalizes on another dimension of the "Goal" of *translatio* to which his own "Studies" are driving him. In addition to echoing Dryden echoing Virgil, he uncovers the site in which Virgil's own echo reverberates, and locates his own poem in that particular Homeric stratum. Although it is not immediately obvious, this is a poem about the withdrawal of a great champion, Harley/Achilles, from the field of battle, about the "living Lays" that his fallen Patroklos/Parnell—"thy Parnell"— still sings to him, and about Harley/Achilles' imminent death.

The fact of death is not, however, what principally interests

Pope or our other poets. Rather, what each poet creates is a death scene dramatizing a structure of relationships. All of these scenes are characterized by a significant breach in the landscape or story. In its turn, this breach or gap coincides with the place of the protagonist's death and of his handing on of the tradition. The place of death, finally, is for all our poets something other than the marking of absence. For all of them, in fact, only place remains, not the persons who disappear into it.

To show how this is so, I will begin by describing the drama of Pope's poem and then reconstructing the setting that gives that particular drama its deepest form. Both the drama and the setting are functions of the poem's opening words:

> Such were the Notes, thy once-lov'd Poet sung,
> 'Till Death untimely stop'd his tuneful Tongue.
> Oh just beheld, and lost! admir'd, and mourn'd!

The word "such" points literally to the volume of Parnell's selected poems, dedicated to Oxford, that Pope's "Epistle" accompanies. It refers most immediately, therefore, to the fact of Parnell's death and the commemoration of that death in the publication of the finest of his verses. "Such" verses give the dead Parnell a way to perform a last office of the living, which is to honor his great friend in a final salutation. This is itself a poignant illustration of handing on, but it too is not the main concern of Pope's poem.

Rather, the drama of this poem begins with its decisive turning away from its ostensible subject, its transformation of the local occasion into an event that is somehow of ritual significance. Pope's opening line stands first and foremost as a separate statement, with no necessary connection to any of Parnell's verses. It is an exclamation of pain which refers in one sense to no particularized object. Pope's line, that is, not only refers to a "once-lov'd Poet," but, more palpably, it invokes the rhythms that structure the rite of passing called elegy.

If we ask for the immediate evidence of this continuity of rite, we find it, as I suggested earlier, in the unmistakable allusions to at least the following lines from Dryden's elegy to Oldham and to the lines in Virgil that stand behind Dryden's:

> Farewel, too little and too lately known,
> Whom I began to think and call my own;
> . . . . . . . . . . . . . . . . . . . . . . . . . . . . . . . . .
>
> . . . farewel thou young,
> But ah too short, *Marcellus* of our Tongue.
>
> ostendent terris hunc tantum fata, nec ultra
> esse sinent.
>
> > (*Aeneid,* book 6:869–70)

The angle of vision on poetry or discourse created by verses like these suggests, self-reflexively, that they are themselves included in the collective transience. At the moment of being written they self-consciously embrace their own condition of being past. Though Pope's "Epistle" is apparently preoccupied with a local occasion, its opening words lament the lost worlds of the past that, for Pope, form one pole of the structure of the present.

Pope's decorum or unity of impact is perfect here because the power of "such," as of "like" in line 22, is double-edged, summoning up both the immediate reality of the poem and its existence within the tradition of passing away into which it is itself passing:

> And sure if aught below the Seats Divine
> Can touch Immortals, 'tis a Soul like thine:
> A Soul supreme, in each hard Instance try'd,
> Above all Pain, all Passion, and all Pride.
>
> > (ll. 21–24)

We cannot arraign Pope for empty hyperbole or special pleading in his tribute to Harley, whom he has earlier criticized quite severely (ll. 7–12).[4] Pope's Muse is "no Prostitute to Praise." He does not, therefore, say that Oxford himself has a supreme soul or that, vying for power in a grossly flawed world, he was singly above all pain, passion, and pride. Rather, just as the word "such" simultaneously points to Parnell's poems and pulls away from them to the greater succession of poetry sung by other dead poets, so the soul that can touch immortals is identified not as Oxford's but as being "*like*" Oxford's. It is only said to be his soul by approximation and mortal succession.

Indeed, if that soul can be said to have any one primary identity, in any one individual, it is with Christ himself, whose soul,
Pope intimates, became incarnate in a tradition of human being.
The phrase "in each hard Instance *try'd*"—meaning *tempted,
proven*—and the allegorical scene evoked not only by "Above all
Pain, all Passion, and all Pride," but also by "The Rage of Pow'r,
the Blast of publick Breath / The Lust of Lucre, and the Dread of
Death" (ll. 25–26), lead suggestively to an image of the man of
the Gospels and of *Paradise Regained*, the greater man tempted
in the wilderness, whose archetype dwarfs the little events of
Augustan England: "In vain," says the Muse to Harley, "In vain
to Desarts thy Retreat is made" (l. 27). Harley has already been
absorbed into a greater Christian destiny. Capturing the beauty of
Pope's understatement is impossible. But we can say that Oxford
is presented here as a distant *imitator* of a "supreme" original.

Pope thus accomplishes much more than inserting an earliest
Christian soul in the links of a classical metempsychosis built on
the play of suchness or likeness. Rather, the Christian intimations
work a recession and dissociation of Harley's individual personality, not only from the local world of the poem but from the
world itself. This is felt also in the easy exchange of Harley's
names: of Oxford for Harley, and then of Mortimer for Oxford.
The supreme soul that is momentarily *likened* to Oxford both is
and is not Robert Harley. The drama of the poem does not consist
in the celebration of Harley or Parnell, either as individuals or
even as individuals who evoke classical or scriptural resonances.
Rather it emerges from the wavering between past and present,
between quotidian reality and spiritual universe, that not only
cuts the poem painfully down the middle but creates an intermediate zone of uncertainty where it is impossible to say, finally,
whether Oxford is dead or alive.

We can take a large step forward in seeing the relation between
Pope's poem and its forebears if we can acknowledge this area of
equivocation in all its troubling dubiety. Harley's "Fall" signifies
much more than a temporary setback. We have suspicions to this
effect from the beginning. Parnell, we are told, is "Dear to the
Muse, to HARLEY dear—in vain!" The ambiguous placement of
"in vain" at the end of the line raises the possibility that Parnell

may continue to be dear to the Muse, which deals in records and memories, even though he very soon, or even now, can no longer be dear, in any sense, to Harley. This suspicion is amply borne out at the edge of the other "in vain":

> In vain to Desarts thy Retreat is made;
> The Muse attends thee to the silent Shade:
> . . . . . . . . . . . . . . . . . . . . . . . . . . . . . . . . . . . . . . . .
> Ev'n now she *shades* thy *Evening Walk* with Bays,
> (No Hireling she, no Prostitute to Praise)
> Ev'n now, observant of *the parting Ray,*
> Eyes *the calm Sun-set* of thy Various Day,
> Thro' Fortune's Cloud One Truly Great can see,
> Nor fears to tell, that MORTIMER is He.
> (ll. 27–40; italics added)

Though with a different finality, Harley no less than Parnell abides now in the condition of "in vain." Harley's ray is departing; a concluding sunset is upon him. Various as it has been, his day is now done. There is accordingly an announcement of doom as well as a kind of immortality in the uttering of the name, perhaps even with puns intended on Latin *mors, mortis* and Greek (especially Homeric) *moros. MORTimer* or *MOR/TIMER,* Death-Timer. This may be set in decisive opposition to the "Death Untimely" in the poem's first sentence.

The verse epistle to Harley is also, in effect, an elegy for Harley as well as for Parnell. Far more than Pope is willing to make obvious, the poem's parting lines reenact the stark conclusion of Dryden's poem for his deceased friend: "Thy Brows with Ivy, and with Laurels bound; / But Fate and gloomy Night encompass thee around." The sphere of death is vastly inclusive. The Nisus who was the first to fall is not mentioned in Dryden's close, much less the older Marcellus; but both of them are *here,* in the moment of death. Indeed, the silence that envelops Dryden in the final instant of his poem is the index of a fate far gloomier than Oldham's. As Parnell is to Euryalus/Oldham, so is Harley to Nisus/Dryden.

The Harley who is seen hazily "thro' Fortune's Cloud" already walks with the dead. This is indicated more or less unmistakably when the line "The Muse attends thee to the silent Shade" is followed seven lines later by "she shades thy Evening Walk with Bays." Before our eyes Harley is passing into the place of *shade*, among the spirits or *manes* of the dead. "All have their *manes*, and those *manes* bear" is the way Dryden translated the controlling doctrine formulated by Anchises (*Aeneid*, book 6:982),[5] who is himself the *manes* burden borne lightly by Aeneas. When Pope writes that the Muse's office is "the brave Man's latest Steps to trace" (l. 29), he is defining in advance the terminal steps of Harley's "Evening Walk" as well as the steps that come after. After evening there is, for the most part, only night. But in the tradition of this poem, unsentimental as it surely is, night is a naught of a special kind. Though Parnell may be dear in vain to Harley (and to the man Pope as well), to the Muse the dearness not only of Parnell, but also of Mortimer, remains. In the instant of parting Harley is reabsorbed into the hereditary title and estate which the Muse heralds for him. MORTIMER is the shade to which Harley's spirit goes out.

## The " 'scape to Wit" and the Landscape of Negation

But what, or more precisely *where*, is the estate into which Harley is passing? Once we have recognized that what is unfolding in these last scenes is the envisioning of Harley's own death, the ending of the third verse paragraph takes on an unexpectedly ominous quality: "And pleas'd to 'scape from Flattery to Wit." We might have wondered earlier why the ending of the third paragraph apparently offers the single exception to the tragic and epic resonances that close each of the other paragraphs: " 'Till Death untimely stop'd his tuneful Tongue"; "to HARLEY dear—in vain!"; "Beholds thee glorious only in thy Fall"; "the Dread of Death"; "Nor fears to tell, that MORTIMER is He." But when Harley is later shown to his final deathly escape by the Muse who abjures flattery ("No Hireling she, no Prostitute to Praise"), our premonitions are confirmed. Yet at least one key question remains unanswered in this account. If Harley's escape to death and to the condition of being "such" is, in fact, the poem's main subject and its own Wit, the " 'scape" to Wit must also reside in

a geography of meanings commensurate with Pope's epic undertaking. But in what landscape is that " 'scape" situated? This map
is most immediately provided, I believe, by the context of Dryden's elegy to which Pope alludes.

The Wit to which Harley escapes in Pope's "Epistle" is the
descendant of the Wit that is said to shine through death in
Dryden's poem. Like Harley, Dryden/Nisus has also experienced
a "Fall," in this case "upon the slippery place" (l. 9). Both Harley's "Fall" and Dryden's stand for failure within striving as well
as imminent death—Oldham's and Harley's, in addition to Parnell's and Dryden's. Standing on the verge of Hades, to which his
friend now descends, Dryden anticipates the gloomy night which
encompasses Oldham, even at the very instant that Oldham continues the race for poetry:

> O early ripe! to thy abundant store
> What could advancing Age have added more?
> It might (what nature never gives the young)
> Have taught the numbers of thy native Tongue.
> But Satyr needs not those, and Wit will shine
> Through the harsh cadence of a rugged line.
>
> (ll. 11–16)

From the first, the fact that Oldham and Dryden are both "Cast in
the same Poetick mould" implies more than their similar natures.
With its emphatic placement at the beginning of the line, "cast"
suggests a violent disposal which, taken together with the funer-
eal garlands of the closing couplet, confers another meaning upon
"mould": for "Cast in the same Poetick mould" we must also
understand "Thrown into the same poetic grave." Dryden and
Oldham are both pointed toward death.

Yet in this poem, at least, pondering the enormity of death is
not an occasion for despair. For Dryden, being encompassed
"around" by "Fate and gloomy Night" is not the same as being
swallowed up or obliterated. Like poetry, life also mellows; it
ripens even as it decomposes, regenerating endless cycles of living and writing. The golden light of Wit shines through lines or
furrows after a fatal fall upon "the slippery place," a fall that is
beautifully recaptured in the word "cadence"—"harsh cadence"

(l. 16)—derived (by a circuitous route) from the Latin *cadere*, to fall. We are not told how, specifically, "Wit will shine / Through" the fall and descent into earth. But somehow "quickness" or spirit is kept alive, the poet affirms, even if the "generous fruits" are "gather'd ere their prime." Here "generous" has its seventeenth-century meanings not only of *free in giving* (as from the "abundant store"), but also of *high-spirited* (which deepens "quickness") and *of noble lineage* (even Oldham's error is called "noble"). This is the rugged line of Euryalus and Marcellus with whom Oldham's soul is collaterally derived in the poem, as is Dryden's soul, more indirectly, by being "near ally'd" with Oldham's.[6] This is the "One common Note" of poetic souls which Dryden derives from Anchises' oracular explanation of the transmigration of Roman souls. Indeed, in his translation of Anchises' key terms (*Aeneid*, book 6, ll. 726–27: "spiritus intus alit, totamque infusa per artus / mens agitat molem et magno se corpore miscet"), Dryden writes of "one common soul" (*Aeneid*, book 6, l. 982).

In the gloomy ending of Dryden's elegy the departure into oblivion images one part of a scene of transmigrating souls. There is, of course, no mitigating the pain and oblivion suffered by individuals, but the oblivion, at least, functions as prelude to the handing on. In Anchises' explanation, the dead must in "Lethe's lake . . . long oblivion taste" so that "the soul may suffer mortal flesh again" (Dryden's translation, book 6, ll. 968, 1020). When Dryden closes his elegy by identifying Oldham as the young Marcellus, he reenacts the painful moment when Anchises identifies young Marcellus in Hades. Dryden's identification inevitably draws after it the ambience of Anchises' fuller explanation which circumscribes even the awesome Virgilian pronouncement, "sed nox atra caput tristi circumvolat umbra" (*Aeneid*, book 6, l. 866).[7]

## Virgil's Slippery Place

Harley's, Dryden's, and Oldham's Falls and the escape to or shining through of "Wit" reconstruct, in overall design and in significant detail, the landscape of the *Aeneid* and the *Iliad*, where other heroes run the race that the fall "upon the slippery place" interrupts. In the *Aeneid* the larger scene that gives meaning to the fall of Nisus is specified in the following way: Aeneas has escaped his deflection to Carthage and Dido only to discover that he has been detoured once more and must return to Sicily, yet another waystation. It happens that this new suspension of the progress of his journey from Troy to Rome occurs almost precisely one year after the death of Anchises. Aeneas decrees funeral games to honor his father's *manes*, to which he will turn even more profoundly in the next book. As we know, and as we will see graphically in a moment, this descent episode interrupts the *Aeneid* at its structural, thematic, and metaphysical center.

Like the journey of the Trojans toward Rome, the two races run by Nisus and Euryalus replicate the handing on or translation ritual of classical culture. The explanatory core of the race symbol is clearly the fact that the fall of Nisus makes possible the continuation and winning of the race. But what, after all, does it explain? Both races remain full of mysteries. In book 5 Nisus and Euryalus are the first, we are told, to answer Aeneas' call to the games (ll. 294*ff*). In book 9 they again present themselves first for the race, this one toward absent Aeneas and toward death. In book 5, however, Nisus falls upon the place made slippery by the blood of ritual slaughter that memorializes Anchises. And in book 9 the two heroes engage in their own brand of ritual slaughter, which is almost as mysterious as the earlier bloodletting, considering that their aim is only to pass through the enemy lines as quickly as possible.

There are irresolvable ethical tensions here which are significantly parallel to Aeneas' destiny of violence and power, up to and including the very last moment of the poem, when, in founding Rome and finally completing his race, he plunges his sword into Turnus' breast. We are not meant to be put fully at ease by the impersonal necessities of sacrifice that Aeneas invokes in this final moment: *Pallas immolat* (book 12, ll. 948–49), he claims. The ambiguities diffused, boundlessly, by this moment are already implicated in Nisus' fall upon the slippery place. Given this abundance of troubling bloodshed, it is no wonder that when Nisus approaches Aeneas, after the first race, all besmeared with gore, Aeneas awards him "an ample shield / Of wondrous art" (Dryden's translation, book 5, ll. 471–72). There is a knot of contradiction in all of this which cannot be cut except by acknowledging that in Virgil's view each of these characters, in some sense, not only falls and fails, but his hopes and projections are significantly negated in relation to values he himself upholds. The slippery place opens wide even within the most noble Roman aspirations.

Without taking into account the placement of these races within Aeneas' (Troy's) larger race toward Rome, with its own bloodletting and its own "fall" into Hades directly at its center— dividing, in fact, the races of books 5 and 9 as well—it is impossible to understand the poem's architecture of division and, specifically, the kind of divided scene that Virgil repeatedly constructs. The slippery place of fall, failure, and violence interrupts the race toward Rome. It is a breach in the landscape, as well as in the ethos, of heroic action. But it is also the place around which the poem's actions are organized. And it finally determines the meaning toward which the poem's characters are being moved. The geography of the slippery place is, I submit, one of the determinative conditions of the classical handing on, although by itself it does not achieve the traditio. The classical poet reaches out to a place which in itself not only is, but always was, significantly ruined and forfeited. In the Iliad, right from the first, Troy hangs on the edge of "devastation" (book 1, l. 2).[8] In the aboveground world of the Aeneid, a pax Romana is a contradiction in terms. In this regard it is surely significant that the "Iliad" half of the Aeneid comes second and last. In the poems of Dryden and Pope that we are discussing, as in their works in general, the new Augusta is already beyond idealization. England is already the "lubrique" or slippery scene, as Dryden puts it in the Killigrew ode, of our "Second Fall" (ll. 63–66). Hell or the nether world gapes wide within the scenes of each of these poems.

There may be no way to avoid the slippery place. It may, however, be possible to mitigate some of its consequences. The possibility of such mitigation derives from the confrontation with and acceptance, in some sense, of the slippery place itself. Thus the Nisus and Euryalus episodes are separated by a simulacrum for the harshest cadence of all, Aeneas' experience of death. And this experience is conceptualized by Aeneas as a form of *pietas*, a conception which, as Viktor Pöschl observes, is "in its several forms . . . the concealed but central motif of the sixth book."[9] In the descent, Aeneas enacts the meaning of the cadence of fall, the meaning that the experience of death within life can bestow upon life itself. Without the knowledge that "immanent Mind" (book 6, ll. 726–27) intervenes in the very interruption of life by death and that this "Mind" is continuous throughout mankind's longing for place, which in the *Aeneid* is called "Rome," the entire Nisus and Euryalus story, I suggest, would be absurd, even grotesque. Virgil's decision to write the death tale of a pair of heroes, rather than a Patrokleia (or Doloneia), derives from a deepening of the logic of human relatedness embedded in the concept of immanent Mind. By accepting the inevitability of the death of self, fallen and blood-stained, the self acknowledges the other who reveals the self's mortality and imperfection.[10] It is clear, however, that the Patrokleia itself already means nothing without the relation of Patroklos to Achilles.

## Homer's "Chalkline" of Death

Before I try to explain how the interruption or spacing of life by death is used to condition the meaning of these poems' apostrophes, I will glance at the landscape in Homer, which is, significantly, the source of Virgil's, Dryden's, and Pope's scenes. All of the constituents of Virgil's context of apostrophe are to be found in the Patrokleia. This is the pivotal moment of the *Iliad*, just as the Nisus and Euryalus episodes and the whole of the *Aeneid* pivot on Aeneas' turn downward to death and *pietas*—and to Anchises' explication of death and *pietas*. Taken together with this contextual parallel it is all the more significant that the apostrophes of the Patrokleia grow out of a scenery of frozen oppositions, with death in the midst. This scenery of irresolvable division is pervasive, even dominant in the *Iliad*. Of course, in a battle poem we cannot be surprised to find numerous figures and figurations of parataxis. But in Homer, as is well known, the symmetries of a structural parataxis become in one way or another the extensive and intensive characteristic of his art.[11] And, I would add, the medial feature of this parataxis—the blank or missing connective between the symmetries—is identified by Homer with a center of conflict which for the most part cannot be visualized. In the *Iliad* the gulf within parataxis is a slippery, unfixable place which is a focus of far more anxious attention than the city called Troy.

In the Patrokleia the repetition of this figure is so frequent that it may strike us as being almost feverish. From the first moment of the telling of the *Iliad* the "division of conflict" (the *diasteten erisante*: book 1, l. 6) both organizes the plot of the epic and locates its atemporal place. This is the place from which the goddess or muse of this poem must "sing." From very much the same place—caught in the division of conflict between Achilles and Agamemnon—Kalchas is told (by Achilles) that he must "speak, interpreting whatever he knows, fearing nothing" (book 1, l. 85). His courage to fear nothing, in the very middle of the deadly division of conflict, leads him to "speak," in Pope's translation, "Truths invidious to the Great" (book 1, ll. 101–2).[12] This is quite possibly the moment that Pope echoes at the end of his "Epistle" when his Muse, also acting with real courage,[13] does not fear to tell of "One truly Great" (ll. 39–40).[14]

This dimensionless midpoint figures recurrence. It describes a standoff that cannot be resolved except by giving way to other standoffs. For this reason at least, it exists as a focus of potential relatedness and solidarity with other human experiences of the nothing. I will offer a few brief examples.

In the book just preceding the Patrokleia, Homer describes the deadly stalemate between the Danaans and the Trojans who are trying to destroy the Danaans' ships:

> as a chalkline straightens the cutting of a ship's timber
> in the hands of an expert carpenter, who by Athene's
> inspiration is well versed in all his craft's subtlety,
> so the battles fought by both sides were pulled fast
>    and even.
>
>                              (book 15, ll. 410–13)

The space filled by corpses and death in this passage is the chalkline or carpenter's line (*stathme*) that has no thickness, the line that in the hands of an expert carpenter, who is guided by the gods, gives form or definition to his materials, so that he may build a structure (itself perhaps an engine of war) as durable as the gods will allow. The same line of death appears in the endlessly attacked, endlessly defended ditch and wall and in the movable corpse—be it Sarpedon's or Patroklos'—over which other doomed warriors endlessly fight.

Later we are confronted by another virtually invisible white line, this one as of a splash of milk soaking into the ground, made by dead Sarpedon:

> No longer
> could a man, even a knowing one, have made out the godlike
> Sarpedon, since he was piled from head to ends of feet under
> a mass of weapons, the blood and the dust, while others
>     about him
> kept forever swarming over his dead body, as flies
> through a sheepfold thunder about the pails overspilling
> milk, in the season of spring when the milk splashes
>     in the buckets.
>
> (book 16, ll. 637–43)

This slippery place, of blood, not milk, occurs in the very midst of the Patrokleia. It is a stark instance of the dimensionless, intervening space in which the Patrokleian apostrophe is conceived. Indeed, we can now recall that the first verse of the book of the Patrokleia opens with a fatal figure of division that could not be more emphatic: "So they fought on both sides for the sake of the strong-benched vessel" (book 16, l. 1). The fighting then proceeds through a long series of confrontations that produce no resolutions but only a movement of standoffs from one point to another: from the "deep-dug ditch" (l. 369) to the encounter, near the end, of Hektor and Patroklos over the corpse of Kebriones. "Like lions / who in the high places of a mountain, both in huge courage / and both hungry, fight over a killed deer" (ll. 755–58), the two champions stand on the borders of the space of division, identified with the death that inheres everywhere in creation. At

this given instant of standoff, there is no difference in power
between the two lions. If no other force were introduced, they
would fight over this intervening space to eternity. Although
Patroklos soon falls, Hektor himself, "whose own death," we
hear, "was close to him" (l. 800), is not the victor. He cannot
close the gap. Rather Zeus, acting through Apollo, has decreed
from "the division in his heart" (l. 652), that the line of division
must structure human being. It is this particular kind of negation,
fixed in a slippery, divided, epic place, that, for Homer, Virgil,
Dryden, and Pope, conditions the lineage of apostrophe.

## Apostrophe and Negativity

Throughout its long history the activity of apostrophe has remained close to its Greek etymology, *apostrephein*, to turn away.
Apostrophe is different from other forms of direct address or from
narrative digressions, because in apostrophe all preceding time
and place are for an instant totally interrupted. Instead a no-time
and no-place is momentarily inserted into the speaker's, and our,
quondam world. So decisive and characteristic is the operation of
apostrophe in our poetry that it is tempting to identify it, as has
Jonathan Culler, with lyric itself. In making this identification
Culler discusses what he calls "post-Enlightenment" apostrophe,
which he understands as "the pure embodiment of poetic pretension: of the subject's claim that in his verse he is . . . the embodiment of poetic tradition and of the spirit of poesy." In Culler's
view the O of apostrophe is an individual "act of will" that is
"devoid of semantic reference" even though it "refers to other
apostrophes and thus to the lineage and conventions of sublime
poetry."[15]

Yet in the classical lineage that we are considering, the poet's
pretension to embodying the tradition is precisely *not* uncondi-
tioned. While this conditioning may not be strictly semantic, if
we understand by that term the language forms traced in historical change, it is eminently semantic in the sense that it is a
function of signs and symbols of division that are external to it
and in which historicity plays important roles. To a great extent,

classical apostrophe occurs under the sign of the tropes of negation and division described above. Whatever the content of a
given apostrophe may be, classical apostrophe does not itself act
as a negation, and it does not act alone. Rather, the framework of
the divided place combines with and conditions the no-time and
no-place created by apostrophe. I will try to show this now.

Of the fifteen narrative apostrophes addressed to mortals in the
*Iliad*, eight are addressed to Patroklos as he moves toward death
in the Patrokleia.[16] This immense pressure of Homeric apostrophe, exerted at a single point, leaves an indelible imprint on
the later life of classical apostrophe. In our texts from Virgil,
Dryden, and Pope, founded in the Patrokleia, we discover a sustained recognition of the relation between that imprint and the
meaning of tradition. Here are the apostrophes (all from book 16)
to Patroklos:

> Then groaning heavily, Patroklos the rider, you answered.
>> (l. 20)

> So straight for the Lykians, o lord of horses, Patroklos,
> you swept, and for the Trojans, heart angered for your
>> companion.
>>> (ll. 584–85)

> Then who was it you slaughtered first, who was the last one,
> Patroklos, as the gods called you to your death?
>> (ll. 692–93)

>> Now
> you spoke in bitter mockery over him, rider Patroklos.
>> (ll. 743–44)

> So in your fury you pounced, Patroklos, above Kebriones . . .
>> (l. 754)

> there, Patroklos, the end of your life was shown forth,
> Since Phoibos came against you there in the strong encounter
>> dangerously.
>>> (ll. 787–89)

He first hit you with a thrown spear, o rider Patroklos,
nor broke you, but ran away again, snatching out
    the ash spear
from your body, and lost himself in the crowd.

(ll. 812–14)

And now, dying, you answered him, o rider Patroklos.

(l. 843)

The contents of these apostrophes differ substantially from each
other, yet a number of things remain constant. Although each
apostrophe interrupts its context, together they form a perfect
continuity. They resonate together in a shadow world, where they
are addressed to a shade among the shadows. One of the semantic
features that is markedly invariable here, indeed, is the iteration
of the name *Patroklos*. The placement of that name within the
*turning away* of apostrophe effectively rips Patroklos untimely
from the world. Like Virgil's "Fortunati ambo!" or Dryden's "O
early ripe!" or Pope's "MORTIMER," this Patroklos is also, already, a dead man. He is the double for the earthly Patroklos.
And he exists in another realm. There he is privy to a whole
universe of secrets that are for us totally sealed and incomprehensible. We feel that we almost glimpse these secrets, as through a
crevice, each time Homer is able to name Patroklos. The force of
this doubling is certainly not negation. Quite the contrary, this
kind of doubling suggests a fully formed world that must exist for
us under a negative sign because the only thing that we know
about it is that it is *not the world interrupted by apostrophe*. It is
therefore a world that moves side by side with our world, in
negativity.

Wolfgang Iser has shown how the presence of blanks and negations in any text creates a "need for combination" of textual
patterns. This is extremely pertinent for understanding the force
of combination generated by tropes of division. Of even greater
relevance for my discussion is Iser's suggestion that the same
need for combination is made deeper yet by the spaces or blanks
of negativity. The functioning of this negativity, he emphasizes,
is not simply negative or negating. Indeed, the whole of Iser's

distinction between negation and negativity applies meaningfully
to the negativity created by apostrophe:

> Blanks and negations increase the density of fictional texts,
> for the omissions and cancellations indicate that practically
> all the formulations of the text refer to an unformulated
> background, and so the formulated text has a kind of unfor-
> mulated double. This 'double' we . . . call negativity.
>
> Unlike negation, negativity is not formulated by the text, but
> forms the unwritten base; it does not negate the formula-
> tions of the text, but—via blanks and negations—condi-
> tions them.
>
> Negativity in the true sense of the term . . . cannot be de-
> duced from the given world which it questions, and cannot
> be conceived as serving a substantialist idea, the coming of
> which it heralds.[17]

Iser's comments could be used to illuminate the ways in which
apostrophe conditions its narrative context. My primary concern
here, however, is not how negativity conditions the formulated
text, but how, via the same blanks and negations, the formulated
text conditions negativity, in this case the inaccessibility or un-
sayability of meaning carried from one apostrophe to another.
Having been enabled by negativity, apostrophe and its framework
of divisions now give a shape to negativity itself. They condition
negativity's relation to poetry and the world. To a great extent, I
believe, this conditioning is the signature of classical and neoclassical tradition.

Each of the apostrophes in the line I have been considering
passes on negativity in this way. Each successive apostrophe is
not only addressed to a "double," but also doubles its predecessor. It keeps alive, and yet does not comprehend, and thereby
dispel, the negativity that it inherits. The identification of *traditio*
with a particular substantialist message is totally voided in this
expounding of tradition. In this placing of negativity we witness
the merger of the place of division, created in the epic landscape,
with the space of interruption, opened up by apostrophe. Here
Mind or Wit speaks out, shaping the world not only into a scene

of boundaries and death, but also into a scene of shades and of *pietas* and of human relatedness.

Some modern commentators have identified a "noetic" interval or "logos" within the visualized elements of Homer's verse. According to such a view, Homer's cosmic scene may in fact be held together by the agency of a particular kind of logos, one that works in the interstices between all objects. This dynamic "Urlogik" is even said both to separate and to bind nature's irresolvable dialectic.[18]

How much of such a defining logos may Virgil have grasped when he gave us his own vision of the forces that define and sustain cosmic relatedness? Is "immanent Mind" Virgil's translation of a Homeric spiritual logos intervening in all being? "Immanent Mind, flowing / Through all its parts and leavening its mass, makes the universe work" (book 6, ll. 726–29),[19] says Anchises from the place of death and *pietas* in which Aeneas meets him. It is possible that the similarity between logos and Mind— and Wit—may in turn help form the definitional or opening character of Homer's and Virgil's—as well as Dryden's and Pope's— apostrophes. And it may help explain the reasons for their association of apostrophe with a landscape of "chalklines" and slippery places. It is as if logos or Mind or Wit speak directly in apostrophe, performing the act of separation and bonding that is required by its ethos of boundary making.[20]

Whatever the nature of Homer's "logos" or the sources of Virgil's "immanent Mind," the classical usage of division and apostrophe is strikingly similar to that of the Logos Divider in the Judeo-Christian tradition, which I have discussed elsewhere with regard to Milton's poetry.[21] It seems possible, in fact, that the similarity between these two traditions has a common philological root.[22] But whether or not this or some other shared source is confirmed, in the case of Pope's "Epistle" the confluence of Christian-Miltonic tropes of division with the classical tropes that they closely resemble strongly enhances the effect of both kinds: it both deepens the gulf of sorrow in which apostrophe speaks and multiplies the doubling of addressees and voices. Virgil's apostrophe to Nisus and Euryalus is perhaps the premier case of apostrophe in the classical tradition, because it is already self-consciously in the posture of handing on, and because it is part of a Virgilian structure of epic that makes that handing on functional:

> Fortunati ambo! si quid mea carmina possunt,
> nulla dies umquam memori vos eximet aevo,
> dum domus Aeneae Capitoli immobile saxum
> accolet imperiumque pater Romanus habebit.

> Ah, fortunate pair! if my poetry has any influence,
> Time in its passing shall never obliterate your memory,
> As long as the house of Aeneas dwell by the Capitol's
>    moveless
> Rock, and the head of the Roman family keeps his power.
>                    (*Aeneid*, book 9, ll. 446–49)[23]

In this slippery place, as in Dryden's and Pope's, a great deal impinges upon the moment of apostrophe. Division here inherits and bequeaths a history and a metaphysics which flow into the breach made by apostrophe. In Virgil's case, the influence of poetry, the magic of a fabulous site of nostalgia upon which the Roman house dwells, and the magnetic power of a family head who propagates enduring relations among the mortal members of that family are all expressions of *pietas* and immanent Mind. What makes this *pair* ("ambo"—*two together*), and all our other pairs, "fortunate" is that they are doubles for the ideas of *relation* and *proportion*. This could only be achieved in division and in the acknowledgment of negativity. In the moment of division and apostrophe, all of these poets give voice to apostrophe's and poetry's power to inherit and to hand onward.

Apostrophe and its framework of division carve out an empty space so that appropriation can—must—occur. What is then appropriated and reappropriated is the empty space—negativity—itself, which, however, can never be made into anyone's substantialist message, anyone's possession. Tradition of this kind is constituted by the acceptance and bestowal of negativity thus marked off.

## Additional Note

Standing at the receiving end of this line of apostrophe handed on by Homer-Virgil-Dryden-Pope, how much may Harley/Oxford/Mortimer have understood of its meaning, especially of its implications for his own passing into the shade, his being "pleas'd to 'scape . . . to Wit"? In the letter that Harley sent to Pope on November 6, 1721, acknowledging the "Epistle," he writes that it "could not but give me great Pleasure, to see you preserve an Old Friend in Memory." His next two sentences make clear that the Old Friend, preserved in Memory, of whom he speaks is himself. And then he adds, "I am contented to let the World see, how well Mr Pope can write upon a barren Subject."[24] Did Harley already understand that the Subject or subjectivity of this poem is for Pope always necessarily "barren"? Had he grasped that this conditioned negativity functions like an awesome tunnel connecting the historical moments of poems like Pope's and Dryden's with those of the *Aeneid* and the *Iliad*? What higher compliment than to be implicated in the light and the darkness at the provisional end of this great line!

## Notes

1. Geoffrey Tillotson, "Pope's 'Epistle to Harley': An Introduction and Analysis," in James L. Clifford and Louis A. Landa, eds., *Pope and His Contemporaries: Essays Presented to George Sherburn* (Oxford: Clarendon Press, 1949), p. 68. A full account of this echoing would have to pay close attention to apostrophes of Catullus, which are alluded to not only by Dryden's elegy but by passages in the *Aeneid* that Dryden here imitates. With regard to the anecdote, mentioned by Tillotson, that it was Swift who first suggested to Pope the use of Dryden's Oldham materials, notice should also be taken of Swift's own extraordinary version of Virgil's apostrophe to Nisus and Euryalus in the closing moment of "The Battle of the Books."

2. The text of Dryden's poem is cited from *The Poems and Fables of John Dryden*, ed. James Kinsley (London: Oxford University Press, 1962); of Pope's, from *The Poems of Alexander Pope*, ed. John Butt (New Haven: Yale University Press, 1963).

3. George Birkbeck Hill, ed., *Lives of the English Poets* (Oxford: Clarendon Press, 1905), 3:119. In his life of Dryden, Johnson had pointed out that "Pope

called Dryden's *Virgil* 'the most noble and spirited translation that I know in any language' " (*Lives*, 1:449). Johnson's praise of Pope's *Iliad* was calculated to return Pope's compliment with interest, as if on Dryden's behalf.

4. See Tillotson, "Pope's 'Epistle to Harley,' " p. 77.

5. Dryden's translation of *The Aeneid* is cited from *The Poetical Works of Dryden*, ed. George R. Noyes (Cambridge, Mass.: Riverside Press, 1950). Virgil's Latin is given according to the Loeb *Virgil*, trans. H. Rushton Fairclough, 2 vols. (London: William Heinemann, 1960).

6. This "line" may also be said to include Homer's Greek Euryalos as well as the slipping of Aias on the dung of Achilles' oxen—those slaughtered to honor Patroklos: *Iliad*, book 23, ll. 677ff and 773ff.

7. For a particularly eloquent description of the "picture" of "nonbeing" in Virgil's Marcellus image, see W. R. Johnson, *Darkness Visible: A Study of Vergil's Aeneid* (Berkeley: University of California Press, 1976), pp. 110–11.

8. Except for one instance, noted below, all citations from Homer are to *The Iliad of Homer*, trans. Richmond Lattimore (Chicago, Ill.: University of Chicago Press, 1961).

9. Viktor Pöschl, *The Art of Virgil: Image and Symbol in the Aeneid*, trans. Gerda Seligson (Ann Arbor: University of Michigan Press, 1970), p. 150.

10. In philosophical terms we can say that for classicism, the making of *traditio* in the space of negativity is its way of dealing with the "problem of the other." How important this attempt may be for the history of literature and thought may be suggested by a parallel in the work of Stanley Cavell. Cavell has explained how the spectator half of the self can function in the achievement of impersonality in a complementarity of incomplete selves. Cavell understands the possibility of such achievement as a rehearsal of "an ancient and recurring intimation of the self" that is effected "out of a present sense of incoherence or division or incompleteness." He shows that a writer can deal with the problem of "doubleness" or "division of self" by interpreting it as "a relation between ourselves in the aspect of indweller, unconsciously building, and in the aspect of spectator, impartially observing. Unity between these aspects is viewed not as a mutual absorption, but as a perpetual nextness, an act of neighboring or befriending"—an act closely related to "acknowledging the presence of the other": Stanley Cavell, *The Senses of Walden* (New York: Viking, 1972), pp. 100 and 63. I would suggest that one of the first occurrences of this ancient doubleness is to be found in the space of negativity where classical apostrophe does its work. The *pietas* and "immanent Mind" named by Virgil are metaphors for the negativity and "nextness" of each such instance of apostrophe. If I am right about the handing on of classicism and neoclassicism, the specificity of this *traditio* is one of the most significant recurrences of such "nextness" that we experience.

11. On Homer's use of parataxis see, for example, J. T. Sheppard, *The Pattern of the Iliad* (London: Methuen, 1922); Bruno Snell, *The Discovery of the Mind in Greek Philosophy and Literature*, trans. T. G. Rosenmeyer (New York: Harper, 1960), pp. 6–7; James A. Notopoulos, "Parataxis in Homer: A New Approach to Homeric Literary Criticism," *Transactions of the American Philological Association* (1949), 80:1–23; and Cedric H. Whitman, *Homer and the Heroic Tradition* (Cambridge, Mass.: Harvard University Press, 1958).

12. *The Iliad of Homer*, trans. Alexander Pope, ed. Maynard Mack et al. (London and New Haven, Conn.: Methuen and Yale University Press, 1967).

13. Tillotson, "Pope's 'Epistle to Harley,' " p. 75, cites Grattan's contemporary remark that writing the poem "required courage."

14. Interestingly enough Kalchas' speaking at this juncture is precisely the passage in the *Iliad* that Heidegger identifies as a lingering "within the expanse of unconcealment," a moving "away," he calls it, "from the sheer oppression of what lies before us, which is only present, away to what is absent." We do not have to be Heideggerians to feel the rightness of this reading: see Heidegger's *Early Greek Thinking*, trans. David Farrell Krell and Frank A. Capuzzi (New York: Harper and Row, 1984), pp. 34–35.

15. Jonathan Culler, *The Pursuit of Signs: Semiotics, Literature, Deconstruction* (London: Routledge and Kegan Paul, 1981), pp. 137 and 143.

16. For a survey of these and other apostrophes, see Elizabeth Block, "The Narrator Speaks: Apostrophe in Homer and Virgil," *Transactions of the American Philological Association* (1982), 112:7–22.

17. Wolfgang Iser, *The Act of Reading: A Theory of Aesthetic Response* (Baltimore, Md. and London: Johns Hopkins University Press, 1980), pp. 182 and 225–29. For Iser's remarks on one kind of two-way traffic between the spoken and the "unspoken" see "The Dramatization of Double Meaning in Shakespeare's *As You Like It*," *Theatre Journal* (1983), 35:307–32. For his conception of negativity as "an enabling structure," see his essay in this volume.

18. See Wolfgang Schadewaldt, *Von Homers Welt und Werk* (Stuttgart: Koehler, 1951), pp. 149–50; and Norman Austin, *Archery at the Dark of the Moon: Poetic Problems in Homer's Odyssey* (Berkeley: University of California Press, 1975), pp. 177–82.

19. The translation is that of C. Day Lewis in *The Aeneid of Virgil* (New York: Doubleday, 1952).

20. The Homeric force of division that concerns us here is perhaps also related to Homer's methods, explained by Gregory Nagy, for retrieving "the transformation of the hero from mortal to immortal," a transformation that was an important part of heroic cult. Noteworthy among these methods, Nagy shows, is Homer's use of cultic formulae of *daiomai*, to divide, apportion, allot, and of formulae of two other words derived from the same root: *dais*, the heroic or divine feast; and *daimon*, the spirit that divides between and straddles the realms of mortal and immortal. The transformation of the hero is achieved by opening up a third realm between mortal and immortal, a realm that comes alive in the ancient formulae of division: Gregory Nagy, *The Best of the Achaeans: Concepts of the Hero in Archaic Greek Poetry* (Baltimore, Md. and London: Johns Hopkins University Press, 1979), pp. 127–29.

21. Sanford Budick, *The Dividing Muse: Images of Sacred Disjunction in Milton's Poetry* (New Haven, Conn.: Yale University Press, 1985).

22. See, for example, John F. Priest, "OPKIA in the *Iliad* and the Consideration of a Recent Theory," *Journal of Near Eastern Studies* (1964), 23:48–56.

23. Here too the translation is from C. Day Lewis, *The Aeneid of Virgil*. I have discussed this apostrophe at some length in an essay forthcoming in *New Literary History*.

24. The whole of Harley's letter to Pope is reproduced by Tillotson, "Pope's 'Epistle to Harley,' " p. 64.

# PERFORMING

# 14

# THE PLAY OF THE TEXT
## Wolfgang Iser

IT IS reasonable to presuppose that author, text, and reader are closely interconnected in a relationship that is to be conceived as an ongoing process that produces something that had not existed before. This view of the text is in direct conflict with the traditional notion of representation, insofar as mimesis entails reference to a pregiven "reality" that is meant to be represented. In the Aristotelian sense, the function of representation is twofold: to render the constitutive forms of nature perceivable; and to complete what nature has left incomplete. In either case mimesis, though of paramount importance, cannot be confined to mere imitation of what is, since the processes of elucidation and of completion both require a performative activity if apparent absences are to be moved into presence. Since the advent of the modern world there is a clearly discernible tendency toward privileging the performative aspect of the author-text-reader relationship, whereby the pregiven is no longer viewed as an object of representation but rather as material from which something new is fashioned. The new product, however, is not predetermined by the features, functions, and structures of the material referred to and encapsulated in the text.

There are historic reasons for this shift in focus. Closed systems, such as the cosmos of Greek thought or of the medieval world picture, gave priority to representation as mimesis because of their overriding concern that whatever existed—even if it eluded perception—should be translated into something tangible. When

the closed system, however, is punctured and replaced by open-
endedness, the mimetic component of representation declines
and the performative one comes to the fore. The process then no
longer entails reaching behind appearances in order to grasp an
intelligible world in the Platonic sense, but turns into a "way of
world-making." If what the text brings about were to be equated
with world making, the question would arise whether one could
continue to speak of "representation" at all. The concept could
be retained only if the "ways of worldmaking" themselves became the referential object for representation. In this case, the
performative component would have to be conceived as the pregiven of the performative act. Irrespective of whether this might
or might not be considered tautological, the fact remains that it
would lead to a host of problems that are not within the scope of
this essay. There is, however, one inference that is highly relevant
to my discussion: what has been called the "end of representation"[1]
may, in the final analysis, be less a description of the historical
state of the arts than the articulation of misgivings relating to the
ability of representation as a concept to capture what actually
happens in art or literature.

This is not to deny that the author-text-reader relationship
contains a vast number of extratextual elements that undergo
processing, but these are only material components of what happens in the text and are not represented by it one to one. It
therefore seems fair to say that representation in the sense in
which we have come to understand it cannot embrace the performative operation of the text as a form of happening. Indeed, it is
striking to note that there are hardly any clear-cut theories of
representation that actually set out the workings necessary to
bring about mimesis.

Among the rare exceptions is Gombrich's idea of representation: he broke up the received notion into clearly distinguishable
phases of a process, starting out from the interaction between
painter and inherited schemata, followed by the correction of the
latter in the painting, and eventually by the deciphering activity
of the beholder, whose reading of the corrected schemata brings
the object of representation to fruition.[2]

The following essay is an attempt to raise play above representation as an umbrella concept to cover all of the ongoing operations of the textual process. It has two heuristic advantages: 1. Play does not have to concern itself with what it might stand for. 2. Play does not have to picture anything outside itself. It allows author-text-reader to be conceived as a dynamic interrelationship that moves toward a final result.

Authors play games with readers,[3] and the text is the playground. The text itself is the outcome of an intentional act whereby an author refers to and intervenes in an existing world, but though the act is intentional, it aims at something that is not yet accessible to consciousness. Thus the text is made up of a world that is yet to be identified and is adumbrated in such a way as to invite picturing and eventual interpretation by the reader. This double operation of imagining and interpreting engages the reader in the task of visualizing the many possible shapes of the identifiable world, so that inevitably the world repeated in the text begins to undergo changes. For no matter which new shapes the reader brings to life, they are all certain to encroach on—and hence to change—the referential world contained in the text. Now, since the latter is fictional, it automatically invokes a convention-governed contract between author and reader indicating that the textual world is to be viewed, not as reality, but as if it *were* reality. And so whatever is repeated in the text is not meant to denote the world, but merely a world enacted. This may well repeat an identifiable reality, but it contains one all-important difference: what happens within it is relieved of the consequences inherent in the real world referred to. Hence, in disclosing itself fictionality signalizes that everything is only to be taken *as if* it were what it seems to be, to be taken—in other words—as play.

The world repeated in the text is obviously different from the one it refers to, if only because, as a repetition, it must differ from its extratextual existence, and this holds equally true of all types of discourse, textual or otherwise, since no rendering can be that which it renders. There are therefore various levels of difference that occur simultaneously in the text:

1. Extratextually:
    a. Between the author and the world in which he or she intervenes.
    b. Between the text and an extratextual world as well as between the text and other texts.
2. Intratextually:
    a. Between the items selected from extratextual systems.
    b. Between semantic enclosures built up in the text.
3. Between text and reader:
    a. Between the reader's natural attitudes (now bracketed off) and those he or she is called upon to assume.
    b. Between what is denoted by the world repeated in the text, and what this denotation—now serving as a guiding analogue—is meant to adumbrate.

The levels of difference are quite distinct, but all of them constitute the basic blank of the text which sets the game in motion.

The movement is one of play in three different respects:

1. On each level distinguishable positions are confronted with one another.

2. The confrontation triggers a to-and-fro movement which is basic to play, and the ensuing difference has to be eradicated in order to achieve a result.

3. The continual movement between the positions reveals their many different aspects, and as one encroaches on the other, so the various positions themselves are eventually transformed. Every one of these differences opens up space for play, and hence for transformation, which even at this early stage of my argument would appear to discredit the traditional notion of representation.

Games head toward results, and when the differences are either bridged or even removed, play comes to an end. The result of the textual game, however, must be highly reductive, since the moves of the game split positions up into multifarious aspects. If we take the result of the textual game to be meaning, then this can only arise out of arresting the play movement which, more often than not, will entail decision making. But any decision will eclipse countless aspects brought to view by the constantly shifting, constantly interacting, and hence kaleidoscopically iterating positions of the game, so that the game itself runs counter to its being brought to an end.

Thus the duality of play comes to the fore. It is directed toward winning something, thereby ending itself at the same time as it removes difference. But it also refutes any such removal of difference, and outstrips its achievements in order to reestablish its own freedom as an ever-decentering movement. In short, it upholds the difference it seeks to eradicate.

These mutually exclusive features inscribe themselves into one another and so turn the meaning of the text into something of a "supplement." The multiplicity of differences that give rise to play and also result from it can never be totally removed but may in fact increase with attempts at eradication. Consequently, the "supplement" arises not only out of the winning of the game (i.e., establishing meaning) but also, and at the same time, out of freeplay—not least because freeplay itself would remain ungraspable if it did not have some form of manifestation. If the "supplement" is the product of these two countervailing features, we may draw two conclusions: 1. The "supplement" as the meaning of the text is generated through play, and so there is no meaning prior to play. 2. The generation of the "supplement" through play allows for different reenactments by different readers in the act of reception—even to the extent that it can be played either as achieving victory (establishing meaning) or as maintaining freeplay (keeping meaning open-ended).

This duality of play—removing and maintaining difference— defies further conceptualization. It cannot be reduced phenomenologically by tracing it back to an underlying cause. Even such one-sided play theories as that of Huizinga assert that play precedes all of its possible explanations.[4] Therefore, the play of the text can only be assessed in terms of its possibilities, by way of the strategies of playing and the games actually played in the text.

As a playground between author and reader, the literary text can be described on three different levels: structural, functional, and interpretive. A structural description will aim to map out the playground, a functional one will try to explain the goal, and an interpretive one will ask why we play and why we need to play. An answer to this last question can only be interpretive, since play is apparently built into our anthropological makeup and may indeed help us to grasp what we are.

We must now look in more detail at the three different levels. First, that of structure. The focus here is on countermovement as the basic feature of play. The operational mode of the counter-movement converts the text from a mimetic to a performative act. It manifests itself by creating what we might call the play spaces of the text which, it must be remembered, both repeats and encap-sulates extratextual worlds whose return is indicative of a differ-ence. In Gregory Bateson's words, it is "a difference which makes a difference"[5]—for a great many differences arise out of the initial one between the components of the text. The difference, as we have seen, triggers the to-and-fro movement, which opens up play spaces between the positions it separates.

The smallest play space is produced by the split signifier, which is stripped of its designating function so that it may be used figuratively, thanks to the text's fictional indication that what is said is only to be taken as if it meant what it said. The signifier therefore denotes something, but at the same time ne-gates its denotative use without abandoning what it has desig-nated in the first instance. If the signifier means something and simultaneously indicates that it does not mean that something, it functions as an analogue for figuring something else which it helps to adumbrate. If what is denoted is transformed into an analogue both triggering and shaping a picturing activity, then something absent is endowed with presence, though that which is absent cannot be identical to the analogue that facilitated its conceivability. Thus the split signifier—which is simultaneously denotative and figurative—invokes something that is not a pre-given for the text, but is generated by the text, which enables the reader to endow it with a tangible shape.

Thus the play movement turns the split signifier into a matrix for double meaning, which manifests itself in the analogue as the mutual interpenetration of the denotative and figurative func-tions. In terms of the text, the analogue is a "supplement"; in terms of the recipient, it is the guideline enabling him to conceive what the text adumbrates. But the moment this becomes conceiv-able, the recipient will try to ascribe significance to the "supple-ment," and whenever this happens, the text is translated into the dispositional terms of the individual reader, who ends the play of the split signifier by blocking it off with a meaning. If the meaning of a text, however, is not inherent but is ascribed and only achieved through play movement, then meaning is a meta-statement about statements, or even a metacommunication about what is supposed to be communicated (i.e., experience by means of the text).

Another basic play space in the text is opened up by the schema. A schema, so Piaget maintains in his play theory, is the outcome of our constant endeavor to adapt to the world we are in.[6] In this respect it is not dissimilar to imitation, since it is motivated by the desire to overcome the difference that marks our relation to the world. First and foremost, it is perception that has to work out these schemata of adaptation.

Once these schemata have been formed, the first vital step is for them to be internalized, so that they may function subcon-sciously. This means that they tend to become ritualized in one way or another, and when this happens, they become separable from the very objects that initially gave rise to their formation. The conventions of art are nothing but sets of such schemata, which lend themselves very easily to new uses, especially when they have been separated from the world of objects.

Instead of facilitating adaptation to the physical world, the schemata may be used to pattern things that are otherwise un-graspable or that we want to bring within reach on our own conditions. Just as schemata enable us to adapt ourselves to ob-jects, so too do they allow us to assimilate objects into our own disposition. When this reversal occurs, it opens up the play space. The schema is dissociated from its accommodating function and, in becoming subservient to the assimilative function, permits whatever is withheld from us to be staged as both present and manageable. This process is immediately evident in child's play. The play movement takes place when the schema ceases to func-tion as a form of accommodation, and instead of taking its shape from the object to be imitated, now imposes a shape on that which is absent. In other words, the schema of accommodation copies the object, whereas the schema of assimilation shapes the object in accordance with the needs of the individual. Play there-fore begins when assimilation displaces accommodation in the use of schemata, and when the schema is turned into a projection in order to incorporate the world in a book and to chart it according to human conditions.

A striking feature of the assimilative use of schemata is that they become subject to disfigurement. This highlights the switch in their function, and also the difference in their application. It is a duality inherent in all textual schemata, where the original function of the schema is backgrounded, though retaining its shape, and now instead of imitating something it serves to represent the unrepresentable.

In this respect, the inverted schema bears a close resemblance to the split signifier. Both form basic play spaces of the text, and set the game in motion. And in both cases, a basic function is transformed into a medium for something else: with the signifier the denotative function becomes the medium for figuration, and with the schema, the accommodating function becomes the medium for shaping the featureless. The original functions, however, are never totally suspended, and so there is a continual oscillation between denotation and figuration, and between accommodation and assimilation. This oscillation, or to-and-fro movement, is basic to play, and it permits the coexistence of the mutually exclusive. It also turns the text into a generative matrix for the production of something new. It forces the reader to play the games of the text, and to finish playing by coming up with what he or she considers to be its meaning. In the final analysis, oscillation is a patterning of freeplay—which may be a feature of nature or even of human nature, but is not one of the text. Oscillation, however, can also restrain freeplay. This is evident when we see how the strategies of the text restructure the manner in which the respective duality of the split signifier and the inverted schema is played out.

There are four main strategies, each of which allows for a different type of game. They are *agon*, *alea*, *mimicry*, and *ilinx*. The mixture of Greek and Latin terms may be jarring, but the expressions have become standard terms in game theory since Caillois,[7] although he himself did not relate them to texts as verbal structures.

Let me first explain the terms and the types of games they cover, in order to ascertain the patterns of gaming that they organize:

1. *Agon* is a fight or contest, and is a common pattern of play when the text centers on conflicting norms and values. The contest involves a decision to be made by the reader in relation to these opposing values, which are in collision with one another.

2. *Alea* is a pattern of play based on chance and the unforeseeable. Its basic thrust is defamiliarization, which it achieves through storing and telescoping different texts, thus outstripping what their respective, identifiable segments were meant to mean. By overturning familiar semantics, it reaches out into the hitherto inconceivable and frustrates the reader's convention-governed expectations.

3. *Mimicry* is a play pattern designed to generate illusion. Whatever is denoted by the signifier or foreshadowed by the schemata should be taken as if it were what it says. There are two different reasons for this: a) the more perfect the illusion, the more real will seem the world it depicts; b) if the illusion, however, is punctured and so revealed as what it is, the world it depicts turns into a looking glass enabling the referential world outside the text to be observed.

4. *Ilinx* is a play pattern in which the various positions are subverted, undercut, canceled, or even carnivalized as they are played off against one another. It aims at bringing out the rear view of the positions yoked together in the game.

Although these play strategies allow for different games to be played, more often than not they link up as mixed modes. For instance, if *ilinx* plays against or is combined with *agon*, there may be two possible types of game: *ilinx* gains the upper hand, in which case the contest between norms and values becomes illusory, or *agon* dominates, and then the contest becomes more differentiated. These strategies can even be inverted, playing against their own underlying intentions. For example, *agon* appears to be directed toward winning the game, but in postmodern literature it is frequently used to play a losing game. This may entail all conflicts of norms and values being deliberately marked as things of the past, thus exposing the closed nature of the systems that gave them their function and validity. It may also show that all forms of meaning are nothing but defense mechanisms designed to achieve closure in a world where open-endedness reigns.

These four strategies of play can be combined in a vast number of ways, and whenever they *are* combined, each of them takes on a particular role. All roles—as we have to remind ourselves—are characterized by an intrinsic doubleness: they represent something they aim to project, and yet simultaneously they lack total control over the intended achievement, so that there is always an element in role playing that eludes the grasp of the player.[8] This applies equally to the play patterns outlined above when they become roles, and so the game to be played may either enhance or restrict the degree of uncontrollability.

Now, no matter what type of game ensues from indulging in the doubleness of role playing, it is always governed by one of two different sets of rules. In game theory these are called *conservative* and *dissipative* rules.[9] With regard to the text, they may be called *regulative* (which function according to stabilized conventions), and *aleatory* (which set free whatever has been restrained by the conventions). Aleatory rules apply to what cannot be controlled by the role in question, whereas regulatory rules organize what the role represents in terms of hierarchical, causal, subservient, or supportive relationships. Aleatory rules unleash what regulative rules have tied up, and thus they allow for freeplay within an otherwise restricted game.

LET ME now summarize my structural description so far: the split signifier and the inverted schemata open up the play space of the text. The resultant to-and-fro movement is patterned by four basic strategies of play: *agon*, *alea*, *mimicry*, and *ilinx*. These in turn may undergo innumerable combinations, thereby turning into roles. Roles are double faced, with representation inevitably shading off into uncontrollable adumbrations. The games ensuing from roles may be acted out in accordance with regulative rules, which make the game basically conservative, or aleatory rules, which make it basically innovative.

All of these structural features provide a framework for the game. They mark off both the limits and the free areas of play, and so represent the preconditions for "supplements"—in the form of meaning—as well as for the playful undoing of these "supplements." Thus there is a countervailing movement in which play strives for a result and freeplay breaks up any result achieved.

The structural features, however, assume significance only in relation to the function meant to be performed by the play of the text. Since play strives for something but also undoes what it achieves, it continually acts out difference. Difference, in turn, can be manifested only through play, because only play can make conceivable the absent otherness which lies on the reverse side of all positions. Thus the play of the text is neither winning nor losing, but is a process of transforming positions, thereby giving dynamic presence to the absence and otherness of difference. Consequently, what the text achieves is not something pregiven, but a transformation of the pregiven material that it encapsulates. If the text highlights transformation, it is bound to have a play structure, otherwise transformation would have to be subsumed under a cognitive framework, thus obliterating its very nature. Should the notion of representation be retained at all, one would have to say that the text "represents" play, insofar as it spells out the individual process of transformation as it is happening in the text.

This process of transformation is common to the literary text, and it unfolds through all the various interconnected phases that we have outlined so far—from split signifier through inverted schemata, and strategic roles of *agon, alea, mimicry,* and *ilinx,* to the mutual interference of regulative and aleatory rules. Although I have separated these phases for analytical purposes, they in fact overlap and interlink, but through them we may observe transformation in slow motion, as it were, thereby rendering this otherwise intangible process perceivable.

Transformation, however, comes to full fruition through the recipient's imaginative participation in the games played, for it is only a means to an end, and not an end in itself. The more the reader is drawn into the proceedings by playing the games of the text, the more he or she is also played *by* the text. And so new features of play emerge—it assigns certain roles to the reader, and in order to do this, it must clearly have the potential presence of the recipient as one of its component parts. The play of the text is therefore a performance for an assumed audience, and as such it is not just a game as played in ordinary life, but it is actually a staged play enacted for the reader, who is given a role enabling him or her to act out the scenario presented.

The staged play of the text does not, then, unfold as a pageant which the reader merely watches, but is both an ongoing event and a happening for the reader, causing his or her direct involvement in the proceedings and indeed in the staging. For the play of the text can be acted out individually by each reader, who by playing it in his or her own way produces an individual "supplement" considered to be the meaning of the text. The meaning is a "supplement" because it arrests the ongoing process of transformation, and is additional to the text without ever being authenticated by it.

In this respect something important is to be revealed by the textual play. As a means of transformation, play does not only undercut the position presented in the text; it also undercuts the status of that which transformation has moved from absence into presence, i.e., the "supplement" that the reader has added onto the text. But the undercutting, even if it may seem negative, in fact is highly productive, because it brings about transformation and generates "supplements." Hence this operation is driven by negativity, which is basically an enabling structure. Negativity is therefore far from negative in its effects, for it lures absence into presence, but by continually subverting that presence, turns it into a carrier for absence of which we would otherwise not know anything. Through these constant shifts, the play of the text uses negativity in a manner that epitomizes the interrelation between absence and presence. And herein lies the uniqueness of play— it produces, and at the same time allows the process of production to be observed. The reader is therefore caught up in ineluctable doubleness: he or she is involved in an illusion, and is simultaneously aware that it *is* an illusion. It is through this incessant hovering between the closed and the punctured illusion that the transformation effected by the play of the text makes itself felt to the reader.

Transformation, in turn, appears to head toward some aim that must be realized by the reader, and so the play of the text can be ended in various ways: one is in terms of semantics. In this case what is paramount is our need for understanding and our urge to appropriate the experiences given to us. This might even indicate a defense mechanism operating within ourselves, as the search for meaning may be our means of warding off the unfamiliar.

Another way in which we may play the text is by obtaining experience. Then we open ourselves up to the unfamiliar, and are prepared to let our own values be influenced or even changed by it.

A third mode of play is that of pleasure. We then give precedence to the enjoyment derived from an unusual exercise of our faculties which enables us to become present to ourselves. Each of these options represents a tendency according to which the play of the text can be acted out.

I NOW come to the final point: what is play, and why do we play? Any answer to this fundamental question can only be in the nature of tentative interpretation. In phylogenetic terms, play in the animal kingdom begins when the space of the habitat expands. Initially it appears to be an activity for its own sake, exploring the bounds of the possible, in view of the fact that everything is now possible. But we may also see it as a would-be action, or a trial run that trains the animal to cope with the unforeseeable that is to come. The more the animal's territory expands, the more important and sometimes the more elaborate play becomes as a means of preparing for survival.

In ontogenetic terms, there is a distinction to be observed in child's play between perception and meaning. When a child rides a hobbyhorse, i.e., a riding stick, he is engaged in a mental action that is quite distinct from what he actually perceives. He does not, of course, perceive a real horse, and so the play consists in splitting the object (horse) and the meaning of that object in the real world. Its play is therefore an action in which a defamiliarized meaning is acted out in a real situation.

What these two instances of playing have in common is a form of staging. But in neither case is the staging carried out for its own sake. In the animal kingdom, it serves to anticipate and prepare for future actions; in child's play, it permits real limitations to be overstepped. Staging, then, is basically a means of crossing boundaries, and this holds equally true for the play of the text, which stages transformation and at the same time reveals how the staging is done. This duality arises largely from the fact that transformation here has no pragmatic outcome: it does not change one thing into another. It is, rather, a purpose that can be properly fulfilled only if its own procedural workings are exhibited.

What is the nature of this purpose? Transformation is an access road to the inaccessible, but staged transformation does not only make available the unavailable. Its achievement is perhaps even more gratifying. It allows us to have things both ways, by making that which is inaccessible both present and absent. Presence comes about by means of the staged transformation, and absence by means of the fact that the staged transformation is only play. Hence every presented absence is qualified by the caveat that it is only staged in the form of make-believe, through which we can conceive what would otherwise elude our grasp. Herein lies the extraordinary achievement of play, for it appears to satisfy both epistemological and anthropological needs. Epistemologically speaking, it imbues presence with adumbrated absence by denying any authenticity to the possible results of play. Anthropologically speaking, it allows us to conceive that which is withheld from us. Interestingly enough, the epistemological and anthropological perspectives do not conflict, even though they may appear to run counter to each other. If there were a clash, it would undo the play, but as there is not, the cognitive irreconcilability in fact reveals something of our own human makeup. By allowing us to have absence as presence, play turns out to be a means whereby we may extend ourselves. This extension is a basic and ever-fascinating feature of literature, and the question inevitably arises as to why we need it. The answer to that question could be the starting point for a literary anthropology.

## Notes

1. See Michel Foucault, *The Order of Things. An Archaeology of the Human Sciences* (London: Tavistock, 1970), pp. 217–49, and Jacques Derrida, *Writing and Difference*, trans. Alan Bass, (London: Routledge and Kegan Paul, 1978); especially the essay on "Artaud." For a detailed exploration of that issue see Gabriele Schwab, *Samuel Becketts Endspiel mit der Subjektivität: Entwurf einer Psychoästhetik des modernen Theaters* (Stuttgart: J. B. Metzler, 1981), pp. 14–34.

2. E. H. Gombrich, *Art and Illusion: A Study in the Psychology of Pictorial Representation*, (London: Phaidon Press, 1962), especially pp. 154–244.

3. Peter Hutchinson, *Games Authors Play* (London: Methuen, 1983), provides a catalogue of the various games played in literary texts.

4. Johan Huizinga, *Homo Ludens. Vom Ursprung der Kultur im Spiel* (Hamburg: Rowohlt 1956), pp. 9–14.

5. Gregory Bateson, *Steps to an Ecology of the Mind* (San Francisco: Chandler, 1972), p. 315.

6. Jean Piaget, *Nachahmung, Spiel und Traum* (Gesammelte Werke 5), trans. Leo Montada (Stuttgart: Ernst Klett, 1975), pp. 178–216.

7. Roger Caillois, *Man, Play, and Games*, trans. Meyer Barash (N.Y.: Free Press of Glencoe, 1961), p. viii.

8. Irving Goffman, *The Presentation of Self in Everyday Life* (Garden City, N.Y.: Doubleday, 1959), pp. 8f, 141–66.

9. Manfred Eigen und Ruthhild Winkler, *Das Spiel. Naturgesetze steuern den Zufall* (Munich: R. Piper, 1985), pp. 87–121.

# 15

# NAUGHTY ORATORS: NEGATION OF VOICE IN *GASLIGHT*

## Stanley Cavell

FILM IS an interest of mine, or say a love, not separate from my interest in, or love of, philosophy. So when I am drawn to think through a film I do not regard the reading that results as over, even provisionally, until I have said how it bears on the nature of film generally and on the commitment to philosophy. I hope you have seen or will see *Gaslight* and will like or respect it sufficiently to be willing to think through it—through certain very limited passages of it of course—with such interests in mind.

I begin with a word or two about why I am drawn to this film. It is one of a number of films I am currently studying that I claim constitute a genre of film, ones that I find share certain preoccupations, or parts of a story—some would say laws. I call the genre the "melodrama of the unknown woman."[1] Apart from *Gaslight* the principle or defining members of it are *Letter from an Unknown Woman* (Max Ophuls, 1948, with Joan Fontaine and Louis Jourdain), from which I have taken the genre's title; *Now, Voyager* (1942, starring Bette Davis); *Stella Dallas* (1936, starring Barbara Stanwyck); *Show Boat* (1936, with Irene Dunne, Helen Morgan, and Paul Robeson); and the earliest, *Blond Venus* (1932, directed by Joseph von Sternberg, starring Marlene Dietrich). The specific systematic connections of these films with one another are, I realize, at first hardly discernible; the impression they make, when one hears them cited together, is likely to be one of arbitrariness. An important pattern within their mutual connections is given in their relation as a group to another genre of film I have studied and, in the light of the new genre of melodrama, continue also to study, to which I devoted the book called *Pursuits of Happiness*—a genre I name there the "comedy of remarriage," a group of films also from the Hollywood of the 1930s and 1940s. The defining members of this genre are *It Happened One Night, The Awful Truth, Bringing Up Baby, His Girl Friday, The Philadelphia Story, The Lady Eve,* and *Adam's Rib.* A system of connections among these films is much easier to see, for various reasons: certainly, because they are individually more famous and more beloved and remembered (though their being beloved and remembered may contrariwise itself result from their system of connections); and because they share their particular directors and their characteristic stars (Katharine Hepburn, Irene Dunne, Cary Grant, Spencer Tracy, Barbara Stanwyck). (Not the least interest, by the way, of *Gaslight* in particular, which was made in 1944 by George Cukor, is that Cukor is also the director of two of the seven central remarriage comedies, *The Philadelphia Story,* three years earlier, and *Adam's Rib,* five years later.) The fit of remarriage comedies with one another is quite perspicuous once you look for what roughly speaking are features they share: for example, they all begin or climax with the threatened end of a marriage, the threat of divorce, and the drive of the narrative is to set the original pair together *again;* whereas classical comedies—at least, so-called "new comedies"—concern the overcoming of obstacles to a young pair's desire to be together in the first place and end in a condition called marriage. The obvious obstacle to marriage in the classical comedies is the woman's father (or some senex, i.e., some older man), whereas in remarriage comedy, if the woman's father is present he is always on the side of his daughter's desire. Moreover, in remarriage comedy the woman's mother is never present (with illuminating exceptions that prove the rule), and the woman of the principal pair is never herself shown to be a mother and is approaching an age at which the choice of motherhood will be forced upon her or forced away from her.

The feature of remarriage comedy that pervades each moment of its texture and mood is the nature of the *conversation* that binds or sweeps together the principal pair. I suppose that this is the feature that comes in for the greatest conceptual development in *Pursuits of Happiness*. Conversation is given a beautiful theory in John Milton's revolutionary tract to justify divorce, making the willingness for conversation (for "a meet and happy conversation") the basis of marriage, even making conversation what I might call the *fact* of marriage; and conversation in these remarriage films is concerned with what religion, in the Book of Genesis, takes as what we might call its myth of marriage, namely the creation of the woman from the man—the story of Adam's rib. In these comedies the creation of the woman—the new creation of the woman, the creation of the new woman, the new creation of the human—takes the form of the woman's education by the man; hence a critical clause in the story these films tell and retell is the discerning of what it is about this man that fits him to be chosen by this woman to provide that authorization of her, of let us say her desire. This suggests a privileging of the male still within this atmosphere of equality. The genre scrutinizes this in the ways, even in this atmosphere, the male is declared, at his best, to retain a taint of villainy. This so to speak prepares the genre for its inner relation to melodrama. And if the melodrama of the unknown woman is "derived" from the genre of the comedy of remarriage, the pervasive feature of equal conversation must have its pervasive equivalent in the melodramas.

The mechanism of "derivation" is what I think of as the negation of the features of the comedies by the melodramas. For example, in the melodrama of unknownness the woman's father, or another older man (it may be her husband) is *not* on the side of her desire but on the side of law, and her mother is always present (or her search for or loss of or competition with a mother is always present) and she is always shown as a mother (or her relation to a child is explicit). With these differences in the presence and absence of parents and children goes a difference in the role of the past and of memory: in the comedies the past is open, shared, a recurring topic of fun, no doubt somewhat ambiguous; but in melodramas the past is frozen, mysterious, with topics forbidden and isolating. Again, to take an odd but interesting feature, whereas in remarriage comedy the action of the narration moves from a setting in a big city to conclude in a place outside the city—called by such critics as Northrop Frye, following Shakespeare, "the green world" or "the golden world," a place of perspective—in melodramas of unknownness the action returns to and concludes in the place from which it began or in which it has climaxed, a place of abandon, or transcendence.

The chief negation of these comedies by these melodramas is the negation of marriage itself—marriage in them is not necessarily reconceived and provisionally affirmed, as in remarriage comedy, but rather marriage as a route to creation, to a new or an original integrity, is transcended, and perhaps reconceived. (It is, I think, the idea of a negation of marriage taking the form of a negation of conversation that produced my title "Naughty Orators," echoing *All's Well That Ends Well* [5.3.253]. This pair of Shakespeare's words invokes one of the Shakespearean puns in the region of the nothing, that between "naught" and "naughty," and arises as a character is explicitly remarking yet another turn in the Shakespearean problematic of marriage; and in *Gaslight* Paula will say, in reaction to the detective's telling her that her "husband" already has a wife, "Then from the beginning there was nothing.") The route to this alternative integrity is still creation, or what I am calling metamorphosis—some radical, astonishing, one may say melodramatic change of the woman, say of her identity. But this change must take place outside the process of a mode of conversation with a man (of course; since such a conversation would constitute marriage). It is as if the women of the melodramas are saying to their sisters in the comedies (they are sisters because both lines of women, as I argue elsewhere, descend from identifiable heroines in Shakespeare and in Ibsen): "You may call yourselves lucky to have found a man with whom you can overcome the humiliation of marriage by marriage itself. For us, with our talents and tastes, there is no further or happy education to be found there; our integrity and metamorphosis happens elsewhere, in the abandoning of that *shared* wit and intelligence and exclusive appreciation." This elsewhere is a function of something within the melodrama genre that I have called the world of women.[2]

That there should be this alternative route to integrity and possibility is hardly surprising, since it is the one taken in char-

acteristic films of the women who represent the highest reaches
of glamorous independence registered in the idea of a star—
classically, by Greta Garbo and Marlene Dietrich, by Bette
Davis at her best, and perhaps by Barbara Stanwyck and Ingrid
Bergman. The persistence of this feature of metamorphosis indicates the cause of these genres as among the great subjects
of the medium of film, since a great property of the medium is its violent transfiguration of creatures of flesh and blood,
its recreation of them, let us say, in projecting and screening
them.

The films represented in the melodrama of the unknown woman
are among those films known to our culture, from the time of
their making until the present, as "women's films" or "tearjer-
kers." And even in very recent years, when a few are receiving
more serious attention from a few critics, they are mostly, as far
as I have seen, treated as works to be somewhat apologized for,
somewhat condescended to. My experience of these films dis-
putes any such condescension, and I regard them as worthy com-
panions of the remarriage comedies from which they derive, hence
among the highest achievements of the art of film—worthy com-
panions in intelligence, in seriousness of artistic purpose, in moral
imagination, and even in a sense in wit. They are of course less
ingratiating than those comedies; but then so much film, and so
much in the rest of culture, is less ingratiating. But a film like
Gaslight is so often the reverse of ingratiating that it becomes
painful to go on watching. Yet I have found the pain of studying
it in the end to have been transcended.

Since the proof of such a claim, or feeling, of value lies nowhere but in the experience of individual films, it is to that
business that we must now turn.

I may perhaps help prepare you for such a film's candidacy as
a worthy companion to the best of the Hollywood comedies of
the sound era by describing both the comedies and the melodramas as workings out of the problematic of self-reliance and conformity, or of hope and despair, as established in the founding
American thinking of Emerson and of Thoreau. The comedies
envision a relation of equality between human beings that we
may characterize, using favorite terms of Emerson, as a relation

of rightful attraction, of expressiveness, and of joy. Emerson's terms are ones he attributes to the work of poetry, which, moreover, he generally understands as metamorphosis. The relation as between human beings is not, in the comedies, perceived as one that pervades society, but it is shown to hold between a pair who are somehow exemplary of the possibilities of this society at large. The melodramas envision the phase of the problematic self-reliance that demands this expressiveness and joy first in relation to oneself. It is a claim of mine that in his essay "Self-Reliance," Emerson explicitly (but somehow unnoticeably) affiliates his guiding idea with the self-consciousness demanded in Descartes' famous *cogito ergo sum* (I think therefore I am), his pivotal answer to skepticism, to philosophical doubt concerning the existence of the world and of oneself and others in it—the thing philosophers have called hyperbolic doubt; I might call it doubt to excess, to the point of melodrama. Emerson's work thus offers nothing less in its proposal of self-reliance than a succeeding proof of human existence, as well as a proof of his right to offer such a proof, namely through his inheriting of philosophy—in this instance of Descartes' *Meditations*—for America.

Why the comedies and melodramas that work out this problematic of American transcendentalism's participation in skepticism themselves concern the achievement or the transcendence of marriage—I mean why from a philosophical, call it even a metaphysical, point of view marriage is their theme—I will merely suggest by quoting loosely one longish sentence from near the end of a companion essay of mine that works out both Emerson's and Poe's differently parodistic inheritance of Descartes' philosophizing, and that relates their achievement in this regard to the criticism of Cartesian skepticism developed in ordinary language philosophy, particularly in Wittgenstein's *Philosophical Investigations* (a criticism whose originality is essential to the later Wittgenstein's philosophical originality as such):

It stands to reason that if some image of human intimacy, call it marriage, or domestication, is [or has become available as] the fictional equivalent of what the philosophers of ordinary language understand as the ordinary, call this the

image of the everyday as the domestic; it stands to reason
that then the threat to the ordinary that philosophy names
skepticism should show up in fiction's favorite threats to
forms of marriage, namely in forms of melodramas and
tragedy.[3]

This takes me to *Gaslight*.

I said that in the case of the unknown woman something in her
language must bear the weight borne by the weight of conversation in the case of her sisters in remarriage comedy. In turning
now to a reading of *Gaslight* I name this opposing feature of
language as that of irony, a negation of conversation, a recognition of one's isolation—a piece of knowledge to which these
women, in transcending marriage, have to show themselves equal.
Sadistic irony riddles the exchanges of *Gaslight*, from the coil of
words with which this husband (Gregory; played by Charles Boyer)
incessantly lashes this wife (played by Ingrid Bergman) ("Paula,
don't get hysterical"—when he's driving her to distraction; "You're
not beginning to imagine things too, are you Paula?"—when all
of his time with her is spent suggesting things for her to imagine);
to the irony of such directions as those of the opening words of
the film, "Stand back. Stand back," said by an anonymous police-
man to a depicted audience outside the house of murder, but in
some viewing bound to be taken by us as directed to us as audience, but in that case ambiguously, ironically, since it could be
meant either as a warning to protect ourselves from what is coming or as a tip to seek a perspective from which to command a
better view; to the full-throated melodramatic climax of ironies in
which the woman confronts her husband alone—brandishing a
knife with which she might free him or kill him, and doing
neither quite, or perhaps both—and delivers to him her *cogito
ergo sum*, her proof of her existence, which this film translates
roughly as "Now I exist because now I speak for myself; and in
particular because I speak in hatred and to you, who have always
pretended to understand me, and pretended not to understand
me, and who I now know will alone understand my every word
and gesture" (as if, in our mysterious world, to exist is to take
revenge). This declaration causes, or is caused by (that is, it is the
same as), her metamorphosis, or creation, which is what one

should expect of the assertion of the cogito that, as in Descartes, puts a close to skeptical doubt.

The melodrama of Gaslight, in turn, reveals the cogito as occurring in an explicit context of irony and madness. The overt content of the wife's declaration to her husband is that she is mad, that she is just what he has suggested she is and driven her to be —or is this itself irony? (I do not know that philosophers have ever spoken explicitly of irony in relation to the cogito, but hardly any have failed to find some demonic bewilderment over it, sometimes speaking of a peculiar circle in Descartes' argument, sometimes wondering whether the cogito is really an argument exactly at all. One is after all apt to wonder: If I am supposed to exist only if I acknowledge that I do, claim my existence, who was I before I acknowledged it, and before whom is it that I claim it, since every other's existence must be under the same necessity of acknowledgment that mine is under? Some such bewilderment must have helped keep the cogito's fascination alive for three and a half centuries; for its life can hardly be due to some as yet unfathomed intricacy of argumentation.) Now the association of the cogito with a scene, or play, of madness formed the crossroads of a notable early moment within the developments of French thought over the past two or three decades that have transformed the study of literary criticism and theory: I mean the crossroads of Derrida's taking up of the treatment of Descartes by Foucault in (Foucault's) *Madness and Civilization: A History of Insanity in the Age of Reason.* I will want to come back to this moment as a way of defining my own early stake in writing of such matters —a stake I am sure was internal to my being drawn to think about film. But first let us get deeper into what this film has to say for itself, how it accounts for the woman's turn to her freedom for the source of energy that allows her to claim her existence at last. What is she metamorphosed into?

That the woman frees herself from her husband in forms of madness and irony suggests that the portrait of marriage we are given in this film is precisely the way of life that the women of both the comedy of remarriage and of the derived melodrama of the unknown woman all shrink from, live so as to find freedom from. In Gaslight we are given the perfect contradiction of the education and creation sought in remarriage comedy: in this melodrama the woman is meant to be decreated, tortured out of a mind altogether.

The imaging of her terror of madness by the lowering and raising of the light in the gas lamps in her room and by the obscure sounds originating over the room are, I have found in discussions of the film, quite unforgettable—people who saw the film only on its first release, over forty years ago, at once identify the film when reminded of these features. But these features are generally falsely remembered as being planned by the husband to drive his wife mad. The devices to this end that the husband plans consist rather of insinuating to his wife, then accusing her, then "proving" to her, that she forgets things and hides things and steals things.

The general order of these events is roughly as follows: After the opening sequence of the young Paula escorted at dusk out of her dead aunt's house, Paula's story is picked up ten years later, with a set of sequences in Italy, opening with her singing lesson with her aunt's old teacher, and closing with the morning after her wedding night with a man she had met some two weeks earlier (he is the pianist, it happens, who had been her accompanist at the singing lesson) to whom she promises the house she owns—uncannily like the house in a little square in London that the man has just intimately confessed to her that he has always dreamed he might live in one day with a woman he loves. Back in London, after reopening the house, and following Gregory's suggestion to board up in the attic all the furnishings of the house, which are associated with Paula's memories of her aunt, Paula's deterioration—beyond her mounting bouts of panic in response to Gregory's various demonstrations—shows in her inability to go out of the house alone for an afternoon walk, in her incapacity to oppose Gregory's violent disapproval of inviting guests into her house, in her failure to make her wishes credible to her servants, punctuated by her being isolated under the fluctuating gaslight. When at a formal party at the house of Lady Dalroy, a friend of her aunt's, Paula publicly breaks down under a fresh private accusation of Gregory's, a young detective from Scotland Yard (played by Joseph Cotten)—a friend of this household and an admirer as a youth of Paula's celebrated aunt—divines the urgency of the situation and seizes an opportunity that night to be admitted into Paula's house after her husband has taken her home and gone out again. The detective contrives to regain Paula's confidence in her memory and then in her own senses and intellect sufficiently to ground her belief in his tale that the man she has accepted in marriage is the murderer of her aunt. Of the countless significantly recountable details in the film, I mention two that occur after the detective leaves Paula to intercept Gregory's usual return to the house: (1) that of the almost deaf cook who, meaning to protect Paula, precipitates what seems a final recurrence of Paula's self-doubt by "confirming" Gregory's wild denials that a stranger had visited the house while he was absent —so the world of women is drawn into conspiring with the maddening world of men; and (2) that of Cukor's homage to Hitchcock, who might have made a film using this material, as the camera stays for what feels like too long a time fixed at Paula's door after she has shut it behind her to await developments as the detective leaves, and then moves as if in Paula's sleep-walking pace, distractedly, to discover Gregory entering the house from above—forcing open the barred door to the attic—an unnerving moment of exposure and vulnerability, as if after all we have been shown, we recognize for the first time that this obsessed maniac has actually been pursuing his obsession just a few feet from the woman victimized by it, by her having to deny it, as if we have also been denying some part of it, some part of our own victimization by it, a late recognition that we are blind to the direction from which danger comes.

Only marriage given an historical development that empowers it to save could have the power of this marriage to destroy. The decreation of the woman works first to destroy Paula's confidence in her memory, hence to destroy her memory. Some of the first words of the film are those of a man (some kind of official guardian, a solicitor one supposes) saying to the young Paula, whose guardian aunt has been murdered, "No, no, Paula. Don't look back. You've got to forget everything that's happened here" (when she has exactly nothing to look forward to); and later her husband Gregory will say to her, "You're becoming forgetful, Paula" (when

she has returned to the scene of her past and wants exactly only
to look forward). So not only individual men are destroying her
mind, but the world of men, in its contradictions with itself, is
destroying for her the idea and possibility of reality as such. This
seems roughly to be what was happening in Freud's treatment, or
in Freud's case history of his treatment, of the patient he called
Dora. (Freud's behavior toward Dora was so described by Steven
Marcus when, in an essay on this case history in 1974, he redi-
rected the attention of American literary-psychoanalytic culture
to this material so prominently featured by Freud and now so
prominently under discussion, particularly in feminism.)[4]

The process of controlled amentia is one that is to render the
woman of *Gaslight* stupid, say self-stupefying: she does not know
what the fairly obvious sounds of tramping are on the floor above,
and she does not know why, hence soon not even whether the
gas lamp is obviously lowering in her room—self-stupefying, but
in such a way that what she imagines cannot be dismissed, either
by her or by us, as ordinary stupidity, any more than Descartes'
suggestion that he might only be dreaming that he is sitting before
his fire can be dismissed by him or (if we follow him) by us as
ordinary stupidity. Let us say that it is in both cases hyperbolic
stupidity. (Of course I am offering a little gag here about what
philosophers have named Descartes' hyperbolic doubt, but I would
not have my gag too simply interpreted. It is meant to question
whether this philosophical description is satisfying; but it is at
the same time meant to affirm that some such philosophical description is at this place necessary.) How is the woman's overcoming of her stupefaction, her access to knowledge, represented?

The access is initiated upon the appearance of the young man,
the man from outside, called the detective, whose access to the
house the woman at first shrinks from. The detective gains her
confidence by producing the match to the aunt's mysterious single glove kept in her case of mementos; this matching is an
adventurous mode of identifying an authentic contact. (This
matching may well prompt us to ask how it was that Gregory first
gained this girl's confidence—it is quite clear that Paula has
known no other man romantically.) The young man confirms the

reality of her sensations (that there is tramping, that the light dims)—call them expressions of the reality of her inner life—and then explores this reality with therapeutically detective-like questions concerning when the light goes down and when it comes up again. Her knowledge dawns, and the night of self-stupefaction ends, on his pressing the question, "You know, don't you Mrs. Anton? You know who's up there," as she confirms his assertion of her knowledge by at first denying it: "No. No. He can't be." Here again there is a remarkable structural resemblance to perhaps the central crux of Freud's treatment of Dora, his insistent claim to her that she possesses a piece of knowledge that she persists in disclaiming (a piece of sexual knowledge, you may be sure).

I cannot say that I am surprised by this early, repeated intrusion of the case of Dora into these deliberations, and since I welcome it, and will cultivate it for a few moments, I should perhaps explain why I am not surprised. I have suggested elsewhere that some internal connection between the discoveries of psychoanalysis and the means of film narrative is argued in their each originating, in the closing years of the nineteenth century, in the study of the sufferings of women. The originating role of women in psychoanalysis is becoming a familiar topic as interest increases in Freud's early cases: besides the Dora case there is principally the sequence of cases, all concerning women, reported in Freud and Breuer's *Studies in Hysteria* (1893–1895). That our interest in film, as expressed in the astonishingly rapid discoveries of narrative technique in the new medium, especially in its adaptations of melodrama and romance, is equally a function of the study of women is not something to attempt to argue for now. I mostly offer the idea as my intuition of the fascination of film, without denying the reasonably obvious fact that human males have also significantly occurred in major films, but suggesting that while men primarily appear in contexts of mutual competition and of uniform or communal efforts (in work, in adventure, in prison, in war) it is individual women who have given film its depth, as if lending it their own fascination. (It is an open question for me whether Charlie Chaplin and Buster Keaton would exactly be exceptions to this idea.)

I begin to speculate about why it is that women play this originating role in both of these developments by way of continuing to think about the history of skepticism in Western culture, particularly about its inception or representation in Shakespeare and Descartes, especially with respect to philosophical doubts about the existence of what philosophy calls other minds—as though both psychoanalysis and film testify that by the turn of the twentieth century psychic reality, the fact of the existence of mind, had become believable primarily in its feminine (one may say passive) aspect. (This should help us to see why in Wittgenstein's *Philosophical Investigations*, in his study of the question of the other, the pervasive example is that of pain.) But doesn't this line of speculation assume that both psychoanalysis and cinema are themselves interested in testimony as to the existence of mind, that it is part of the value of both that they provide modern testimony, testimony acceptable to a modern sensibility, as to psychic reality? Yes.

Freud's brutal insistence to Dora of her knowledge precipitates her termination of the analysis, and part of the crux of her case is whether her leaving is a realistic rebuke to Freud's bullying or whether it is a denial that confirms the truth of his claim. Another part of the crux (taking up Freud's reporting of the case as one in which he learned of the power of countertransference, having failed to take into account his identification, call it, with the woman) is the extent to which psychoanalysis is, and presented itself to Freud as, the theft of women's knowledge, that knowledge which, suppressed, caused the conditions psychoanalysts were first asked to see, conditions of hysteria. Gregory's "Don't get hysterical, Paula," is said to her suggestively, so this figure further encodes a resemblance to psychoanalysis in the man's power of hypnosis or suggestion, and it thus invokes the—again current—criticism of the scientific pretensions of psychoanalysis, that it coerces the confessions it claims as its evidence. And, to be sure, if all psychoanalysts were, and were by the psychoanalytic process compelled to be, essentially like Gregory Anton, the criticism would be valid. (Why, one should accordingly ask, is this such a critic's picture of the psychoanalyst?—recognizing that a Gregory Anton might also ask *that* question.)

A last line of comparison I invoke between *Gaslight* and the Dora case concerns the sense in Freud's account that the woman had been handed over to him by her father, as if to help continue her obedience to, or subservience within, the world of men. This might at first seem to be Paula's case as well, as she moves from the hands of the lawyer into that of the singing teacher, and from there into the hands of the piano player. But both Gregory and the detective arrive as from Paula's aunt, thus from a connection with the world of women (called for by the genre of the unknown woman): it is surely because of Gregory's association with the aunt's singing teacher that we imagine his general route into Paula's confidence; and the missing glove is a direct sign of the bearer's having been *sent* by the aunt, as if to overcome false emissaries. That the glove is also presented as if by a child, the boy to whom the aunt has entrusted the memento (a sign of an undoubted memory), is also to the point: it invokes in the child another figure called for by the genre, and at the same time it presents the young detective as not quite or just another grown man; he is in effect a part of Paula's childhood.

Her childhood is invoked poignantly the night of Lady Dalroy's musicale and dinner party. The anticipation of the evening gives Paula courage for the single time in the process of her decreation to oppose Gregory and to command the obedience of the scornful maid Nancy, declaring her intention to go to the party alone if necessary. Then, the opening exchange with Lady Dalroy gives a vivid picture of Paula in command of her faculties: "You're Paula Anton; I'm sure you don't remember me." "Indeed I do, Lady Dalroy. I was at the children's party here, and there was a magician." The combination of her powers of decision and command and of her intact memory, in particular her memory of her childhood, within the orbit of a powerful woman, poses a threat to Gregory's plan, and he uses this outburst of Paula's confidence, the show of the woman she might have been, might be, as the occasion to crush her hopes at their strongest. His defeat of her on this critical ground prepares her for the crisis, in which she accepts her fate of being declared and confined as mad. This sequence thus repeats the rhythm of the maddening established by Gregory in the preceding sequence, where he had counter-

manded Paula's invitation to the inquisitive neighbor (the spinster figure, Miss Thwaites, played by Dame May Whitty) to come
into the house, and then bullied Paula, with sweet reasonableness, into agreeing that she *could* have had the woman in if she
had *really* wished it (thus suggesting that Paula's problem is her
own metaphysical, intellectual occultism, and not social and psychological violence; it is what metaphysics chronically suggests).
Then out of the blue Gregory announces, having somehow begun
playing a tune from *Die Fledermaus* on the piano (to change the
mood, or cover it), that they are going out to the theater this
evening, so clearly there is no time now for a visitor. Paula is
stunned with elation, and Gregory charmingly, teasingly gets her
to deny, as if it were the reverse of the truth, the childish thought
that he is a bad man who keeps her a prisoner. As she lets her
spirits extend into a whirling dance to his music, and fills the
room with painful laughter and uncertain singing—it is the only
recurrence of her singing voice since the early lesson with Signor
Guardi—Gregory breaks off the music and begins a methodical
strangling of Paula's rising spirits by accusing her of the meaningless action of having taken a picture from the wall and hidden it.
(The passage into and out of dancing is one of immense cinematic
and theatrical bravura, on the part both of actress and of director.
I find in it an allusion to the passage in *A Doll's House* near the
end of act 2 in which Nora is being instructed in dancing by male
piano playing. Nora's husband is replaced at the piano by Dr.
Rank, friend of the house, who encourages a wilder dancing
which her husband then puts a stop to, saying, "This is sheer
madness. . . . You've forgotten everything I taught you"; and
having just said, "Nora darling, you're dancing as if your life
depended on it," which she confirms. The power of demonic
piano playing possessed by a foreign or invasive male with some
shadow over him is a figure that appears in several of Cukor's
films.)

It is worth noticing here, for those who still have difficulty
believing just how well made movies can be, that Paula's memory
of the magician plays ironically into her blindness to Gregory's
strategy at the party, which is precisely to make a watch magically appear. He had earlier held her bag open, and waited (as if

keeping the camera running) until she turned to see him, unmistakably, drop the brooch he had given her into her bag—a perfectly ordinary bag. The new trick of making the watch appear matches and caps the trick of making the brooch disappear. His feeling around the outside of the soft bag until he discovers the outline of the hard watch (in close-up) is in a sense his most intimate gesture toward her since their embraces in the opening sequences of the film.

Here we might consider that we witness the gaslight dimming only in her bedroom. (We witness its return to normal only at the last, in her husband's room, near the end of her interview with the detective. Artfully, the return to normal is shown to be as much the cause of fear, as much an event to be aghast at, as the dimming.) It is specifically her bedroom that her husband twice abandons her in, or to, in extreme terror—the first time in terror, as she puts it, "of this house, of myself," the second time in terror of her sentence to a madhouse, I mean to a different madhouse. (She had described her house to her new husband, the place to which that husband has already confined her, as "a house of horror.") What goes on in her bedroom with him are scenes of psychic torture, prepared by the woman's sense that she is fated to horror, that her desires are twisted and incomprehensible to the one figure in her life who now defines reality for her, that these normal, human desires are by no means to be satisfied but to be deplored and humiliatingly confessed. This is figured in the opening sequence of Paula's and Gregory's guided tour of the Tower of London (preceding the sequence of their viewing the Crown Jewels), as Paula discovers that the brooch Gregory had given her is missing, and the institutionally confident voice of the tour guide (continuing in voice-over) accompanies her imagination as he picturesquely describes the method of torture on the rack. Gregory's impotence seems to me implied in various ways; for example, by his nameless fear of the young man; by his flirtatiousness in response to the overtures of the housemaid (played by Angela Lansbury); by his implying, when he asks the maid to explain her makeup secrets to his wife, that his wife is unattractive to him; and by the gross, general displacement rendered in his obsession with jewels. But I am not here concerning myself

with Gregory's story. It is in a sense inessential. (The essential or
first question in considering his relation to Paula is whether he
does or does not recognize the thing that everyone else knows
who knows Paula well—that she strikingly resembles her aunt.
That we are not given the means to know whether Gregory fully
recognizes this, or cares about it, suggests to me the irrelevance
of this man's story—as if there is nothing remarkable in this
telling of its twistings, as if all women face equivalent turns in
the men to whom they give themselves in marriage.) And I urge
that before coming further to terms with what the sequences in
her bedroom may betoken—in particular before proferring some
obvious Freudian symbolism of jewels and Gregory's fetishizing
of them as all this film knows of the relationship between this
man and woman—we have more evidence to ponder concerning
how that relationship is to be described.

The detective describes it as one in which Paula is "being
systematically driven out of her mind," and grateful as we are for
his practicality and enlightenment, here and hereafter, he does
not satisfy our more speculative, or let us say dramaturgical interests. For example, when Paula asks how her husband could be up
in the attic, the detective answers by describing the path he takes
"over the roof," rather than responding to her evident wish to
know how her husband could be doing such a thing at all. A way
of describing the mode of torture that is systematically driving
Paula out of her mind is to note that she is being deprived of
words, of her right to words, of her own voice. Sometimes this
happens by her being made ashamed to describe what she sees
and hears (the dimming light, the noise—one might disgracefully
call them fragments of a primal scene); sometimes by her being
made to know that her protestations of innocence will not be
believed, and her desire for companionship will not be heard;
and sometimes by her being offered a simple description, such as
"My watch is gone," and being invited to supply the speech-act
of blaming, as if every fact accuses her.

The idea of deprivation of the right to words alerts us to the
way the therapeutic process is pictured in this film. Upon the
detective's confirming the dimming of the light, the woman says,
"You saw that too? Then it really happens. . . . Now I can tell

you. Every night when my husband goes out. . . ." She stops, startled by hearing her own words. The man continues for her, carrying on her words: "The light goes down. Then what?" And she is able to go on: "I hear things. . . . I watch. . . . Then the light goes up." A hesitation again, and again the man continues: "And he comes back." And again she can take the words on: "Yes. Always quite soon after." A dog would have had no trouble making such a connection. Only a human being could be *prohibited* from making it, from subjecting herself to her own words, having her own thoughts. In *The Claim of Reason*[5] I call something like this "having a voice in your own history," and compare the ways by which one may be so denied (deny oneself) in philosophy and in politics. This denial of voice is not the loss of speech, a form of aphasia, but a loss of reason, of mind, as such — say of the capacity to count, to make a difference. The image of this denial that haunts Paula—and that men keep telling her to forget—she reveals to Gregory moments after they reopen the house in London, as she recites her discovery of her murdered aunt: "She had been strangled. . . . Her lovely face was all—No! I can't stay here!" The young detective, in giving her an explanation, in a sense, of what she saw, bringing her back from strangulation, reintroducing her to language (demonstrating that her words are not shameful, but ordinary and perfectly credible, that the act of speech is hers to define), returns her to her voice—becoming, one can say, her voice teacher.

Here something of the uncanny power of the medium of film —its natural surrealism and violence—shows through. Suppose we take the film as an exploration of the question Paula asks her singing teacher in the film's first sequence proper (after the brief prologue): "I have no voice, have I?" The maestro answers: "The trouble is not with your voice alone. Your heart is not in your singing any more." He does not answer the question of her having a voice so far as it concerns a special talent or gift that Paula is questioning in herself, and he goes on to suggest that she is in love, and tells her to forget tragedy (alluding to her aunt's murder, but also somehow to the meaning of singing), and urges her to take the chance of happiness—which, he adds, is better than art, thus explicitly raising the question both of what happiness is and

what art means. The question of the possession of a voice and of
the meaning of singing is set up by the prologue, in which, more
fully, the vaguely official man says to the child Paula, as they
drive in a hansom away from the house:

> "No, no, Paula. Don't look back. You've got to forget every-
> thing that's happened here. That's why you're going to Italy,
> to see Signor Guardi. He was the best friend your Aunt ever
> had and he'll be yours too. Perhaps Signor Guardi will make
> you into a great singer as she was. Wouldn't you like that?"

The young Paula (who when we next see her in Italy ten years
later seems barely twenty years old) continues to look bewildered
and speechless, as well she might. Where in the history of (let us
say legitimate) theater could one imagine a play opening with
words such as: "Perhaps Signor Guardi will make you into a great
singer. Wouldn't you like that?" One could imagine Groucho
Marx saying it to Margaret Dumont, or W. C. Fields to a ten-year-
old brat whom he fears and despises and offers to strike. But film
has the power also to slip past comic censorship and to design
for us a fantasy we are to find our own way out of.

From the interrupted singing lesson with Signor Guardi Paula
goes to meet Gregory in the corner of a courtyard flanked by
barred windows, where he says, "I've waited for you so long,"
and she replies, "We've only known one another two weeks"—
to which he counters, "I've waited all my life," his words steep-
ing language in ironies from which it may never recover. After
her later voice lesson from the young detective she goes again to
meet Gregory, this time ascending forbidden stairs alone, as if
into her mind—literally into the space above her bedroom from
which the maddening noises originated, and finds the man roped
to a chair. She asks the detective to let her speak to her husband
alone, eagerly locks herself together with her husband in the attic
room as the detective reluctantly leaves, and launches into her
aria of revenge. Signor Guardi had stopped the early, literal singing lesson with the words, "This opera is tragedy, Signorina, a
thing you seem incapable of understanding. Did you never hear
your Aunt sing Lucia? You *look* like her." "But," responded
Paula, "I don't sing like her." Now, at the end of the film, we are

given her version of the mad song, prompted, as in *Lucia*, by the violent end of her marriage, and bearing certain earmarks of her aunt's performance.

We know that her aunt performed so that only one person in her audience knew the secret of what she was hiding in plain view: the royal jewels sewn into her gown among worthless stones. Now, Paula uses her voice so that her husband (or someone who is, as it were, identified with his position—who is, say, fixed to a chair; in reversed roles with her; subject to her vengeance; us) alone is in a position to know the open significance of her spectacle of madness, of what is sewn into her mind. She intones:

> "Are you suggesting that this is a knife? I don't see any knife. You must have dreamed you put it there. . . . Are you mad, my husband? Or is it I who am mad? Yes. I am mad. . . . If I were not mad I could have helped you. . . . But because I am mad I hate you, and because I am mad I have betrayed you [thus she defines the speech-act of her voice lesson with the detective], and because I am mad I am rejoicing in my heart without a shred of pity, with glory in my heart."

Her *cogito* thus comes to the singing of her existence, and she chants this existence, accepts herself, as mad. Nor is she, so far as I understand, recovered from this state as the film ends. After calling the detective back into the attic room to "Take this man away," she has only two or three small sentences left to say. Walking out onto the roof balcony of the house with the detective (the route she refused to cut her husband free, in cutting herself free, to take) she says, "This will be a long night"—something madness can know about itself. This time the detective speaks allegorically (one hopes), as melodrama will, about the weather: "It's already starting to clear." But this is a mere courtesy. His going on to ask, "Will you let me come and talk to you sometime?" is a subtler and more practical courtesy; he does not expect that Paula will talk to him. She is back where she started, or stopped, at best—the place from which she was to be rescued from her fears and her ignorance of the world by marriage to a mysterious stranger. Her identification, through the aria, with her

dead aunt has rescued her from that rescue, but the world of
women here seems to hold no further hope; it cannot conceive of
it. Women's options in this universe—apart from the exceptional
aristocratic title (such as that possessed by Lady Dalroy) and
outside the state of matrimony (if these women are indeed to be
understood as being outside, rather than serving as further figures
for present states of matrimony)—are the flirtatiousness of the
maid, the deafness of the cook, or the shocked spectatordom of
the spinster; a set of options perfect for maintaining the perfect
liberty and privilege of the male.

The figure of a magician and piano player who exercises a
hypnotic control over a singer is bound at some stage to invoke
Svengali, a figure from the late nineteenth century that has also
been associated with the early practice of Freud and Breuer. But
Svengali loved Trilby, and the voice upon which he lavished his
unearthly skill was hers. In his cultivation of it he took control of
it, but the world-historical singing that resulted is no more accurately described as his voice ventriloquized through her, than as
her voice possessed by him. The joint inhabitation here is no
doubt at best a parody of love, but it is not a parade of hatred:
distinctions are to be made. It is a parody, moreover, this sharing
of the same voice, that comedies of remarriage look for a sane
version of—that is, show it to be worth looking for a sane version of.

Another association to mysteriously absorbed singing keeps
impinging on my consciousness, doubtless because Svengali is a
Jew, and surely because this particular material began coming
together during my time in Jerusalem (on and off through the
spring of 1986). The events of Kafka's story "Josephine the Singer,
or the Mouse Folk," are generally accepted, I believe, as modeling
something about the Jews, I suppose about the dispersion of the
Jews, particularly in the story's relation to prophecy. My association turns on two thoughts in the story: on Kafka's question
whether the singer creates the people for whom she sings, or the
other way around; and on his question whether a singer can, as it
were, express a people who did not themselves already sing, and
hence whether one should really call what she does singing, since

it is not different from what goes on every day—whether we call it chanting, or beseeching, or saying. The allegory drawn this way seems no more apt for the relation of a prophet or perhaps a philosopher to a people than for an artist (of a certain stripe) to a public, and perhaps especially, as I will suggest, to a movie public (where the public is apparently openly *all* of the people, the populace, whose lives are not different—are they?—from screened lives).

IT WAS the conjunction of film with madness, skepticism, and the *cogito*, together with the issues of discipleship and of the finding of one's voice, that prompted my earlier citing of Derrida's review of Foucault. Articulating this conjunction of themes forms one sort of response to a question repeatedly directed to me, in various guises, which I might formulate in this way: What is film that it invites you to discuss philosophical issues of this kind, and why specifically do you wish to accept the invitation from film (when there are so many other places)? So I will spell out this response a little in terms of a fragment or two in answer to another demand equally often pressed upon me in recent years— to say how I understand my relation to philosophical developments in France over the same years as those in which I have been doing my work, say the past three decades, especially to that of Derrida. I hope that these fragments will provide an efficient measure of the level of discussion that my concluding descriptions of this woman and her film will lay claim to—that is, the level my descriptions will claim that this woman and her film lay claim to.

I note two autobiographical moments in Derrida's reflections on Foucault's *Madness and Civilization*, moments in his lecture of March 4, 1963.[6] I may be the last person I know to read this lecture of Derrida's and I dare say he is past interest in the reactions it elicits. But I have claimed that American intellectual time is in any case different from European, beginning with the birth of American thinking in Emerson, who in the 1840s and 1850s was writing as if before the post-Kantian split between the German and the English traditions of philosophy—as if it need

not have taken place. One could say either that I am still a
generation late, or else that I am, as in a good tragedy, working
my way backward to a recognition.

The first of Derrida's autobiographical moments I note is his
opening ironic declaration that "having formerly had the good
fortune to study under Michel Foucault, I retain the consciousness of an admiring and grateful disciple" (p. 31); the second
moment is his closing declaration that "I philosophize only in
terror, but in the *confessed* terror of going mad" (p. 62). These
moments cast, in their elaboration, an uncanny light on certain of
my own preoccupations in those years around 1960—preoccupations, or a facet of my preoccupations, that there would still
perhaps be no particular point in stressing, no ready circle of
interest in, apart from the delayed resonance of contemporary
intellectual developments in France (which is doubtless part of
the reason why I am now questioned particularly about my relation to them). Derrida speaks of discipleship (unironically, I take
it) in terms of "start[ing] to speak," or, shall we say, finding a
voice:

> The disciple's consciousness, when he starts, I would not
> say to dispute, but to engage in dialogue with the master or,
> better, to articulate the interminable and silent dialogue which
> made him into a disciple—this disciple's consciousness is
> an unhappy consciousness. . . . As a disciple, he is chal-
> lenged by the master who speaks within him and before
> him, to reproach him for making this challenge and to reject
> it in advance, having elaborated it before him. (p. 31)

And Derrida, in confessing the terror of going mad, is responding
to his characterization of philosophy as "perhaps the reassurance
given against the anguish of being mad at the point of greatest
proximity to madness" (in the preceding sentence he had spoken
of the philosopher's reflecting of the *cogito* for the other, i.e., for
oneself, as a relationship in which "meaning reassures itself against
madness and nonmeaning" [p. 59]).

The title essay of my first book, *Must We Mean What We Say?*[7]
(from a talk delivered in 1957), characterizes the ordinary lan-

guage philosophers—whose work I therein claim to inherit, specifically by placing myself in the relation of discipleship to Austin—as "continuing—while at the same time their results are undermining—the tradition of British Empiricism: being gifted pupils, they seem to accept and to assassinate with the same gesture" (p. 21, n. 19). The gesture, in particular, is one of "reminding ourselves of *what we should say when*," which turns out to be a matter of reinserting or replacing the human voice in philosophical thinking, that voice that philosophy finds itself to need to deny, or displace. (It is this denial of voice that, for me, determines philosophy's drive to the hyperbolic. How this relates to Derrida's findings concerning the denial of writing is no small matter, at least for me.) Four essays later, in the context of thinking about Beckett's *Endgame,* I characterize philosophical profundity as taking the shape of madness, and summarize Wittgenstein's philosophical procedures as declaring, or confessing, that there is "no other philosophical path to sanity save through madness" (p. 127). These statements about replacing the voice and about the mad itinerary of sanity could be the epigraphs to *The Claim of Reason.* That book of mine is about skepticism as sketched, for example, in Descartes' *Meditations*—skepticism interpreted as the repudiation of language (or reason) by itself—and about the recovery from this repudiation as the return, if it is possible, from tragedy, say from the community's expulsion. But this early congruence of Derrida's and my interests in discipleship, voice, Cartesian skepticism, and madness takes place within as yet immeasurable differences.

A banal but decisive difference between us lies—or did, all those unknown years ago—in our accounts of Descartes' hyperbolic doubt (something we both contrast with what we both call "natural" doubt). For Derrida this is a turn to excess or exaggeration (and hence oddly resembles Austin's view of the matter, as when Austin says: "Some philosophers are prone to argue that because I *sometimes* cannot know that therefore I *never* can");[8] whereas for me the hyperbolical is a turn to emptiness (sometimes I say a craving for nothingness), a wish to exist outside language games—not so much as it were beyond language, perhaps, as before it. Both excess and emptiness express the human wish to escape the human—the desire for the inhuman, or the demonic.

A sublime difference between us lies—or did—in our conceptions of philosophy, a path of difference drawn, to my mind, by an affinity, one hard for me to characterize, one that takes philosophy to exist only in its questioning of itself, its threats to itself. The difference is suggested, in those of Derrida's reflections that I confine myself to, in his division of nonphilosophy from philosophy: "Foucault would be correct . . . if we were to remain at the naive, natural, and premetaphysical stage of Descartes's itinerary, the stage marked by natural doubt" and not come to "the properly philosophical, metaphysical, or critical phase of doubt" (p. 52). I would like to say: For me there is no itinerary, say no approach, to philosophy; rather philosophy comes upon me, approaches me, like a conversion. This may seem a trivial difference, but it is to my mind as important as the division as such between philosophy and nonphilosophy. The difference may be read in that strain or moment of philosophizing when philosophy does not recognize itself as having a history. Being a master of (whatever else) what may be thought of as the history of Western philosophy, Derrida recognizes (or did) himself and philosophy as having something like a history, preceded by a line or lines of thinking beginning with the Greeks. I believe that no American (North American? Middle American?) conceives this of himself and his or her philosophy. (Derrida might perhaps reply that he does not assume history, especially not one continuity of history, but rather plays with, or plays off, history. Then I might reply: No American philosopher plays off history. If Emerson does something of the sort, it is not out of a sense that the history may be taken to be his, but in the knowledge that it is not.) Analytical philosophy is of course made, as science is, always to escape its history. On this ground, where the myth of pure thought dwells, Thoreau is for once and in full irony at one with the later Americans, as when he says: "The oldest Egyptian or Hindoo philosopher raised a corner of the veil from the statue of the divinity . . . and I gaze upon as fresh a glory as he did, since it was I in him that was then so bold, and it is he in me that now reviews the

go in for leaves us beside ourselves in an insane sense, which he specifies as despair; we would say depression, or melancholia.

Now, since in Emerson's and Thoreau's world philosophers have not yet as a group separated themselves from the community, they cannot assume that they are writing for identifiable philosophers, and so they are reticent about declaring their own fears of madness—put this as the threat that they will not be able to guide, or ride out, their accession to ecstasy. Reticent not for themselves but because of the directness of the implication (they call it the conviction) of their fellow countrymen: one would not want too openly to invite another to the risk and party of madness who has not already shown his or her readiness for it. They leave themselves dismissible, protecting society from wrong access to them, if they can, as when the writer of *Walden* successively identifies himself with the bird of awakening (the rooster), the bird of prophecy (the owl), and the bird of madness (the loon): you may take him or leave him alone, which is where and what he is. In a land without an edifice of thought, in which the first cabins of thought are still under construction, there is no question of wishing to go back, as if historically or pedagogically or archaeologically, to the day of thought's founding—its metaphysical point of departure from chaos, or emptiness, or madness. The question is rather one of detecting these departures and arrivals each day. (Emerson's founding question he can express, in the opening sentence of "Experience," by asking "Where do we find ourselves?")[10] So, for example, when in *The Claim of Reason* I interpret certain famous parables in Wittgenstein's *Investigations* (that of the idea of a private language, and the related one of the person who insists on saying that there must be something boiling in a picture of a boiling pot), I say that they are meant to draw out the bits of madness or emptiness that philosophers, being human beings, are subject to under the pressure of taking thought (p. 336). And if Wittgenstein's interlocutors in those places (which is to say, any of the voices Wittgenstein contends with in himself, as a philosopher) suffer moments of madness and emptiness, then where not in the moments of the *Investigations*, where not in the event of philosophy? I go on to say that a philosopher's failing to recognize these outbreaks, to confess their madness, as it were, is itself a sign that the outbreak is shared. Moreover, since I am there placing myself in opposition to certain standing interpretations of those parables of Wittgenstein's, I am naming certain fellow professors of philosophy as sharing these outbreaks or bits of madness. That I mean this naming impersonally, and include myself within this term of criticism, will not altogether set aside the suspicion that I am stepping beyond the bounds of academic manners, even if my remarks are seen as a compliment to philosophical genuineness. Were my immediate audience Foucault— and, say, Artaud, or Bataille, Blanchot, or Lacan, or Deleuze or Derrida—the issue of the bounds of manners would itself be shared. But as matters stand the cultural (or say stylistic) distance between American and French intellectual life sometimes strikes me as maddeningly untraversable; too near to ignore, too far to go. So, naturally, I am reticent in my self-revelations, as I am reticent in giving away the positions of my masters, Emerson and Thoreau. (Then what am I doing now? Why now?)

Derrida's weaving of irony and openness in his claims for discipleship bears further thought. Since I find our voices passing and repassing in the experiments I have made with certain of the passages of an early essay of his, and of certain others, I am led to take his reflections on discipleship as, more generally, or more specifically, reflections on reading at its most faithful—as if at its most faithful reading consists of this competition or mutual inhabitation or mutual subjection of voices. Then one had better be careful of what it is one is drawn to read faithfully. This takes me back to my interest in film—I mean to my practice of working out such concepts as I am invoking here sometimes in relation to film and to films, and specifically back to the mad song in *Gaslight*.

I APPROACH it by inquiring into the film's title, into gaslight. In a definitive remarriage comedy made three years earlier, Preston Sturges' *The Lady Eve*, a supporting character tells the lady (Barbara Stanwyck) that he has just conned the film's sucker/hero (Henry Fonda) with the story of "Cecelia, the Coachman's Daughter," which he calls a "gaslight melodrama"; this character goes on to describe it as one of those impossibly old-fashioned popular productions about innocence and villainy set in a dualistic, heav-

ily symbolic universe, dealing in events of dispossession and of
the loss and the finding of identities, and so on—the sort of thing
that sophisticated con artists like themselves laugh about and are
beyond believing. The bigger and better laugh for us, more or less
implicit, is that *The Lady Eve* is thus declaring a certain relation,
to be defined, between the con game(s) of its own depiction and
the equally venerable con game(s) of melodramatic narrative. Our
*Gaslight* is such a production as Sturges comically alludes to,
with this decisive difference; it is a film, yet one, let us say, that
is lit by the same light as gaslight melodramas (by the same mood,
transfigured)—as is declared in the opening shot of a lamplighter
lighting a street lamp, which illuminates the screen. (Cukor's own
*Adam's Rib* analogously declares its affiliation with classical
melodrama in depicting a mock film melodrama—an imitation
two-reeler called a "Too Real Epic"—of villainy and innocence
and the rescue from dispossession. Since this affiliation is not
just alluded to but shown within film itself, and still within a
certain mode of comedy, the melodrama is itself presented comically, in this case as a home movie, thus attesting to the underlying unity of the world of film as well as to the domestic provenance of a certain genre of melodrama.) But what is this "decisive
difference" of film? What is the work of film? (I will not here take
in evidence the fact that an arc lamp projector is directly a form
of gaslight.) If this film belongs among the defining members of a
genre, it ought to tell a piece of this difference.

Following the cue of the light, of the rising and falling of the
light as a cause of madness, and considering that this rising and
falling is the light by which *we* see the figures on the screen, we
have to ask whether there is something in the light of film that is
inherently (not, of course, inveterately) maddening. Here I think
of my emphasis, in speaking of photography, of photography's
metaphysically hallucinatory character, its causing us to see things
that are absent: it makes things present to us to which we are not
present. For this reason I call film a moving image of skepticism.
In viewing film we know ourselves to be in Paula's condition of
victimization, in need of ratification, if so far without her bad
luck—as if to be human is to be *subject* to the madness of skepticism. An acknowledgment of film's maddening light is expressed

narratively in *Gaslight* as the connection between the wife's incomprehensibly (to her) fluctuating light and the apparently (to us) all too comprehensible actions of her husband. The film links Paula's fear of hallucination with the idea of hypnotism. ("Don't look at me like that," she cries, shielding her eyes. Have we stood back from that, from looking at her like that?)

But another feature of this narrative of rising and falling light is quite readable. That gas lighting works throughout a given household in such a way that one jet lowers or rises according to whether another jet, elsewhere in the house, is raised or lowered, is a phenomenon drummed in by the dialogue. We are never shown Paula lighting her own, or any other, lamp; hers waxes and wanes (inversely) with her husband's. Read this as: the woman's supply is drawn off by the man's unacknowledged need of it, and specifically by his unacknowledged, assumed power to demand it (his literal draining of her is not even part of his conscious deviousness). Then, in addition to the theme of hallucination as an interpretation of hypnotism, we are given the theme of vampirism; one life the sapping of another's, an interpretation of a certain state of human intimacy.

Emerson has an extraordinary account of what I understand this state to be, in his great essay "Fate":

> Jesus said, "When he looketh on her, he hath committed adultery." But he is an adulterer before he has yet looked on the woman, by the superfluity of animal, and the defect of thought, in his constitution. Who meets him, or who meets her, in the street, sees that they are ripe to be each other's victim.[11]

Emerson's gesture here, following Jesus' internalization of the law, is to interiorize the matter further—unless characterizing the condition as "fate" externalizes it. Either way, this mutual victimization, sapping of one another, vampirism, is what Emerson spots as adultery; and since this state is to be seen between a pair in the common street—I take the scene as one of encountering them together, or putting them together, any ordinary day— we see the state of public intimacy (call this marriage) as itself a state of adultery. Put into Emerson's structure of Fate, what this means is that the given or conforming condition of marriage as adultery is what we are fated to. Hence this condition is exactly something that self-reliance calls upon us to challenge, to turn upon through our equally primitive capacity to think in aversion to the given: Fate is not itself our metaphysical fate, but an opening choice; we *can* (this is the Kantian fact of reason) turn the account into freedom, which is thus always an eventual condition. Strictly, I suppose, adultery would be the name of any given, fixed relation to others (the word *adultery* stems from a word meaning *other*); in Emerson's understanding of conformity, it is the sapping of self-reliance, of acting from one's own light. Then marriage, as it is given, would be the perfected state of this adulterating, conforming fixation.

What are the conditions under which the woman of *Gaslight* starts to act in her own light, takes on her voice, the power of voice sufficient to turn upon her husband, terminate her marriage (call it her marriage to fate), a voice found in the power of freedom, initially, of madness? A practical fictional condition, as befits the help of the good young detective, is that her husband is, let us say, disarmed and restrained—that is, roped to a chair. A psychological fictional condition is her assumption of identity with her aunt. But what does this identification consist in? I have said that Paula's mad song, her aria of revenge, succeeds or inherits her aunt's mad song from *Lucia*. This implies that the camera and its transfigurations, under projection, can turn, for one thing, human speech into singing. So the question becomes: How has this star, this human figure of flesh and blood, call her Ingrid Bergman, called upon the camera to lend her this transfiguration? Part of the answer would be to say what a star is, what it is about such human beings that invites this favorable photogenesis. It is not knowable *a priori*, but this film should be consulted on the matter.

We are told that the aunt's performances were double: a public one, and simultaneously a private one, in which the precious tokens of intimacy she was concealing from her public were displayed in plain view. A public is, logically, required for something to be hidden in plain sight; the concept of intimacy in question is accordingly that of secrecy; it is the concept of inti-

macy that Gregory would steal. Paula performs for her husband
fictionally in isolation, but with the knowledge that what is in
plain view can never be displayed for him; he was always turned
from it; what is in plain view is herself, her appeal for intimacy.
Is she hiding her existence? Even if we see how to say yes to this,
she is not keeping it a secret from Gregory; so for that very reason
he is not in a position to penetrate it. And we might also say that
what is concealed from him is revealed to and by the camera and
its director, from whose hiddenness is determined what of the
woman will be rendered to her public as in plain view—in view
of which it is up to each of us to turn toward her and her film, in
intimacy, knowing the gifts we render one another, or to turn
from her and her film, in more or less common, appreciative
ignorance. So both Svengali and Gregory are types—radically
opposed types—both of the director and his or her camera, and
of what you might call a film's dispersed public.

One moral to be drawn from this allegory—whether you think
these relations healthy or unhealthy, escapable or inescapable,
worth or not worth the fame and ecstasy they provide—is that
what attracts the favorable powers of the camera and the projection of its work is a certain willingness and capacity of the star
for exposure—say, for making herself visible with, as Paula puts
it, "glory in her heart." A certain willingness for visibility is the
way Emerson puts his version of the *cogito*'s demand in his
taking on of Descartes for America and his claim that we are
ashamed to say "I am," afraid of the exposure of ourselves to the
consciousness of others (say, of otherness, so of exposure to ourselves); from which Emerson draws the conclusion that we mostly
do not exist, but haunt the world, ghosts of ourselves. When the
detective first sees Paula, he says he thought he saw a ghost. He
is registering her resemblance to her dead aunt, of course, a
resemblance we have already learned from Signor Guardi, and
from the portentous portrait of the aunt in costume, to be striking;
but the detective is surely also responding to a quality of Paula's
own bearing—of, let us say, her being bound but unclaimed. The
price of Descartes' proof of human existence, of the mind's inability, as it were, to doubt itself, to doubt that it doubts, is that our
relation to our bodies is attenuated; the price of Emerson's proof

of human existence, our exposure to the consciousness of otherness (say our subjection to surveillance), is that our relation to
ourselves is theatricalized, publicized. It is no wonder that it is
in melodrama, and in movies, that such matters are worked out.

Not only there, of course, so I have still not answered why it is
there among other places that I seek to trace their working out.
What then is my more general interest in film as such beyond, as
it were, my interest in particular films? I will answer here and
now, in concluding, by stating five assumptions in three plus two
sentences.

I assume that movies have played a role in American culture
different from their role in other cultures, and more particularly
that this difference is a function of the absence in America of the
European edifice of philosophy. And since I assume further that
American culture has been no less ambitious, craved no less to
think about itself, than the most ambitious European culture, I
assume further still that the difference everyone recognizes as
existing between American and European literature is a function
of the brunt of thought that American literature, in its foundings
in, for instance, Emerson and Whitman and Poe, had to bear in
that absence of given philosophical founding and edifice, lifting
the fragments that the literature found, so to speak, handy and
portable. Finally, I assume that American film at its best participates in this Western cultural ambition of self-thought or self-
invention that presents itself in the absence of the Western edifice
of philosophy, so that on these shores film has the following
peculiar economy: it has the space, and the cultural pressure, to
satisfy the craving for thought, the ambition of a talented culture
to examine itself publicly; but its public lacks the means to grasp
this thought as such for the very reason that it naturally or historically lacks that edifice of philosophy within which to grasp it.

Its film prepared to satisfy the craving for thought, and its
public therefore deprived of recognizing the economy of its satisfaction, American culture casts its film and its film's public in the
relation that is described in "Josephine the Singer" as existing
between Josephine and her public. Each will think that it is the
creator of the other; and film's public, for all its periodic adora-
tion of its art, will fall to doubting the specialness and beauty of

its art, and its own need for it; it will even come to doubt that its art is an art—that it sings—at all.

## Postscript (1988)

The allegory of spirit through images and consequences of gaslighting may, if it does not put one off, put one on to wanting some (further) explanation of the connection. (The founding connection, for the work represented in my text, is always the fate of spirit as the fate of voice; so that strangulation and vampirism— the victimizations, respectively, of the aunt and of Paula—are psychically linked thefts, say of freedom, or separateness, difference.) Beyond specifying the connection of rising and dimming gaslight with the ideas of vampirism, and of the husband's obliviousness of his need, and of the woman's fear of the normal, I have suggested a connection with the man's incessant accusations or insinuations of the woman's metaphysical obscurity (described by him variously as her behaving "meaninglessly," as her "sleep-walking," finally as her being "mad"). Here I note his final announcement of his own metaphysical obscurity: "Don't try to understand me. . . . The jewels were a fire in my brain." (The *American Heritage Dictionary* provides the meaning with which "gas" was coined by the chemist van Helmont [d. 1644] as "an occult principle supposed to be present in all bodies"—like, say, certain ideas of the mind.) Derrida, in response to my presentation, observed that "gas" and the fateful German *Geist* ("spirit," "mind," etc.) are related words. So, of course, are further variations I have signaled within my text—Paula's being marked as a ghost and her fear (or amazement) at events of rising and falling gaslight describable as her being aghast at them. Derrida's observation was not meant as an explanation of the connection, but it increases the pressure for one.

The extent to which, or sense in which, such domestic melodramas are ghost stories—a matter coming to another head, in Ibsen, in *Ghosts*—is laid out in the question the detective asks the constable after they have followed Gregory only to have him disappear into the fog, like a ghost: "You don't suppose he could have gone into his own house do you? . . . Why should a man

walk out of his own house, all the way around the corner, just to
get back where he started from?" If we translate this as: "Why
would he wish to enter his house unseen?" the answer is irresist-
ible: in order to haunt the house, which is a way of inhabiting it.
Here the path is opened for considering Paula to be responding to
lowering lamps and noises in the attic as to a ghost story, or ghost
play. (Then where does that place us?) This suggestion is confirmed by Gregory's last accusation of Paula, that her madness is
inherited from her mother, who, he claims to have discovered,
died in an insane asylum—himself now the fabricator of a ghost
story, fictionalizing Paula's history as well as her perceptions. (In
not considering Gregory's own story, I am not considering the
extent to which he seems to come to believe his fabrications.)
Paula had said to Gregory the morning after their wedding night
that her mother died in giving birth to her, and that she never
knew her father. It is a very questionable tale, not to say a haunting one, since Paula's "aunt" might have had her reasons for
telling Paula the story: it could cover such a fact as that Paula's
mother was indeed mad; or the fact that Paula is the "aunt's"
child, whom it would have been most inconvenient for a famous
actress, in a secret liaison with a royal figure, to acknowledge as
hers (as theirs?). But the question for us is what Paula thinks of
the story, why she speaks of it as knowing no more than these
few words about so massive a matter of her life. She attaches great
feeling and significance to the memory of her aunt's going over
for her, on special occasions, the stories associated with her collection of theatrical mementos; but the child seems not to have
asked about, nor to have had, mementos associated with the
figure she calls her mother. As if she does not feel she has the
right to know something, or as if she already knows something.
Now consider again: Who does Paula know to be in the attic?
And before all: Who did she know was there before she knew?
(And who am I to want to know what Paula knows—to speculate,
for example, about Freud's observation, in discussing second
marriages in his 1931 essay "Female Sexuality," that a woman's
problems with her [first] husband will repeat her problems—
Freud says, "disappointments"—with her mother.)

Explanation of the connection between gaslight and spirit would

have, for example, to account for the possibility of such an explanation as that given by the cook Elizabeth when Paula, drained,
manages to scream down the stairwell for Elizabeth to come up.
Entering Paula's room and, in response to Paula's question, assur-
ing her that there's no one in the house to cause any dimming,
Elizabeth adds: "But the gas comes in pipes; and I expect there
gets more gas in the pipes at some times than there does at
others." Paula sees the possibility: "Yes. Yes. I suppose that
could explain it." It does not explain the ensuing noises, however, and it does not really in itself match what calls for an
explanation: it does not connect the specific conduits between
the seen and the unseen. (And can film do what Kant could not
do?) But the dimension Elizabeth's explanation invokes of gas
coming in pipes, and of having more or less gas put into the
pipes, and not ones joining merely the rooms within this house,
but one's linking this house with numberless other houses, is the
dimension of a social organism in which this house functions,
bound in the networks of dependence of a vast city. Hence the
dimension is an allegory of those features of (modern) life that
Gregory can depend upon, without planning, that support the
deference and secrecy his plans require—the obedience of servants; the nightly visits to a "studio" where he does mysterious,
unsharable work; power to exclude all other people and all other
places from his marital privacy. I do not have to say that his
occupations are, allegorically, characteristic of the society that
supports them to observe that his evil is, for all its exotic trap-
pings, utterly, unutterably, unoriginal—like the preoccupations
of melodrama.

My putting Gregory's unoriginal power to inflect the possibilities of ordinary social exchange toward mystery and evil, together
with his devotion to metaphysical obscurities, betrays perhaps
my memory of a conjunction Austin records in his "Other Minds":
"The wile of the metaphysician consists in asking 'Is it a real
table?' (a kind of object which has no obvious way of being
phoney) and not specifying or limiting what may be wrong with
it, so that I feel at a loss 'how to prove' it *is* a real one. . . . *What
are you suggesting?*" (Austin's emphasis.) To which Austin ap-
pends the following footnote: "Conjurers, too, trade on this. 'Will

some gentleman kindly satisfy himself that this is a perfectly ordinary hat?' This leaves us baffled and uneasy: sheepishly we agree that it seems all right, while conscious that we haven't the least idea what to guard against." Let us grant that Austin is too quick to invoke "the wile of the metaphysician" as the cause of our "feeling at a loss how to prove" reality. Evidently Austin would exempt himself, and his more candid philosophical procedures, at a stroke from the tendency of human unguardedness to mount systematic defenses, at devastating intellectual cost, against philosophical "suggestion" ("I cannot see all of any object so I cannot know with certainty that there is a table here"). Still, the condition of unguardedness and suggestibility that Austin isolates is traded on by psychological torturers (as often as not, no doubt, self-torturers)—a more extensive species than professional metaphysicians and magicians. Austin's philosophical animus in his appeals to ordinary language is explicitly to counter the skeptic, portrayed in the guise of trickster. But if skepticism reappears as (self-)torture, then Austin's portrayal does not reveal steps by which skepticism is to be defeated, but, on the contrary, the ground of its continued success, its open threat, say our openness to suggestion. (This should be related to a common criticism of deconstruction, that it partakes of the metaphysics it seeks to overcome. I have said that Austin underestimates the craving of metaphysics [ours for it, its for totality]. Does one believe [really] that Derrida underestimates the craving?)

On the subject of obviousness and oblivion, or light and darkness, I pose again a question for those with the fixed idea that Hollywood film of the golden age (whose trade is, let us say, obviousness and oblivion) *cannot* know and explore the subjects I have been working out here, cannot, as it were (whether or not it recognizes itself in the terms in which I have described it) assume responsibility for itself. Is there evidence for this idea? Should I regard what I have written here as evidence against it? But if indeed the conviction in Hollywood's metaphysical or magical ignorance is a fixed idea, then nothing would count as evidence for or against it. One would have instead to locate some spiritual trauma that has caused the fixation. It must be a late version of the trauma sustaining the idea that Emerson cannot

know what he does, that to know his work just cannot be his
work. It is a point on which America's admirers and its detractors
eagerly agree.

## Notes

1. Stanley Cavell, "Psychoanalysis and Cinema: The Melodrama of the Unknown Woman," in Joseph H. Smith and William Kerrigan, eds., *Images in Our Souls: Cavell, Psychoanalysis, and Cinema* (Baltimore: Johns Hopkins University Press, 1987), pp. 11–43.

2. *Ibid.*

3. Stanley Cavell, "Being Odd, Getting Even: Threats to Individuality," in T. C. Heller, M. Sosna, and D. J. Wellbery, eds., *Reconstructing Individualism: Autonomy, Individuality, and the Self in Western Thought* (Stanford, Calif.: Stanford University Press, 1986).

4. See, e.g., Charles Bernheimer and Claire Kahane, eds., *In Dora's Case: Freud —Hysteria—Feminism* (New York: Columbia University Press, 1985).

5. Stanley Cavell, *The Claim of Reason: Wittgenstein, Skepticism, Morality, and Tragedy* (Oxford: Oxford University Press, 1979).

6. Jacques Derrida, "Cogito and the History of Madness," in Derrida, *Writing and Difference*, trans. Alan Bass (Chicago: University of Chicago Press, 1978). Page references will be cited in the text.

7. Stanley Cavell, *Must We Mean What We Say? A Book of Essays* (Cambridge: Cambridge University Press, 1976). Page references will be cited in the text.

8. J. L. Austin, "Other Minds," in Austin, *Philosophical Papers*, ed. J. O. Urmson and G. J. Warnock (Oxford: Oxford University Press, 1961).

9. Henry David Thoreau, *Walden*, ch. 3, "Reading."

10. Ralph Waldo Emerson, "Experience," in *Emerson: Essays and Lectures* (New York: Library of America, 1983), pp. 469–92.

11. Ralph Waldo Emerson, "Fate," in *Emerson: Essays and Lectures* (New York: Library of America, 1983), pp. 941–68.

# CONTRIBUTORS

**HENDRIK BIRUS** is professor of Comparative Literature at the University of Munich. He is the author of *Poetische Namengebung: Zur Bedeutung der Namen in Lessings "Nathan der Weise"* and *Hermeneutische Positionen: Schleiermacher, Dilthey, Heidegger, Gadamer.*

**GERALD L. BRUNS** is White Professor of English at the University of Notre Dame. He has written *Modern Poetry and the Idea of Language, Inventions: Writing, Textuality, and Understanding in Literary History,* and *Heidegger's Estrangements.*

**SANFORD BUDICK** is Professor of English and Director of the Center for Literary Studies, the Hebrew University. He is the author of *Dryden and the Abyss of Light, Poetry of Civilization, The Dividing Muse: Images of Sacred Disjunction in Milton's Poetry,* and a forthcoming book on English classicism.

**STANLEY CAVELL** is Walter M. Cabot Professor of Aesthetics and the Theory of Value, Harvard University. Among his books are *The Claim of Reason: Wittgenstein, Skepticism, Morality, and Tragedy, Disowning Knowledge in Six Plays of Shakespeare,* and two studies of film, *The World Viewed* and *Pursuits of Happiness: The Hollywood Comedy of Remarriage.*

**JONATHAN CULLER** is Class of 1916 Professor of English and Comparative Literature, Cornell University. Among his books are *Structuralist Poetics, The Pursuit of Signs, On Deconstruction,* and *Framing the Sign.*

JACQUES DERRIDA is Professor of Philosophy at the École des Hautes Études en Sciences Sociales, Paris, and Visiting Professor of the Humanities at the University of California, Irvine. His books include *Of Grammatology, Dissemination, The Post Card: From Socrates to Freud and Beyond,* and *The Truth in Painting.*

GEOFFREY H. HARTMAN is Karl Young Professor of English and Comparative Literature, Yale University. Among other books, he has written *Wordsworth's Poetry, The Fate of Reading, Criticism in the Wilderness,* and *Saving the Text: Literature/Derrida/Philosophy.*

NEIL HERTZ is Professor of the Humanities at Johns Hopkins University. He is the author of *The End of the Line* and a forthcoming book on George Eliot.

WOLFGANG ISER is Professor of English and Comparative Literature at the University of Constance and Professor of English at the University of California, Irvine. His books include *The Implied Reader* and *The Act of Reading,* as well as *Laurence Sterne, Tristram Shandy,* and a forthcoming collection of essays called *Prospecting: From Reader Response to Literary Anthropology.*

FRANK KERMODE is King Edward VII Professor of English Literature, Emeritus, and Fellow of King's College, Cambridge. Among his recent books are *The Genesis of Secrecy, The Art of Telling, Forms of Attention,* and *History and Value.*

STÉPHANE MOSES is Professor of German and Comparative Literature, the Hebrew University. He is the author of a book on Jean Paul and Thomas Mann, as well as *Système et Révélation: La Philosophie de Franz Rosenzweig* and *Spuren der Schrift: von Goethe bis Celan,* and the forthcoming *Une autre histoire: Rosenzweig, Benjamin, Scholem.*

GABRIEL MOTZKIN is Lecturer in History, Philosophy, and German Literature at the Hebrew University. He has published articles on secularization, neo-Kantianism, and Heidegger, and is currently a fellow at the Wissenschaftskolleg zu Berlin.

SHLOMITH RIMMON-KENAN is Associate Professor of English and Comparative Literature at the Hebrew University. She is the author of *The Concept of Ambiguity: The Example of Henry James* and *Narrative Fiction: Contemporary Poetics.*

JON WHITMAN is Senior Lecturer in English, the Hebrew University. He is the author of *Allegory: The Dynamics of an Ancient and Medieval Technique* and articles on medieval and Renaissance literature.

SHIRA WOLOSKY is Senior Lecturer in English and in American Studies, the Hebrew University. She has written *Emily Dickinson: A Voice of War* as well as articles on Celan, Frost, and Derrida.

# INDEX

Absolute, vs. the relative in *Romance of the Rose*, 266

*Adam Bede* (Eliot), 281

Adorno, Theodor W., 140-64; and aesthetic form, 144-45; and art history, 142; and Beckett, 142, 146, 147-48; and Barthes, 158; and Being, 146; and Benjamin, 143, 145, 157, 158, 160n12; and Berg, 154; and Bloch, 153; and Celan, 148; compared to Derrida, 149-51, 161n16; and dialectics, 142, 148, 150-51, 153-54, 155; on the essay, 156, 157-59; Habermas on, 158, 161n16; and Hegel, 142, 145, 148; and Heidegger, 143, 149; and history, 148; and Husserl, 145, 148; justification of aesthetics, 154; and Kant, 147; on literature, 141, 146, 154; on Lukács, 160n9; and Lyotard, 162n27; and mimesis, 142; Nagele on, 161n16; and negativity, xiii; and Nietzsche, 147, 150; and Proust, 154; and Stendhal, 147; and Stravinsky, 158; on psychoanalysis, 147; on theology, 146; and transcendence, 146, 153; and utopia, 148

*Aeneid* (Virgil), 298, 309-11, 314-20; Dryden's translation of, 301, 306, 308

Aesthetics: aesthetic form and Adorno, 144-45; Adorno's justification of, 154; and the author, 145-46; classical aesthetics, 145; and dialectics, 145, 155-56; Hartman on, 232; and negativity, 140-64; aesthetics of reception, 204; vs. aesthetics of production, 145-46; vs. philosophy, 155; vs. theology, 146

"Aesthetic Dignity of *Les Fleurs du Mal*, The" (Auerbach), 190

*Aesthetic Theory* (Adorno), 140-64

Agassiz, Louis, 72

*Aids to Reflection* (Coleridge), 365

Alan of Lille, 262

Allegory: Benjamin on, 145, 233; and Blake, 233; crisis of in *Romance of the Rose*, 269; de Man on, 205, 233; and dislocation, 259; in Eliot, 291; and modernism, 204; and unsaying, xviii

Allemann, Beda, 61

"All Strange Away" (Beckett), 169

*All's Well That Ends Well* (Shakespeare), 343

Alonso, Damaso, 190

"Amos Barton" (Eliot), 280-81

Analogy, problems of, 272-73, 276

Apophasis, xv, 4, 27-29, 31, 42-43, 45, 53, 73; and Beckett, 176-78, 184; and Hegel, 30; and history, 39, 48-49; and irony, 73, 76; and negative theology, 5

Apostrophe, xvii, 297-322; of Catullus, 320n1; and intertextuality, xvii; lyric, 314; and negativity, xvi-xvii, 318-20; and ontology, 297; and Swift, 320n1

Apotropism, in Beckett, 165

Promise, 14-16; in Heidegger, 55; politics of, 24; and the trace, 38
Proust, Marcel, Adorno on, 154
Psychoanalysis: Adorno on, 147; and film, 351-53; and hypnosis, 360; and literary criticism, 291; and women, 351, 352
*Pursuits of Happiness: The Hollywood Comedy of Remarriage* (Cavell), 341

Question, 66n12

Raymond, Marcel, 190
Realism, in *Daniel Deronda*, 280, 291
Realm, 80-81; and city, 79
Reference, 27; and dislocation, 259; and God, 28; and Heidegger, 108-09; and Nothing, 112-13; and the Other, 29; and transcendence, 113-14
Repetition, 48; and the law, 68n19; and the neutral, 290; in *The Sound and the Fury*, 247, 249, 251-53; and the text, 327; and time, 232
Representation: end of, 326; functions of, 325; Gombrich on, 326; and mimesis, 326; vs. play, 327, 328; and "worldmaking," 326
*Republic, The* (Plato), 31-34, 172
Revelation: and Blake, 232; in Celan, 216-17; and negativity, 216, 222-23; and Nothing, xv; and secularization, 223; and the Shofar, 222; Sinaitic, 212, 215, 219
Rhetoric, and philosophy, 163n37
Rickert, Heinrich, 98
Ricoeur, Paul, 121
Rilke, Rainer Maria, 228
Rimmon-Kenan, Shlomith, xix
*Romance of the Rose* (Guillaume de Lorris and Jean de Meun), 259-79; and crisis in allegory, 269; authorship of, 259-61; and closure, 274; and *Complaint of Nature*, 262; God in, 260; and the Good, 263, 272-73, 275; and irony, 264; and nothingness, 267; and philosophy, 269-73, 275-77; and point of view, 275
Rorty, Richard, 156; on Derrida, 163n37

Rosenzweig, Franz, translation of the Bible, 213
Rousseau, Jean-Jacques, Derrida on, 85
Russian Formalism, 143

Sartre, Jean-Paul, 87
*Schelling* (Heidegger), 69n25
Scholastics, and transcendence, 99-100
Scholem, Gerschom, xv; on Kafka, 222-23
Schopenhauer, Arthur, and Beckett, 183
Scotus, Duns, 100
Seal, 50-51
Searle, John, Derrida on, 85
*Seasons, The* (Thomson), 237
Secret societies: and deconstruction, 18-19; and negative theology, 18-19; sharing of the secret, 25
*Sein und Zeit* (Heidegger), 55, 149
Self: Cavell on, 321n10; and grammar, 181-82; Hertz on, 199; loss of in Baudelaire, 199-201; in Lacan's mirror stage, 242; and the Other, 96; unity of, 182-83; *see also* Subject
"Self-Reliance" (Emerson), 365
*Sense of an Ending, The* (Kermode), 71, 72, 81-89, 93
*Senses of Walden, The* (Cavell), 321n10
Sermon, 47
Shakespeare, William: and Blake, 225; and Descartes, 52; and marriage, 343
Shibboleth, 24
Shklovsky, Viktor, on ending, 87-88
*Songs of Innocence* (Blake), 235
*Sophist* (Plato), 34, 177
*Sound and the Fury, The* (Faulkner), 241-58; and the body, 241-42, 244-45; and difference, 250; and loss, 242-58; and *Othello*, 254; and repetition, 247, 249, 251-53; the subject in, 241-45; and time, 249-50
*Sound and Sense* (Perrine), 195
Spenser, Edmund, and Blake, 225
Spitzer, Leo, 241